Transcribing Class and Gender

CLASS : CULTURE

SERIES EDITORS

Amy Schrager Lang, Syracuse University, and Bill V. Mullen, Purdue University

TITLES IN THE SERIES:

The Syntax of Class: Writing Inequality in Nineteenth-Century America
Amy Schrager Lang

Vanishing Moments: Class and American Culture
Eric Schocket

Let Me Live
Angelo Herndon

Workin' on the Chain Gang: Shaking Off the Dead Hand of History
Walter Mosley

Commerce in Color: Race, Consumer Culture, and American Literature, 1893–1933
James C. Davis

You Work Tomorrow: An Anthology of American Labor Poetry, 1929–41
Edited by John Marsh

Chicano Novels and the Politics of Form: Race, Class, and Reification
Marcial González

Moisture of the Earth: Mary Robinson, Civil Rights and Textile Union Activist
Edited by Fran Leeper Buss

Grassroots at the Gateway: Class Politics and Black Freedom Struggle in St. Louis, 1936–75
Clarence Lang

Natural Acts: Gender, Race, and Rusticity in Country Music
Pamela Fox

Transcribing Class and Gender: Masculinity and Femininity in Nineteenth-Century Courts and Offices
Carole Srole

An Angle of Vision: Women Writers on Their Poor and Working-Class Roots
Edited by Lorraine M. López

Michael Moore: Filmmaker, Newsmaker, Cultural Icon
Edited by Matthew H. Bernstein

Hog Butchers, Beggars, and Busboys: Poverty, Labor, and the Making of Modern American Poetry
John Marsh

American Socialist Triptych: The Literary-Political Work of Charlotte Perkins Gilman, Upton Sinclair, and W. E. B. Du Bois
Mark W. Van Wienen

Transcribing Class and Gender

Masculinity and Femininity in Nineteenth-Century Courts and Offices

CAROLE SROLE

The University of Michigan Press
Ann Arbor

First paperback edition 2012
Copyright © by the University of Michigan 2010
All rights reserved
Published in the United States of America by
The University of Michigan Press
Manufactured in the United States of America
⊗ Printed on acid-free paper

2015 2014 2013 2012 5 4 3 2

This book may not be reproduced, in whole or in part, including illustrations, in any form (beyond that copying permitted by Sections 107 and 108 of the U.S. Copyright Law and except by reviewers for the public press), without written permission from the publisher.

A CIP catalog record for this book is available from the British Library.

Library of Congress Cataloging-in-Publication Data

Srole, Carole, 1948–
Transcribing class and gender : masculinity and femininity in nineteenth-century courts and offices / Carole Srole.
p. cm. — (Class : culture)
Includes bibliographical references and index.
ISBN 978-0-472-07055-8 (cloth : alk. paper)
1. Working class women—United States—History—19th century. 2. Stenographers—United States—History—19th century. 3. Masculinity—United States—History—19th century. 4. Femininity—United States—History—19th century. 5. Social classes—United States—History—19th century. I. Title.
HD6073.S582U67 2009
305.38'9623097309034—dc22 2009018640

ISBN 0-472-05055-9 (paper : alk. paper)

Photo: A female stenographer working for an actuary in 1897.
Courtesy Metlife Archives.

To Kenneth S. Star, the good

Acknowledgments

The number of people who have helped me along the way has expanded more than I could imagine. I thank you all, even the ones I have failed to mention here.

I received funding through creative leave and sabbatical awards from California State University, Los Angeles. The quantitative materials were based on a grant from the Department of Labor. Generous assistance was provided by staff from the New York Public Library; the New York Historical Society; Harvard; Yale; the University of California, Los Angeles; the Massachusetts Department of Vital Statistics; and the *Boston Globe.* Marshall Jorpeland, director of communications for the National Court Reporters Association, went beyond the call of duty by supplying citations and current issues of the *Journal of Court Reporting* and taking the time to calculate membership numbers.

Research assistants and family members helped find citations and documents: I thank Sam Vong, Irma Valdivia, M. Gwin Wheatley, Amy Ver Berg, Greg Srolestar, and Julianna Coco. I could not have finished this book without the computer consultation of Ken Star and Matthew Srolestar.

Friends and colleagues supplied help in countless ways. Cindy Aron, Jesse Batton, Wendy Gamber, Marc Silberman, Rennie Schoepflin, and Scott Wells shared documents and citations. Thomas Alvarez, Marilyn Boxer, Jim Cullen, Angel Kwolek-Folland, Karen Lystra, Bill Rorabaugh, Joan Severa, Sarah Stage, and Eileen Boris and the anonymous readers at *Feminist Studies* offered advice on parts of chapters or conference papers. Cindy Aron, Tom Dublin, Nancy Page Fernandez, Wendy Gamber, Glenna Matthews, Ken Star, and Lillian Taiz read all of the chapters. Anthony Bernier, Lesley Kawaguchi, and Greg Srolestar commented on the entire manuscript more than once.

I have been fortunate to have a number of communities who have given advice and moral support. The members of a U.S. women's history reading group in Southern California provided an intellectual community that I treasure, comprised of Nancy Page Fernandez, Jill Fields, Jennifer Hillman Helgren, Karen Lystra, Lois Nettleship, Emily Rader, Donna Schuele, and former or sometime participants Victoria Brown, Mary Lou Locke, Peggy Renner,

Margaret Rose, and Sarah Stage. I value the friendship and "old girl" network of the many participants in the yearly Teaching Workshop on Women's History. I especially thank Emily Abel, Patricia Cohen, Mary Felsteiner, Jill Fields, Estelle Freedman, Jo Goodwin, and Marge Lasky, who brainstormed titles and publication strategies, searched for records, and introduced me to the University of Michigan editor. I cannot thank Karen Lystra and Nancy Page Fernandez enough for spending days helping revise the introduction and title and clarify my ideas and for graciously putting up with my phone calls and e-mails.

Family and friends enlivened my research trips to the east. My aunt, Esther Srole, generously provided bed and board and family stories in New York. In the early years, Ted Byers, Judy Taylor, and Marion Bloch put me up in Boston, and Myrtle and Saul Srole supplied room, board, and guided trips throughout the Washington, D.C., area.

I appreciate those historians who have given moral support and encouragement over the long haul: Stanley Burstein, Nancy Page Fernandez, Nancy Fitch, Karen Lystra, and Lillian Taiz. I also appreciate former students who willingly discussed my work: Anthony Bernier, Torrie Hester, Jennifer Langdon, and Lydia Otero.

I am indebted to the support and advice of University of Michigan Press editor LeAnn Fields; the editors of the Class: Culture series, Amy Schrager Lang and Bill V. Mullen; and the anonymous readers for the press.

Most important of all, I thank Kenneth Star, to whom this book is dedicated, for never losing faith in me.

Contents

Introduction

Returning to his office from an out-of-town job as a legal stenographer, Mr. Carossal finds himself at the scene of a murder committed in an adjacent office building. Horatio Kabb, a bookkeeper for a stockbrokerage firm, the J. B. Grafton Company, has been found "tumbled head-foremost half way down the K Street stairs, sprawling face downward in a pool of blood." Kabb has been "shot through the lungs, from the front, and at close range," and the company safe has been broken into and emptied of thirty-three thousand dollars in cash and securities. A crowd has gathered, and the police have begun interrogating the occupants of the adjoining offices. As J. B. Grafton relates the gruesome details of these discoveries to police detectives, Carossal scans the room and makes a disturbing observation: "My eyes were busy, with increasing perturbation, upon a hurried survey of his office. One end of his filing cabinet had been swung out a little way from the wall, and I saw with astonishment and horror that behind it there was a large hole through the wall, leading into my room."[1]

The prime suspect in the case is young Burt Anderson, a taciturn and scruffy-looking, but competent, young man, who works for Trafton during the day as an amanuensis and general clerk and assists Carossal in the evenings, transcribing legal reports and turning out clean copy "at a uniform rate of more than sixty words a minute."[2] Despite mounting evidence to the contrary, Carossal feels certain of Anderson's innocence and speculates that the indecipherable shorthand notes found at the scene of the crime would prove the key piece of evidence and exonerate Anderson. The police have the notes copied and examined by professional stenographers all over the country, but while many theories are advanced as to their meaning, no one could decipher them. Carossal makes the first breakthrough in the case. Reasoning that "stenographers generally are a law-abiding lot and erudite burglars are by no means common," he deduces that the script might actually be a simple cipher that even an uneducated criminal could read.[3]

Searching for a possible culprit, two undercover policemen accompany Carossal to a disreputable saloon in the neighborhood. In the bar, they find Ross Ruggler, "a tall, bony man [whose] wolfish ugliness was accentuated by a great scar that drew up one corner of his mouth, exposing the teeth." He is loud and inebriated and carries in his pocket a "fat roll of paper currency," from which he is freely buying drinks for the crowd in the bar.[4] When he boasts that he can read shorthand but not write it, it becomes clear to Carossal that he committed the crime and that he had an accomplice. Shocking everyone, including the police inspector, Carossal deduces that the brains behind the operation was none other than the dead bookkeeper Kabb, who wrote the ciphers as instructions to his partner in crime before the brutish Ruggler accidentally shot him during the heist.

"The Trafton Tragedy," printed in the spring of 1906, was among sixty-six short stories about stenographers and typewriter operatives published in the *Phonographic World* between 1887 and 1907 (this magazine had several names over the years; see appendix). The tales were obviously meant to amuse, inspire, and educate shorthand students and practitioners, but a closer reading reveals how their inscriptions of class served to shape the middle-class contours of office occupations at the end of the nineteenth century. Authors represented some male and female stenographers in these stories as respectable and professional by imbuing them with class characteristics commonly associated with the middle class. Some clerical workers came across as merely competent and a few as entirely unsuitable for office or court work because of their stereotypical working-class traits. In this way, the stories served to clarify for readers the complicated mix of characteristics necessary to build a secure, middle-class identity in this quickly burgeoning employment.

A case in point are the three office workers who appear in "The Trafton Tragedy": a bookkeeper, a shorthand amanuensis, and a law stenographer. Bookkeeper Horatio Kabb seemed quiet, self-possessed, and without vices. He "moved a good deal in the best society" and is clever enough to devise and execute a plan to break into Trafton's safe and implicate Carossal's assistant.[5] Of course, as a criminal, he lacked real decency, and the author, writing under the pen name A. B. Wrighter, used Kabb to warn readers about the dangers of false appearances in blurring the boundaries of respectability in the office. Kabb meets his death because his criminal accomplice mistakes him for an innocent office employee entering his own place of employment during the burglary. Kabb poses as respectable and dies because of that outward presentation.

The amanuensis, Burt Anderson, looks odd and scruffy and does not conduct himself as an "amiable fellow." However, he is energetic and efficient, punctual, "quick-witted, well educated, and an indefatigable worker." Wrighter makes it clear that Anderson does not belong among the expert, elite stenographers, because he uses the same improper grammar as the incompetent police inspector and the murderer and lacks the proficiency to figure out the meaning of the mysterious note from the crime scene. In contrast, Carossal, a legal stenographer, adroitly solves the crime, while hundreds of "writers of every system," including a "genius," fail to decipher the script and distinguish between it and real shorthand.[6] Carossal's superior intelligence and logic lead eventually to his becoming a judge years later.

Many of these stories, whether the characters are male or female stenographers, take place in business offices and attempt to define and portray competence and respectability in that setting. Yet there are striking differences between the depiction of male and female stenographers. While a third of the male protagonists embark on adventures, invent gadgets, or solve crimes, at least half of the plots about women revolve around romance. In "Wanted—a Stenographer," a young law student outwits his junior partner, Fred Hartley, who favors hiring an incompetent but attractive stenographer "who caught [his] fancy." She is a "tall, dark and rather forward young woman," who "flashed her black eyes and laughed and chatted with . . . [the men] quite familiarly." The law student, Mr. King, prefers a more experienced, competent, and respectable candidate, Eleanor White, who looks "rather slight and pale."[7] When Mr. Hartley dismisses Miss White without viewing her dictation and typing test, Mr. King tracks her down and arranges for her to meet the senior partner, who recognizes her skills and hires her on the spot. A few years later, King becomes a partner in the law firm and marries Eleanor.

While the story attempts to delineate the competence and respectability necessary for stenographic employment, its nearsighted treatment of its female characters threatens to undermine those distinctions. The inept applicant's appearance and forwardness confirms her unsuitability for the position, while the well-qualified Eleanor White deserves the job and eventual marriage to the conscientious young partner. However, the two female job candidates also share some surprising similarities. Just as the "brunette's" appearance prompts Fred Hartley's selection, so does Eleanor's looks drive Mr. King's estimation of her suitability: he calls Eleanor's the "sweetest face I ever saw" and says she "looks so pretty," before she proves her competence for the position.[8] Further, both women enjoy the same ultimate fate. When Eleanor leaves her position for marriage, the incompetent stenographer replaces her and seems posed to wed the other junior law partner. Although the author makes distinctions between the two couples, it is clear that beauty and romance were central concerns for women in the office.

While "The Trafton Tragedy" and "Wanted—a Stenographer" both illustrate how shorthand magazines tried to brand stenographers as middle-class, they also expose the problems in delineating criteria for ranking and evaluating class. Contemporaries of this period may have thought that they could easily identify middle-class men and women, yet reliable markers for defining class remained elusive. Too many conflicting and imprecise measures, including formal and informal education, social manners, consumer items, occupation, and attitude, could symbolize the middle class.[9] As a result, authors sometimes strained to formulate boundaries that would clearly flag middle-class membership. In the first story, Wrighter recognizes the difficulties by contrasting the false appearances of the characters Kabb and Anderson with their real behavior and attitudes. However, he also endows his villain and his hero with some of the same admirable traits—for instance, linking Kabb's shrewdness in devising a convoluted plot with Carossal's talent in uncovering it. In the second story, the problems of drawing distinctions between the two women multiplied, as their drastically different levels of competence nevertheless leads to similar outcomes in their lives.

Moreover, in both stories, the protagonists' exemplary traits risked becoming liabilities. Wrighter admired the astute reasoning of Judge Carossal, echoing the common middle-class privileging of the mind over the body. However, Kabb might have remained alive if he had developed a brutish physicality to match his sinister mind. Instead, he compensated for his lack of brawn by turning to a goon for an accomplice, who shot first and asked questions later. In the second story, a bit of beauty and romance proved a woman's respectability, but too much disqualified her from the office. Finding that perfect balance was not so easy.

Transcribing Class and Gender: Masculinity and Femininity in Nineteenth-Century Courts and Offices addresses these stories and other materials from the many nineteenth-century shorthand magazines, textbooks, and conferences that catered to students and practitioners of stenography. The proliferation of shorthand posts in business and courts, stenographic schools, and the shorthand press in the last decades of the nineteenth century set the stage for this study's explanation of how men and women sought to construct a gender balance to consolidate their positions in the middle class. Both men and women tried to strike a certain combination of contemporary masculine and feminine traits that embraced elements of conventional definitions of both manhood and womanhood and carved gender difference out of both, sometimes leaning toward feminine delineations and sometimes toward masculine ones. This book not only will catalogue the feminine and masculine characteristics appropriated by men and women in fashioning a working gender balance but will explore how those traits carried class connotations. By interrogating the efforts of historical subjects to fabricate such balances, especially as the fulcrum shifted during times of major cultural change, the book's approach provides a method for analyzing the fashioning of gender as well as class.

Since gender shaped class, gender balancing enabled the molding of the middle class.[10] Nineteenth-century bourgeois culture designed the upper and working classes as gender extremes: working-class men appeared as brutish or hypermasculine, upper-class men as dependent and foppish, that is, excessively feminine. So, too, upper-class women looked too dependent and frivolous—that is, unduly feminine—while working-class women seemed overly forward, sexual, and independent, sometimes too masculine and other times too feminine.[11] The middle-class ideal sought to balance gender and class together, finding the perfect middle ground. *Transcribing Class and Gender* shows how both men and women embodied a middle-class identity by locating a balance within each gender repertoire. As the centerpiece of the story, professionalism became the New Man's version of economic manhood and the New Woman's rendition of public womanhood.

To understand the shorthand press's steadfast efforts to forge a middle-class construction of the profession of stenography requires dissecting the interrelations and conversations between various groups of participants. This study of the shorthand world explores how the complex affinities between business stenographers and court reporters, as well as shorthand publishers and educators, affected class and gender sensibilities.[12] Let us begin with business stenographers, followed by court reporters and law stenographers.

The advent of business stenography in the nineteenth century and its essential partner, typewriting, brought profound changes to office jobs in the United States by rationalizing, mechanizing, feminizing, and commingling the classes. Most office occupations were revamped after the Civil War, when department stores, insurance companies, manufacturers, and other sectors of the economy developed new methods of internal communication that reorganized office practices and began to replace handwork with machinery. To fill the new positions of subdivided and mechanized work, employers hired large staffs of typewriting operators, stenographers, clerks, and bookkeepers, who often came from working-class backgrounds. While both men and women secured these office assignments, women predominated, especially in business stenography and typing, as the numbers of workers performing such tasks skyrocketed. Bookkeeping's female composition grew rapidly in the twentieth century, while clerking remained a male occupation, though altered by routinization and mechanization. Not until the end of the late twentieth century did women monopolize, or feminize, professionalized accounting and court reporting, as well.[13]

These changes in business stenography, typing, bookkeeping, and eventually clerking challenged the assumption of such positions as middle-class work. For men, the middle-class, manly ideal of economic independence became increasingly less tenable. For women, any employment retained an association with the working class. Additionally, the growing proportion of working-class men and women in these jobs further confounded efforts to maintain clerical employment's middle-class image.

While the transformations in business stenography jeopardized its middle-class standing, court reporters and law stenographers continued to build their own practices in the traditional, male, middle-class model. However, the proliferation of positions in business stenography threatened to overshadow the occupation of court reporting. Reporters grew concerned that the depreciated status of business stenography would rub off on them. They feared that people would confuse them with business stenographers and not recognize that they were a largely male workforce with high earnings and considerable economic independence. In response, they sought to fortify the differences between themselves and business stenographers, a difficult task because of the actual similarities in their training and initial work experiences.[14]

Moreover, business stenographers appropriated variations of the techniques that court reporters employed to elevate themselves. The growing professionalism of the male-dominated field of court reporting inspired those in the predominantly female field of business stenography to adopt professional language and launch their own organizations. The presence of business stenographers in professional associations led to more varied types of such organizations, reflecting complex meanings of professionalism. These bonds between the different shorthand occupations exacerbated the intense conflict over gender and class as court reporters tried to reify the fluid boundaries between legal and business stenography.

In addition to business and legal stenographers, shorthand boosters (the media, textbook authors, and educators) shaped the directions and meaning of shorthand employment by pursuing their own business goals. Inexpensive magazines devoted to shorthand proliferated when improvements in printing technology and transportation drove down costs, expanding circulation in the antebellum years that peaked in the last two decades of the nineteenth century.[15] They sought to boost interest in shorthand, especially since most editors also published shorthand manuals, some founding magazines to raise money for releasing their books.[16] A few ran shorthand schools. The desire to sell shorthand infused their publications and was intensified by competition among advocates of different shorthand languages in the second half of the century. Existing business schools and those devoted to teaching shorthand supplied formal training that also grew in the same years. These shorthand promoters influenced shorthand employment similarly, although they were not always involved in the same ways.

As a result, the shorthand media and educators also contributed to molding shorthand's middle-class contours. Each sought to attract readers and students by convincing them that shorthand offered middle-class economic and social opportunities. To potential students, they held up court reporting as a model of economic independence and mobility. Through the publication of brief biographical sketches of successful stenographers (often legislative, law, or official court reporters), the shorthand media promoted the type of proficiency and work ethic that accounted for the fictional Judge Carossal's rise from a law stenographer to a judge. They also encouraged women to consider shorthand by promising that they would retain or acquire middle-class status and, like Eleanor White, might meet and marry men of promise and means.

Shorthand magazines provide an especially useful source for revealing the gendered middle-class constructions, because they attracted a wide range of readers. They offered practice exercises in shorthand, examples of first-rate shorthand styles by prominent stenographers, employment tips, and advertisements for materials for home study. The magazines were aimed not just at students but also at the professional needs of active practitioners. They spoke to business stenographers, especially those with hopes of becoming court reporters or legal stenographers, by offering advice and connections to other shorthand practitioners. Some magazines, such as the *Philadelphia Stenogra-*

pher, the *Metropolitan Stenographer,* and the *Phonographic World,* served at times as the official organs of various shorthand professional associations. Their pages addressed the efforts to forge a national professional association; publicized professional meetings and debates; provided summaries of association proceedings, prospective laws, and court cases; and carried other relevant information.

This study examines the vocabulary of clerical work through a reading of shorthand magazines, educational publications, stenography conference materials, and popular fiction. The language and messages contained in these materials drew on familiar images of working women and men. While older discourses set the framework, new conditions, such as the growing presence of middle- and working-class women in offices, influenced which of these older conversations would gain currency and in what form. Instead of automatically determining which older images and languages became prevalent, debates about these depictions helped mold stock characters that informed the reactions of actual stenographers and that would prevail eventually to become symbols of the twentieth-century office worker.

The popular fiction that proliferated in shorthand magazines provides an especially useful source for unraveling gender and class dynamics. The concrete images within these stories expose class and gender assumptions and helped create a binary of stock female office characters. First, they established the character of the typewriter girl, a floozy who cared more about dressing to find a husband, especially a rich one, than her job, like the incompetent brunette in "Wanted—a Stenographer." This character type had its roots in the mass market melodramas and dime novels about working-class women that began in the 1840s and took off in the 1870s.

Primarily written for working-class women (although some middle-class women read them as well), dime novels often struck the middle class as tawdry and low-class. The typewriter girl replicated the romantic themes that many in the middle class viewed as cheap and sensational. The shorthand magazines took working-class types, dreamed up by the middle class to entertain the working class, and divided them into two new office stock characters: the working-class typewriter girl and the professional businesswoman. While pillorying the typewriter girl, shorthand magazines formulated an alternative character who embraced dime novel themes of pride in work and independence. They forged the stock heroic white-collar woman as competent and businesslike, the epitome of the middle-class professional woman, whose neatness and service reimagined domesticity and nurturance. Eleanor White met some of these criteria, with her rapid, neat, and accurate transcription and prompt arrival for the interview.[17] In other instances, fiction that appeared in shorthand magazines borrowed from dime novels' capers and tales of self-reliance to fabricate prototypical male office types, such as the self-made bureaucrat and the office professional who combined technical mastery, intellectual innovation, and endurance, like the young Carossal.

Fiction's role in shaping the vocabulary of clerical work departed somewhat from other texts in the shorthand library. Male authors of fiction who wrote about men in shorthand magazines tended to discuss their manly escapades and physicality rather than the scientific and artistic qualities of professional stenography, probably because of the stories' roots in the dime novel genre. Fictional stories about women privileged dime novel themes of love and adventure rather than the leitmotiv on ambition common elsewhere in shorthand texts. They also more frequently portrayed women's competence, rather than their professional expertise, although they ultimately did both.[18] Shorthand magazine fiction exhibited a style that catered to working-class audiences more than did the proceedings of shorthand professional meetings and magazine letters and articles, probably because the authors of the former were not necessarily practitioners but writers for mass magazines that aimed at working-class audiences. In contrast, nonfiction in stenography magazines and textbooks reflected the goals of editors and authors to attract men and women willing to make the substantial effort to learn shorthand. Not surprisingly, conference materials from stenography associations also privileged images of expertise common among emerging professionals. Despite the differences between fiction and nonfiction, both served to conceive new models of the middle class.

Transcribing Class and Gender uncovers the changes in gender balances in the stenographic world as working women and men forged their own blends of masculine and feminine language to assure their respectability.[19] Women and their supporters borrowed what contemporaries thought of as male qualities to demonstrate female suitability for work. In the mid-nineteenth century, personal independence was the only masculine trait considered marginally acceptable for women. By the end of the century, shorthand magazines employed similar vocabulary for both men and women, appropriating a male lexicon as women made inroads into the masculine domain of the office. The magazines frequently deployed the concept of the self-made man: they billed stenography as an opportunity for women, like men, to achieve upward mobility, and they used words like *ambition* and *independence* to describe both men and women. Moreover, women took this talk seriously. They quickly joined and even founded professional organizations, adopting the vernacular of professionalism, but there were limits that produced feminine versions of professional competence and service.

Men borrowed from women's vernacular as well, but less directly. At midcentury, they accentuated their own virile independence but portrayed self-study as a form of morality, choosing a middle ground between more manly working-class styles and the more feminine forms of morality. By the end of the century, male appropriation from womanhood included performing refined leisure with wives and coworkers at the meetings of their professional associations. By participating in such activities within a professional context, men appropriated the propriety associated with womanhood that protected them from appearing like popular images of the crude working class, but without appearing effeminate.[20]

Nevertheless, historical subjects do not easily settle on a gender balance. The instability of the languages of class and gender means that concepts and words can have multiple meanings, sometimes privileging gender or, at other times, class. For example, common notions like respectability and professionalism contained both class and gender definitions but could imply either, depending on the context. When respectability meant middle-class propriety, it signified class. When associated with gender, respectability leaned toward femininity, while professionalism tilted toward masculinity. To add further complications, the same language took on different meanings for men and women. When women joined men's attacks on the typewriter girl as flirtatious, they impugned her middle-class decency, using gendered wording to stand for class. However, when men challenged women, whether typewriter girls, business stenographers, or women court reporters, gender and class merged, with gender becoming the dominant feature. Now, the undesirable traits that the middle-class associated with working-class women applied to all women.[21] The analysis of these unstable gender balances through the vocabulary of clerical work forms the core of this project.

Transcribing Class and Gender reveals that the community of court reporters, stenographers, typewriter operators, commercial media, textbook authors, and educators enshrined middle-class identities by constructing usable gender balances. At midcentury, when shorthand's popularity took off, the gender balance for middle-class men centered on increasingly unstable definitions of independence. Male clerks, bookkeepers, and stenographers weighed competing images of independence, finding career self-improvement as a middle ground between the working-class excitement of urban life and middle-class, feminine, moral respectability. Students of shorthand embraced it as a sign of their ambition and hence their independence. Women's midcentury gender balance marked female copyists as degraded. By the end of the century, they and female stenographers had become symbols of the masses. When women poured into shorthand and typing positions during the last few decades of the century, the midcentury images of female office workers as degraded and the newer concerns about them as symbols of the masses challenged men's gender equilibrium and class status. In response, men sought to secure a new middle-class identity by pursuing different images of manhood. Those who worked as business stenographers might imagine themselves as reframed self-made men, climbing the steps of the new corporate bureaucracies. Male stenographers could also try to maintain their own decorum through clothes and behavior. Even more appealing, court reporters led the way in associating themselves with the increasingly popular middle-class language of professionalism.

Male court reporters and some business stenographers often chose the terminology of professionalism to strike a usable gender balance, with the support of commercial educators and the stenographic press. Expertise became the new rallying cry, despite the legal stenographers' lack of theoretical training or advanced credentials in their field. To proclaim their expertness, they recast the long-standing privilege of mental over manual labor to fit the vocabulary of professionalism. They also blended middle-class manhood with working-class physicality, implying that mental work required endurance. This definition of manhood excluded working-class upstarts who might lack the capacity to do mental work, as well as women deemed too physically weak. But manhood required more than cultural contrasts. Men had to prove that they were not womanly and that their occupation was not feminine. To do so, they tarred female competitors with the long-standing image of employed working-class women as immoral and incompetent.

Critics of women workers in the 1880s and 1890s accused typewriter operators and business and court stenographers of working-class frivolity and gold digging, behavior inappropriate for serious middle-class employment in the workplace. Even supporters of women office workers joined in lampooning the inappropriate female office worker. In response to the critique, women and their advocates tried to present female office and court personnel as ladies. However, ladies were just as rhetorically ill-suited for the offices and courts as gold diggers, because they lacked an appropriate work ethic. As a result, the shorthand press and educators adopted the model of the businesswoman, whose ambition and lack of sentiment made her almost perfect, except that she seemed too masculine. To address the flaw in the businesswoman type, women, the shorthand media, and commercial educators whittled working womanhood into a more feminine ideal by turning, like male court reporters, to professionalism. They blended the ambition, independence, and self-control of the businesswoman with the modesty and caring of the lady. Both men and women stressed their professionalism through professional organizations that performed domesticity as respectability. Men now found the gender balance that safely softened their hardened expertise and virile endurance, and women could prove their competence in a new feminine ideal, the turn-of-the twentieth-century New Woman. Gendered professionalism became the basis for discourses about ideal working women and men in offices and courts well into the twentieth century.

In discussing the struggle for gender balances, *Transcribing Class and Gender* maps out various strategies for cultural change. If we are to understand how manhood and womanhood interrelated in a society that used separate spheres to define male and female domains, we need to name and study the methods used by participants to reconfigure presentations of gendered identity. Sometimes, participants engaged in reframing, in which they justified new behavior by referring back to conventional articulations. For example, the shorthand magazine portraits of male business stenographers at the end of the century used the jargon of the self-made man to cast career moves within or between corporations as advancement, instead of a continuation in dependent wage labor. The magazines' use of older idioms discloses a cultural discomfort with the new bureaucratic job structure. Typically when participants draw on a new vocabulary to refashion their behavior, even to describe older styles of conduct, they reveal real cultural change. Employed women refashioned as ambitious New Women demonstrated how much they embraced newer values. Moreover, that both men and women maneuvered to depict their work in ways that conformed to the lexicon of professionalism conveys how much the culture had changed. Gendered professionalism had become the language of the New Man and the New Woman.

The first and second chapters of *Transcribing Class and Gender* examine the mid-nineteenth-century gender balances of manhood and womanhood, including those that carried into the end of the century. Chapter 3 moves entirely to the late nineteenth century and identifies the changes for business, legal, and court stenographers, explaining men's growing concerns about their middle-class identity as independent men and their inadequate methods for elevating themselves above the masses. Chapter 4 explores the model of the professional man as the new fulcrum that middle-class men might use to rise above the masses. Chapters 5 and 6 turn to women's attempts to find an equilibrium for employed womanhood. Chapter 5, which interrogates women's struggle to balance traditional femininity with a proper work ethic, emphasizes the role of class in debates over working womanhood. Chapter 6 looks into professionalism as the reformulated gender balance for the working New Woman. Chapter 7 discusses how both men and women performed professionalism. It compares the more traditional professionalizing goals and practices of the elite court reporters with the more inclusive mainstream organizations. The epilogue relates the continuity of the stock characters and discourses of the professional man and woman and the typewriter girl throughout the twentieth century, even as offices and courts underwent dramatic changes.

Court reporters, business stenographers, and others in the shorthand world help us rethink historical interpretations of the New Woman and New Man as professionals who represented middle-class manhood and womanhood. They expose the complexity of professionalism and extend its meaning beyond the professionalization of an occupation, the forging of a middle-class identity, and the infusion of the terminology of expertise and efficiency common at the turn of the twentieth-century culture, to include how professionalism simultaneously crafted a new badge of gender.[22] By piecing together identities drawn from the interwoven dialects of class and gender, shorthand discourses contributed to the increasing popular usage of the term *professional* as a synonym for occupation.

Moreover, court reporters, business stenographers, typewriter girls, the shorthand media, educators, and reformers remind us that negotiating gender balances is the heart of gendered cultural change. Men and women constantly struggle to pin down gender equilibriums, which are impossible states to achieve. When women invade male space, or vice versa, the scramble over gender boundaries and balance intensifies. Their battles over gender often deploy the language of class, while they frequently wrestle over class in the parlance of gender.

The story of court and office workers discloses the changing meanings of clerical work, the creation of professional labor, and the simplicity of our current vocabulary of gender and class in the context of the middle-class workplace. Modern stenography spanned over a century and exemplified the complexity of class and gender in the work force and the prototypes of the twentieth-century New Woman and New Man.

Some terminology requires clarification for the purposes of this book. *Copyists* or *scriveners* copied letters and business information by hand. When the typewriter began to replace copying, the writers were initially called *machine copyists* and then *typewriters* or *typewriter operators.* Shorthand practitioners went by a number of names. Until Gregg shorthand appeared at the end of the nineteenth century, the vast majority were disciples of Isaac Pitman, or *Pitmanites,* who called themselves *phonographers.* Initially, the term *amanuenses* referred to those who worked for court reporters, reading and transcribing their shorthand notes. With time, it referred to stenographers in business. I use the terms *amanuenses, business stenographers,* and *office stenographers* interchangeably. *Official reporters* worked in a particular venue, such as a court, a legislative branch, or an organization, although the term *official reporter* came to identify government reporters primarily. I often refer to court and legislative reporters as *court reporters* and *official reporters,* since mostly these terms overlapped. *Court reporters* worked either for the press, covering trials, or as official reporters for the courts. I employ the term *court reporters* to denote the latter. The term *expert reporter* often meant a court reporter or anyone who could write verbatim, that is, who could take dictation fast enough to record common speech.

Let us now turn to the antebellum years, when phonography first made a splash in the United States.

I. INITIAL HOOKS

CHAPTER 1

Performing Independence: Male Clerks, Bookkeepers, and Stenographers from 1820 to 1870

Shorthand has a long history going back to the ancient Greeks and Egyptians but it did not spread across the West until the sixteenth and seventeenth centuries. Europeans brought it to the New World, where some colonists—like Roger Williams; John Winthrop Jr. and his wife, Martha; ministers; and some court personnel—wrote shorthand. In the eighteenth century, Thomas Lloyd recorded the first congressional debates and George Washington's inaugural address. American shorthand in the late eighteenth and early nineteenth centuries continued to follow popular English styles, such as Samuel Taylor's and Thomas Gurney's systems and their adaptations. Shorthand became more commonly used in the United States with the popularization of Englishman Isaac Pitman's phonics-based "phonography" as part of an international movement to simplify language, with phonetic principles as its central feature. From his 1837 book, *Stenographic Soundhand,* phonography dispersed to English-speaking countries, spreading throughout the United States after Pitman's younger brother Benn's immigration in 1852 and establishment of the Phonographic Institute in Cincinnati.[1]

Phonography took off in the United States within the context of efforts to reframe clerking in a changing middle-class world. Well before midcentury, a tension emerged: clerical workers depended on their families and employers, either as mercantile apprentices or employees, yet they hoped to remain in the middle class by becoming economically independent as proprietors. Until then, they chose among conflicting definitions of independence to maintain a middle-class male identity. For some young clerks living in the urban boardinghouse districts, independence meant freedom from parents and respectability. Both the excitement of city life and involvement in working-class leisure intensified the feelings of autonomy. In contrast to this tougher, more manly characterization, other clerks embraced a respectable middle-class connotation of independence, which advocated self-control over unrestrained license and development of character. This rendering, however, acquiesced to female standards of morality and gentility, although some young men managed to reframe respectability to account for their freer behavior. A final, more practical meaning of independence made room for both urban adventures and decision making by emphasizing movement, whether geographic or social mobility. Simple exercises in self-study could demonstrate steps toward improvement, the hallmark of a middle-class manhood that balanced manly mental preparation and morality. Stenographers eventually became associated with this last definition of independence, although they initially had their own unique ties to middle-class notions of progress.[2]

YOUTHFUL DEPENDENCE

In the antebellum years, clerical workers were poised in a liminal space between youthful dependence and adult independence.[3] Whether they worked in offices, sold in shops, or combined both types of labor as salesclerks, clerks were boys and young men in the process of preparing for owning a mercantile or manufacturing business. Despite the weakening of mercantile apprenticeship, many still depended on the paternalism of familial networks, especially fathers negotiating job placements and arranging and financing proprietorships. Once employed, these young men were supposed to absorb skills on the job by gradually learning increasingly complex tasks, from tallying packages to copying letters and invoices to duplicating letters. Even mundane errands of message and merchandise delivery and distributing handbills introduced them to commercial rhythms and connections.[4]

As these young men plodded along in hopes of advancement, popular culture reinforced their liminality by questioning the middle-class manhood of those employed as retail clerks. According to historian Brian Luskey, contemporary cartoons ridiculed their eagerness to negotiate with and advise female customers about frivolous consumer purchases in a job some thought better suited to women. Conversely, when clerks toted goods, either in offices or stores, they risked appearing like lowly Irish or African American porters. In either case, these gender and class challenges reminded clerks of their precarious position.[5]

This status uncertainty emanated from the recognition that their expectations for proprietorship might not be met, as large proportions worked in occupations that did not lead to self-employment. In 1821, nearly four of every ten Boston clerks (whether in sales, office, or mixed positions), accountants, bookkeepers, scriveners, and secretaries worked for a branch of government or a bank (see appendix, table A1). Clerks in government and, to some extent, those in banking did not become proprietors without leaving their jobs. Government clerks generally stayed year after year as employees, eschewing proprietorship. For example, Moses Bass merely transferred from the collector's office, where he was working in 1821, to the city treasurer's office by 1834. William Rowson, a customhouse clerk for at least ten years, died without ever advancing to proprietorship. Of those government clerks traced from 1821 to 1834 in Boston city directories, none advanced beyond more responsible positions in the same bureaucracy or left the government and established a business, although some did in the next ten years (see appendix, table A3).[6] Not surprisingly, government clerks felt defensive about their jobs, despite earning relatively high salaries.

Men in these institutions hoped to earn enough money to invest, buy a business, or make connections. Those who already had succumbed to bankruptcy hoped to find less-risky commercial adventures to ease their way back into proprietorship. Even dead-end jobs could appear as apprenticeships by providing opportunities for training in skills, raising funds, and networking. The fading of youth, however, exposed their dependency. Clerks in their thirties must have felt pressure to settle down. Once they reached their forties and still worked as employees in offices, they undoubtedly worried about their futures, for they could no longer pretend that they were still apprentices. In 1860, 13.6 percent of clerks, 10.3 percent of bookkeepers, and 25 percent of accountants in Philadelphia and 37 percent who worked for the federal government were forty or over.[7]

For apprentices and employees, dependence cast a shadow over their work lives. Both aspired to independence: apprentices to advance and government clerks to finance their own businesses. Once economically independent, they could achieve respectable, middle-class manhood; until then, they remained youths or failures.[8]

INDEPENDENCE

Despite their economic dependence as apprentices or employees, antebellum male clerical workers became a symbol of potential economic independence. In the early nineteenth century, both manual and nonmanual workers continued to embrace the eighteenth-century belief in the importance of economic, political, and familial self-rule as a major component of manhood. As economic changes throughout the nineteenth century curtailed economic self-sufficiency for both groups, each struggled to hang on to some autonomy. By the antebellum years, Christian fiction and advice aimed at boys and young men shaped the self-made man as a symbol of the middle-class version of manly independence.[9]

Prolific authors like Freeman Hunt, Timothy Shay (T. S.) Arthur, and then Horatio Alger focused on the actions of the autonomous man, in contrast to the dependence inherent in the paternalism of the family and apprenticeship system. They collapsed the various stages of apprenticeship into a process of individual effort. A youth leaving home as an apprentice turned into a young man seeking his fortune in the city or an abandoned orphan struggling alone in the teeming metropolis. Instead of absorbing the craft from an employer, he now prepared to improve himself. Each act of mastering a skill was recast as solitary decision making and effort. Individual acquisition of increasingly complex skills, first as an apprentice and then a journeyman and possibly a master, now signified movement, especially upward mobility. Initial jobs mattered very little, for he slowly climbed the rungs of a career ladder from one learning opportunity to the next. By choosing the right path, he ultimately succeeded both financially and morally, moving to a respectable and comfortable station in society, often as a merchant, sometimes as a manufacturer, but always upward until he reached the middle class (and sometimes beyond), all accomplished "on his own."[10]

The maturation of the ideology of the self-made man in the antebellum years corresponded with a rise in commerce that inaugurated a shift in the availability of clerical work. As the economic expansion from the 1820s to the 1850s rocked the eastern seaboard states, the work of jobbers, brokers, wholesale traders, and storekeepers expanded, multiplying the number of proprietors, the ideal goal for the middle-class man. The clerking populace kept pace. The years between 1821 and 1844 saw a steady rise in the number of clerking positions in Boston, doubling between 1821 and 1834 and rising 35 percent between 1834 and 1844, more than tripling the total who were household heads in Boston between 1821 and 1834.[11] Mercantile clerking grew at a faster pace than government and bank clerking.[12]

As emphasis on the possibilities for success for those with initiative grew and as the number of new jobs in cities rose, many clerks became potential self-made men who grew restless and anxious to take advantage of these opportunities. Some rushed to acquire training. Young men like Edward N. Tailer Jr. relocated from job to job, impatient with the pace of the work and the slow stride of advancement. Such men wanted more money and responsibility sooner than clerks of a generation before, because they feared missing out. To keep their employees, merchants reassured their own clerks that they would soon become businessmen and advised young men about the importance of loyalty.[13]

However, even in this heyday of mercantile clerking, the number of positions for clerking employees began to outpace the opportunities for proprietorships. The growth of commerce in the 1830s and 1840s initially boosted prospects for office workers, until midcentury, when supply outstripped demand. The number of clerks in Boston multiplied tenfold from 560 to 5,165 between 1846 and 1855, far surpassing the number of merchants and opportunities for economic independence. A smaller number of clerical men reached proprietorship in the 1850s than in the 1840s in Utica and Poughkeepsie, New York. With so many clerks, the proportion becoming merchants fell. Merchants began to perceive of their assistants as employees, not potential partners. The social distance between them increased, as office workers seldom boarded with their employers. Employers treated clerks impersonally and complained publicly about their dishonesty. In 1855, *Hunt's Merchants' Magazine* compared mercantile clerks to wives for their dependence. By the 1840s, clerks complained in their diaries about the boredom at work. Copying, in particular, already earned a reputation as wearisome. Advisors warned that remaining too long as a clerk might dull a man's senses. His brain would become "weary" while "living in an unnatural state, doing what was really of no advantage nor delight to any human being."[14] Men rushed to leave clerking for independent positions as soon as possible.

Even while waiting for promotions, these antsy clerks sought to define themselves as independent by deciding their own educational and employment futures. If they relied less on their fathers and merchant masters, paternalism lost some of its impact. Along the way, these young men could imagine themselves as active risk takers, strengthening their own sense of autonomy. The next section explains how clerks transcended dependence to become the epitome of aspiring independent middle-class men by choosing and balancing varied gendered definitions of independence.

MEANINGS OF INDEPENDENCE

In affirming autonomy, clerks shaped their own meanings. Some who moved to the cities and lived in boarding houses defined independence as establishing freedom from parents and respectability, especially by participating in male-centered working-class forms of leisure. Others embraced the more feminine moral respectability by avoiding such forms of leisure. These men identified independence as exercising self-control and developing character. Still others found ways to reframe respectability to account for their new behavior. Lastly, the characterization of independence as movement, or steps toward success, had the greatest appeal, since it could blend with the other meanings.

City Freedoms: The Manly Working-Class Model

Clerks who lodged with relatives or employers remained integrated in household leisure activities, whether playing chess or whist in the parlor or ice-skating nearby. However, at midcentury, large numbers of unmarried urban clerks resided in the new boardinghouse districts of the burgeoning cities, such as New York and Boston, unsupervised by employers and family. Some felt homesick and anxious about this new independence, but they sensed the freedom of the city's energy and leisure. Vendors chanted rhymes to hawk their goods, while labor and patriotic parades, strikes, bare-knuckle fighters, street urchins, beggars, squealing pigs, rumbling trolleys, and petty crime filled the streets with color, pageantry, and spectacle. Horatio Alger's stories beginning in 1867 recounted the urban dangers of crime, traffic accidents from trolleys, and moral distractions, such as gambling, drinking, and oyster bars, all of which made life risky for the uninitiated. Alger also pointed out that these same dangers energized the city by offering entertainment for patrons of theaters, parks, hotels, restaurants, and sights, such as museums, hospitals, churches, the post office, banks, the city hall, the police department, the hall of records, and the Cooper Institute. Traffic noise and noxious odors added to the tumult.[15]

Clerks pursued their own leisure enjoyment in this fast-paced busy atmosphere, without parents or employers to dampen their delight. Nineteen-year-old William Hoffman visited Fowler's Phrenological Cabinet, with its "Busts and Skulls of many distinguished characters," as a break from looking for a clerking job. Robert McCoskry Graham, a Parisian-educated clerk, wrote in his 1848–49 diary about the excitement of the "perfect jam" that he missed when Henry Clay came to New York. The next day, he reported that two hundred thousand onlookers lined the streets to witness a "melancholy pageant" as the remains of John Quincy Adams were carried through the crowds. Edward N. Tailer recorded the "bonfires, fireworks, illuminations, torchlight processions, and noisy speeches" during the 1848 election.[16]

Only in the city could clerks view such a variety of novelties, some of which crossed the line of respectability. Since they lived in working-class districts and boarded with working-class men, clerks could participate in the urban leisure of the male working class, with its rowdiness, fighting, drinking, and theatergoing. Harry Hodges marveled at the "noise and excitement" but worried that it "causes a person almost to forget every thing he ever knew."[17] Benjamin Tilton also felt uneasy that the "temptations and allurements of a populous city" offered "rare enjoyments to the unsuspecting youth" in a "more enlarged sphere of action."[18] Henry A. Patterson placed bets with his fellow clerks, winning a dinner of oyster stew. In 1848, Edward N. Tailer, son of a wealthy merchant, celebrated the Fourth of July with his "cannon and horse pistol" and fired over sixty packs of firecrackers. To build muscles through gymnastics and boxing, he joined a gymnasium aimed at the middle class, but in a less-than-respectable milieu. Some clerks joined working-class men in firehouse companies, drinking, brawling, and participating in "ritualized displays of strength." Clerks in the 1840s and 1850s also attended raucous theater performances where working-class single men in the audience hissed and booed and threw garbage and rocks at performers. Tailer enjoyed the Olympic Theater, especially the character Mose, who he viewed as "a true specimen of one of the [Bowery] B'hoys." He might have even seen the play *Glance at New York,* about middle-class men reveling in the adventures of working-class urban life.[19]

Along with other young men, clerks indulged in the "sporting culture," where they visited houses of prostitution and purchased the "licentious press" that gossiped about prostitutes, crime, and the theater. According to historian Timothy J. Gilfoyle, "sporting-male culture broadly equated sexual promiscuity and erotic indulgence with individual autonomy and personal freedom." For example, Richard P. Robinson clerked for New York City merchant Joseph Hoxie, a relative. Despite Hoxie's advocacy of moral uplift for clerks and despite the presence of two other cousins at work, Robinson led a secret life of dissipation. In his leisure time, he became a regular client, the lover, and the presumed murderer of prostitute Helen Jewett, and he was not the only clerk who patronized her services. In big cities like New York and Boston, clerks frequented the new burlesque houses, admiring their spectacle of female bodies—legs, legs, and more legs. They continued to attend burlesque even after the late 1860s, when these shows shifted from respectable middle-class to working-class male entertainment. The dangers of the city—murders, fighting, pauperism, pool, betting, and prostitution—titillated the young urban middle class. Clerks could easily sample this world.[20]

Many young clerks enjoyed this freedom of urban leisure, engaging in the forbidden male, working-class activities of drinking, whoring, gambling, and fighting. Those who lived on their own in the new boardinghouses, apart from parents or employers, appreciated the license to explore the city and the freedom from genteel restraint. The usually dutiful Henry A. Patterson refused his parents' request to move from Mrs. Fitch's to Aunt Mary's because he thought "the reason insufficient," although he was staying at Uncle Morrison's a few months later. Maybe Henry's parents feared the lack of oversight and Henry's pleasure in the freedom from family controls.[21] The exhilaration of danger exaggerated the clerks' sense of liberation. By traversing from middle-class to working-class leisure, they ventured into a world that tantalized, horrified, and ultimately separated them from the moralists and the sedate evening activities of married folks like their parents. Slumming heightened the adventures and reinforced their independence from parents and family. Now they participated in a male working-class culture, rather than the genteel and feminine middle-class world of their families. Independence for slumming clerks meant freedom from the constraints of respectability but also a step in their direction of self-making.[22]

Respectable Independence: Middle-Class Models

Urban freedoms troubled advice writers, merchants, parents, and Christian reformers. Advice peddlers reminded their readers that success required postponement of gratification. Ministers and reformers warned clerks and other youth to eschew gambling, the temptation to steal from an employer, and the immorality of unearned wealth. Parents also counseled their sons about the dangers of the city.[23] The father of the accused murderer of prostitute Helen Jewett wrote to his son expressing fears about the "thousand temptations" in New York City, while in 1833, Sarah Sheldon of Vermont admonished her son to stop chewing and smoking tobacco and to choose his friendships carefully.[24]

Young middle-class men responded to these pleas differently. Some renounced the activities of the urban working-class culture. Others found ways to reconcile their behavior with respectability through reframing and waited until adulthood to turn completely away from the working-class behavior of rowdiness, drinking, and promiscuous sexuality. By exercising some self-control, they chose the second meaning of independence, which underscored their middle-class identity as autonomous men implicitly embracing the feminine cast of nineteenth-century morality.

Popular writers and advisors joined Christian reformers, merchants, credit reporting agencies, and parents to assert a definition of independence that embraced moral choices of respectability, rather than working-class rowdiness. As youths moved further from parental controls, an explosion in didactic literature, from novels to advice manuals, spread the ideas of late eighteenth-century middle-class individualism, despite continued acceptance of paternalistic guidance. Three-quarters of eighteenth-century guidance manuals and over half of nineteenth-century ones addressed adolescents exclusively or partially. The topics of these targeted nineteenth-century works expanded to include lessons about relationships, character, employment, and religious practices, rather than merely manners. The most popular of these nineteenth-century didactic writers sought to direct and contain youthful license, while still buttressing individualism. This approach more directly bound clerks to middle-class independent manhood by emphasizing the values of self-mastery and self-making.[25]

Both male and female authors endorsed parental or employer instruction, but with different spins. Middle-class female novelists assumed that family direction remained important for sons' success, as the home became increasingly a feminine preserve. They encouraged morally superior women to nurture their sons', brothers', and husbands' successes and even their independence by providing happy, calm homes. Slightly differently, male writers praised merchants' traditional oversight of clerks' work and free time and scolded young men scrambling upward who lacked loyalty to their employers. To them, men in a hurry stole supplies, money, and business secrets, only to launch competing businesses well before they were ready to go it alone. Advisor Freeman Hunt circulated merchants' complaints that they could no longer regulate the comings and goings of their clerks, who wandered around the seamy districts of the city with its theaters, taverns, and prostitutes, wasting time reading novels and throwing away money on cigars. Didactic male novelists also criticized what they viewed as the excesses of capitalism. For example, in *The Way To Prosper*, T. S. Arthur censured unchecked individualism by damning a family where each brother independently and selfishly acts in his own interests and by praising a family of brothers who help each other survive in a difficult world. Elsewhere, Arthur admonished his readers to be wary of other capitalist values, such as overvaluing money, impatience to succeed, conspicuous consumerism, and cutthroat competition at the expense of customers and partners.[26]

Even as popular writers and speakers damned unbridled individualism and warned young men to heed their good advice, they endorsed clerking autonomy by instructing young men to cultivate individualistic character traits—

such as loyalty, sobriety, and frugality—as the correct path to prosperity. In novels, melodramas, and biographies, heroes who were hardworking, disciplined, independent, modest, and generous always succeeded. Each of T. S. Arthur's many midcentury preachy novels celebrated different character traits presumably necessary for success. In his 1853 novel, *Sparing to Spend,* Arthur lauded thrift and unpretentiousness. The "humble" clerk Archibald Lofton and his principled wife, Ellen, who live within their means, slowly, ethically, and steadfastly accumulate the rewards of success. Conversely, the villain and his conspicuously consuming wife eventually learn from the humiliation of bankruptcy that spending wastefully, extravagantly, and selfishly to build a false impression of affluence does not pay commercially, socially, or morally.[27]

By counseling young men to develop personal qualities, didactic novelists and advisors bridged paternalism and individualism. At the same time, their use of the vague concept of character redefined independence to refer less to economic self-sufficiency than to individualistic traits. In doing so, they inflated the pool of potential self-made men. Any young man could imagine himself someday as an independent middle-class man, if he had the right character.[28]

Advisors employed a narrative strategy to advance a set of moral choices through which their charges could develop and demonstrate character, which also highlighted individualistic behavior. They set up dichotomous obstacle courses for clerks by sketching a map with privations on one side and dangers on the other. In each of Horatio Alger's or T. S. Arthur's stories, the hero chooses between the paths of righteousness and wicked corruption, and the reader decides between hero and antihero. Scruples entailed sacrifices. For example, hero Edward Claire in *True Riches; or, Wealth without Wings* accepts a pay cut and loss of a potential partnership rather than continue employment with immoral Mr. Jasper, who expects his clerks to cheat customers. Edward also endangers his health by taking a second job at night to support his family. By making the correct moral choices, protagonists like Edward chose to develop the sterling character that held promise for success.[29]

Some clerks took these warnings to heart. To demonstrate their good character and hence their independence, they embraced respectability, with its implied feminine morality. They often tried to assure their parents and even themselves that the big cities would not tempt them. Bradford Morse comforted his parents that he spent his time alone, and William Hoffman reported, "I always had an aversion . . . against anything that would tempt to moral depravity and disregarded looseness."[30]

Some male clerks participated in wholesome activities that kept them busy, like joining musical societies, organizations, and churches.[31] Historian Bruce Dorsey reports on dry goods clerk Gideon Burton's busy weekly schedule.

> He arose before breakfast on Sundays to distribute tracts in the market. From there he proceeded to a Bible class at St. Andrew's Episcopal Church. Following the morning service, he took a twenty-five-minute walk to Southwark, where he taught in the mission Sunday school. Burton then made his way back to St. Andrew's for afternoon services at 3:30. He also attended all weekly services, including evening prayer meetings and lectures. Squeezed between these commitments were his committee and managers' meetings for the tract and Sabbath societies.[32]

While Gideon Burton had little time for getting into trouble, he also demonstrated respectable values of piety, enterprise, and usefulness. Other clerks joined the Young Men's Christian Association, which sought to protect and uplift young clerks migrating to the cities by providing them with wholesome activities based on evangelical religious values.[33]

Others waited to embrace reform associations as an alternative to working-class styles of manhood, sowing their wild oats first and then marrying. Dorsey finds that in the 1830s, white temperance associations in Philadelphia attracted young married men, over twenty-five, often with young children. They lamented the temptations of "drinking, sexual licentiousness, and greed" and a lifestyle of "aggressive masculinity." These clerks had chosen the second definition of independence, moral respectability.[34]

Such men did not explicitly acknowledge the feminine influence on respectability-based independence. Moral choices did not necessarily connote femininity or manliness, unlike the manly working-class style of leisure. When women advice writers promoted morality, they expected women to have greater influence over sons and husbands, while male advisers intended to continue a male paternalism. Nonetheless, middle-class society accepted that women represented greater morality, which explains why male politicians tried to attract women's support to demonstrate their own integrity. Moreover, when men performed respectability, their actions fit more within a female-influenced world, even as male reformers tried to develop manly pious institutions, like the YMCA, as an alternative to feminine piety. By embracing piety and sobriety and scorning the sporting culture, young clerks chose the respectability of the middle-class home, the world of their mothers.[35]

Other clerks demanded the benefits of respectability even if their behavior failed to meet the expected standards. Often, they reframed their questionable conduct as proper by attacking others. Historian Brian Luskey describes New York clerk Samuel Edgerley's 1859 attendance of a "mid-week prayer meeting or bible 'class' at his church" before spending the night with friends at a brothel. Edgerley saw no contradiction between his repeated sexual exploits and his imminent respectable marriage. Henry A. Patterson's attitudes and experiences as a seventeen- and eighteen-year-old clerk blended moralism with his broadened horizons. On a number of occasions, he criticized the moral behavior of others as "illmannerly" [*sic*]." He even sniped at a congregation for so much clapping and stomping, "much more like a theater than a place for the worship of god," while also reporting his own visits to the Park Theater, known for its raucous audience behavior. Besides joining in wholesome family entertainment and gawking at fires, Patterson attended more controversial happenings, like a speech by radical Fanny Wright at the Masonic Hall, where he observed a brawl. Six months after practicing boxing "almost every night after work," he watched a fight between a butcher and five or six of his crew. Soon after he participated in these activities, his family requested that he move back with a relative.[36]

Henry Patterson justified his own behavior by accusing others of acting much more inappropriately and with less self-control. He wrote in his diary that one of his reasons for leaving his employment as a clerk with James Robinson was that "the boys in the store are anything but respectable." Patterson complained about the drunkenness of his fellow clerks but engaged in suspect behavior himself. At times, he drank "hot whisky punch," "some first rate cider," learned to toast, and even got "tipsy" on champagne wine. Patterson differentiated himself from the other drinking clerks, like "Andrew [who] was so drunk this afternoon that he could scarcely walk"; Patterson claimed that he had only become "tipsy." A few years later, Patterson reported that he was "eating and drinking in moderation."[37]

Patterson's comments seem typical of men who asserted their own respectability by distinguishing themselves from others. At times, ex-clerks who became forty-niners expressed disgust at the conduct of others, especially men of color, while implying their own relative propriety. Sometimes, they portrayed themselves as overcoming temptations, like the man who qualified his momentary risk of falling as "only once, and then only for a few minutes." Such men labeled themselves sober and others as drunks or identified themselves as manly or civilized and others as either effeminate or savage. By contrasting their self-discipline to others, men reframed their own behavior and announced their class identity.[38]

Since young clerks enjoyed the benefits of working-class urban life yet still wanted the advantages of respectability, they looked for other ways to temper manly unrespectable behavior. They might drink but still carefully attend to their attire, rather than wear the clothes of the dandy. Or they might dress like dandies only for leisure pursuits or at opportune moments, such as clerks did to support Richard Robinson during his murder trial. To maintain respectability and continue to enjoy the masculine metropolis, clerks often gravitated to a final definition of independence: self-improvement for career advancement. This definition actually appealed to everyone, whether they also defined independence as freedom, moral choice, or reframed respectability.[39]

Mobility as Independence

Since young men found it difficult to prove their promise for economic success, ambition became the cultural marker of potential accomplishments and middle-class manhood. But drive was equally difficult to substantiate. According to historian Scott A. Sandage, credit reports evaluated loan applications in moralistic language, equating virtue with aptitude for achievement. Didactic writers also confused morality with economic triumph. These same sources, however, can furnish an alternative means to evaluate enterprise: constant movement. Now, clerks as well as stenographers could convince themselves that every action, from keeping journals to studying bookkeeping or shorthand, prepared them for employment, confirmed their eagerness, and demonstrated their progress toward independence, a more manly middle-class form of morality.[40]

Didactic fiction portrayed potential self-made men as hopeful lads on the move. They might not achieve wealth by the end of the book, because all that mattered was constant progress. For example, Horatio Alger's hero Ragged Dick in his first adventure works casually as a bootblack and lives on the street wasting his money and life. After a chance meeting with a successful businessman, Dick resolves to change his own life. Through sheer willpower, he reinvents himself. He begins to dress in respectable and clean clothes, save his money, and, most important, study. When the opportunity arises, Dick is ready to accept a clerking job as a reward for bravery. Although this story ends here, Dick's future prospects look promising. As he climbs upward, Ragged Dick renames himself Dick, then Richard, and finally Richard Hunter, Esq., signs of his increasing middle-class respectability. While Alger emphasized the importance of good character, he also told a story of steps toward success.[41]

Mid-nineteenth-century narratives of failure also illustrate this characterization of independence as career mobility. Many fictional failures had stopped moving forward and remained permanent clerks. Men who were in their forties or were fathers of teenagers and still worked as clerks or bookkeepers had let down their families. Tragically, daughters of such men regularly needed to find jobs. Mary Clemmer Ames, a proponent of employment for women, described Morna in her novel *Victorie* as the daughter of an unsuccessful but respectable bookkeeper who "lived and died a common man," leaving her fatherless and unprotected. An 1869 *Harper's New Monthly Magazine* article supporting jobs for women referred to a hypothetical young woman whose father, "a mechanic, or perhaps a clerk," does not earn enough for the family to live comfortably and respectably. Fiction also presented younger clerks headed in the wrong direction. Mr. John Skiddy, a clerk at the Messrs. Fog and Company counting room in Fanny Fern's novel *Ruth Hall,* is a dreamer, not a doer, and ultimately a loser. A henpecked husband, he botches a love affair and efforts to find gold in California and ends up abandoned by his wife. He is left rocking a screaming baby while wearing the crumbled clothes of a respectable clerk, a "limpsey dickey and collapsed shirt-bosom."[42]

While Ames illustrated the older man who never reaches independence and while Fern depicted the younger man heading in the wrong direction, Herman Melville portrayed the essence of nineteenth-century middle-class failure in the character Bartleby in 1853. This most famous office worker in nineteenth-century literature descends into literal immobility. When asked by his new employer to "examine a small paper," the once extraordinarily productive clerk issues his famous words, "I would prefer not to." Increasingly, this "motionless young man" refuses to do anything, even leave the building. When his employer relocates to another office to escape him, Bartleby lingers. Eventually dragged to prison, he dies. How stationary could one become![43]

Each of Bartleby's fellow clerks characterize a step in his descent. The youngest, Ginger Nut, a twelve-year-old errand boy, appears quick-witted and awash with energy and potential. The twenty-five-year-old Nippers is already impatient with the "duties of a mere copyist" and ambitiously ventures to move on. However, his sins foreshadow a fall. Although he "dressed in a gentlemanly sort of a way," his leisure activities tell a different story—his visitors include "fellows in seedy coats, whom he called clients." The eldest, Turkey, sputters downward: "not far from sixty," he works like the blazes until noon but slowly loses energy and prudence afterward. Together, these three office men chart the path from hopeful vigor to degeneration, with the inert Bartleby as the nadir.[44]

These literary clerks not only flounder at commerce; they die prematurely. Moire's father succumbs to the tragic death of a consumptive clerk. Bartleby, the "pallidly, neat, pitiably respectable, incurably forlorn" scrivener (copyist), also ultimately perishes, "huddled at the base of the wall, his knees drawn up, lying on his side, his head touching the cold stones." Because of their failure to rise up, death is the only honorable solution for these dependent and immobile men. Even real clerks learned that "to become stagnant is to die."[45]

Immobility proved a lack of ambition and, therefore, of middle-class manly character for Bartleby and his coworkers and the other narratives of failure. George William Curtis's old bookkeeper in his 1856 novel *Prue and I* has become "content to remain a deputy book-keeper." With his ambition tempered, he spends his time fantasizing about castles in distant lands, leaving work early in the afternoon to stroll along the Battery, even imagining meeting the fictional Bartleby. His own character explains why he remained a clerk for so long.[46] A man with ambition would learn and grow from his experiences on the job, no matter how boring or degraded the job. Character, not the work itself, determined dignity.

Training and Education

The market economy's proliferation of commercialized education provided clerks with a site for proving their ambition, whether or not they embraced the feminine moralism of respectability. In the two decades before the Civil War, an expansion in two forms of preparation, book learning and classroom instruction, supplemented on-the-job training and stood ready to challenge traditional apprenticeship and authority relations. Although the time and money necessary for formal schooling often made young men more dependent on their parents, the growing availability of books for self-study and formal training actually provided young men with some independence by weakening employers' monopoly of knowledge. Instead of relying entirely on their employers to regulate and dispense information, young men could turn to books or schools as aids in promotion. By furnishing an alternative to employer dependency, education strengthened clerks' sense of their own self-reliance, proof of ambition. They could now move their careers forward and "make" themselves into middle-class men by defining their preparation as mental and purposeful. Their moral behavior rested on manly discipline, mental activity, and study.[47]

Clerks could choose from varying means to improve themselves. They might acquire formal and even extensive educations, graduating from colleges, but completion of the seventh grade was usually more than enough. All they needed was to meet very simple educational requirements: speak English; possess general knowledge of arithmetic, spelling, grammar, composition, and punctuation; and write neatly and legibly.[48]

More important than acquiring formal education, clerks needed evidence of mental training, since mental labor defined middle-class men's work. Success literature championed purposeful self-study, a gendered form of reading that bolstered masculine individualism and marked middle-class manly status. To move upward, learning must meet the criteria of determined manly study, rather than the feminine form of novel reading for leisure.[49] T. S. Arthur and Freeman Hunt, among others, regularly censured novel reading. Arthur distinguished between "well-directed study" and fiction reading that would lead to "puny intellectual growth." "Self-education," Arthur argued, "requires prolonged and laborious study," the behavior of men, not women.[50] For example, Horatio Alger's hero, Ragged Dick, studies reading and writing nightly to prepare to enter the middle class. T. S. Arthur explicitly advised young men to learn "figures and account-keeping" and improve their handwriting. Clerks recognized the need for individual initiative if they expected to advance. Bradford Morse made sure to write his parents to say, "I spend my time mostly in reading and studying," and he advised his brother, who had just found employment as a clerk, "Study your school books the same as if you were in school."[51]

The simplest strategy of self-improvement required men to track their own behavior. Literary scholar Thomas Augst finds that nineteenth-century clerks kept diaries to monitor their own activities and insights, as guides for evaluating and ordering their lives. They incorporated the Christian tradition of self-reflection as necessary for salvation by contemplating on their progress at milestones, such as birthdays, New Years, and anniversaries with a particular employer. These diarists built a "fund of wisdom on which they might draw" for reference in the future. But self-scrutiny was not enough, and enterprising young men turned to other sources for training.[52]

Materials for purposeful study became more widely available with changes in factory production, mass marketing, advertising, and distribution during the printing revolution. If a clerk wished to prepare himself to learn about the uniformity of procedures, attention to detail, and the general workings of business by studying bookkeeping, he would find that self-instruction had grown easier. The antebellum commercial explosion in publishing had expanded the number of resources available, such as James Bennett's forty-one editions of *The American System of Practical Bookkeeping*, issued between 1820 and 1862, and B. Wood Foster's eight editions of *A Practical System of Bookkeeping*. Future reformer Henry George remarked in an 1857 letter, "I commenced last evening to take lessons in penmanship, . . . I have taken your advice and am trying to improve myself all I can. I shall shortly commence to study book-keeping."[53]

Henry A. Patterson, who enjoyed the urban working-class leisure of drinking, theater, betting, and boxing but still insisted on his respectability, maintained focused study and reading throughout his early years of clerking. He began studying bookkeeping at his grandfathers' six months after starting to work as a store clerk. He and five others met weekly for thirteen months. He frequently noted who lost interest and dropped out, again comparing himself to others: he wrote, "Uncle William has given up," after one month; and after nearly a year, his brother Turner's attendance became spotty, before he finally quit. Besides bookkeeping, Patterson periodically practiced writing with Turner, read on his own, and joined the Mercantile Library Association. By preparing themselves at night, such young men strengthened their sense of individual responsibility.[54]

New institutions also enabled young men to engage in purposeful self-improvement. Like Patterson, some clerks joined mercantile libraries to promote self-study and affirm their middle-class identity. These dozens of libraries, which grew in the years before the Civil War, initially sought to attract merchants' clerks and young men desiring careers in business. *Hunt's Merchants' Magazine* praised the mercantile library for teaching "order, dignity, self-respect, [and] business tact" through writing constitutions and following rules of order. The New York Mercantile Library promoted itself as a "training ground for business organization," according to literary scholar Thomas Augst. Active participants wrote mission statements in the annual reports, and they learned about cost-benefit analysis and developed an appreciation of the "law" of supply and demand as they decided which books to purchase.[55]

For two dollars per year, young men could join the New York Mercantile Library and acquire knowledge and the confidence that they had made decisions to improve not only their business future but also their moral standing. The library enabled clerks to use their leisure hours "profitably." Reading for study promised to cultivate character by transforming men's evaluation of texts into a type of morality, rather than merely work for money, according to Augst. The annual addresses of the presidents portrayed reading as an investment for discipling the minds of young men and protecting them against catastrophes. In the 1840s, the New York Mercantile Library promoted the social aspects of reading through institutionalized discussion sessions, conversation rooms, and lectures. These programs helped young men engage in purposeful study, while also keeping them too busy for more dangerous diversions.[56]

Beyond reading philosophical or practical books on business practices, clerks increasingly studied with tutors and attended classes to master office skills. Private tutoring and business schools teaching bookkeeping had been around since the eighteenth century, although their numbers remained small until the expansion of mercantile clerking. In the 1820s, there were a number of small private commercial schools in Boston. Most notable was Foster's Commercial School, which offered morning, afternoon, and evening classes in penmanship, rapid writing, arithmetic, and bookkeeping. Foster charged twelve dollars for single and double bookkeeping lessons, quite expensive for a young man on his own. Public schools introduced single-entry bookkeeping in Boston when the English School opened in 1821. Six years later, the state of Massachusetts used Boston's curriculum as a model by requiring courses in single-entry bookkeeping in towns of five hundred families or more.[57]

After the 1830s, commercial schools became plentiful. In Boston, Comer's Commercial College (1840), French's Business College (1848), and Bryant and Stratton Commercial School (1860) were established. The last two were originally part of the Bryant and Stratton chain, which organized more than fifty schools nationwide between 1853 and 1866. This trend of proliferating commercial instruction in bookkeeping continued in the 1860s and 1870s, when private commercial schools nationally swelled from 30 in 1860 to 1,620 in 1880. The public schools also continued to appeal to business-minded students. In 1866, Boston's Girls High School instituted courses on double-entry bookkeeping. Three years later, Boston's evening school first opened its doors, with bookkeeping becoming its most popular course: 42 percent of the subjects taught in the night school were commercial. By 1875, all Boston high schools offered a second-year bookkeeping course and an additional elective in business. Pittsburgh even launched a commercial high school department as early as 1868, with a program aimed at boys.[58]

These new opportunities to acquire office skills enabled young men to initiate career moves, evidence of individual effort. Reading materials, tutors, and courses decentralized knowledge, undercutting employers' monopolization of the necessary skills, while also affirming individual initiative. When young men from small towns and rural communities left home to attend commercial schools or when city youth spent time and money for such training, they appeared responsible for their own success. Job preparation through manly middle-class self-study or seeking out commercial training enabled men to envision their actions as steps forward, proof of their ambition. Such conduct demonstrated independence, whether the young men totally adopted a respectable lifestyle or not.[59]

This version of independence embraced a softer and therefore more respectable manliness than that of the riotous city clerks. Without entirely adopting feminine moralism, purposeful study gave men a form of respectability that still elevated and differentiated them from women's leisurely reading and working-class men's mechanical labor. The self-made man was the midcentury's balanced manhood.

STENOGRAPHIC INDEPENDENCE

Stenography developed within this framework of middle-class manly improvement. From 1830 to the 1870s, stenographers shared an even greater appreciation of their craft as a sign of independent ambition and progress. Unlike other clerical occupations, stenography grew out of the antebellum spelling and phonetic reform movements before becoming a moneymaking position. For many early practitioners, shorthand was a crusade for human progress. Their social activism reinforced an image of self-reliance. For others, shorthand was a hobby that encouraged self-study. Even stenographers who earned a living practicing their craft for newspapers, legislatures, or the courts could imagine their work as a step upward.

Like their English counterparts, many nineteenth-century stenographers in the United States became interested in shorthand through phonetics and spelling reform as a means to modify the irregularities of the English language, improve communication, and disseminate information and knowledge. Building on the eighteenth-century studies of scientific classification, language reformers like Augustus French Boyle sought to codify sounds using a "utilitarian" alphabet with no capitals, script, or printed characters. Boyle had developed a "reformed system of spelling" and was looking for a publisher when he heard about Stephen Pearl Andrews publicizing Isaac Pitman's more systematic phonography system, which used lines and squiggles to represent individual sounds. Andrews and Boyle and other early proponents of phonography advertised this "more perfect" system as a sign of progress.[60]

Since phonography's advocates believed it improved language, they viewed their teachings and writings as reform work. Boyle and Andrews founded the *Anglo-Saxon* and Andrews the *Propagandist* as a crusade to promote phonography by "increasing the number of teachers, . . . aiding teachers to introduce it into schools, and . . . supplying reading materials for phonographers."[61] They compiled lists of teachers and potential pen pals to enable isolated phonographers to practice their skills. By 1850, Andrews estimated that 80,000 people could scribble a smidgen of phonography, that about 300 wrote a hundred words per minute or faster, and that 102 taught phonography. The 80,000 figure reveals more about Andrews's grand hopes than about success at midcentury.[62]

Because spelling reform was an "essential counterpart of phonographic writing," early publications devoted considerable space to language theory and wrote English in phonetic spelling, as in "Fenetiks iz diveided intui fonotipi and fonografi" (Phonetics is divided into phonotypy and phonography). Entire publications were written in phonetic spelling. However, by the 1870s and 1880s, spelling reform declined in shorthand periodicals and devolved into merely leaving out silent letters like *e* in "have" or "are," while diehards continued with a few more substitutions, like using "az" instead of "as."[63]

Language reformers who identified phonography as an example of human progress also belonged to the more radical antebellum reform movements. Isaac Pitman was a vegetarian activist and a member of the Swedenborgian spiritualist sect. Augustus F. Boyle and Theron C. Leland became adherents of the philosophy of Charles Fourier, a utopian socialist believer in perfectibility and progress.[64] Boyle's partner Stephen Pearl Andrews, an ardent abolitionist and agent for the Liberty Party, brought Isaac Pitman's phonography to the United States from the World Anti-Slavery Conference in England in 1840. When he read through the materials, he "resolved to become a propagandist of [*sic*], the Pitmanian project." Later, he developed his own universal language, Alwato, before becoming one of the most notorious "free lovers," a founder of the Long Island utopian community Modern Times, and a leader of the International Workingmen's Association established by Karl Marx in the 1870s.[65] Oliver Dyer was an abolitionist, a Swedenborgian New Church lay preacher in 1868, and then a clergyman in 1876. Edward F. Underhill signed the "Declaration of Sentiments" at the first woman's rights convention at Seneca Falls in 1848. John Brown Smith boasted adherence to temperance, water cure, and vegetarianism and was an opponent of state power. A publisher of early phonograph pamphlets and books, Fowler and Wells, was a well-known supporter of reforms like phrenology, temperance, water cure, mesmerism, and psychology.[66]

The reformist beginnings of phonography in the United States made stenography different from other clerical jobs. Reformers, or "propagandists," as Andrews called them, optimistically viewed shorthand as proof of human progress. They even worried that men studied phonography for "selfish motives" rather than "to learn and help spread Phonotypy" (the printing of phonography) and phonography itself. However, with time, the reformist impulse among stenographers diminished dramatically, although not entirely dissipating. These reformist motives for learning phonography distinguished it, especially before 1870.[67]

Phonography's mystery and novelty also attracted adherents. Shorthand magazines liked to report how men marveled at phonography's strange dots and dashes that were uniform enough for others to read and translate into longhand. Like visitors to dime museums, who gaped at the bearded lady and other freaks of nature, phonography at first "attracted considerable attention and curiosity." Because few people had come into contact with this new style of fast writing, early practitioners reported how it astonished classmates and left ministers whose sermons they copied in awe. Young men remembered their first sightings of phonography, whether among the books of an elder brother, uncle, or fellow worker or even in "the show window of a law stationer." With time, more people encountered stenography in newspaper offices, the army, and school.[68]

These new methods of fast writing attracted middle-class men and even women who never imagined themselves as office employees or intended to use shorthand as a stepping-stone to business ownership. Some took up study just for the fun of it or as a "pleasing accomplishment," with "no intention or expectation of using it for business." Theodore F. Shuey recalled how a visiting clergyman introduced him to shorthand as a suitable recreational activity for a boy.[69]

Nonetheless, stenography magazines promoted shorthand's usefulness. In the inaugural issue of the *Propagandist* in 1850, Stephen Pearl Andrews touted phonography for "those who are seeking to educate themselves." He particularly encouraged it as a tool for "stocking your own mind with the most useful kind of information" that "you can acquire by your own exertions."[70] Many young men agreed, immediately recognizing shorthand's utility for self-improvement. Some read up on phonography on their own while at school. John Brewster secretly traded his algebra book for a copy of Benn Pitman's manual. He pored over shorthand texts into the wee hours of the morning while his parents nagged him to "put away that book and go to bed."[71] College students were even more likely to study stenography outside of formal classrooms, like Truman J. Ellinwood, who learned phonography from another Central College classmate. Students often practiced taking notes from lectures in college. Phonography's use as a tool for learning facilitated its association with a career step-up.[72]

Although the shorthand press framed phonography's advantages to improve their own bottom line, they did reveal that young men recognized the advantages of shorthand for journalism and law. A journalist with stenographic training could report verbatim political speeches, congressional sessions, trials, or any number of political events. The Senate acknowledged the job opportunities for such journalists when it contracted with the leading Whig and Democratic Party newspapers in Washington, D.C., in 1848 to publish all of its debates in their entirety. The stenographic press reminded readers of the potential for advancement for journalists who could write in shorthand, since newspapers printed many speeches and proceedings in their entirety. Some young journalist apprentices learned "rudimentary and practical knowledge" at work, like other clerical workers traditionally did. Stephen O'Meara began studying stenography in 1872 to improve his career prospects as a newspaper man: "I found to my surprise that in the office a high value was placed upon the very slight knowledge of shorthand which I possessed. . . . As a consequence I was pushed immediately into such work as required shorthand." He might have been sent to cover trials, a common assignment that evidently led to the term *court reporter.* Printers, too, recognized stenography's usefulness.[73]

Very early on, before courts generally hired legal stenographers, lawyers and judges kept notes of the court proceedings. Shorthand proponents, like the *Propagandist,* appealed directly to lawyers, "who require it so much." Some lawyers and even judges studied stenography after they were well established professionally. Law students especially took up the study of shorthand to improve their note taking. Some, like Charles B. Collar in 1848, then found themselves more in demand as court reporters and switched fields. This interchange between lawyers and stenographers continued into the twentieth century.[74]

Shorthand reporters began to offer their services to lawyers, providing transcripts of trials in exchange for fees. In 1868, the "Office of Osgooby & Gilbert, Stenographers and Law Reporters" advertised that they would save lawyers time and money. Louis Feeser's advertisement explained that his transcription would "free" counsel from the "distracting" "mechanical process" of "taking minutes," so his "mind can be solely occupied with the mental process of a trial." This division of mental and mechanical labor would haunt stenographers in years to come. Court reporter Philander Deming, who wrote short stories about life in the Adirondacks, mirrored the arguments calling for court stenographers in an 1865 story, "The Courts." His protagonist convinces a judge to allow him to take shorthand notes for free in order to prove their value. When a dispute arises over testimony, the stenographer's transcript settles the controversy and wins over the reluctant defense attorney.[75]

Increasingly, young men perceived of stenography as a means to advance beyond the "ordinary clerk," "make more money," or become law stenographers, as encouraged by the shorthand promoters.[76] Frank F. Wood had read a copy of George Odell's *Odell's System of Shorthand* while at an academy but had lost interest until hired by legal reporters Dement, Gray, and Company in 1874 as a longhand copyist. He very quickly had a "relapse of the shorthand fever," acquired a copy of Andrew Jackson Graham's *Handbook,* and began "inwardly digesting that ponderous volume."[77] Whether as a reform, a novelty, a tool for self-improvement, or an opportunity for employment in journalism, printing, or law, shorthand became associated with progress and ambitious mobility, the most useful and gender-balanced definition of middle-class independence.

Stenographic training accentuated individual initiative by relocating the transmission of skills away from the work site and the employer. Increasingly, young men could learn shorthand outside of work, although at first, students had to seek out instructors. The early promoters of phonography studied with the inventors and the few who had procured copies of Isaac Pitman's manuals. The rare men possessing knowledge of phonography then trained a few select students. Stephen Pearl Andrews recalled his early years as a stenography teacher when he taught "before I was sure of writing a hundred words correctly." Soon, he, Oliver Dyer, and Augustus French Boyle published the *Anglo-Saxon,* a magazine that provided information on phonography and texts for transcribing practice. Boyle taught "classes, . . . five hundred strong, meeting at five-o'clock in the summer mornings—so great was the enthusiasm."[78] Others followed Boyle's lead and gave lectures in makeshift schoolrooms. In 1847, Theron C. Leland, a utopian, traveled throughout central New York organizing and teaching classes of forty pupils for six lessons based on Andrews and Boyle's *The Complete Phonographic Class-Book* and *The Phonographic Reader.* Three years later, he was appointed instructor for the New York Mercantile Library Association; in the same year, the Boston Mercantile Library Association also engaged a phonography teacher. Slowly, a few public schools introduced shorthand, but often on a temporary basis. Thomas J. Griffin taught his public school students shorthand after school. For a few years, Oliver Dyer trained a group of prominent court reporters and law stenographers at Philadelphia's Central High School. The proliferation of new classes provided more opportunities to learn shorthand.[79]

Prospects for studying shorthand also improved as more publications about phonography became available. Some phonetic advocates and legislative and judicial reporters revised Pitman's language and created their own versions. They then authored pamphlets and books and founded magazines to promote their own dialects. The new publications multiplied the types of reading materials for home study, especially mail-order lessons and dictation practice. Andrews and Boyle's *The Complete Phonographic Class-Book* and *The Phonographic Reader,* Benn Pitman's *Manual of Phonography,* and Andrew Jackson Graham's *Standard Phonography* proved especially popular. Low-cost phonographic materials also attracted more readers. Oliver Dyer remembered Andrews and Boyle's texts selling for thirty-seven and a half cents and twenty-five cents, respectively—a good price compared to the average of ninety-one cents for business books, but still requiring some savings compared to six cents for a sporting weekly in the 1840s. In 1856, Benn Pitman's *Phonographic Reader* sold for twenty-five cents, his *Phonographic Copybook* for ten cents and rising to twelve cents by mail, his *Phonographic Magazine* for one dollar per year, and his *Phonetic Primer* for ten cents. Early shorthand magazines typically included exercises for transcribing from phonography to English, advice on form, and model script. Most shorthand journals were short lived, but beginning in the late 1850s through the 1870s, a few survived and lasted for over twenty years.[80]

The proliferation of books and magazines by proponents of competing shorthand dialects plus the increased circulation of Pitman's manuals meant that more prospective stenographers could study on their own. For example, Jay Thomas had heard about fast writing and seen a copy of Andrews and Boyle's version of Pitman, but he recounted that when a friend showed him Longley's *Manual of Phonography,* "here was a revelation! . . . a book that said positively that he could learn this wonderful art without a teacher." He immediately ordered a manual from the publishers and later concluded that within a short time, he had become a "fair writer of the corresponding style." John H. Fazel also recounted how he began to study Pitman's *Manual of Phonography,* but after failing to learn on his own, he entered a correspondence with Benn Pitman and took mail-order classes, which enabled him to farm during the day and study at night.[81]

Despite these greater opportunities to study stenography, only those willing and able to devote the long hours to drills could master the skill. Many young men encountered shorthand but did not become interested enough to practice until years later. David Wolfe Brown studied shorthand in Oliver Dyer's Central High School classroom, but by the end of school two years later, he had forgotten much of it. Not until experiencing the monotony of a $2.50-per-week clerking job did he become serious about learning. He then studied books written by Benn Pitman and R. P. Prosser and implored his family to dictate to him. When their patience wore thin, Brown used "some small savings of my own and the cash advances of my parents" to hire boys as readers. He then continued honing his skills by reporting sermons and public addresses for over two years.[82]

Some young men arranged for out-of-state apprenticeships. After studying on his own, David Wolfe Brown headed for Washington to work in the Senate under Richard Sutton and Dennis F. Murphy. Application, practice, and travel to find training enabled shorthand writers to see themselves as independent despite the help of families and fellow workers.[83]

The investment in preparation bolstered the image that only ambitious men with initiative, determination, and industry would succeed. Stenography proponents encouraged this view. An 1860 volume of the *Phonographic Magazine* noted that "the lazy man would not give it enough practice to acquire speed or correctness." Shorthand manuals repeatedly assured readers that phonography students would acquire the character traits useful for work. In 1855, Benn Pitman's *Manual of Phonography* plugged his dialect as a means to improve the mind and encourage "habits of patience, perseverance, and watchfulness" as well as "precision" and "vigilance." In 1864, Elias Longley repeated the promise of phonography as an "improvement of the mind," that manly middle-class requirement.[84]

Early stenographers' career paths also reinforced their image as ambitious independent men. There were few stable appointments until the 1870s, even though Congress created a permanent staff of shorthand writers to record debates during the Jefferson administrations, and the first official reporter positions appeared in the 1850s.[85] In most cases, men hustled for jobs from city to city. William F. Fitzgerald, born in Columbia County, New York, took a series of jobs throughout upstate New York until he "became infatuated" with stenography.[86] From then on, the scope of his traveling widened. In 1879, he served as a private secretary for the Mobile and Montgomery Railroad in Mobile, Alabama; he was back in Albany the next year, but by March, he headed south again to Florida, then back to Troy, New York. Others oscillated between jobs, using their shorthand skills to report for newspapers about government legislative bodies, conventions, and trials or to chronicle, on their own, the proceedings of conventions or conferences of religious groups, learned societies, and medical associations. From 1849 to 1862, Edward F. Underhill found work with the *St. Louis Republican,* the *Reveille,* the *National Intelligencer,* the *New York Times,* and the *New York Tribune* before turning to legal transcription and eventually becoming an official court reporter. Charles B. Collar worked for the *Boston Globe* from 1850 to 1858. Between 1850 and 1856, he joined the corps of official reporters assigned to the House of Representatives. At the same time, he assisted in recording the proceedings of the constitutional conventions in Ohio and Virginia in 1850 and in Massachusetts in 1853. Constitutional conventions in almost every state between 1820 and 1870 provided employment opportunities for stenographers who would pick up and move for a few months. In 1858, Collar formed a partnership with Andrew J. Graham for reporting patent cases in the U.S. Courts, while continuing to freelance lectures, sermons, public meetings, constitutional conventions, and political addresses for newspapers. Finally, in 1863, he became one of the early official stenographers for the Supreme Court in New York City, a position that he held for over thirty years until his death near the end of the century. Collar's career path illustrates the fluidity of reporting in the 1850s and the slow expansion of secure positions in the 1860s and 1870s.[87]

Stenographers' early history strengthened their identity as middle-class men. Their unique association with reform and mystery linked them to middle-class values of progress and perfectibility. Shorthand's potential as a skill for future learning contributed to stenographers' self-identity as men who made themselves. They could see each action as movement forward. Their efforts to seek out new material and courses, practice to build speed, and travel for employment enhanced their image as ambitious, autonomous men.

CONCLUSION

Stenography developed as a language reform and then an occupation during the antebellum years, when clerks struggled to construct a new class and gender identity. Despite male clerical workers' dependence at work as apprentices or employees, clerking was associated with middle-class manly independence. This image of independence flourished with new economic opportunities. Some clerks found independence by embracing urban, male, working-class styles of leisure. They often lived apart from their families and engaged in exciting activities that differed from those at home. Since enjoyment of male working-class leisure in the city jeopardized their respectability and middle-class status, some clerks took another road to independence. They embraced the more feminine moral respectability by joining religious groups or the YMCA. Through such groups or on their own, they assured themselves that their self-discipline proved that they had made a choice to follow a difficult but moral path for character development. Alternatively, some clerks reframed their new behavior to fit with respectability. The most appealing definition of independence demanded ambition through simple steps of mobility, which young men could acquire through new forms of training and education. Each step symbolized initiative and individual choice. Stenographers, too, identified with the self-reliant middle-class man, although their connections at first differed from other clerical workers. This last meaning of independence enabled men to find a middle ground between the moral respectability associated with women and the exhilarating independent leisure activities of working-class men. In the last few decades of the century, when opportunities for mobility declined further, stenographers and other clerical workers rethought their definitions of independence and failure, as we will see in chapter 3, after first examining women's midcentury gender balance and their role in the changes.

CHAPTER 2

Treasury Girls and the Masses: From Degraded Women Workers to Employees

"STANDING in the doorway of the *National Theatre,* a few nights ago, watching the audience leave the building, we heard a young snob near us exclaim to his companion, 'Let us go now, Tom! We've seen all the ladies! The rest of these women are only Treasury Clerks!'" John B. Ellis thus gleefully disclosed the dark side of government clerking, treasury courtesans, even when ostensibly exonerating them: "The majority of them are [ladies], but it is a melancholy fact that many of them are either suspected of immoral practices, or looked down upon by the Washingtonians as being of a lower order."[1] Ellis's division of women government employees into either socially respectable ladies or disreputable clerks exposed the problem for the rising numbers of middle-class women clerks—how to maintain their social position while holding jobs outside of the home.

Since the woman's sphere revolved around the home, the midcentury gender balance defined respectable women as dependent and family-oriented, though personally spunky. Personal qualities that featured independence were acceptable so long as they did not interfere with women's primary duties. By constraining women's individualism to the personal arena, however, the midcentury feminine balance only valued women's employment that comfortably fit within the true woman's sphere of the home. As women and men came to share similar (if not identical) jobs, women's labor and employed women themselves were viewed as degraded. Their image as pitiful and dependent laborers who performed debased work made way for their positions as employees. By the end of the century, they had become symbols of the masses, the modern employee in the corporate bureaucracies.

TRUE WOMANHOOD AND INDEPENDENCE

Since the mid-nineteenth century, middle-class men and especially women valued both dependence and independence in women. Contemporary nineteenth-century fiction depicted both values as well. Besides praising women's dedication to home and family and dependence on fathers and husbands, novelists and writers of short stories also respected autonomous women who shared with men the traits of resourcefulness, initiative, and agency. While woman's rights advocates fully embraced the economically self-sufficient woman, others were more tentative until near the end of the Civil War.

The nineteenth-century view of independence as the essence of manhood defined womanhood as its opposite, a symbol of dependency. The shift of some economic tasks from homes to factories and shops helped reinvent eighteenth-century notions of women's sexual and political dependence, although the process was not simple or unidirectional. As the market economy of the early nineteenth century transformed labor and gender relations, the metaphoric concept of separate spheres became a means to explain the effects of these economic changes on male and female relations. Gendered spheres divided human relations, associating men with the institutions that seemed to drive the new industrial world, including work, politics, public life, and money. The rhetoric about women crystallized around the symbols of family and private life, with the home symbolizing the repository of traditional human values and of women as dependents on men.[2]

Nineteenth-century Americans applauded women's selfless devotion to their families. A middle-class woman's worth lay in her adherence to the requirements of a lady. A True Woman was modest, compassionate, forgiving, pious, and accomplished in domestic skills (like cooking and sewing); she loved children and beauty, especially flowers; she valued neatness and sincerity, dressed simply, and nursed the sick. Even Fanny Fern's economically independent heroine Ruth Hall, in the controversial 1854–55 novel of the same name, cared for her ailing daughter Daisy and her husband, Harry, as well as for Deacon Gray and Mrs. Rice's child. When her husband died and the family failed to help out, Ruth struggled to survive but still found time to appreciate beauty, flowers, and poetry and to play with her children, eventually securing a home for them.[3]

Since members of the middle class expected husbands and fathers to support their families, they assumed that women sought employment because men failed as providers, and they were mostly correct. Throughout the century, a father's death precipitated the most devastating economic crisis for any family, forcing both middle-class and working-class daughters to seek employment. In New England, when such a family crisis occurred, sons and daughters left rural communities and small towns for work in Boston, "the Hub." Working-class women also held jobs, even if their fathers were still present, because their families relied on the contribution of every member of the family. Wives often kept boarders, and daughters either helped their mothers or found wage labor. From the middle-class view, all women appropriately worked for pay when the family system of support floundered because fathers died or earned too little. Since women sought employment due to men's economic shortcomings or death, employed women symbolized men's failure to care for their dependents.[4]

In the antebellum years, respectable women's employment had generally been framed as victimization, not opportunity. Women, the thinking went, should be useful to their families. If a family needed a woman's income, she should have the training and health to help out. In other words, serving others and sacrificing for her relatives—not a desire for economic self-sufficiency—justified a woman's paid work. A True Woman should not burden others by her dependence. Even women mill workers writing in the *Lowell Offering* portrayed themselves as "republican daughters" supporting rural communities with dignity. However, if ambition drove a woman's desire for remuneration, she came across as cold, calculating, and unwomanly, because enterprise implied agency and a rejection of the status quo rather than victimization. According to historian Wendy Gamber, midcentury fiction and credit reports criticized milliners and dressmakers who did not exhibit helplessness and dependence. As long as women worked only because of family need, rather than out of aspirations, paid employment was acceptable.[5]

Although True Womanhood served as the touchstone for cultural respect, since the antebellum years, nineteenth-century women recognized the cultural value of independence. Women authors admired independent-spirited women, especially in middle-class characters. Literary critics Frances Cogan, Janice Hume, and Amy Gilman find that heroines in novels and short stories exhibit resourcefulness, initiative, and agency. They have spunk, gumption, drive, and ingenuity to rise above "unfortunate" circumstances or troublesome superiors. Emily Graham of Maria Susanna Cummins's popular 1854 novel, *The Lamp-*

lighter, justifies giving her ward a "good education . . . to make her independent of all the world, and not simply dependent upon us."[6] Some heroines even possess the qualities of self-made independence that characterized middle-class manhood. In Susan Warner's blockbuster 1850 novel, *The Wide, Wide World,* heroine Ellen Montgomery makes her way by "her own resources." When Ellen's cruel aunt refuses to let her attend school, Ellen engenders "a sudden resolve": "I'll study by myself!" she proclaimed, and she "sprang up stairs to her room" to do so. Ruth Hall, in Fanny Fern's novel, struggles to support her children after her husband's death. She moves from dependence on him and then her in-laws to a successful career as a journalist and, finally, ownership of her own home.[7] Like middle-class heroines, working-class protagonists on their way to the middle or upper class also display pluck, determination, bravery, and defiance of authority. In *The Lamplighter,* the resourceful Gertrude brings along India rubbers to navigate the damp meadow, unlike the fashionable, arrogant, and helpless Belle Clinton.[8]

Even the calls for women's economic independence and ambition that would become more common at the end of the century had their antecedents in the antebellum years. While the Democratic Party press disapproved of expanded career opportunities for women, the antislavery Free Soil and Republican parties accepted some women's employment. Harriet Beecher Stowe's female characters in *Uncle Tom's Cabin* have the talent to manage farms profitability and even do confectionary work;[9] by 1856, Milly in *Dred: A Tale of the Great Dismal Swamp* is able "to provide a very comfortable support" for the children. Antislavery editor Jane G. Swisshelm also encouraged work opportunities for women because women professionals "could provide better food for their families" and reject problematic marriage proposals. Nonetheless, these antislavery women's beliefs in gender difference led to a continued preference for women remaining "engaged in home duties."[10]

In contrast, the more radical abolitionists and their offshoot, woman's rights activists, called for gender equality. They agitated for expanding the acceptable reasons for female employment and financial independence. In the 1850s, Amelia Bloomer, for example, extended the general view that women should be useful by calling for them to "occupy their hands and minds in some useful business occupation" as opposed to a "life of idleness or . . . frivolity." She critiqued "dependent and helpless" women and encouraged them to learn "to rely on themselves and less upon man." Bloomer insisted that a woman must have "aspirations for a nobler destiny" and "make herself a name and fortune by her own energy and enterprise" in order to be happy and content with life. Like other advocates for woman's right in this era, she believed in equality: "A girl's hand and head were formed very much like those of a boy; and, if put to a trade at the age when boys are usually apprenticed, . . . she will master her business quite as soon as the boy." Champions of property rights for married women even promoted their employment by blaming financial dependence for their lives of household drudgery. Paulina Wright Davis and Elizabeth Cady Stanton wanted higher wages to free women from the home.[11]

The image of clerical work as an employment possibility for women goes back to these years. Support for hiring women in dry goods stores and offices spread, even from the conservative press, who labeled clerking jobs as potential female positions. In the 1830s, large stores in Boston and Philadelphia began hiring female clerks. In 1853, the conventional *Godey's Lady's Book* endorsed indoor work as quintessentially feminine because it "harmonize[s] with her natural love of home and its duties." So, too the conservative Democratic press in 1858 acknowledged that the "natural characteristics of women fit them for the duties of a clerk more than those of the other sex." A stenographic magazine in 1858 quoted a Philadelphia newspaper, that asked, "And what should hinder young ladies from becoming phonographic amanuenses to merchants . . . and literary men?" The next year, this same shorthand publication printed an advertisement that read, "A Secretary Wanted: Wanted, a person of either sex, to act as secretary to a physician and lecturer." So, by the 1850s, some approval of clerical positions for women emerged.[12]

During the 1860s and 1870s, the various justifications for female economic independence began to converge. Women were still encouraged to learn a trade to help out their families in a crisis. Yet, the concept of usefulness at times broadened beyond the family. In Ella Rodman's "An Angel of Murphy," Helen Jimpson lambasted "the silly, useless life I led—without aim and without reward" in contrast to "the honorable life of labor and usefulness before me."[13] Writers still insisted on the naturalism of women's dependence and lamented the necessity of paid work for widowed mothers and orphaned daughters who had sacrificed their loved ones to the war. Images of helpless women struggling to find respectable sources of income in the crowded world of female jobs received even more attention.[14]

Female authors published more frequently about working-class characters as victims of industrialization and urbanization who wallowed in poverty and moral decay during the war and early postwar years. Working-class women who sought employment, they wrote, faced sexual threats from lascivious employers who paid low wages for long hours and dangerous working conditions that led to starvation and death. In the 1860s, a growing number of short stories and articles portrayed working-class women as "sentimental victims of violence." The women suffered from the scarred heredity of parents damaged by drink and mill work and then finished off by mill accidents and fires. These working-class characters often chose feminine selfless sacrifice, rather than the bravery of the dime novel heroines. Advice books and government studies also depicted working-class women as victims. In her 1869 book, *Think and Act,* reformer Virginia Penny characterized the working-class woman as a "beast of burden," a slave in domestic or industrial life. Since women's employment itself often stood as a metaphor for industrialization and hence victimization, it seemed to reinforce notions of women as dependent and needing rescue. Nonetheless, working women received more attention than before the war.[15]

At the same time that writings about working women as victims flourished, some authors included a more assertive tone about economic independence. An 1869 *Harper's New Monthly Magazine* article began with the typical justifications for women's need for employment, calling for education, the right to "work at any employment for which she has physical or mental capacity," and equal pay for equal work. Eventually, however, the author went further, recommending that women "make a business" of their work, something "as if for life," not "for a few months, or at most, years, and then to be laid aside, never to be resumed." She admonished women, "Don't be afraid of being called strong-minded," which was "better than to be called weak-minded."[16]

More significantly, fiction aimed at female working-class readership took off in the 1870s with more assertive and independent heroines. The working-girl tales first appeared in the 1840s as short stories in magazines and then inexpensive paperbacks aimed at a working-class audience. In the mid-1870s, publishers of inexpensive and formulaic fiction developed a genre for working-class women. These dime novel plots emphasized love, jealousy, romance, defense of virtue, and marriage, with heroines who risked seduction, fell victim to kidnapping, and needed heroic rescuing. Yet the employed heroines exhibited pride in their work and agency. As early as the 1860s and 1870s, western heroines could adeptly rope, ride, and shoot, as well as rescue. Eventually, working girls also invariably escaped traps and rescued others from "near fatal accidents." Adapting male modes of action, working-class heroines in dime novels actually came to blows with villains and bailed out others. They fought off evil and danger and defended their morality, especially against elite men.[17]

From midcentury to the 1870s, female writers applauded both conventional femininity and independence. Despite this range of opinion, the nineteenth-century gender balance still favored dependence, family, and home, but it made room for personal independence. A few woman's rights supporters leaned more radically toward independence. Generally, however, respectable female employment required dependent women forced into unwanted independence. Although writers, including dime novelists, were slow to give up women's need for sacrifice and economic dependence, they increasingly encouraged economic self-sufficiency in the 1860s and 1870s.

GENDER, CLASS, DEGRADATION, AND WORK: WOMEN AS DEPENDENT EMPLOYEES

The antebellum characterization of women workers as dependent helped shape an image of their labor as degraded and made them good candidates for temporary jobs that lacked opportunity and required repetition. This image of women's labor as degraded, along with their low wages, accounts for their entry into office work before and during the Civil War. From the 1840s to the 1870s, women copyists stuck permanently at the bottom of the office hierarchy became symbols of degraded monotony, implying that the job debased the worker, rather than the popular notion that the worker's character debased the job. In doing so, they edged the occupation closer to the working class.

In the antebellum years, male clerks performed varied office tasks that included duplicating letters and other documents for internal record keeping. In contrast to the ubiquitous Renaissance clerk, very few men copied business materials exclusively without engaging in other work or received the job titles *copyist* or *scrivener.* An 1845 Boston Census counted only eight male copyists in comparison to 479 clerks. The number of men listed as copyists remained small through the 1870s.[18]

Copyists held relatively low status. Some clerks complained that copying kept them from tasks that would lead to their advancement. William Hoffman, for example, resented being "'kept at the desk,' writing bills, recording transactions, and making change," rather than "mak[ing] a sale or two."[19] The work itself could be performed by a low-paid office boy with a letterpress machine or by temporary workers. When the superintendent of the U.S. Patent Office repeatedly requested more clerks, his superiors only allowed him to hire temporary copyists, first in 1827 and then four years later when the office fell behind in recording patents. These latter copyists were housed in a barnlike room without seats or heat. Their prospects for social mobility remained dim, like those of the 1853 fictional law scrivener Bartleby.[20]

The low status of copying opened the way for female employment in the 1840s. In these antebellum years, women were already associated with monotonous and repetitious labor. Their work in mills and factories had became symbols of dreary and degraded industrial toil. Critics of factories portrayed women as victims of debased work, with long hours of boredom, regimentation, and low pay. Nathaniel Hawthorne referred to factories as "the demons of machinery [that] annihilate . . . the human soul." Herman Melville, in his 1855 short story "The Paradise of Bachelors and the Tartarus of Maids," described how the tedium of factory work transformed the "young fair brow" to "ruled and wrinkled" as "mere cogs to the wheels." Reformers, like Fourierists and other utopian socialists, extended their criticism of factory labor to nonmanual jobs changed by division of labor, with copying as the initial symbol of repetitive and mechanical office work.[21]

As business and correspondence increased at midcentury, women moved effortlessly into copying partly because they could perform the simple requirement of good handwriting at home. Although penmanship had been associated with educated manhood, handwriting became feminized with the "graceful lines and curves" of the Spencerian and other popular mid-nineteenth-century styles of penmanship. The perception of handwriting as a "mechanical process" also encouraged employers to believe that women could perform this simplest of tasks. By 1850, Charles Dickens considered copying so easy and so unskilled that even fictional David Copperfield's child wife, Dora, who could not manage a small household, and his simpleton friend, Mr. Dick, copied at home.[22]

Employers appreciated women's temporary work status and reliance on family, which meant they could be paid less than men. By the 1840s, the U.S. Patent Office hired women for copying as temporary home workers, a dominant form of female labor in these years. Unlike a freelance male copyist paid twenty cents per hundred words in 1825, Annie Goodrich Ellsworth earned ten cents per hundred words in 1843. The numbers of at-home copyists grew to sixty-five by 1869. Initially, women's salaries were half those of men, but that changed as women's pay increased and men's fell.[23]

The expansion of employment of women in offices also relied on their potential as temporary replacements. In 1854, the soon-to-be-famous nurse Clara Barton found employment in the U.S. Patent Office as a confidential clerk for fourteen hundred dollars but worked mostly as a copyist. When the superintendent of the office left for a year, his superior, the Secretary of the Interior, removed her. Upon his return, the superintendent rehired Barton, but as a temporary copyist mostly working at home, depending on the political resistance from the male staff.[24]

When government agencies sought temporary replacements for soldiers during the Civil War, the association of women with repetitive work, temporary labor, and dependency enabled their employment. The Civil War and its rapidly expanding government functions precipitated a dramatic acceleration in the number and proportion of female clerical workers in all levels of government. The war's costs forced the federal government and the Confederacy to cut corners while expanding their staffs. The federal government hired women to cut, sort, and clip Treasury notes in 1861, for what looked like temporary positions to pay for the war and substitute for soldiers. The Confederacy accepted women in the post office as well. An 1869 *New York Times* article justified women's employment for redirecting letters in the Post Office as "merely mechanical work." In 1869, the U.S. Patent Office engaged women on government premises to replace the at-home copyists. Now, the government specifically employed dependent women forced into the labor market by the death or injury of male relatives during the war, paying them less than male workers.[25]

By 1870, well before the typewriter, copying had become a growing female position. In Boston, the number of copyists had climbed to forty-eight, with women comprising 84.5% of the total. The report of selected occupations from the 1875 census of Massachusetts included eighty-nine female copyists in Boston but left out that category for men because of their low numbers.[26]

Once women made inroads into copying, the existing discourse condemning female factory work as degraded labor reinforced copying's low status. In the 1860s, fiction painted an image of women tediously copying. Rebecca Harding Davis, a strong supporter of employment opportunities for women, described Margaret Howth, in an 1862 novel by the same name, as a respectable woman victimized by the slow dragging hours of the "long day" as "a sluggish, hackneyed weariness creeping into her brain." She sat on a "high office-stool" and copied "from one to other as steadily, monotonously, as if she had been used to it all her life," even though these were the "first pages" on her "first day" at the job. Even after "an hour or two," her motions had become "mechanical." Her future looked bleak, like "an old woman, hard, mechanical, worn out."[27] Copying performed by women came to symbolize tedium and degraded work.

Women's dependence also gendered the concept of degradation, although their employment in men's jobs threatened to blur the male and female versions. Since middle-class men were expected to move upward from low-level positions, their own character, not the job itself, degraded them. In contrast, female dependency and, hence, permanent job immobility meant that paid employment could victimize even respectable women. For example, at the all-male Chicago Stenographers' Second Annual Dinner, Mr. M. H. Dement explained that women did not belong as stenographers because of the "drudgery of transcription at night . . . [and other hardships that] will quickly destroy all their grace and beauty." For some critics of female employment, paid work itself damaged women by limiting their chances of learning household skills; for most, a job with a masculine image diminished femininity.[28] Degradation for women, however, meant more than repetitive labor, because of the linkage of feminine debasement with immorality and the working class.

TREASURY COURTESANS: MORAL DANGERS OF GOVERNMENT WORK

Once it was acknowledged that women's presence debased work and that work degraded women, the public cause of that debasement transformed mere dependence to something more sinister and amorphous. The presence of women now threatened to mark their jobs as dangerous for innocent women and as attractions for immoral women, such as the working-class prostitute. Hence, there emerged a strong undercurrent of hostility toward government employment for women, ranging from a seeming concern about women clerks' welfare to downright assaults on their virtue, despite some enthusiastic approval of widening economic opportunities for women in the 1860s. Some male employees blew smoke at women, loafed, and were generally impolite. After 1864 congressional hearings on the Treasury Department linked embezzlement, seduction, and promiscuity, conservative journalists led an attack that impugned women's morality. They lambasted the "experiment" of integration of the sexes in the public arena of government offices for deprecating innocent feminine virtue. Government clerking symbolized the latest employment to threaten the reputations of women working outside of the home, especially women living alone.[29]

Conversations about the perils of government clerking for women borrowed from story papers and dime novel narratives of seduction and working-class morality that defined virtuous and predatory women. Beginning in the 1840s, mass-marketed stories revived the seduction narrative that had its roots in eighteenth-century English novels and their American imitators. Both the earlier fiction and the mass-marketed modifications portrayed women as victims of male deception, especially wealthy men of leisure who schemed to violate young, naive women. In the earlier versions, innocent but morally weak women failed to resist temptation and succumbed to ruin, pregnancy, sometimes insanity, and ultimately death, while pure and noble women avoided wealthy cads plotting fiendish deeds. When newspaper stories, dime novels, and female moral reformers revitalized the narrative plot of seduction, poor but respectable women successfully resisted immoral entreaties from employers, especially merchants. In a typical factory-girl novel, *The Factory Girl; or, Gardez La Coeur,* written in 1847 by A. I. Cummings, two virtuous factory girls avoided the debauched son of an affluent merchant and his friend, the son of a moneyed planter. Such fictional wealthy cads were potential employers of female clerks, strangers who played the confidence game.[30]

Critics of government clerking jobs for women warned that this type of employment would ruin women by exposing them to corrupt men who might force them to sell their virtue for employment. In his guidebook to the excitement and dangers of Washington, *The Sights and Secrets of the National Capital,* John B. Ellis warned, "Government clerkship by a woman is her first step in the road to ruin. If she is young and pretty, she is surrounded by men who seek her moral destruction." Corrupt supervisors would hire a woman for a "pretty face . . . and ankles" rather than for her clerical skill. Like seduction narratives, these "men oftentimes high in position . . . surround her with flattery, with temptations of every description, and when these fail, threaten her with a dismissal." Her economic situation compounded the intimidation. As an orphan or without a father, she had to provide for herself or her family. The few low-wage jobs available for women, which failed to cover the high cost of living, plunged her into poverty and cast her at their mercy, "until she is nearly driven mad, and—she yields." This language of seduction melded with bribery and influence peddling in the exposés of government corruption in the 1860s and 1870s.[31]

Twenty years later, in 1891, Lewis Vital Bogy, a clerk in a U.S. Bureau of Pensions office and the son of a former senator from Missouri, wrote just such a novel about government moral corruption, with some minor modifications accounting for the passage of time. In his novel *In Office: A Story of Washington Life and Society,* Bogy focused on the government corruption of Reconstruction and echoed the disclosures of his time, noting that the events of his novel took place "during an earlier period of Civil Service reform," when depravity reigned in the government offices. However, he blended the storyline with later changes in offices, enabling the heroine to eventually become a typewriter operator, a job generally unavailable until the 1880s. Tula Fairleigh, an impoverished, fatherless young woman, migrates alone to Washington, D.C., with the hopes of supporting her invalid mother and younger brother. Like typical dime novel heroines isolated from female friends and family, Tula evinces stock middle-class respectability with an emphasis on virtue, yet this heroine embodies more features associated with sentimental middle-class fiction. Tula is the daughter of a failed merchant, whose downfall from speculation and death devastate the family. Although poverty compels her to dress shabbily, Tula maintains respectable middle-class values: she wears appropriate conservative clothing, plays the piano inspiringly, reads and discusses books intelligently, writes home regularly, sends money to her family, and ultimately possesses enough strength to withstand temptations, an essential trait of dime novel heroines.[32]

Once in Washington, Tula meets lecherous men who exploit their economic and political power for sexual favors from innocent and helpless young women. Her fifty-five-year-old employer and nemesis, aptly named Colonel Letcher Thompson, plies Tula with flowers, arranges for beneficial social connections, walks her home regularly, and eventually promises a raise in return for sexual favors. When Tula rebuffs the colonel's advances, he retaliates by relocating her to his office, demoting her to the more physical task of filing, recording unsatisfactory reports about her work performance, and slandering her with rumors that she is the mistress of a congressman. Tula's female coworkers turn against her, isolating her from feminine companionship. When Tula applies to General Twining, ex–postmaster general, for help, she encounters more of the same. In the war between virtue and starvation, one lascivious man of power after another tempts her to trade chastity for a secure job. At the brink of despair, a friend helps Tula secure private employment. Still, she refuses to marry the young man she loves until she unexpectedly inherits a fortune, a common dime novel ploy that enables her to marry for love.[33] By resisting upper-class promiscuity, the potential victim proves her moral worth.

While seduction narratives like this sought to protect innocent young women from the hazards of government clerking, commentators often blamed women themselves, accusing them of naively engaging in dangerous flirtation or donning inappropriate office attire. They were said to wear "extravagant dress" because they "fail[ed] to see the distinction between business and social life" and so "drag[ged] the drawing-room with them, with its coquetries, on to and into the office." These remarks reflected the middle-class critique of working-class women's morality and conflated working women with working-class women. Critics denounced working-class women's more public displays of affection and flirtation in an urban street culture where both men and women participated. The masculine tone of the street culture reinforced this image of working-class as sexually available.[34]

Some writers even indicted female government clerks as treacherous predators who preyed on innocent men, linking inappropriate sexual power with working-class women. Fiction and nonfiction narratives of the prostitute portrayed her as a sexually dangerous woman who roamed the streets searching for naive young men to debauch, rob, and snare into a world of vice. Commentators worried that treasury courtesans masqueraded as ladies to seduce and blackmail men. The middle-class critics conflated prostitution and "working class women whose dress, demeanor or actions transgressed bourgeois notions of propriety and respectability," according to media scholar Robert C. Allen. Identification became even more difficult in the late 1860s as some middle-class women began dyeing their hair blond and wearing heavy makeup like working-class women. Since treasury courtesans hid behind masks of innocence and mingled with true pure women, they tainted all women, exposing even the virtuous to suspicion.[35]

In Bogy's novel, Tula befriends two treasury courtesans, the second of whom typifies the predator. The first, Dollie Dangerness, initially looks seductively toxic with her painted "colored cheeks," "full red lips," and "good figure and splendid hips." Women hate her; men admire her, gossip about her, and shower her with presents, clothes, flowers, and trips to the opera and theater in private boxes. Despite her sins, Dollie reforms through Tula's respectable goodness. She "followed her [Tula's] example in everything": she "read the same books, took the same walks, dressed as plainly," and she spent time "sewing at the little table in Tula's room." The really dangerous courtesan turns out to be a fellow boarder, similar to the stock villainess of the dime novel, although she seeks money and power, rather than love and revenge. Lizzie Buck "dressed elegantly, went shopping in a coupe, and seemed to have solved the problem of securing most of the luxuries of life on an income of six hundred a year." She lives a life of ease by trading roses, an undemanding job, and money for sex. Ignorant of Lizzie's true lifestyle, Tula turns to Lizzie for counsel when tempted and tormented, but "Miss Buck laughed lightly," advising her to "give it to him" and explaining, "My dear, virtue in [this] office doesn't pay. What do you get by it? Hard work, poor pay, persecution, and the constant fear of dismissal." Lizzie enumerates the benefits of promiscuity: "You have a good salary, nothing to do, lots of attention from men, and plenty of fun. All you have to do is to keep quiet. You don't have social recognition, but you wouldn't get that anyhow, and you don't want it." She then lists the kept female government clerks in Washington and scolds Tula, "If you are dismissed, it will be your own fault, and I won't feel one bit sorry for you."[36]

These assaults on female government clerks' virtue arose for many reasons. In general, all women's work was suspect since the ideology of domesticity defined labor as public and therefore as the opposite of the moral home. Most women did work within the confines of a home, either their own (as "given-out" workers, independent laundresses, or seamstresses) or someone else's (as domestics, governesses, or companions). There, in theory, brothers and fathers implicitly shielded women's virtue and guided sisters and daughters, like those who worked for family businesses as office and salesclerks. When women deviated from the typical locations of female employment and residence, they appeared more vulnerable to immoral influences and became susceptible to attacks.[37]

This traditional household labor initially became the context for women's involvement in clerical work. Since colonial days, shopkeepers' wives and daughters assisted in family businesses by keeping their husbands' and fathers' legal account books and handling sales. In 1787, Benjamin Rush called on women to study bookkeeping to assist their husbands. Middle-class women were also expected to learn how to keep household accounts and periodically were encouraged to prepare for emergency employment in case their husbands or fathers died. T. S. Arthur advised women to adapt bookkeeping into "everyday uses and pursuits," like cooking and cleaning. Generally, women worked at men's tasks under the rubric of the family, which in the nineteenth century defined women's economic activities for the family as proof of service and love.[38]

Skills that later became office skills were also performed by women for social reasons, rather than economic benefits. Mid-nineteenth-century "fashionable" women cultivated writing skills for daily correspondence to enhance their sociability, neighborliness, and pride in individualistic accomplishments. In 1845, James French opened a writing room, promoting a "new and elegant epistolary hand writing" for "the most fashionable ladies." Women wrote letters for illiterates or the non-English-speaking, occasionally earning cash for their efforts. Some female stenography students hoped to improve themselves by learning an art, while others studied to take better notes of sermons for moral study, all appropriate feminine pursuits.[39]

Women involved in the early years of stenography also maintained connections to the home by following the traditional pattern of partnerships in husband-and-wife teams, mainly as wives of school owners or phonography boosters, although a few actually practiced stenography. One significant teacher of stenography, Mrs. Jane Pitman, came to the United States from England in 1853 with her shorthand-promoting husband, Benn. Here, she taught classes in phonography as her husband's assistant. Margaret Vater Longley, wife of Elias, began studying in 1849 after their marriage. From 1850 to 1851, she instructed reading using the phonetic alphabet. When the Civil War broke out, she and her husband worked as reporters. Later they taught phonography. Her husband authored a stenography textbook primer, and she penned an early textbook on typing fingering. These women were helpers in the family business. As in other crafts from science to printing, husband-and-wife teams granted women access to higher status positions. However, these women also lived in the shadow of men, gaining little if any financial or social remuneration for their labor. Even when they worked for pay, they retained their association with home and dependency, as "helpers," not workers. By teaching, they contained their use of shorthand within the most respectable employment for middle-class women, one that presumably prepared them for motherhood.[40]

Even a stenographic woman who became a prominent reformer, emerging from the shadow of her husband, found employment in teaching. In 1844, Eliza Boardman Burnz, a twenty-one-year-old widow with an infant to support, became a teacher and later the director of the Bolivar Female Seminary. After reading about phonography, she began to correspond with prominent shorthand leaders Stephen Pearl Andrews and Isaac Pitman. In 1849, she and her new pastor husband became enthusiasts of spelling reform and phonography, preaching and teaching across Ohio to the Great Lakes. Burnz taught varied subjects, including shorthand, while her husband attended medical school. In 1868, she opened a phonography school in Cincinnati. A year later, when they moved to New York, Burnz took charge of the stenography classes at the New York Mercantile Library on Astor Place. She offered free evening classes at Cooper Union beginning in 1872 and published the *Phonic Shorthand*. Even before her husband's death in 1874, Burnz was recognized as a phonography leader in her own right. Like other women in the field, she worked with her husband; unlike them, she transcended his interest, making the field her own specialty.[41] Similar to many of the early prominent stenographers, Burnz rarely practiced shorthand herself, mostly encouraging other women to learn stenography for pay.

In contrast to these early stenographers, women who worked outside of the domestic arena as mill workers, saleswomen, and nurses risked that their virtue would be slandered. Employment outside of the home posed risks for women. There, they encountered male "strangers" as supervisors. In factories, stores, and offices, men trained and managed female staff; they served as guides and mentors and exercised authority over their female crew. The middle class and working class feared, sometimes correctly, that such men would take advantage of their young charges. A supervisor could require sexual favors as a kickback for full-time employment or good working conditions, wages, or hours, just like Letcher Thompson and U.S. Treasury Department supervisors in 1864 did.[42]

While women who worked in mills, garrets, and schools labored primarily with other women and might have avoided male "strangers" (other than foremen), office space belonged to men. It was an unprotected male world, symbolized by male crudity, cigars, cusswords, whiskey, and cuspidors. As busy thoroughfares of commerce, the office exposed a lady to a male world of "strangers"—from errand boys to clients and bosses—who could sexually harass women with bawdy language, indelicate subject matter, or sexual proposals. It is not surprising, then, that federal government departments in Washington, D.C., initially hired women copyists to work at home in the 1840s through 1860s.[43]

Unfortunately for their female coworkers, male clerks' unsavory reputation tarnished women's own standing. As seen in chapter 1, many young men who were newly independent from their families traversed between middle-class and working-class worlds as they roamed the liminal space between respectability and rowdiness. Theft became a symbol of clerks' questionable reputation. Beginning with the 1830s, the popular press regaled its readers with stories about dishonest, disloyal, and immoral clerks, like the Treasury Department clerk caught embezzling in 1866 to repay lost bets on a New York election. Clerking thefts became so standard a type that an article in *Frank Leslie's Illustrated Newspaper* on the city courts in 1872 included "clerks in the confidence of bankers" in its clichéd list of those commonly arrested. Merchants' and advisors' concerns about their clerks reinforced the debauched image of male clerks.[44]

Another source of clerks' notoriety involved sexual dalliances associated with the sporting life. In the 1830s, female moral reformers portrayed clerks as symbols of "young men gone wrong." The midthirties publicity of the murder of prostitute Helen Jewett by her lover, a clerk, continued into the 1850s, especially when he died, although later reports did not mention his occupation.

Male government clerks were charged with patronizing houses of prostitution and converting boardinghouses into informal brothels. Clerks continued to receive bad press in the 1860s, such as when Mary Harris murdered Treasury Department clerk Adoniram J. Burroughs for breach of promise of marriage. Male clerks' sorry reputation as embezzlers, prostitutes' johns, and seducers tainted their female coworkers. Such men would not have objected to working with treasury courtesans; nor would immoral women have minded associating with such men. However, respectable families might have worried about their daughters serving in such sexually charged conditions in the 1860s and 1870s, even though relatively high salaries made this a plum job financially. Male attention jeopardized any woman's reputation, whether a saleswoman, nurse, or office worker.[45]

According to middle-class fears, living alone further aggravated those risks, since the dangers women faced were so great. In theory, women adrift lost access to the advice and protection of family and friends, chancing sexual promiscuity. It is no accident that all three women in Bogy's novel, the heroine and the two treasury courtesans, lived alone. Without a family and true friends around, Tula almost becomes a victim by turning to a stranger (her lecherous boss) for guidance, because she cannot differentiate between honorable and confidence men. She misreads Letcher Thompson's and General Twining's attentions as paternalistic direction and nearly succumbs to temptation, becoming a victim of male seduction and licentiousness. Ultimately, family correspondence, female friendship, and inheritance save Tula, while the two other female characters fall into debauchery by living alone in boardinghouses. A threatening world gnawed at the reputations of women adrift, whether working-class factory girls and Bowery "g'hals" or middle-class government clerks.[46]

Even more than other employed women, clerical workers and especially government clerks had left home to seek employment in the big cities, the state capitals, and Washington, D.C. For women, traveling itself implied moral danger and supposed dependence, although their journeying increased throughout the century. In 1860 and 1870, one-third of women clerks in Boston lived alone or with relatives other than parents or siblings (see appendix, table B3). Historian Joanne Meyerowitz found that clerical women were much more likely to be adrift in 1880, a trend that reversed by 1910, when more working-class clerical women lived with their parents. In Washington, D.C., in 1880 and 1900, 36 percent and 33 percent of the female clerks resided on their own, while in Boston, where the numbers of government clerks were fewer, 35.7 percent of single women in 1880 lived alone.[47] In cities they lived "hundreds of miles distant, where everybody [is] a stranger." Enough lived alone to fuel concern for their safety.[48]

Middle-class fears of city life as dangerous, mostly as sexually corrupting, also colored the perceptions about female government clerks who moved to Washington, D.C., or to state capitals, such as Boston, for employment. Contrasts between country life as simple and wholesome and the city as dangerous intensified fears that naive and trusting country maidens were ripe fodder for the sophistries of the city slicker. Sexual immorality symbolized and subsumed all urban dangers: scantily dressed children, lascivious gazes, and sexually charged language lobbed at women passersby. These concerns about urban dangers for the woman adrift underpinned the criticisms of government clerking as dangerous for women, especially in the early years of the 1860s and 1870s. However, the image of the government courtesan had a life of its own, as seen in the publication of Bogy's book in 1891 and in repeated references well into 1910.[49]

Even attempts to champion female government clerks reveal assumptions of their immorality, when women needed to appear bound to the cocoon of the protective middle-class family. These defenses reveal the narrow scope for working women from midcentury to the early postwar years, when respectability provided the only acceptable defense for working women. Clerks, journalists, and bosses writing in the 1860s and 1870s utilized four common rhetorical themes of respectability. The first defense trotted out family credentials to insist that such women already came from respectable families. Backers demonstrated middle-class status by reciting fathers', husbands', and even uncles' occupations, as in references to a chaplain's daughter, a military officer's widow, the niece of two governors, and the daughter of a nationally known surgeon. Advocates also recalled a male relative's military service in the recent war, especially if he had lost his life in battle. Only rarely did women's references include their own achievements; exceptions include an opera singer and a woman who aided General Sheridan at the Battle of Winchester. A second explanation of respectability portrayed these women as the advocates' class equals, who they could "invite to my house to meet my wife" and "walk the length of the avenue with."[50] A third rationale stressed women's victimization and need for protection by blaming overcrowding and lack of ventilation for female government clerks' "pallid" complexion and calling for higher wages and civil service reform to protect respectable women from temptation and sexual corruption. Still, they insisted on women's right to work.[51] Finally, defenders asserted female clerks' purity and impugned men's respectability by condemning critics as "brute[s]" and seducers lacking the "instincts of . . . gentlemen."[52] Such advocacy for women employed outside of the home branded them as distinctively feminine by guarding their respectability, while also preserving clerking's masculine identity.

WOMEN AND WORKING-CLASS EMPLOYEES: THE MASSES

Business and government changes in the last forty years of the nineteenth century finished off construction of the modern office employee and set the stage for stenography's move to the spotlight. This well-known story deserves a brief retelling as a prelude for understanding the male stenographers' responses discussed in the following chapters. These years solidified the trend toward an abundance of permanent clerical employees, when government and then businesses reorganized and began hiring even greater numbers of office workers. Women's image as low-cost, dependent workers contributed to their employment, especially as business stenographers and typewriters, in the newly mechanized office. As the number of women clerical workers and especially those from the working class skyrocketed between 1880 and 1910, they epitomized the modern clerical employee as a symbol of the masses.[53]

In response to the economic downturns of the 1870s, 1880s, and 1890s, companies consolidated and employed new cost-saving measures. They organized pools, trusts, trade associations, and mergers to control prices, productivity, and labor. They also vertically integrated production, distribution, and some services all within each company and reorganized their offices, procedures, and staffing to reduce costs. Written communication mushroomed to coordinate the many parts of these large corporations and to facilitate information exchange with other companies as well as with government. With larger operations and less personal contact between employer and employee, managers adopted circulars, manuals, in-house organs, reports, tables, forms, and memos. To speed up record keeping and communication, managers subdivided tasks and adopted new equipment, such as typewriters, carbon paper, and adding and billing machines. When looseleaf binders enabled more than one person to work on an account, old jobs like bookkeeping were split between accounts receivable and billing and ledger clerks.[54]

To handle the expanded clerical tasks, governments and the new corporations hired ever-increasing numbers of office workers. Nationally, only one in forty employed adults worked in offices in 1870, with that number leaping to one in twenty-five by 1900. In cities, the numbers climbed even higher; in

Boston, for example, the number increased by seven times from 1870 to 1900, from 3,068 to 22,264 (see appendix, table C1). Nationally, male bookkeepers, accountants, clerks and copyists, and stenographers and typewriters tripled during that period, growing from 288,761 to 751,854.[55]

In some ways, stenographers followed the same general trend as other clerical men in salaried positions, when newly trained shorthand writers found corporate jobs with railroads, insurance companies, tool companies, foundries, and sugar processing firms. Like other newly subdivided and mechanized occupations, stenography and typing rapidly intertwined to reorganize business practices. They sped up the mechanical labor of copying by changing the work process and mechanizing communication. Businessmen who had composed their own letters before began dictating to stenographers. Even railroad superintendents who had once barked orders to foremen sent directions transcribed by stenographers and typewriters instead. Amanuenses also replaced clerks who wrote letters by hand or followed form letters. Together, the typewriter and amanuensis stimulated even more paperwork communication and demand for their services.[56]

As efficiency became the standard for the new horizontally and vertically integrated corporations, the stenographer and the typewriting machine and operator symbolized modern organization. Stenography advocates presented shorthand as a boost to the economy and office proficiency. Though slow at first, typing also came to represent efficiency through its association with speed. Promoters of the typewriter sponsored speed contests to advertise the fastest typist and machine. Employers shared this optimism and calculated prospective savings if they replaced hand copying with a typewriting machine that squeezed more words on a page, thereby reducing the number of pages used. The American love affair with technology and mechanization also guaranteed the typewriter's association with progress and modernity. As early as the mid-1880s, employers without typewriters in their offices were derided as "old fogies" and men "behind the times."[57]

Despite the typewriter's crucial role in creating and expanding business stenography, the linkage also posed problems for stenographers. Too much of the stenographer's workday seemed devoted to typing. Advisers recommended that workers exercise constant care, cleaning machines in the morning and evening to prevent smudging and learning to "repair slight breakdowns." Stenographers actually spent more time typing than writing shorthand, and their regular "wish" was for "more shorthand work to do." Moreover, employers seemed to notice flawed typing more than shorthand mistakes, asking schools and employment bureaus to send "a typewriter operator who can write shorthand," rather than a stenographer who can type.[58]

Like other clerical jobs, business stenographers became part of the rationalized, mechanized modern office. However, those whose workday varied from taking dictation, indexing letter books, keeping up accounts, writing checks, phoning for their employer, addressing letters, affixing stamps, and mailing at the post office could choose to interpret this range of tasks as learning a business or as independence, rather than as degraded monotony; others, though, viewed the many tasks as overwork. The availability of employment and the possibility for evaluating the stenography's workday as a time of independent decision making and commercial preparation kept men flocking to these jobs throughout the 1880s and 1890s, although their share of the positions dropped dramatically.[59]

The existing images of women as dependent, temporary workers and lower salaries, as we shall see in chapter 3, enticed employers who turned to women to fill these new office positions. The increased use of typewriters and amanuenses hastened women's presence in the office. At first, women found employment where they could be hired as assistants, such as in bookkeeping, often in the offices of professionals, trade, and government. Since low-paid women already dominated copying, they transferred easily to typing. From there, they moved into stenography, encouraged by the many stenography promoters. Typewriting and the broadened use of business stenography facilitated women's entrance into sectors of the economy that had been closed to them. Banks and railroads, slow to employ female clerks, hired them as typewriters and stenographers; professionals who needed one or two clerks replaced them with female stenographers and typewriters. Openings for women spread to manufacturing, transportation, insurance, real estate, and finance, and the numbers of women in these fields grew. The 1870 federal census first recorded stenographers, listing 7 out of 154, or 4.5 percent, as female. In 1880, an estimated two thousand women comprised 40 percent of stenographers and typewriters. By 1890, the number of female stenographers and typewriters multiplied nearly ten times, to 21,270, or 63 percent of the total; and ten years later, in 1900, the number had climbed to 86,118, or 76 percent. In northeastern cities, women's dominance of stenography and typing occurred sooner, rising from 46 percent in 1885 to 86 percent in 1900 in Boston (see appendix, table C2).[60]

The late nineteenth-century reorganization of the office and its concomitant job explosion set the stage for a shift in the overall makeup of clerical workers. Nationally, in 1870, women constituted 3.1 percent of all clerical workers; by 1900, their participation multiplied more than ninefold, to 29.3 percent, and it had nearly doubled to 49.6 percent twenty years later, in 1920.[61] In Boston, female clerical employment accelerated earlier, from 9.0 percent in 1870 and 10.6 percent in 1880 to 17.5 percent by 1885. It had increased twofold, to 35.4 percent, by 1900 and grew to 57.2 percent by 1920. The percentages do not do justice to the enormous expansion in the number of women. Nationally, the numbers of women in clerical jobs multiplied eightfold between 1880 and 1900, from 30,344 to 245,517. In Boston, there were only 524 female clerical workers in 1880, but their numbers soared to 4,217 in 1890, 7,885 in 1900, and 26,243 by 1920 (see appendix, table C1). The large-scale employment of women in offices, along with the rising working-class composition of the clerical workforce, helped transfer the image of the degraded copyist to the typewriter and office worker and affirmed their position as dependent and unremarkable employees, symbols of the masses.

In addition to the growing employment of women, a reconstructed class composition of male and female office workers contributed to supplanting the image of clerical workers from men potentially on the make to low-status office employees, threatening to mark all clerical workers as degraded. First of all, the higher class among clerical men began to disappear. In 1870, 7.7 percent of young clerical men in Boston were sons of professionals and business executives; this number fell to only 3.6 percent thirty years later, despite the more than fivefold increase of professionals during these years (see appendix, table A2). The appeal of clerical work for affluent men waned because education, especially college, offered alternate routes to the professions and management. During the last decades of the nineteenth century, college attendance swelled faster than the population, intimately bound with professionalization of white-collar labor, particularly law, engineering, architecture, medicine, and business. With the expansion in the number of law schools and business programs, formal training increasingly became the key to career achievement, and clerical work no longer supplied the best route to career mobility. Instead, elite young men spent more years in school and a shorter time doing on-the-job training as preparation for professional or managerial careers.[62]

Along with this decline in well-born men, the working-class share among clerical men and women climbed upward. Among clerical men in Boston, increasing numbers were sons of manual workers, from 51.3 percent in 1870 to 65.1 percent in 1880, despite the dramatic overall surge in nonmanual employment (see appendix, table C3). The decline in a predominantly third-generation male clerical workforce from 70 percent in 1870 to only 50.2 percent in 1880 further illustrates the receding middle-class male clerical population, since nativity served as a measure of class as this time.[63]

Among women, the working-class share of the clerical population in Boston grew even greater, from 56.3 percent to 71.9 percent between 1870 and 1880 (see appendix, table C3). Generational data also showed an increasing working-class composition. In 1870, 4.9 percent of clerical women were immigrants, while 79.1 percent were at least third-generation; by 1880, 7.3 percent were immigrants, and only 65.9 percent were at least third-generation. This trend continued through the end of the century. From 1880 to 1900, middle-class women continued to fall behind the growing numbers of working-class women seeking security and prestige in the office, despite the static proportion of fathers in traditional working-class occupations among clerical women with fathers present, at 71.9 percent and 73 percent (see appendix, table B2). The rising proportion of working-class men in clerical and sales work at that time undermines the usefulness of this traditional middle-class marker, as does the many women without a father present. Instead, generational changes furnish the strongest indications of the escalating working-class presence in clerical work. Although the female immigrant population in Boston remained constant between 1880 and 1900, the proportion of clerical women who were immigrants doubled, from 7.3 percent to 13.6 percent, and the share of third-generation and longer Americans among clerical women skidded from 65.9 percent to 40.3 percent (see appendix, table B1). By 1900, clerical work had become the domain of the working class in Boston despite the continuation of a strong middle-class component. What happened in Boston was not unique.[64]

This increase in the working-class composition of the clerical field, however, varied by position. Stenographers experienced class changes, albeit at a different pace than bookkeepers and typewriters. For example, in Boston by 1900, more female typewriters and bookkeepers were immigrants and children of immigrants than were female stenographers, 51.5 percent, 49.6 percent, and 39.1 percent, respectively (see appendix, table C4). Among men, even more typewriters than bookkeepers and stenographers were immigrants or children of immigrants: 57.6 percent, 43.6 percent, and 30.9 percent, respectively.[65] The very high first- and second-generation population among typewriters stood as a harbinger of the future of stenography.

The stenographic and popular presses acknowledged this rise of a working-class clerical constituency, transforming them into symbols of the masses. One shorthand periodical reported in January 1881 that the editor "had expected our circulation to be limited chiefly to literary and professional persons—the 'cultured classes.'" Instead, the magazine attracted "young men in workshops, factory-girls, and the laboring people." For example, William Thorpe, a horseshoer and inventor, proudly wrote to *Browne's Phonographic Monthly* about studying in "my spare moments," utilizing "Phonographic books worth $50, and all kinds of Phonographic materials." The shorthand press's frequent attacks on the "awful surplus of the wrong sort" criticized the working class's general educational skills and shorthand competency, lamenting the change in class constituency, as we shall see in chapter 4. Mass-market newspapers and magazines, like the *New York Sun*, the *Chicago Daily News*, the *Post-Intelligencer*, and *Tid-Bits*, spread images of female clerical workers as the embodiment of the degraded masses, by caricaturing "typewriter girls" as frivolous, flirtatious, and not too bright, as we shall see in chapter 5.[66]

The growing presence of middle-class and especially working-class women as both real and symbolic dependent employees helped transfer the image of the degraded female from copying to typewriting and sometimes to business stenography. At times, even the shorthand press portrayed the work as monotonous and routine. Even some of the short stories commissioned for the *Phonographic World* at times used the common trope of the tedium of work. In "A Mistake in Identity" Evelyn Harvey's "life had become very dull and very humdrum." She longs for a vacation or maybe romance. In another story, Eleanor Lee "leaned her tired head on her hands . . . [as] her overtaxed brain, and the bewildering shorthand characters kept up a dizzying whirl before her tired eyes." Still others refer to their work as "the daily grind" or drudgery. The sound of the click-click symbolizes overwork as well as modern productivity.[67]

CONCLUSION

This new female, often working-class population of clerical workers who arrived amid the reorganization of the growing government and corporate bureaucracies embodied the modern business methods of efficiency. They were typewriters who operated the new office technology, assistant bookkeepers who recorded business transactions, and amanuenses who facilitated communication—all relatively skilled workers at the bottom of the office hierarchy. The many women contributed to the solidification of the image of modern office employees, working at desks in large bureaucracies with no possibility of promotion to proprietorship. Women as symbolic dependents turned office workers into emblematic employees.

The midcentury gender balance of womanhood explains this shift. The definition of respectable womanhood as family-centered and economically dependent, with a tad of personal independence, led to the characterization of women's clerical employment as degraded positions, despite new conversations emerging in the 1860s and 1870s. While images of female dependency promoted their employment, women office workers inherited the discourse of degraded work from factory work in the 1850s to 1870s. Their presence in low-skilled copying stamped women's office work as monotonous and routinized labor, which spread to government and then corporate positions and solidified the connection between degradation and employees. The work then cast these working women as debased, especially when working-class women held these jobs.

For men, monotonous work itself might not necessarily devalue them. Yet contemporary arguments also assumed that certain jobs suited people with inferior capabilities; that is, degraded workers performed debased work. This meant that if men did the work appropriate to women, they descended and also became damaged. Hence, once women entered copying, men wanted to distinguish it from other clerical work by naming female office workers "copyists." Federal government documents in the 1860s and 1870s referred to women as "copyists" or "employees" and to men as "clerks," even though they performed the same tasks. By the 1880s, low-paid government men also were called "copyists." Such efforts to isolate women may explain why men willingly located to different work spaces in the government, to protect their reputations as much as women's.[68]

When a job was in transition between male and female work, the work had the potential to demean both genders. Women's presence in men's jobs threatened to mark the job and worker as degraded, transferring their lessened employment status to men and demeaning all beginning clerking jobs by blurring the distinctions between degraded work and degraded worker.[69] As women entered and then monopolized typewriting and business stenography in the last two decades of the century, their image as modern employees, symbolic of the masses, seemed to extend degradation to these jobs and possibly to all shorthand work. They threatened men's middle-class identity by exposing the inconsistencies with the image of clerks as men on the make. For the next two chapters, we turn to male stenographers to observe their reactions.

II. FINAL HOOKS

CHAPTER 3

Stepping-Stones and Short Ladders: Men's Faltering Independence

A 1901 article referring to office malcontents cited a bookkeeper who lamented "the mistake of my life when I learned to keep books." He explained, "I was a good bookkeeper at 25 and was proud of it. I am a good bookkeeper now at 50 and am ashamed to tell anybody that I am a bookkeeper. Draftsmen talk the same way, and stenographers, [too]." The article's author then reminds readers that "the railroad presidents and corporation presidents and the great captains of industry today were almost without exception bookkeepers or draftsmen or stenographers at some time in their careers."[1] These passages reveal three common themes at the turn of the century: male office workers' heightened fear of failure, the herculean efforts made to alleviate their anxiety by reframing the self-made man to fit within the new corporate job structure, and the assumption that male bookkeepers and stenographers shared the same experiences and concerns.

To understand the first two themes, it is necessary to examine the third, about the uniformity of office experience. In some ways, stenography did epitomize the archetypical transformations of routinization, mechanization, and feminization in clerical work. Women and some men found new opportunity for employment, although in subdivided work. However, men risked the dependency and immobility that characterized antebellum clerical failures when more became stuck in salaried positions at the second half of the century. Declining opportunity for proprietorship especially troubled men who competed with women, symbols of dependence, powerlessness, and degraded labor. The presence of women, correlated with falling salaries in business offices, proved the flash point.

However, despite these similarities between stenography and the classic story of routinization, mechanization, and feminization, shorthand men lived through a more complex experience. As a newly subdivided job, business stenography provided many new office positions that quickly belonged to women. In contrast, male bookkeepers worried that divided tasks might induce assistants to usurp their work, but many found positions as head bookkeepers with female assistants. This dramatic feminization of business stenography (along with typing) caused the new feminine, mass image of clerical work discussed in chapter 2 to matter more to male stenographers (and typewriters) than to other clerical workers at the end of the nineteenth century.

Moreover, unlike other clerical jobs, shorthand employment outside of business offices shaped male stenographers' reactions to these changes. During the last forty years of the century, stenographers who worked for the courts and legislative bodies experienced their own version of rationalization of work, affording them more positions, especially liminal semisalaried court work. Still, they earned relatively high incomes in an occupation overwhelmingly populated by men. Despite these differences between business shorthand and court reporting, the two occupations were not entirely separate. The overlap enabled the shorthand press to portray business stenography as a stepping-stone to court reporting and allowed some male business stenographers to imagine a career in the courts that would meet their hopes for independence. Conversely, declining salaries in business stenography, along with the growing image of business shorthand as feminine work, frightened male court reporters about the few women in the courts. Exacerbating fears that they could not cauterize the bleeding from business shorthand to court reporting, these concerns upped the overall level of anxiety about women's presence.

The stenographic press amplified the concerns of business and court stenographers, yet they, along with court reporters and educators, helped frame a new definition of middle-class manhood: rising above the masses. They advertised shorthand as a means for men to advance beyond the common man or woman by turning to older discourses of respectability and a reframed self-made man. However, the two approaches proved troublesome and failed to reassure male stenographers that they had indeed risen above the masses of male and female stenographers and typewriters.

PROPRIETORSHIP, BUREAUCRACIES, AND LIMINAL MEN

For most clerical workers, the trend toward an abundance of permanent office work and midmanagement positions in the growing government and corporate bureaucracies meant that the traditional goal of proprietorship became less viable. Stenographers, however, still found paths to proprietorship because of the route from business amanuensis to court stenographer, even if they had less independence than their predecessors. By lobbying governments for more stable employment and income, legal stenographers transformed court reporting into semisalaried situations that balanced the independence of a business with the dependence of salaried work. Some actually preferred these semisalaried government situations, continuing to envision these new jobs as opportunities.

In general, late nineteenth-century economic conditions limited the options for proprietorship for all men, including stenographers. Economic growth tripled the number of businesses. National figures show the percentage of men in nonfarm businesses rising from 8 to 8.2 between 1880 and 1900. Some small businesses thrived by moving into new economic niches and even developed into large corporations. Nonetheless, in certain regions, proprietors lost out. In Boston, the percentage of male merchants and dealers among employed men dipped from 10.8 in 1880 to 8.1 in 1890, falling significantly to 5.4 in 1900. Moreover, existing proprietors suffered when large businesses capable of absorbing temporary losses cut costs and drove out small competitors. Erratic economic cycles, with two long and difficult depressions in the 1870s and 1890s, made business life even more precarious, especially for those competing directly with the new industrial or commercial giants, such as department stores, insurance companies, or large manufacturing companies. Between the 1840s and 1880, from 32 to 60 percent of companies lasted less than three years.[2]

With small businesses falling behind the exploding numbers of clerical workers, the opportunities for clerical men to become proprietors declined. Historians Clyde and Sally Griffen found the expected avenues to proprietorship obstructed for skilled and clerical men between 1870 and 1880. This access eroded even further for men who worked in offices and stores in Boston between 1880 and 1905. In 1885, 27.9 percent of clerical men located in the 1870 census owned their own businesses. The percentage of proprietors dropped to 22 percent for men traced between 1880 and 1895 and to 16.7 percent for men followed from 1900 to 1915. For sons of manual workers, the drop came sooner, falling from 17.7 percent between 1870 and 1885 to 6.8 percent and then 5 percent, respectively (see appendix, table A4). The exponential growth in office jobs had further limited men's chances of becoming proprietors.[3]

Although the rise in corporate employment restricted possibilities for proprietorship, some men still continued to view corporate posts as a chance to save money for future ownership. Most men flitted from one job to another, looking for better positions and producing a high turnover rate. Among the few who persisted, incremental mobility made long-term careers as middle managers possible. As the likelihood that clerical men would own small businesses fell, men still looked forward to new opportunities but worried even more about failure.[4]

Like others following the common pattern, many male stenographers held out for proprietorship, even at the end of the century. Some quickly abandoned shorthand to teach and, if possible, operate their own schools, ranging in size from a lone teacher to the Bryant Stratton's national chain. Some were temporary affairs, like John H. Fazel's four-year spell as principal of the Fazel Brothers' Shorthand Institute of Winfield, Kansas. Not too many could expect to run their own schools, with only six business colleges (as they called themselves) in Boston between 1840 and 1870, thirteen between 1876 and 1888, and eleven between 1889 and 1895. Yet over one-quarter of the 1,292 national shorthand teachers in 1884 worked on their own as private instructors.[5] Others gave up practicing shorthand and started publishing manuals and journals but struggled to stay afloat. A few founded companies to sell office supplies, like typewriter ribbons, carbon paper, and typewriters.[6]

Beyond these more traditional career paths from stenography to school proprietor, publisher-editor, or office suppliers, which entailed foregoing the practice of their craft, shorthand men scaled to the summit of their occupation as either independent legal stenography entrepreneurs or official government reporters in the courts or legislative bodies. Legal stenographers who owned their own businesses retained the only independent commercial position for practicing shorthand writers. In the countryside, a single reporter often ran his own business, traveling between circuit courts, taking notes, and then transcribing them at noon and during evenings. Stenographers such as these often scrambled to find enough work. One complained of less than sixty days per year. In large cities, reporters worked longer seasons, "sit[ting] practically all of the time," about two hundred days per year. In both regions, reporters enlisted contract labor to replace them when they were unavailable. In the countryside, they paid for substitutes when their assignments conflicted. In the cities, they hired temporary replacements when they fell behind in their commitments.[7]

Like clerks who apprenticed to merchants a generation before, young shorthand writers assisted legal reporters before the lucky ones advanced to partners or sole proprietors. Well before the typewriter, legal reporting firms engaged amanuenses to read notes taken by a court reporter and then transcribe them into longhand. In the 1870s, William Wyckoff sent back his notes to Utica, New York, for his assistants to transcribe while he continued on the circuit, so that they would be ready when he returned. Sometimes, the reporter or an amanuensis dictated the notes in longhand to copyists.[8]

With the adoption of typewriters in the late 1870s, the division of labor sped up even further. In one company in 1889, "several stenographers . . . dictated to two typewriters [operators] at once." A stenographer read one sentence from a recently dictated book. While the operator typed that sentence, the dictator read a sentence from another book to the second typewriter. Court and legislative reporters found other ways to subdivide labor by sharing dictation. In 1891, Frank Burt and his partners and coworkers, Saidee Swift, W. L. Haskel, E. W. Harnden, and Rev. F. G. Morris, apportioned the tasks, with one taking dictation and the others transcribing. Legal reporting companies sometimes distributed a convention assignment among six or seven recorders, each of whom took notes for five minutes, with thirty minutes to write out and send their portion to the newspaper office.[9]

By the end of the century, staffs grew larger and relationships more businesslike, especially in cities. In 1875, Dement, Gray, and Company of Chicago, a large firm of its day, retained nine reporters and eight regular copyists. At the turn of the century, Walton, James, and Ford in Chicago employed thirty in a suite of fourteen rooms with six telephones. Not surprisingly, legal reporters in business for themselves viewed their stenographic staff as employees.[10] According to Joseph Howard Jr., "They come to you raw, green, awkward. They know nothing of literature, . . . absolutely unable to correct the faintest mistake. They tire you, they weary you, but little by little they improve, and in the course of a year or two are worth what you pay them."[11] These legal stenographers behaved like other employers and even formed employer associations. An independent shorthand writer complained that a group of fifteen law reporters formed a "combine" in 1885 to keep prices up, insisting on "$10 per day and 50 cents per page of 250 words for transcripts," but cut rates against competitors. One employer reportedly locked out his three amanuenses who struck for higher salaries.[12]

To expand their work and provide stability, these self-employed legal reporters successfully lobbied state legislatures to require the appointment of court reporters. In 1860, Edward F. Underhill and David Dudley Field succeeded in convincing the New State legislature to establish official reporters for the first judicial district courts. By 1866, four states had adopted such laws, rising to twenty-nine in 1879. An 1870 Massachusetts law established official reporters for courts in Suffolk County. Seventeen years later, in 1887, the legislature extended appointments to the Superior Court for civil business in every county. In the next year, the legislature allowed the enlisting of reporters at inquests. Some stenographers sought official positions to guarantee commissions for their own private legal reporting firms. In Chicago, the company of Ely, Burnham, and Bartlett lobbied for official stenographers and then prospered when each was appointed. They dominated legal reporting until the Chicago Fire of 1871, when their assistants pressured for revisions in the laws. Elsewhere, opponents to the creation of official court reporters echoed the concerns of the Chicago assistants that "one man [might] gobble" up more than one court, like Frank Burt, whose position as official reporter for Plymouth County Superior Court in 1886 expanded to include Norfolk County in 1887.[13] More jobs did not, however, guarantee job security, since the courtroom judge could still hire and fire at whim, a concern shared by even those reporters who held their positions for decades.[14]

Beyond seeking greater access and job stability, law reporters wanted more secure payment than independent contractors. At first, both self-employed legal stenographers and official court reporters received their only income directly from the lawyers themselves, for the number of pages they transcribed (as they still do today) as well as a per diem rate. However, reporters struggled to get paid, especially when tension between attorneys and clients existed. Court reporter Charles H. Requa's song for the Term End Club echoed stenographers' concern: "Trust not the lawyer till the fee be proffered. Lest ye repent of it and never see the money." To stabilize compensation and avoid competition with each other, stenographers lobbied state legislatures to mandate price structures, beginning with setting fees. In New York in 1863, the state legislature amended an 1860 law to add a yearly salary of fifteen hundred dollars paid by the appropriate government body. Payment schedules varied considerably by state. By 1904, thirty-nine of the forty-five states had such laws. Most (69 percent) mandated transcription fees, generally at ten cents per folio (a hundred words). Already 38 percent of states paid salaries as well, ranging from one thousand to thirty-six hundred dollars per year, with New York disbursing the highest by far.[15]

Increasing centralization and standardization of the fee structure gave stenographers the greater security that they wanted, but it also nibbled at their autonomy by locating them between the old-world proprietor and the new manager employee. Since state legislatures set the fees, they could just as easily cut salaries, as Montana did and as California and New York contemplated doing in 1895. They could also listen to appeals of well-connected legal professionals who sought to reduce their transcript payments. By 1906, New York laws enabled judges to deduct from a reporter's salary if he or she missed a session without a good excuse. Salaries transformed official stenographers from independent contractors to proto-employees. The state of New York required free transcripts for the courts, took control of hiring replacements, and gave judges power to suspend errant reporters. Court reporters now worried about overwork, like employees. In the 1890s, Essex County official stenographer Charles D. Gay lobbied for a bill to "relieve the stenographer from the burden of reporting every case." But the bill was killed in the Senate. Years later, in 1913, a reporter complained about the humiliation of having to provide receipts for expenses and the inability to charge what the market would bear, especially in times of inflation. Court reporters' goal of economic stability curtailed their independence by ceding the dominant voice to the legislature and the court.[16]

Despite their increasing economic dependence, official court reporters tried to maintain their independence. They organized their offices like those of independent legal stenographers, where the most senior members hired, trained, and managed lesser-skilled amanuenses and typewriters, who transcribed and typed from the notes of the official reporter. Between the 1860s and 1900s, legal stenographers also attempted to blur the boundary between employees in government bureaucracies and proprietors on their own, trying to hold on to the official reporter's security and the proprietor's independence through combining official positions with reporting on speeches, conventions for newspapers, and public meetings. One well-paid reporter testified to netting two thousand dollars per year from salary and fifteen hundred dollars from "outside work."[17]

As a group, stenographers were on the cusp of business changes. Some men still followed the older paths toward proprietorship. Others stood on the edge of the corporate bureaucracy. Still others vacillated between the two. Court reporting was among the best new semibureaucratic jobs, with relatively high pay, some independence, and local prestige within the stenographic community. The male legal reporter inhabited a liminal space, neither entirely dependent nor completely independent, but blending elements of both. Whether he received a fee set by the state or a salary paid for by local government, he held a middle ground between the middle-class independent proprietor and the government employee.

BLEEDING ACROSS OCCUPATIONS AND SEXES

While the liminal court reporter appeared different from the business stenographer, the two were not entirely distinct. Legal stenographers themselves trained some amanuenses to become court reporters by hiring them to read and transcribe their notes. For instance, in 1876, Charles H. Bender entered the office of Slocum and Thornton, official stenographers in Buffalo, New York, like a traditional apprentice. By late 1877, he had been promoted to amanuensis, transcribing on the typewriter the notes taken in court by the two partners and two other court stenographers. He began to report in the criminal courts one and a half years later, in 1879, and in the superior courts later that year. Two years later, he took a job at a general reporting firm in Grand Rapids, Michigan, becoming partners with his boss and, within a few years, an official court reporter.[18] Some stenographers moved back and forth between court and office endeavors. After serving as an official reporter, Mr. Thorne decided that he preferred reading to writing, so he found situations transcribing to three typewriters.[19]

Court reporters and amanuenses sometimes performed the same tasks. Some business stenographers employed by firms and big corporations like railroads took notes during trials and depositions.[20] Official stenographer Arthur Head complained that lawyers engaged office clerks to do "difficult legal work" that "should only be undertaken by the trained professional reporter."[21] As a result, some court reporters worried that experienced amanuenses could do their work and replace them or that the legislatures would reduce their payment, especially during the 1890s depression, because they were worth less.[22]

This interrelationship between business and court stenography enabled the shorthand press and some educators to assert that business stenography provided a stepping-stone to court reporting, while still reassuring court reporters that they would not suffer from too much competition. Biographical sketches, announcements of job changes, and advice implied that business stenographers who learned to write fast enough might become court reporters and own a business, earn higher incomes, and work in an occupation overwhelmingly populated by men. Moreover, at times, the press treated the two occupational groups as if they were identical, especially for women.[23]

This bleeding across jobs also meant that changes in business stenography affected court reporting as well. Salary declines that occurred among male business stenographers in conjunction with a growing female presence shaped men's interpretation of women's entry into the courts. Now, each group of men shared similar fears of failure, imagining female competitors as the degraded masses who undermined the independent businessman. They panicked that they might sink to femininity, weakness, and degradation.

Clerical Men's Salaries

Declines in male business stenographers' salaries exacerbated fears that they had or might descend to the status of women as degraded failures. For men precariously balancing between dreams of elusive success and nightmares of permanent dependence, unstable salaries during the frequent downturns in the last three decades of the nineteenth century made the loss of independence more acute. Now, they were becoming like women.

Business cycles best explain the fluctuating salaries, as wild oscillations took place in the last thirty years of the nineteenth century. Sharp economic slumps in the 1870s, mid-1880s, and 1890s dragged down clerical salaries. The rise of women in clerical positions, however, compounded the causes of these swings, since tradition and their reliance on family enabled employers to justify paying them 25 percent to 45 percent less than their male counterparts. Those occupations with large numbers of women, especially typewriting and business stenographing, suffered drastic cuts, which both threatened young men's plans for saving money as a step toward independence and challenged their masculine middle-class identity, narrowing the distance between degraded work and themselves.[24]

A summary of studies by the U.S. Commissioner of Labor on bookkeeping, typing, and business stenography in northeastern firms reveals a variety of salary shifts. For male bookkeepers, women's presence was a mixed blessing, benefiting those who became head bookkeepers and hurting the others (see appendix, table D1). After the depression of the 1870s and into the mid-1880s, men's wage rates in bookkeeping continued to recede although employers still hired less than a handful of women. The depression, not the arrival of women, undermined male wage rates. When the economy improved and wage rates stabilized from the mid- to late eighties, northeastern employers in these studies more than tripled their force of male bookkeepers to 236 and introduced a strong contingent of forty female bookkeepers. During the dark days of the depression of the 1890s, wage rates plummeted again. By the end of the decade, when wage rates rose, employment patterns had changed. Employers now preferred female assistant bookkeepers, probably for routinized tasks, and the men who stayed earned actual wage rates above those of the seventies but in constant dollars considerably lower than those of the seventies or eighties.[25]

A second occupational group, typewriters, fared less well (see appendix, table D1). By 1885 to 1889, when typewriters rapidly invaded offices, female wage rates were already closer to male wage rates, at $1.60 per day for women and $1.81 for men in northeastern states, with women earning 88 percent of men's rates. Men drew such low compensation because they competed with women in a feminized occupation.[26] While male and female typing rates followed business cycles, the number of men in these same companies virtually disappeared, plummeting from a high of twelve during the dog days of the early nineties to two in the halcyon years of the later Gay Nineties, so low that comparisons become meaningless. By sliding in tandem with women's wages, men's wage rates did not receive a downward jolt. However, with such low wage rates, men surely wondered if they could ever support themselves adequately; and with so many female competitors, their manhood was at stake.

A third group of male workers, business stenographers, slid toward the vanishing male typeriwters, which explains why they registered the loudest complaints in the last two decades of the century. Their wage rates suffered the greatest impact from both business cycles and feminization. From 1885 to 1889, male stenographers' daily wage rates were already below those of the male bookkeepers, likewise falling in the 1890s, from $2.48 to $1.61 in constant dollars. At the same time, though, the number of female stenographers tripled, contributing to a lower base wage rate. So, when other wage rates revived in the late nineties, male stenographers' barely inched upward, from $1.61 to $1.88 in constant dollars. In 1895–99, their daily wage rates in constant dollars had fallen to 75.8 percent of those in 1885–89, while male bookkeepers' rates only dropped to 89.4 percent. As part of transforming the labor force and lowering salaries, employers replaced women with cheaper female typewriters. Comparisons with women reinforced the deteriorating position of these male stenographers. The gap between male and female stenographers' income in constant dollars narrowed from seventy cents in 1885–89 to forty-eight cents in 1895–99, with a 71.8 to 74.5 gender gap in contrast to the 50 percent gap between male and female bookkeepers by 1895–99, as the proportion of male business stenographers plunged from 53.1 to 17.6 percent.[27]

Naturally, these conditions worried male stenographers. They repeatedly denounced their earnings, especially low starting pay. They complained about employers who forced them to "work . . . for a song" and other stenographers who willingly labored for the low rate of six dollars per week, the stereotypical female remuneration. Incensed by a want ad he read in the *Philadelphia Public Ledger,* Oliver B. Harden scribbled a note to the *Phonographic World* that very day. The advertisement offered a "thoroughly competent" stenographer-typewriter for only seventy-five dollars a month. Harden insisted that "[a] thoroughly competent stenographer and type-writer ought not to receive less than $100." The *Phonographic World*'s editor agreed and entitled the clipping "Cheap Stenographic Labor." A seven-month exchange in 1897 in the *Phonographic World* about low earnings began when Roy Shoemaker blamed "young lady stenographers . . . [for] keeping down the salaries of young men." He explained that after quitting a job, his employer replaced him with a lower paid woman who supplied her own machine; moreover, a potential new employer also hired "a young lady." George Lucas supported Shoemaker and blamed "girls for greatly decreas[ing] my opportunities."[28]

Male shorthand reporters who bemoaned women's wages, symbolized by the six-dollar-per-week woman, expected to earn low starting salaries but worried about decreasing pay rates. They feared that their earnings might continue to slide, bottoming out at a female wage. Although depressions instigated declining salaries, the growing presence of women did contribute to men's insecurity about their pay, future, and status. The frequent depressions brought, at least, temporary slumps that were easily confused with the entry of women and their low income. While some male bookkeepers found a niche as head bookkeepers with generally good salaries, men's rates mostly receded, especially stenographers' rates. Similar remunerations blurred the boundaries between male and female office workers, reinforcing men's fears of being stuck in degraded occupations, unable to save enough money to advance and prove their ambition and middle-class manhood.[29]

Women Court Reporters

The blurring of business and court stenography and reduction of male business stenographers' salaries added to male court reporters' worries that women's entry into the courts and legislature might replicate their dominance of business stenography. Despite their relatively small numbers in nineteenth-century court reporting, women appeared poised to invade the occupation.

Official reporters themselves paved the way for female competitors by hiring them as amanuenses to assist in transcribing dictation and by teaching them skills that prepared them for court work. For instance, while reading the minutes taken by official stenographers D. C. McEwen, Ormsby, and others, Miss Offen learned to read "several systems besides Munson's system, which she writes."[30]

Slowly, a few women received official appointments themselves. In 1870,

Abbie Pulsifer of Maine, daughter and sister of court reporters, became the first woman to serve as an official court reporter. Twenty-three years later, in 1893, women held 56 of the 544 official positions in the United States. Most states enlisted only one or two women, such as two out of twelve in Massachusetts and still only Miss Pulsifer out of eight in Maine. In California and Nebraska, none of the forty and thirty-eight official court reporters, respectively, were women. However, in a few states, women had made major inroads, comprising 47.1 percent of the seventeen reporters in Ohio and 41.7 percent of the thirty-six in Indiana. New York had the most interesting record. None of the forty-six court reporters from the surrogate's courts, supreme court, superior courts, court of common pleas, city court of New York, county courts of general sessions and oyer and terminer, or district courts were women, while the only federal district court reporter and 13 percent of the sixty-two county court reporters were women. It is not surprising that New York male court reporters engaged in the fiercest battles, since the prospects of retaining these situations only for men looked dim. In this light, some men in the courts, as well as the offices, expressed fears about women's presence.[31]

Men's Failure and Women's Power

Anecdotal evidence suggests that men made the connection between women's presence and male failure. In 1882, William Dale Owen's success manual depicted the ultimate failure, a lowly clerk in his wife's hat shop. Fifty years later, according to historian Clark Davis, a company in the 1930s in Los Angeles sought to humiliate men who did not keep up with its standards, by giving men with the lowest sales records "pink unmentionables" (women's underwear) tacked underneath their pictures.[32]

Stenographic sources in the eighties and nineties were less direct but just as conclusive. Men rarely explicitly equated failure or dependence with womanhood and at times even praised women stenographers, as we shall see in later chapters, but some actually articulated that women diminished their manhood. In 1893, court reporter John B. Carey assigned typing exclusively to women "or a very small man," supposedly with tiny hands. However, his explanation revealed his true meaning: "No decent, self-respecting [male] stenographer of education and ability would for a moment think of stooping to it. I am aware that this work is done and often done by strong, able-bodied men, and effectively done, perhaps, well." Going for the jugular, Carey made a backhanded complement to men who did women's work, that is, reversed roles: "Some men can wash dishes, and very good dishwashers they make too." Carey announced that "woman's place is at the typewriter and in the office," rather than the courts. Conversely, typing emasculated men, just like housework, because it was women's labor. Even a woman author's satirical look at the office includes an emasculated "weak-eyed" man who "paints and powders his face, wears all sorts of rings, has several small mirrors about his desk, a comb, a tooth brush, a nail file, and a box of tooth-picks." She says, "We all like him, he's *such a handy fellow* in an emergency, and is so generous with his outfit."[33]

Some male fiction writers in the stenographic press portrayed women as dominant in courtship, reinvigorating the centuries-old discourse of women's power through sexuality and anticipating the popular critique of the New Woman in the 1910s. Office women reversed roles, becoming more powerful than men. In love stories, male authors depicted men who feared women's power to refuse. Robert Barr wrote about wealthy and successful Richard Denham, who "had not the courage" to propose to Miss Gale, with her "somewhat independent air." Fearing he would be "stricken dumb" if he called on her at home, Mr. Denham composed a series of letters using business terminology to suggest a romantic relationship. In other office stories, love turned good men's minds into mush. In Arthur J. Monro's story, Nick had excellent business sense but made one mistake when he "enclosed his personal letter in Miller & Co.'s envelope, while the figures on the New York job had gone to his lady-love."[34]

In other stories written by men, female office workers possessed so much power that male bosses dreaded firing them. Ellis Wood, a prolific author of fiction in stenographic magazines, criticized women's power when the hard-nosed employer who "runs over the boys like a willopus-wallopus" would never "say anything to a woman." The boss grumbled, "When a clerk got funny, I just fired him, and preserved my dignity as head of this concern. But I can't fire a woman. Caesar's ghost! She's the boss here, instead of me!" A republished article by an anonymous author also complained that womanly qualities, incompatible with the workplace, gave women inappropriate power. An employer avoided hiring a qualified woman because when he tried to discharge a young typewriter, she wept for an entire week, upsetting the entire staff "to a point where business was being neglected." Ultimately, the boss agreed to engage the young woman under the condition "if you'll make a solemn promise to go without a single weep if you don't suit."[35]

Author Wood named the source of women's power as sexuality. In a story discussed fully in chapter 5, a new office worker's sex appeal of "puckered" lips "so red and tempting" shook up the law office to the point that the lawyers lost sight of their commitments.[36] Another of Wood's stories features a "high-heeled, honey-tongued little thing" whose every movement attracted her male coworkers' attention so that "every time she moved we all looked up." Even her frivolous behavior "changed the gait of the world for all of us" when "Mr. Attorney gave a second look at the Babe" and she "looked at him . . . [with] the gleam . . . in her eye." In the end, she saved the "weak-kneed" boss's failing business. Wood's authorial voice sums up his views by warning that despite women's "lack of size and strength," "providence . . . gives her a curve somewhere, more potent than armies with banners," so that "it is no use to oppose her." "The man who does so," he explains, "comes out . . . flattened."[37]

This alarm at women's power through sexuality, love, or tears mirrored common nineteenth-century fears of role reversal between men and women. Antisuffrage plays and political cartoons typically depicted voting women smoking cigars and wearing bloomers (symbolic of male trousers) while men were reduced to caring for babies. Their rhetoric demanded that men oppose woman's suffrage to preserve the natural order of things. Women's power meant men's dependence, which was frightening and unnatural. Male writers for stenographic magazines echoed those sentiments, and so did some male stenographers themselves. The presence of women threatened not only men's jobs and salaries but their middle-class manhood as well. Male business and court stenographers risked becoming like women employees—debased, dependent, and powerless. Their fears that demeaning labor as employees marked them as degraded led men to search for ways to rise above the masses, that is, above women and the working class.[38]

PROBLEMATIC SOLUTIONS FOR MALE STENOGRAPHERS

Men might have chosen to quit or eschew stenography, but they did neither until the 1910s.[39] Instead, they looked to improve and rationalize their situation with older discourses of respectability and independence, as frameworks that justified a new definition of middle-class manhood: rising above the masses. Shorthand magazines sought to convince men that phonography still offered them opportunities to surge past the masses, as long as they engaged in proper behavior, worked and studied hard, and possessed ambition. However, this old-fashioned advice now sounded less convincing. With the presence of growing numbers of women workers, how could men insist that their respectability made them especially suited for these jobs? Moreover, phonography promoters' reframing of the self-made man to fit within the new corporate model did not build male stenographers' confidence about what they would find at the top of the career ladder.

Respectability

While middle-class clerks had long since used respectability as a means to elevate themselves above working-class men, stenographers now had to face a new threat in finding the right manly balance. Propriety favored women, who would not let men forget it, often describing them like the middle-class stereotypes of crude working-class men. As a result, when the shorthand press and male stenographers discussed sobriety and dress, they conveyed their hopes that respectability would forge a path for them above the masses, but they also faced risks with such a strategy.

Male stenographers could make genial fun of drunks, as long as they could separate themselves from such men, like clerks in the past had tried to do. In 1891, court reporter John B. Carey published *The Oddities of Shorthand; or, The Coroner and His Friends*, on the adventures of coroners, lawyers, stenographers, and court reporters. One of his stories told of a stereotypical comic tramp, who entertained the coroner and his cohorts with tall tales about his adventures and philosophized about spelling, adverbs, phonography, and war and peace, while downing the hosts' beer. When he finished, the coroner and his buddies debated whether the tramp was a liar or not, with the stenographer alone insisting that he was a scholar. "I know he is a stenographer, and hence a gentleman," he argued, exposing his own poor judgment.[40]

Joking about drunk stenographers became more of a challenge for men with the growing number of working-class men and women in shorthand. While male phonography writers, such as Frank Rutherford, admitted that the "differences between a male and female stenographer" included that a man "sometimes drinks, smokes, and occasionally chews [tobacco]," women would not let men easily escape the implications of that behavior. They trotted out these negative working-class stereotypes to accuse out-of-control young men of lacking the proper work ethic, in contrast to sober, respectable, female stenographers. In an 1897 debate about women's wages, Kate Armstrong, an official court reporter from Illinois, lambasted young men for "prefer[ring] to be free [from marriage] to carouse as they like." In her tirade, she accused men of drinking, using tobacco, gambling, and "lots of other reprehensible things." In an 1890 debate about women's propriety at work, a writer using the name "Ohio" weakly tried to defend "the . . . dozens of honest, earnest, hard-working men in the profession who *don't* do these things," against critics who "condemn" all "male stenographers because many of them drink until totally unfit for work or bet on fast horses, or go mad over some variety actress." Such vices had always risked undermining men's claim to respectability. Now, the presence of female stenographers threatened to exacerbate that danger.[41]

In addition to writings about sobriety, talk about men's dress also disclosed the challenges of employing respectability to stand above the crowd. In 1879, before large numbers of women entered shorthand, a speaker at the all-male Second Annual Dinner of the Chicago Stenographers recalled that president John R. Ritchie was recognized for his "ancient and venerable silk [hat,] . . . the first . . . known to the profession west of the Alleghenies," in his early days as a stenographer in Chicago: "Ancient, weather beaten, time honored, battered and napless, it was still a silk hat, and its effects upon the profession was magical . . . and shed a cosmopolitan luster around the wearer and upon us all (laughter). . . . if Ritchie could wear silk hats, why not we? And from the advent of that historic old hat may be dated the golden age of shorthand in Chicago. (Laughter and applause.)"[42] The all-male audience thought it funny that an old-fashioned tattered hat could mean refinement.[43]

Twenty-one years later, stenographers could still laugh at men's clothes and respectability. Now, middle-class men in general expected clothing to prove a more rugged manliness. Male office workers, like other middle-class men, turned to new styles of business clothing at the end of the century. The boxy sack suit, with its padded chest and broad shoulders, exaggerated men's physique, in contrast to the earlier, elongated styles of the effeminate "dude." The popular advertisements featuring the Arrow Collar Man accentuated broad shoulders, "muscular hands," a square jaw, and chiseled features that retained the refined face of the gentleman.[44]

As court reporters and business stenographers donned the sack coat and Arrow Collar uniform, with its masculine respectability that distinguished its wearers from working-class men and all women, the shorthand press focused its didactic advice about male respectability on neatness and cleanliness. The *Phonographic World* published a story that again borrowed from the popular genre of the comic tramp. Under the guise of a "true story," the author tells of a tramp stenographer who amazes his coworkers and employer by performing more competently than the other candidates for a railroad job. This tramp, however, understands his place and eventually quits—over the protestations of the boss—after twelve days on the job. When pressed, he sardonically explains his departure: "I wouldn't disgrace the profession by staying in this town." The ending has an O. Henry twist in which the tramp turns out to be an intelligent, well-educated stenographer. The gimmick worked because readers could not imagine a stenographer with an "unkempt head of hair," "a week's growth of hair on his face," a "shabby dress coat," and an "unlaundried [*sic*]. . . collar." Competent stenographers were supposed to be knowledgeable and refined, that is, middle-class.[45]

Even more concretely, the shorthand press explicitly described how to dress neatly and cleanly for middle-class jobs as stenographers. In one didactic short story, the slovenly unemployed protagonist, Raymond, cannot find a job until he invests time and money to spruce himself up. With pressed and clean clothes, a boxed hat, and a "clean" shave and "neatly trimmed" haircut, his demeanor and job-hunting fortune change for the better. Now, he looks ambitious and ready for employment, "spurred by the moral support that accompanied the knowledge of being presentable." As the story concludes, Raymond has learned "that one of the very necessary requisites for a stenographer's success is neatness in person and dress."[46] This advice on neatness and sobriety cautioned men to steer clear of the traits that the middle class associated with the working class in occupations increasingly populated by them.

While the clothes men wore accentuated a masculine respectability, these discussions about neatness spoke in a feminine accent about clothing, playing to women's strengths, rather than men's. If respectability required male stenographers to maintain sobriety, order, and cleanliness, they were in real trouble. Such traits and refinement in general were associated with women, not men. If women were assumed to dress neater and cleaner and behave better than men, how could respectability raise men above the masses of women stenographers and typewriters. Moreover, a man overly concerned about style might well be mocked as an effeminate "dude" or dandy. Even the fictional Irish keeper of the boardinghouse where Raymond lives cannot understand why a working man needs to "dress up like a 'dude.'" With respectability privileging femininity, manhood might be better grounded in traditional manly independence.[47]

Career Ladders and Maintaining a Language of Independent Manhood

At the close of the century, middle-class men still clung to the language of independence. Even husbands and their wives who wrote letters begging John D. Rockefeller for loans tried to convince him of the men's worthiness, using the "standard idioms of business," according to historian Scott Sandage. Their insistence on perpetuating the lexicon of independence displays an almost

Pollyannaish faith in the promise of business success. Even throughout the 1910s, 1920s, and 1930s, corporate employers continued to encourage their male employees to view themselves as self-made men. Historian Clark Davis shows how managers sought to build a sense of employee security to discourage workers from flitting between jobs in search of opportunities. In exchange for employee loyalty, management offered limited mobility and prodded workers to see themselves as corporate salesmen and ambassadors. Even before such documented managerial efforts, shorthand educators and promoters and stenographers themselves sought to fit the self-made man within the corporate world. In the 1880s and 1890s, they contributed to reinventing the self-made man by reframing the new conditions to accommodate older definitions of manhood.[48]

Stenography publicists still often wrote in the rags-to-riches idiom, maintaining that even poor boys "with a common-school education" could acquire "success, independence, and prosperity" as official federal stenographers, "auditors, vice-presidents and managers of large businesses."[49] For example, a shorthand press biography of errand boy Henry J. Gensler's introduction to phonography sounds like a Horatio Alger story: having "found a check on [*sic*] the United States Treasury for $10,000," he "at once restored the draft to Colonel Robinson, who gave him a suitable reward." His honesty was soon rewarded by a position. From a second "coincidence," Gensler met, subsequently trained with, and was employed by the official reporters for the U.S. Senate. By 1897, he was also president of the Standard Automatic Machine Company of Washington, secretary and treasurer of the Roanoke Navigation and Water Power Company of North Carolina, and a director for the Columbia Filter and Union Building companies.[50]

In conjunction with self-help advice books that still flourished late in the century, the shorthand press and phonography schools paved the way for the male stenographer to reconcile his dependent status with the middle-class ideal of independence by glorifying shorthand as a stepping-stone toward success for an ambitious man. As proof of the possibilities, the press published announcements and biographies of successful stenographers, especially court reporters. Some told of traditional mobility to the professions, like J. R. Baldwin's climb from stenographer to lawyer. Others described promotions within corporations, such as William Harrison's ascent from a railroad office to president of the Montana Granite Company or George Tuttle's rise to general manager of the Rockford Division of the Sugar Trust Company. Shorthand and typing teacher H. L. Andrews wrote that a young man "may rise to such a height that he will employ others to transcribe his notes, and perhaps occupy an executive position where he will take no dictation at all." As late as 1915, Gregg Publishing Company distributed a booklet, *Shorthand, the Open Door to Opportunity*, which boasted of the many famous men who practiced stenography, including President Woodrow Wilson, senators, congressmen, judges, lawyers, business executives, railway officials, authors, and financiers.[51]

Shorthand boosters and stenographers themselves defined ambition and independence by reframing jobs in bureaucracies as steps up a career ladder toward success. They joined corporations and other white-collar men in hailing small advancements up the corporate ladder and attributing promotions within corporate hierarchies to men's effort and self-reliance. J. F. M'Clain advised young men that if they wrote "neatly and correctly," soon the boss would "sign . . . [their] letters without reading them." Next, the stenographer would sign them himself after the boss departed. Eventually, he would compose the correspondence himself and even "employ an assistant and . . . dictate instead of being dictated to," until, assures M'Clain, "your name hangs over the door." Mr. W. W. Finely wrote in 1888 of his employment history, beginning in 1873 with assorted low-level railroad jobs for different railroads, from which he rose after three years to the position of stenographer in the vice president's office, followed by another move up to receiver's secretary after nine months; he spent one year as a secretary to the trustees' agent, four years as a chief clerk in the general freight department, two-and-one-half years as an assistant general freight agent for the Texas and Pacific division of the Missouri Pacific Railroad, one-half year as an assistant general freight agent for the receiver with the Texas and Pacific Railroad, and almost two years as general freight agent for the receiver with the same road.[52]

This reframing of the corporate employee as a self-made man continued to claim ambition and independence as a product of a man's character. An 1891 biographical sketch of W. T. Crenshaw in the *Phonographic World* portrayed his move from a wealthy childhood to a managerial position as a story of self-sufficiency. Despite birth into a pedigreed family and education at Harvard and at the law school of Washington and Lee University, he attributed his success to "diligent work, close and untiring attention to business and the highest type of strictest integrity." After engaging in insurance, he climbed the railroad corporate ladder from the superintendent's clerk to secretary and treasurer in two years. At the time of the sketch, he worked for Remington Standard Typewriter with six clerks under him, and "with the spirit of the proprietor," he also oversaw hundreds of subdealers.[53]

Some short stories in the *Phonographic World* recast the familiar tale of upward mobility through middle-class effort. The hero still moves up incrementally, but now in a large company. For example, eager stenographer Nick comes to the office early every morning, learning how the business worked, "questioning and cross-questioning everyone who would give him information as to the goods and their different uses," and "his spare time was spent in ransacking the catalogs and other printed matter to learn something new in that way." After a mistake, he redeems himself by saving his firm money and underbidding a competing company for an important and lucrative contract. Nick receives his just rewards: the partners promote him to branch office manager. Initiative pays off in advancement to management, although not yet partnership. By demonstrating character—that is, hard work, initiative, and mobility as proof of ambition—a man could still take responsibility for his rise, but now within the corporate hierarchy. The new incremental steps within the new corporate bureaucracies were reframed to fit with the traditional success myth.[54]

Even with limited opportunities for the traditional goal of proprietorship as economic independence, the shorthand press, phonography schools, and, at times, business and court stenographers themselves continued to promote shorthand as a stepping-stone to economic success. They all embraced the morphing of the self-made man into the career-ladder bureaucrat. This language of stepping-stones and ladders slid easily into a newer hierarchical discourse about "room at the top," above the masses.

Rising above the Crowd

Social Darwinism, with its ranking of societies, human types, and human beings, encouraged men to expect to raise themselves above others, but male stenographers were not entirely confident about their prospects at the top of the stenographic heap. Instead, they wanted reassurance of their middle-class manhood—that they had surpassed other shorthand writers, whether female or working-class male. As the century closed, they became more adamant about the antebellum promise that education, bookkeeping, or phonography would help them "rise above the great mass," that is, the ordinary clerk. Despite promoters', private educators', and some stenographers' repetition of the mantra that there was always room at the top, not everyone agreed on the meaning of "the top."[55]

Shorthand educators and boosters insisted that superior stenographers could always find room at the top. Educators wanted to convince young men to continue to seek business training in shorthand, so they regularly advised them not to worry about female competition. In a seven-month debate about women's salaries in the 1897 issue of the *Phonographic World*, . T. A. Hayes, probably a teacher at the Cedar Rapids Business College in Iowa, tried to convince men that if they "possessed . . . necessary business qualities . . . [and] determination, . . . the minor positions are to be filled by the ladies," while "they will prepare for the top." John L. Peer also insisted that there was "plenty of room at the top . . . [for] those . . . willing to work."[56]

Despite the frequency of these assertions, stenographers did not always share this optimism. In a complaint against proposals to teach shorthand in public schools, stenographer J. B. Reid called the common rejoinder "that there is always room for more—at the top" sheer "nonsense." He expounded, "What is the top! The top of the grandest spire only holds one bird. . . . You mean topward. Then, that is just the overcrowded locality we are now hustling each other about in. There isn't too much room up the phonographic tree just now. . . . There are enough fellows up there now for the number of cherries to be picked."[57]

The speeches and writings of a Brooklyn official stenographer, Colonel Edward B. Dickinson, reveal concerns that even the elite court reporter did not rise above the crowd. He expressed his fears for the future of middle-class clerical men in an 1888 paper delivered at the annual meeting of the New York State Stenographers' Association, over which he presided. He asked, "Does the profession of Shorthand offer any inducements to the man of ability and culture?" His speech lamented the limited opportunities for "cultured men" in stenography, ignoring working-class men and the female half of his audience, who men viewed as temporary and therefore unambitious. Dickinson repeated the well-worn assumptions correlating middle-class men with ambition, when he asserted that "most [cultured] stenographers take up shorthand as a stepping stone to something else." "By prudence and self-denial," he explained, they "may lay aside a competence [for retirement] . . . when the fingers and brain can no longer do their work." But after marriage and children, Dickinson mourned, such men "find it extremely difficult to take the next step." For Dickinson, the risks of failure became too great for family men. They waited and waited, and eventually it was "too late to begin again."[58]

Dickinson worried that men entrenched in shorthand could realize neither fame nor wealth since the general public lumped all speed-writers together: "With most men, one stenographer is as good as another; the highly educated man finds no recognition of or compensation for his acquirements. . . . The mass of mankind does not draw any distinction between the cultured stenographer and the uncultured amanuensis." Even the most "famous" shorthand writers who "have reached the very top of the professional ladder" within the occupation, like Dickinson, remained unknown to outsiders. "Who ever heard of or knew a distinguished stenographer? . . . We know him, but no one else does," Dickinson observed, adding, "Is not the ladder on the topmost rung of which they stand, after all a very short ladder?" Dickinson reported at the previous annual convention of the New York State Stenographers' Association, that he had overheard a demeaning comment when a "gentleman" described another by saying, "Oh, he's only a *stenographer*!" To his fellow reporters, Dickinson bemoaned, "I never knew or heard of but one wealthy stenographer; and he made his money in real estate speculations, and not in stenography." To Dickinson, the unlimited fees that doctors or lawyers could earn far overshadowed the base $2,500 yearly court reporters' salary in New York or even the peak $10,000 that a few earned. In short, Dickinson answered his own query with a resounding no, contending that except as a stepping-stone, shorthand itself did not offer a future to the man who might choose law, medicine, the ministry, or mercantile or agricultural pursuits.[59]

Dickinson's own career history hints at the causes of his fears that even court reporters did not look ambitious by rising above the masses of stenographers. As one who prepared for Harvard by attending the elite Boston Latin School, he held high expectations for himself. When the Civil War came, Dickinson left school to join the army and climbed to the rank of colonel, a prestigious title he continued to use long after the war ended. Next, he studied and practiced dentistry with his father, until becoming disenchanted and turning to law. Eventually, he settled on shorthand and became the official stenographer and secretary of the national Democratic conventions from 1876 to the 1890s. At times, he served as stenographer of a U.S. circuit court, then for the Brooklyn Surrogate's Court, and maintained a private practice. He also became a leader within the shorthand community. These achievements were not sufficient. Edward B. Dickinson felt entitled to stand above the crowd, gaining higher status than his occupation, military title, or leadership within the stenographic community afforded.[60]

As a result, Dickinson tried to elevate some stenographers above others. He distinguished between the "cultured," "ambitious" men and those who chose shorthand as their final goal because they had "no ambition" and were "content with small incomes and short ladders." These men, according to Dickinson, were happy: "leading quiet, unostentatious lives, respected by their neighbors, possessing their little homes, on which there is no mortgage, frugal in . . . habits and tastes, who shall say that they are not the ones to envy?" Others agreed with Dickinson. Shorthand and typing teacher H. L. Andrews of Pittsburgh also differentiated between stenographers with drive and the men who "work along in the same groove for a lifetime," conceding that "surely that would be no disgrace." For Andrews, men who became court reporters moved up sufficiently to satisfy their aspirations. He concluded, "We cannot all be kings or court stenographers." Men like Andrews and Dickinson shared the assumptions of the prevailing success literature that some were born to lead and others to follow. Despite Dickinson's feeble attempt to acknowledge those who did not advance but accepted their place in life, he made very clear that only leaders who rose to the top truly succeeded. Men like Dickinson wanted to believe that their respectability as reinvented self-made men lifted them to the zenith of their field, above men without ambition (presumably from the working class) and women, but they were not convinced.[61]

CONCLUSION

Changes in the last forty years of the nineteenth century for clerical workers in general and stenographers in particular contributed to Dickinson's lament. Traditional prospects for independence looked less promising for business stenographers when the rise of corporations and growth of government expanded the pool of permanent positions, undermined possibilities for proprietorship, and reduced salaries. While male stenographers might still become semi-independent court reporters or leave stenography, they faced the increasing presence of women in business and even court work, where the latter threatened to reinforce the image of male employees as debased and dependent men in degraded jobs. These changes situated male stenographers precariously between their old aspirations of independence through the dream of self-made upward mobility, on the one hand, and the new uncertain possibilities of bureaucratic hierarchies, on the other. Now, men in both the offices and courts worried about losing the prestige of middle-class manhood.

Two solutions that leaned back to a bygone era appeared less convincing for resolving these concerns. Respectability, which had long since enabled men to share the presumed morality of womanhood, now seemed to favor their female competitors, rather than bolster men's prestige. The reframed self-made man, whose incremental steps up the corporate ladder or to court reporting would lead him to the top, looked more promising as a means for maintaining middle-class manhood. But men now worried about what it meant to get to the top. It is no wonder that Dickinson's speeches aimed to bolster the drive for professionalization of court reporters to distinguish clearly between the elite men at the top and other stenographers. He, along with other court reporters and some business stenographers, turned to the language of professionalism to elevate themselves above the crowd and most amanuenses, as we shall see in chapter 4.

CHAPTER 4

The Male Stenographers' Solution: The Language of Professionalism

On 23 May 1878, C. C. Herr of Bloomington, Illinois, fired off a letter to *Browne's Phonographic Monthly* in response to an article in the *Shorthand Review* praising the Scovil system of shorthand. Herr derided "the idea of comparing the speed of a system of shorthand by the number of lines" as "trying to mislead the poor little innocents." In contrast, he tallied the number of motions used in the Munson and Scovil systems: "In his [Scovil's] 11 lines, he has used 31 strokes and 106 liftings . . . in all 437 motions; in the 14 lines of Munson . . . 280 strokes and 125 liftings . . . a total of 405 motions, leaving a difference of 32 motions in favor of Munson."[1] By counting hand movements to prove the superiority of Munson's system, Herr depicted the scientific thinking of nineteenth-century stenographers and the competitive backbiting about shorthand systems that was common for the first hundred years of modern stenography. More important, their competitors' emphasis on speed and simplicity exemplifies the unique characteristics of the shorthand fraternity's efforts to garner prestige through professionalism.

For hundreds of years, Europeans adopted professionalism to assert occupational prestige. In the United States, professionalism grew throughout the nineteenth century, reaching a critical mass at the end of the century. Middle-class men made it a sign of their class and gender status by accentuating educational and intellectual features more available to the middle class and physical characteristics uniquely associated with men. Court reporters and, to some extent, male business stenographers followed suit, fashioning professionalism as a new equilibrium for middle-class manhood.[2]

Men like Colonel Dickinson (discussed at the end of chapter 3) appreciated professionalism for its prioritizing of mental qualities long associated with middle-class manhood. By emphasizing intellect, they could tout their superiority over the working-class male masses and the throng of women who dominated business shorthand and were poised to invade the courts. Reason and logic supposedly required the self-control that middle-class men uniquely possessed, in contrast to feminine emotionalism and working-class lack of discipline. For court reporters, who still identified as independent businessmen, these manly cerebral attributes proved more attractive for elevating themselves above the masses than did feminine respectability and the reconfigured self-made man.[3]

Like others in the middle class, court reporters and law stenographers espoused the newer professional ethic as a means to inflate their authority, garner honor and prestige, elevate themselves above competitors, and maintain an appropriate class identity. While doctors, lawyers, architects, engineers, and accountants strengthened their association with mental work and named themselves as experts in their fields, court reporters transformed themselves into language experts. Like other incipient professionals, they imposed a connection to science and technology and mixed the practical and theoretical, although identifying more with the creativity of the arts. Court reporters and other stenographers also shared the professionals' commitment to education and training.[4]

However, unlike other emerging professionals, who demanded extended specialized college or postbaccalaureate schooling to master the expanded theoretical foundations within their fields, court reporters limited their requirements to a vague middle-class intellectual and educational standard, constrained by the competitive world of shorthand teaching.[5] Without the professional's advanced educational relationship to the manly sciences, court reporters needed a usable muscular professionalism that defined their intellectual work to be as virile as physical labor. As a result, when middle-class men began glorifying their corporeal features, shorthand educators, the press, and legal stenographers chimed in to praise court reporters' endurance and strength. The new strenuous manhood fortified their gender and class position by asserting their superiority to the working class and women and investing toughness as a hallmark of middle-class manhood. To make these connections between intellect and virility, despite their limited education, court reporters and shorthand promoters (educators, the press, and dialect authors) interpreted four sets of opposites as identical pairs: experts and beginners, judgment and mechanical work, the educated and incompetents, and endurance and weakness. Now, they could construct court reporters as middle-class, manly professionals standing above the masses in a new hierarchy based on expertise, judgment, education, and endurance.

EXPERTS AS MENTAL WORKERS

Court reporters, along with the shorthand press and educators, sought to raise the status of legal stenography. Reporters coveted the prestige and admiration of their higher-status coworkers, the lawyers and judges who controlled the courtroom proceedings. Shorthand periodicals and educators also encouraged professionalizing legal stenography to enable the field to attract potential students. They even maintained that court reporters' skills superseded those of other professionals in the courthouse. In a short story, "Betrayed by Voices: Liars Are Unable to Deceive the Stenographer's Ear," the narrating court reporter employs his trained stenographic hearing to identify liars on the witness stand from the quiver in their voices, even when juries and court professionals fail to distinguish the truth. In seeking prestige and authority, court reporters and their cheerleaders spoke like other up-and-coming professionals—as well as less-prestigious groups, such as insurance salesmen, salesclerks, and telegraphers—who privileged mental over mechanical work while maintaining a pride in the practical as well. They refashioned the assumptions of mental labor's superiority into the language of professionalism, with expertise as a key component.[6]

Court reporters believed that their expertise derived from both practical craft techniques and theoretical knowledge. Edward F. Underhill delineated their many intricate skills: "they must know the proper ink to use and must have a copying press, with tank and tablets and dryers and ink and chemicals, and . . . the skill to use them to make one, two, and even three press copies." Legal stenographers advised each other on how to increase their speed by choosing the "best" dialect, hand position, types of paper, and writing implements, as well as by rubbing their hands and joints with pomatum or Vaseline every night.[7]

Despite their pride in craft skills, court reporters and the shorthand community focused on the mental features of the work. The late nineteenth-century shorthand community extended earlier writings about phonography as mental labor to refashion legal stenographers and court reporters as new professional mental workers, or experts, the antithesis of the mechanical performance of beginners. Instead of merely defining experts as seasoned veterans, the shorthand press and court reporters named them as men possessing judgment as a sign of their intellect, in contrast to the rotelike degraded labor of the masses of working-class men and especially women.

Since at least midcentury, shorthand authors depicted phonography as both an art and a science. Benn Pitman called it an "art of representing spoken sound by written signs." Court reporters and the shorthand press continued to portray phonography as an art practiced by creative men, imbued with mental gifts. In 1892, official reporter Edwin Gardiner spoke lovingly of shorthand's artistic features as "a beautiful, ingenious, and methodical . . . art; . . . the handmaid of culture." He praised its "wonders and its beauties and its subtle-ties [*sic*]." Others besides court reporters shared this view. A didactic article advised amanuenses to "aim at . . . beauty of the transcript."[8] Shorthand books and magazines also stressed stenography's scientific order and harmony. Midcentury textbook writers discussed the science of phonetics and its relationship to phonography. Elias Longley told readers that Isaac Pitman based "Phonography" on the scientific theory of phonetics, "the science which treats the different sounds of the human voice, and their modifications." Isaac's brother, Benn, referred to the markings as "geometric signs." Both Pitman brothers and those who modified phonography, like Andrew J. Graham, touted their own systems' orderly principles for their "Scientific Form and Manner" and criticized their competitors' systems for arbitrary rules that followed "no settled principles of orthography."[9]

Building on these earlier notions of phonography as an art based on a science, the late nineteenth-century shorthand press and court reporters joined other professionals in updating the long-standing preference for mental over mechanical labor, but without the manly benefits enjoyed by other professionals. They continued to stress shorthand's objectivity and capability to reveal the truth and parroted scientific language, which had become popular for professions as scientific discoveries like germ theory transformed medicine and health. The new scientific language appeared more objective and less emotional than earlier forms of education.[10] However, the shorthand press's and court reporters' notion of science continued the midcentury emphasis on classification of principles, rather than the newer, physical and natural scientific definition as discovery based on testing from hypotheses. This failure to adopt the recent scientific standards differentiated stenographers from professionalizing accountants, who used modern mathematic and scientific modeling as a springboard to mandate university training and left male stenographers without the same manhood balance embraced by other professionals.[11]

Instead, late nineteenth-century shorthand proponents edged closer to the humanities. The shorthand press and court reporters now praised the intellectual skills of shorthand writers by presenting the most advanced stenographers as language experts in spelling, grammar, composition, and even linguistics. The shorthand community also embraced the nineteenth-century belief that language was the basis of intellect. At an 1892 meeting of the New England Shorthand Reporters' Association, Edwin Gardiner explained to the assembled legal stenographers how the rote work of copying, rereading, and revising the words of the masters taught reporters about the structure of communication. Reporting the sermons and orations of great speakers enabled phonographers to analyze their sentences, styles, and expression and to "understand the power and the structure . . . of . . . [their] native tongue." As high school and college students, the most educated among them had copied and studied quotes from Greek and Latin thinkers; as shorthand students, they often practiced recording the speeches of ministers. Now, as legal stenographers, they extended their educations by reporting the words of lawyers and politicians. Who, after listening to a brilliant lecture with "toilsome . . . logic," would not "giv [*sic*] much," Gardiner gushed, "for the power to stamp it into permanence, to mold it into a visible form which he could examine leisurely and in detail?"[12]

Stenographers, especially court reporters, appreciated shorthand's connection to the arts. They often boasted that men of letters, such as Charles Dickens and Dr. Ben Johnson, knew shorthand.[13] Men (and women) of letters chose stenography, like teaching, to earn a paycheck while they pursued their dream of writing. For instance, to support himself as an author, Charles W. Chesnutt taught high school until discouraged, when he switched to legal strenography. As a court reporter, he penned *The House behind the Cedars, The Marrow of Tradition, The Conjure Woman, and Other Conjure Tales,* and other collections of short stories, becoming the premier African American author of his day. Edward F. Underhill, Philander Deming, and John B. Carey also combined court reporting and publishing, the latter two drawing on their experiences in the courts.[14]

The shorthand community increasingly praised stenographers' creativity and inventiveness. While accounting texts touted their systems' abilities to discover the existing world, like scientists, the shorthand press published short stories that depicted intellectual capability and creativity as proof of the mental superiority of stenographers. Much of the *Typewriter and Phonographic World*'s turn-of-the-century fiction, modeled after dime novel adventures, portrayed imaginative male and female stenographers, who outwitted crooks, bosses, and even rivals in love. Stories about men often took place outside of the office, where they became involved in mysteries and adventures, as in "The Stenographer and the Mermaid: A Six Months' Trip in the Depths of the Sea and the Discovery of the North Pole."[15]

The shorthand press also presented stenographers as inventors whose skills extended far beyond the mere mechanical. Like the inventors characterized in popular advice writings as self-sufficient, solitary figures who exhibited ingenuity, resourcefulness, genius, and entrepreneurship, inventor stenographers showed their mettle. A futuristic story taking place in 1930 captured this image of stenographers perfectly. Judge Carossal (the same young shorthand writer who solves the murder mystery discussed in the introduction to the present study) tells a tall tale about his youthful days as the quickest stenographer. He develops a shorthand dialect that relies on tiny colored pens and a microscope to limit the number and size of his strokes and increase his speed to the astronomical rate of 576 6/7 words per minute, more than four times faster than the best stenographers. Like the larger-than-life John Henry, the hero beats six other shorthand writers to achieve the honor of "The Most Wonderful Stenographer" and fittingly rises to judge. Carossal's genius lay in his ability to devise a shorthand language and design, not just construct the special pens themselves.[16]

Late nineteenth-century phonography magazines also frequently lionized real stenographers who devised their own systems. Some published regular columns of inventions, memorializing early reporters like Thomas Towndrow, who developed his own shorthand system in 1830, and commemorating Isaac Pitman, who was knighted in the 1890s. Like all inventors, these stenography innovators were painted as men of intellect who transformed their occupation. They epitomized the independent man, laboring alone in a struggle for "progress."[17]

While lauding the expert stenographers' intellectual, scientific, creative, and aesthetic abilities, court reporters, their supporters, and even other shorthand writers disdained mechanical, repetitious work. They resented when attorneys called shorthand "merely mechanical," and they insisted that stenography was "not merely a mechanical art" and that "mechanical contrivances" were "worthless."[18] Court reporters' protests reflected fears that their many hours of rote copying and typing and their respect for speed looked like mechanical labor. While science, speed, and efficiency also regimented work, court reporters reconciled the routine characteristics of their work by touting their mental skills, their thinking and judgment. They did so by using the middle-class conversation about the relationship between the head and the hands.

While court reporter Gardiner insisted that "the head and hands of a skilful [*sic*] phonographer [must] . . . do the work," Colonel Edward B. Dickinson explained the primacy of "the head." He began by asserting that machinelike workers could not be professionals, before laying out the "paradox: that the more intelligently the stenographer is able to do his work, through becoming more expert, the more mechanical is his performance." Dickinson reconciled this contradiction by comparing stenography to piano playing, both of which required "wits" and "thought and reflection" for "rapid fingering." By insisting that the execution of perfunctory skills needed thinking, court reporters subsumed the rote components of their work to the mental by adopting the vocabulary of other professionals.[19]

In an 1886 paper on the distinctions between robotic and intellectual reporting, written for the International Convention of Shorthand Writers, official reporter Fred Irland exposed the difficulties of making such distinctions. While court reporters prided themselves in their ability to reproduce rapid testimony for a sustained period of time, Irland claimed to worry about a young assistant who wrote down every word uttered in the courtroom, including all the irrelevant information, repetitions, "yes, sirs," and much more. Irland sent copies of this transcript to colleagues throughout the United States: nine male court reporters responded. Seven called the transcript "laugh-able," an example of "machine reporting" or "mechanical reporting." For them, an expert exercised judgment, the distinguishing quality of intellectual reporting, by eliminating extraneous words in noncrucial testimony. Two insisted that court reporters protect themselves by writing down everything of value, despite disagreements about what was important. One, however, expected stenographers to fix up grammatical errors, bolstering the position that the stenographer is not "merely [a] mechanical assistant."[20]

Even when court reporters used machines like typewriters or Graphophones, they generally viewed them as an assist to the amanuensis, rather than as undermining their own work and skill. In the 1890s, machines for taking dictation became available for business offices and courts. Even when a reporter used a Graphophone, he read his notes into the machine, from which the amanuensis then transcribed onto the typewriter. In other words, court reporters' own note-taking and transcribing skills remained intact.[21]

To more easily distinguish themselves from mechanical work and assert their cerebral identity as professionals, court reporters distanced themselves from business stenographers and typewriters, who they labeled the real rote workers. They regularly deemed office shorthand as repetitive and called the

"$12 or $15 per week stenographer" a "mere machine," referring to typing as "merely mechanical and requir[ing] no unusual intelligence."[22] To many male court reporters, the two jobs of office stenography and typewriting symbolized the routine work suitable for women. Some court reporters tried to reserve the courts for men, since they believed that men naturally ascended to the apex of jobs requiring intellect. They assumed that men would climb to elite posts as court reporter, while "anybody of ordinary intelligence may be a stenographer and write correctly at a low rate of speed." They argued that women, "though skillful and satisfactory in the domain of office duty," were "utterly incompetent to cope with the difficulties of court reporting." These attempts to raise a wedge between office and court stenographers mirrored those of lawyers who viewed the court as a public world and the office as private.[23]

Male business amanuenses employed these same criteria to elevate themselves above women stenographers, by allotting the most "routine" jobs to women and saving "the most desirable positions in our mercantile, banking, insurance, and manufacturing concerns" for men. A stenographer from Seattle, Washington, captured these gender-assumed differences in an 1899 article: "Business to most of [women] is work, and the kind of work that is drudgery. . . . They perhaps have the knowledge and technical skill necessary to make them powers in the business world, and yet they fail in most cases because they have no [imagination]." The writer attributed this lack of creativity to women's recent entrance into the business world.[24]

Business stenographers also wanted to differentiate themselves from other office workers, especially typewriters. Although amanuenses regularly typed and acknowledged "manuscript transcription" on a typewriter as a crucial job requirement, they reminded employers that they were not typewriters. Men delighted in the frequent assumption that they were stenographers while women were typewriters, even though they both did the same job. The masthead of the *Phonographic World,* which pictured a female typewriter and a male stenographer, fed those presumptions (see fig. 1). For these male shorthand writers, women were accepted in the office but relegated to manual positions, the unthinking, unpromotable, and routinized work.[25]

Some women questioned these gendered and occupational binary divisions but maintained the criticism of rote work as drudgery. At times, they joined men in chastising newspapers for lumping shorthand and typewriters together or for dubbing female stenographers as typewriters. One female amanuensis lamented, "I want the great and glorious right to be called a 'stenographer' when I am one, and proud to be one, and not . . . called a TYPE-WRITER."

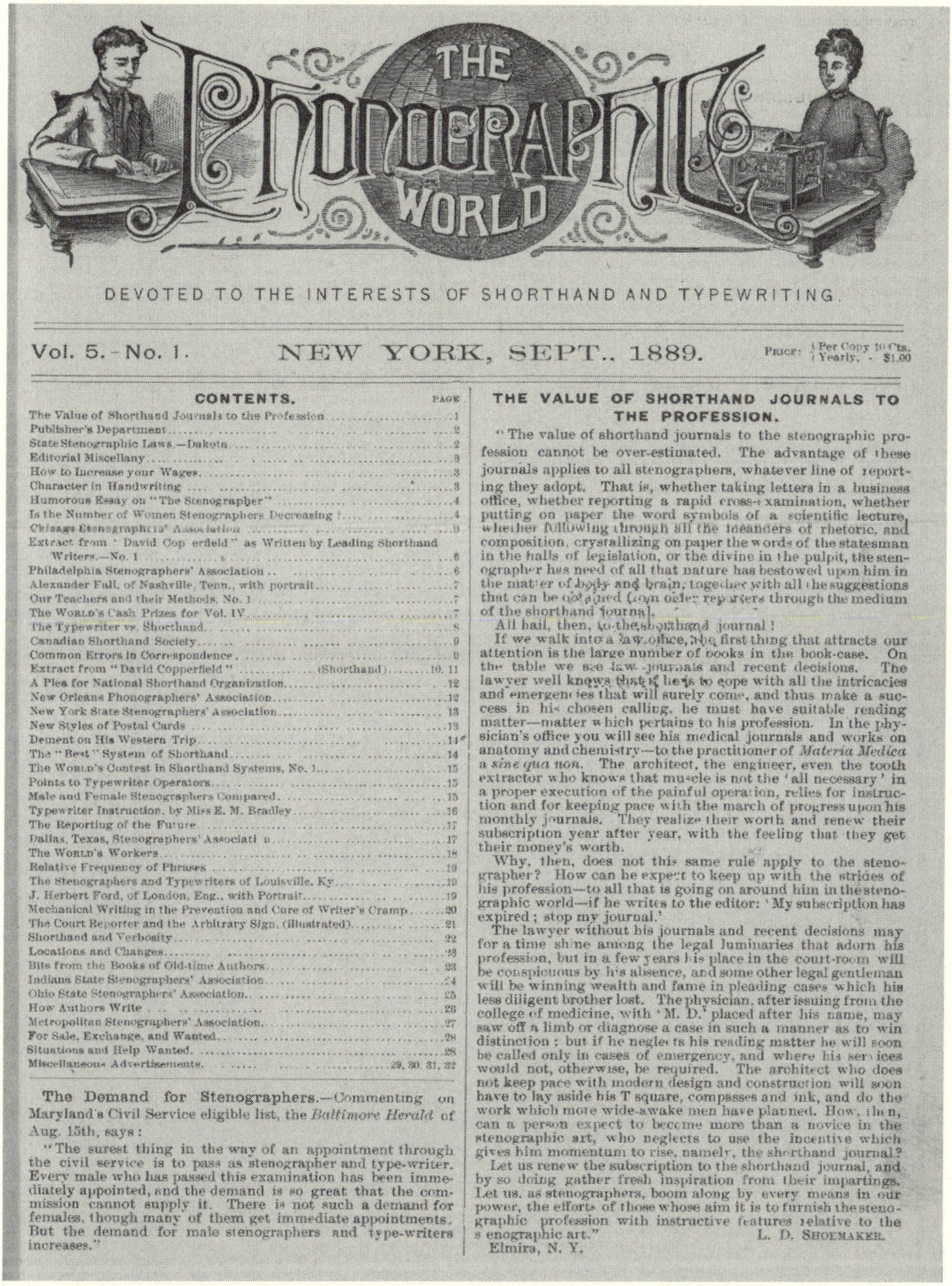
THE PHONOGRAPHIC WORLD

DEVOTED TO THE INTERESTS OF SHORTHAND AND TYPEWRITING.

Vol. 5.–No. 1. NEW YORK, SEPT., 1889. PRICE: { Per Copy 10 Cts. / Yearly, - $1.00

CONTENTS.

The Demand for Stenographers.—Commenting on Maryland's Civil Service eligible list, the *Baltimore Herald* of Aug. 15th, says:

"The surest thing in the way of an appointment through the civil service is to pass as stenographer and type-writer. Every male who has passed this examination has been immediately appointed, and the demand is so great that the commission cannot supply it. There is not such a demand for females, though many of them get immediate appointments. But the demand for male stenographers and type-writers increases."

THE VALUE OF SHORTHAND JOURNALS TO THE PROFESSION.

"The value of shorthand journals to the stenographic profession cannot be over-estimated. The advantage of these journals applies to all stenographers, whatever line of reporting they adopt. That is, whether taking letters in a business office, whether reporting a rapid cross-examination, whether putting on paper the word symbols of a scientific lecture, whether following through all the meanders of rhetoric, and composition, crystallizing on paper the words of the statesman in the halls of legislation, or the divine in the pulpit, the stenographer has need of all that nature has bestowed upon him in the matter of body and brain, together with all the suggestions that can be obtained from older reporters through the medium of the shorthand journal.

All hail, then, to the shorthand journal!

If we walk into a law office, the first thing that attracts our attention is the large number of books in the book-case. On the table we see law journals and recent decisions. The lawyer well knows that if he is to cope with all the intricacies and emergencies that will surely come, and thus make a success in his chosen calling, he must have suitable reading matter—matter which pertains to his profession. In the physician's office you will see his medical journals and works on anatomy and chemistry—to the practitioner of *Materia Medica* a *sine qua non*. The architect, the engineer, even the tooth extractor who knows that muscle is not the 'all necessary' in a proper execution of the painful operation, relies for instruction and for keeping pace with the march of progress upon his monthly journals. They realize their worth and renew their subscription year after year, with the feeling that they get their money's worth.

Why, then, does not this same rule apply to the stenographer? How can he expect to keep up with the strides of his profession—to all that is going on around him in the stenographic world—if he writes to the editor: 'My subscription has expired; stop my journal.'

The lawyer without his journals and recent decisions may for a time shine among the legal luminaries that adorn his profession, but in a few years his place in the court-room will be conspicuous by his absence, and some other legal gentleman will be winning wealth and fame in pleading cases which his less diligent brother lost. The physician, after issuing from the college of medicine, with 'M. D.' placed after his name, may saw off a limb or diagnose a case in such a manner as to win distinction; but if he neglects his reading matter he will soon be called only in cases of emergency, and where his services would not, otherwise, be required. The architect who does not keep pace with modern design and construction will soon have to lay aside his T square, compasses and ink, and do the work which more wide-awake men have planned. How, then, can a person expect to become more than a novice in the stenographic art, who neglects to use the incentive which gives him momentum to rise, namely, the shorthand journal?

Let us renew the subscription to the shorthand journal, and by so doing gather fresh inspiration from their impartings. Let us, as stenographers, boom along by every means in our power, the efforts of those whose aim it is to furnish the stenographic profession with instructive features relative to the stenographic art." L. D. SHOEMAKER.

Elmira, N. Y.

FIG. 1. The masthead of the *Phonographic World* portrays men as stenographers and women as typewriting operatives. The table of contents for this issue from September 1889 shows the variety of topics the magazine covered and its mission to set professional standards for both office and court stenographers. (Courtesy of the New York Public Library.)

Women also insisted that business shorthand writers needed "more than mechanical ability but 'judgement,' intelligence enough to straighten out a much muddled dictation, print a business letter properly, and above all a well balanced mind."[26]

Others recognized that men, too, performed drudge work. When court reporter John B. Carey applauded "self-respecting" men who would not "stoop" to typing, commercial educator H. L. Andrews complained that Carey's pronouncements only applied to a select few, "the official reporter who [was] no longer compelled to typewrite his own notes." Rather, most men filled a "long apprenticeship of office and general work before . . . secur[ing] positions . . . where they are not compelled to typewrite their dictation." Andrews pointed out that "these young men . . . do just as much typewriting as the young ladies." He likened typewriting to other "menial positions" along the steps of a young man's apprenticeship, although "a trifle above" bookkeepers, clerks, and salesmen. He acknowledged that unambitious men might "possibly work along in the same groove for a lifetime," but he said "that would be no disgrace," since "we cannot all be kings or court reporters." Colonel Dickinson agreed that it takes "many years of drudgery . . . to become 'competent.'" In other words, men performed drudge work in the early years of their career. With experience, the character of their labor would improve, unless they lacked ambition.[27]

Sometimes typewriter operators and sellers resisted the categorization of typing as rote work. Typewriters were often called "experts" and occasionally referred to typewriting as an "art." Typewriter manufacturers especially sought to depict their product as nonmechanical. A 1905 fictional story advertising the Remington typewriter presents a young, struggling male author who temporarily acts as a secretary and wins his boss's daughter in marriage. The hero's intelligence is partially responsible for his success, but so is the machine, whose ease and legibility neatens the work and encourages letter writing. For his success, the hero credits his "wits and a talisman," the Remington typewriter, which "through his hand worked miracles." Instead of a mere machine, the typewriter becomes magical.[28]

Such privileging of the mental over the mechanical among even typewriter promoters echoed the language of professionalism among stenographers, who portrayed themselves as scientific and artistic experts to elevate their intellect and denigrate rote work. By defining the expert as a man who exercised judgment, in contrast to beginners who were suitable for mechanical work, court reporters reinforced the middle-class and gendered nature of their work.

EDUCATION

As the discourse favoring the mind continued to define the middle class at the close of the nineteenth century, formal education became more available and increasingly a mark of middle-class status. The new meaning of such schooling for middle-class identity led doctors, lawyers, accountants, and others who sought professional status to require extensive education—especially at the college level—that would furnish formalized expertise for excluding competitors.[29] Unlike other aspiring professionals, court reporters balked at imposing a bachelor's degree or other extended training as a qualification. Instead, they retained the older celebration of the man who studied on his own, and they ridiculed the elite college student who lacked vigor and practical knowledge. They thus echoed late nineteenth-century success manuals and autobiographies and even writings of some professionals.[30] This older language endured in the stenographic community because of its own unique conditions, challenging the court reporters' goal of separating themselves from business stenographers.

Even so, extended formal schooling opened education to a wider population, just as institutional training for professionals grew near the end of the century. In particular, the rise of public high schools and vocational education meant that more young people of all classes remained in school longer. For the "respectable" working class, institutional instruction also signified self-improvement in the abstract as well as real employment opportunities. Concurrently, clerical workers, especially stenographers, lengthened their on-site training at private commercial schools and public high schools.[31]

As more practitioners studied shorthand and typing at schools, the role of education loomed larger in the identity of amanuenses and court reporters. Now, more men and women could interpret their training as signs of cultivation and identify themselves as mental workers. Moreover, competition among shorthand educators reinforced similarities in the instruction of court reporters and the growing numbers of business stenographers, which hampered the use of education as a bar. Instead, the language of education, which could open shorthand to anyone willing to study, buttressed court reporters' professionalism and affirmed all stenographers' middle-class status. Now, learning and educating became the center of stenographic debates.

General Education

During the last quarter of the nineteenth century, clerical workers spent more time in school or studying than most other workers, although the amount varied by class and family circumstances. Compared to the general population, clerical workers were slightly more educated. In Boston, only 9 percent of the boys fourteen to seventeen were enrolled in school in 1875 and 1885. Other than office boys, clerical workers generally remained in school until fourteen (seventh or eighth grade), with some taking an additional year or two of high school. Stenographers were even more educated, but with a wide range in formal educational backgrounds. By the end of the century, even the least educated devoted time to formal education, as classes replaced home study.[32]

During the years before the explosion of amanuenses in the late 1880s and 1890s, stenographers were exceptionally well educated, as illustrated in the short one- to three-page biographical sketches published in a number of stenography periodicals. Among fifteen stenographers born in the 1860s and profiled in the *Phonographic Magazine, Browne's Phonographic Monthly and Reporters' Journal,* and the *Phonographic World,* the vast majority attended academies, some high school, and even some college. For example, Charles H. McGurrin was educated at private and parochial schools until the age of sixteen; W. C. Martin graduated from San Francisco Boy's High School, in the classical course, before preparing to attend a state university. A second, smaller group dropped out of school between thirteen and fifteen because of financial misfortune or family deaths. These men came from middle-class households where informal education prepared them for clerical work. According to historian Ileen DeVault, young people from white-collar families became clerical workers whether they graduated from Pittsburgh's Commercial Department or not. Merely by living in educated families, they learned to speak, read, and write in polished English, even without formal schooling. Along with these advantages and family connections, they could easily find clerical positions. For example, William D. Guthrie, son of a "citizen of prominence and in comfortable circumstances," was born in San Francisco and lived in France and England. But when his father met with "financial reverses," Guthrie quit school at age fifteen. While working as a messenger boy and office boy, he studied shorthand on his own and eventually became a stenographer. By age twenty, he had attended Columbia Law School and was admitted to the bar. We cannot know how crucial Guthrie's family connections were, but certainly his extensive informal education prepared him. Informal and formal education together drew the credit for middle-class successes. A third group of male stenographers were sons of farmers and artisans who left school at thirteen and fourteen to apprentice as printers or newspapermen or to labor on the family farm. These men had the least formal and informal education but often worked around books. Their limited educations, however, were typical of other clerical workers.[33]

By the close of the century, as high school education grew nationally, increasing numbers of working-class youths remained longer in school and moved into what later became known as white-collar employment. Not surprisingly, working-class students who earned good grades continued in school longer and graduated in higher numbers. Through formal schooling, they could secure white-collar jobs. Boys from working-class families in Somerville, a neighboring suburb of Boston, moved into white-collar positions if they attended high school. If not, they worked in blue-collar occupations. Working-class women who became clerical workers also used formal education to launch new office careers. Of the clerical women located in the Boston school records in the 1880s, daughters of manual workers were more likely to graduate from high school than their white collar counterparts, at 35.6 percent and 28.6 percent, respectively. Working-class youths who attended special commercial programs also moved into nonmanual employment. Almost three-fourths of sons (and two-thirds of daughters) of men in unskilled and skilled jobs who attended Pittsburgh's Commercial Department in the public schools found office employment as first jobs. Private commercial schools attracted large numbers of second-generation immigrants by 1880. By earning good grades, remaining in school, or attaining special training, working-class young men and women in late nineteenth-century could access clerical jobs.[34]

Education distinguished all clerical workers, since they were somewhat more educated than the general population. Among stenographers, that distinction was even greater. Most had unusually strong educational training, either formally or informally. Even the least formally educated had a connection to books and learning, and formal training grew by the turn of the century.

Shorthand Training

In the second half of the nineteenth century, autobiographers still proclaimed their self-education. Biographical sketches of stenographers in shorthand magazines did so as well. Yet they still reveal the expansion of formal educational training. Before the mid-1880s, most stenographers learned shorthand on their own. Of eleven stenographers born before 1860 who became presidents of shorthand associations, all initially studied on their own. Two then worked with traveling teachers who led ad hoc classes and peddled their phonography manuals to interested students. Even among those born in the 1860s and trained as late as the mid-1870s and early 1880s, most still began to read up on shorthand without a teacher. Among fifteen such stenographers, eleven began preparing on their own, commonly reading manuals. For example, W. H. Pritchard and Thomas F. King started studying stenography with a teacher at age fifteen while still in school; O. C. Gaston learned it on his own while teaching in a district school; and Thomas P. Hanbury learned it while working as a compositor.[35]

As occurred in other areas of education, the last quarter of the century saw growing numbers of institutional settings available for learning shorthand and typing. Many of the existing private business schools and public schools expanded their curricula to meet the demands for more stenographers and typewriters, replacing much of the home training. Stenographers also opened schools that specialized in shorthand and typing, sometimes to advance their own shorthand dialects. Nationally, the number of students in private commercial education rose from 26,109 in 1875 to 47,176 in 1885 and 81,898 in 1900, with stenography and typing accounting for much of the growth. Only 6.7 percent of teachers worked in public institutions in 1884, but by the 1910s, public schools taught most of the business education.[36]

Increasingly, students of shorthand acquired some of their training formally. Many young men spent a year or two at low-level clerical jobs while saving money. To advance, or "improve themselves," they sought additional training by taking formal courses at private commercial or public evening schools. Some turned to business schools to speed up training and find help with job placement. For example, Louis E. Schrader, born in Wheeling, West Virginia, in 1860, left high school at fourteen and worked for five years in a law office, where he "took the dictation and did the office clerical work." "When the boss was out," he recounted, "I would put in a little time making 'p,b,t,d,' etc., in shorthand." Realizing that he still needed to learn more shorthand, Schrader saved money and traveled to Cincinnati to spend "a term with the Cincinnati School of Phonography," then "returned to Wheeling and opened a general reporting office." Three of the previously mentioned fifteen stenographers born in the 1860s followed this newer pattern of taking courses to complete their training or studied entirely at school. By the late 1880s and 1890s, younger men and women began to acquire commercial skills in short three- or six-month courses in the private schools and in the growing number of high school programs, rather than spending years working in offices. The majority of these shorthand students were female.[37]

Formal business schooling furthered the identification of clerical work with education by conflating it with training. The schools known as business colleges were taught by instructors who established their own professional organizations. Their pedagogy also conformed to nineteenth-century styles of instruction. Students of stenography and typing memorized the basic principles of shorthand, common phrases, or positions of the typewriter keys and then practiced dictation and/or typing. Like elementary and even high school students, they learned by rote. When business schools taught spelling and vocabulary and issued diplomas to their graduates, they further obscured the differences between education and training and advanced the connections between clerical work, education, and the middle class. Public schools themselves also muddied the boundary between training and education, when they responded to the clamor for more classes by expanding their commercial programs.[38]

In sum, as the expansion of business colleges and high schools institutionalized shorthand training in the late nineteenth century, students challenged the dominant pattern of studying on their own. The institutionalization of stenographic preparation reinforced the association of shorthand with education, by equating shorthand instruction with professional training. This development enabled stenographers to imagine themselves as professionals.

Who Belongs: Debates over Education and Class

As formal education grew in importance in middle-class America, it became pivotal to stenographic debates about who belonged in the shorthand fraternity and how much education they needed. These controversies primarily centered around class, as business competition actually reduced the amount of training needed. Yet they show a consensus that stenographers should possess knowledge of grammar, common phrases, punctuation—in other words, good English skills that mostly the middle-class and academically inclined working-class students could achieve, while rejecting a college education as a requirement.

How Much Education?

Court reporters agreed that members of the reporting fraternity should acquire "a good education," although they parsed the meaning of that phrase. Colonel Dickinson cited a dictionary definition of the term *profession* as "an employment requiring a learned education," but he added, "It is not . . . essential to go into the question of how learned the education must be; it will suffice . . . that some learning is essential to equip a stenographer for his work." Others preferred more extensive schooling. Four years earlier, in 1890, the president of the Kings County Shorthand Society, Thomas S. Lewis, advocated "a wide course of reading, a general familiarity with many subjects, . . . some language other than English, particularly French and Latin." His recommendations bolstered stenography's ties to the learned professions of law and medicine, which still counted the classics as a symbol of an elite branch of knowledge. Lewis was not alone in wanting to set a standard for court reporters as lettered men who read and wrote in French, Latin, or German and studied rules of civil procedure, *Gray's Anatomy,* and legal chemistry, along with a wide variety of subjects. At a meeting in Chicago in July 1893, the World's Congress of Stenographers adopted a resolution encouraging college education by calling for the "establishment of professorships for shorthand at the Universities." However, unlike other nascent professionals, few stenographers pressed for a college education. Even Lewis concurred that court reporters did not have to graduate from "one of our colleges, such as Harvard, Princeton, Yale, Columbia or Amherst."[39] In general, the stenographic press and court reporters rejected the need for a classical education or professional training and continued to believe in self-improvement, similar to advice in contemporary success manuals.[40]

The press still promoted self-improvement to sell their texts for at-home study. In an 1882 satirical piece, stenography promoter, editor, and educator D. L. Scott-Browne criticized shorthand schools that advertised that their students needed no skills; instead, he contended that shorthand writers must have intelligence, although he assumed that formal education was not necessary. Scott-Browne poked fun at the presumption that farm boys, artisans, and immigrants had no brains, and he insisted that these men had knowledge, whether from schooling or on their own. Shorthand periodicals, in general, applauded stenographers who grew up on farms or first became artisans and valued studying. For example, court reporter Theodore C. Rose, who had lived on a farm and readied himself to be a carriage ironer, was rendered in a biographical sketch as possessing "an average common school education" and a "love of reading . . . [which fueled] his efforts to learn everything possible." For these men, studying still counted more than formal education.[41]

Leading court reporters from artisanal backgrounds also disliked the college model, resenting the elitism of enhanced education. An unusual pair of speeches by the son of a printer reveals the hidden class tension embedded in the discussions over how much schooling a court reporter should have. In 1890, soon after Colonel Dickinson gave his paper decrying the plight of "cultured men" in stenography, one of the guests in attendance, James M. Yerrinton, began to formulate a rebuttal defending men (and women) without extensive formal education. In 1892, shortly before his death, this early president of the exclusive New England Shorthand Reporters' Association lamented, at an association conference, his lack of "educational advantages in my early life that many of you gentlemen have had." Yerrinton turned this handicap into an advantage, as advised in Gilded Age success manuals, by portraying himself as a self-made man whose "knowledge or skill . . . has been attained by hard work." Later in the conference, the intent of Yerrinton's speech became clearer when he overtly disparaged the increasing emphasis on so much education. He scolded an author who insisted in a stenographic magazine that a successful shorthand reporter must "understand Greek and Latin, French and German,—and, for aught I know, Sanscrit [*sic*], Chinese, and Russian,—and have a knowledge of all the sciences." Yerrinton reminded his audience that such a stenographer would need the training of "all the professorships in Harvard College." Instead, he asserted, "The members of our profession . . . [need] fairly good English education, . . . a strong physical constitution, acute faculties of perception and comprehension, and . . . the fundamental quality of all—*good sense.*" Yerrinton preferred intelligence and even brawn to extensive formal education, available only to the upper middle class. Like others with artisanal or farming roots and some older leaders, he expressed the general disapproval of college education as a requirement, typical of other male professionals.[42]

Pressure for Speedy Training

Shorthand educators and the market for quick training also placed limits on the educational requirements for stenographers. While educators in other professions expanded the theory and knowledge necessary for preparation, shorthand educators promoted practical education. Competition among shorthand educators preparing the growing numbers of business stenographers circumscribed shorthand training as they morphed the promise of teaching speed into speedy teaching. Since court reporters took the same preparation as business stenographers, they could not escape the competitive shorthand market's push for simpler and faster training, instead of the slower, more complex, and exclusionary education that other professionals built.

Speed mattered more than theory to stenographers. Employment, promotion, and prestige within the occupation depended on how fast they could write. Speed distinguished beginners, amanuenses, and experts, or "verbatim" writers, who could write rapidly enough to catch every word. Shorthand trade magazines delighted in reporting the rate of dictation of the leading legislative or court reporters. A typical article written about Dennis Murphy, a reporter for the Senate, described how he kept up with Senator Plumb, who "moves his jaws . . . like a corn-sheller run by electricity . . . at the rate of 200 words per minute." Some leading court reporters felt compelled to prove themselves and advocated speed contests, a practice that carried over to typewriters as well. When John Robert Gregg wanted to gain legitimacy by proving the usefulness of his shorthand style, he prepared his best practitioners to compete. Even state exams focused on speed.[43]

Phonography boosters promised practitioners that they could write faster than in longhand and even reach verbatim speed. Succeeding revisions of shorthand dialects guaranteed greater velocity, while the shorthand press and business school proprietors assured prospective students that they could quickly reach a pace suitable for employment. Shorthand language spokesmen voiced these claims because saving time through winged writing was stenography's promise, making it central to stenographers' identity.[44]

However, reaching a pace rapid enough to take dictation, let alone court testimony, took time. First, students had to master the complex symbols and rules. For example, Benn Pitman divided the study of consonants into "Explodents," "Continuants," "Liquids," "Nasals," "Coalescents," and "Aspirates." For each step, he had complicated rules, such as rule 43: "When a vowel is placed on the right-hand side of an upright or sloping letter, or below a horizontal one, it is read *after* the consonant. See page 33, lines 1 to 4. When a vowel is placed on the left-hand side of an upright or sloping letter, or above a horizontal one, it is read *before* the consonant."[45] Then, students had to practice writing in shorthand and transcribing their notes into English.

Students had little patience for the many hours of practice necessary to build speed. They hoped to spend a few months learning (instead of attending a year or two of high school) and quickly look for employment. Often, they did not finish the commercial college programs either. Historian Jerome P. Bjelopera found that in the early 1900s, only one-fifth of students completed the recommended six to nine months of schooling to graduate from Peirce College, a business college, in Philadelphia.[46]

In advertising their schools, private commercial educators appealed to this desire for quick rewards. For instance, Eastman National Business College in Poughkeepsie, New York, encouraged parents to send their sons and daughters there instead of "keeping them in the treadmill of the common schools going over the same studies." In ten weeks at $100 or twenty weeks at $150, they could learn shorthand and then start working, according to the advertisements. These business colleges sought to convince students (and their parents) that they could acquire skills rapidly, but once the students memorized the rules, the schools pressed them to take more classes to pick up their gait, rather than dropping out to get a job.[47]

Business school and dialect advocates each publicized their own system as the simplest and easiest to learn. They loved to tell stories of students who started to study a more difficult dialect but changed to theirs. *Browne's Phonographic Monthly* wrote about William Milligan, who first took on Taylor's shorthand but switched to Benn Pitman's *Manual*, "which he recognized as superior to the cumbersome and arbitrary system he was endeavoring to learn." John Robert Gregg also explained, in the introduction to his 1888 book, how he had simplified the previous systems by eliminating "shading or thickening, the use of longhand-type strokes, "the objectionable obtuse angle," "the unnatural zig-zag motion," and the "words on, above or through the line," while inserting "vowels in their natural order without lifting the pen," Gregg's supporters boasted that his system had cut Pitman's nearly two hundred rules and three hundred exceptions to only thirty rules. Gregg assured his readers that his method was "so simple as to be readily acquired by [those with] the humblest capacity, and those possessed of little leisure, and yet rapid enough to reproduce verbatim the fastest oratory."[48]

These battles over who taught faster reflected idealism as well as cutthroat competition among shorthand styles and business colleges, which led to efforts to discredit rivals' systems and teaching. The conflicts began when Benn Pitman refused to adopt Isaac Pitman's tenth revision of his dialect, leading to silence between the brothers from 1857 to 1882. Without a "true" phonography, ruthless competition grew. In the late 1870s, stenography system promoter, publisher, and school director Andrew Jackson Graham took rival D. L. Scott-Browne to court three times, accusing Scott-Browne of accepting students' money but failing to send the promised textbooks. They continued to fight until Scott-Browne's death in 1893. Graham had also sparred with Benn Pitman from 1862 to 1872, charging him with claiming credit for improvements in phonography; and Scott-Browne skirmished with Frank Harrison. Gregg named others as "enemies" in private letters. These textbook publishers and business college proprietors demonized their competitors as "frauds," quacks, and charlatans.[49]

Amanuenses, court reporters, and the general press weighed in to condemn some teaching as bogus. Business stenographers and court reporters who felt frustrated by their inability to limit the newly trained competition joined with the general press to condemn the traveling professors and "crooked" business colleges that turned out stenographers and typewriters after a three-month course. These criticisms echoed middle-class advice to country youth to avoid strangers in the city, notice to students of telegraphy and medicine to beware of trade schools, and the general concern about frauds, fakers, and shysters. Using sentimental vocabulary, critics castigated those who "seduced" "innocent young men" with "flaming advertisements" guaranteeing to teach them the "art of verbatim reporting . . . in thirty days"[50] or who would "cheat poor girls" by promising them a shortcut to the altar.[51] They damned the "merits of Prof. Write-like-the-devil's lately discovered system"[52] and those fakers who "took fifty dollars from the labor worn hands of the poor creature, [and] gave her a certificate." One claimed, "Eternity is too short and Hell is too chilly for these charlatans."[53] Miss Parrish, a twenty-year veteran now a teacher, denounced "bogus professors" for taking women's money and failing to prepare them for the business world. In a speech before seventy-five women in New York, she exclaimed, "If I had the makings [*sic*] of the laws, I would hang every bogus professor of stenography as high as Haman" [the villain in the Jewish story of Purim]. The audience roared its approval.[54]

The similarities among shorthand styles contributed to this ferocious competition. Such phonography writers as Andrew Jackson Graham modified Isaac Pitman's system, sometimes with his permission and sometimes without. Their new methods were also adapted. For example, while slightly over half of court reporters in 1893 practiced Graham's system and about one-sixth practiced Benn Pitman's, one-sixth mixed approaches, usually a combination of Benn Pitman's and Graham's. At times, the revisionists displayed some collegiality. Benn Pitman chose his own successor, Jerome B. Howard, and the two published refinements together. David Wolfe Brown thanked all of those authors whose works he found "more or less useful," including both Pitmans, Graham, Dement, Barnes, and Munson.[55]

The distinction between frauds and reputable commercial schools blurred, however, as they all competed to fill their classrooms. Even the more well-known business schools succumbed to the same temptations as the so-called frauds by offering more than they could deliver: foreshortened classroom time, easy-to-find employment, and high-paying jobs. Scott-Browne, who railed against stenographic quacks, assured prospective students that they could learn his system in less than three months (six months faster than in the public schools) and hasten their entry into the paid workforce. He explained that he could teach shorthand quicker than fakers because his system was the most advanced and modern. Such tactics narrowed the difference between "reputable" and "dishonest" schools, undermining the credibility of all private business colleges. All schooling bolstered student hopes for accelerated study and undermined the opportunity for court reporters to use shorthand training to distinguish themselves from business stenographers.[56]

As private business colleges and shorthand language boosters competed to train amanuenses by promising quick rewards, debates in Boston and New York developed about whether the public schools should teach stenography, with private proprietors opposing and public school teachers and administrators supporting. The Boston debate at first seems to explain distinctions between training court reporters and amanuenses, but it ultimately discloses the commitment to practical education for both. In their discussions, the two sides examined the purpose and nature of shorthand education, while ignoring the economic consequences for private commercial educators.

William E. Hickox, the proprietor of the well-known private Hickox Shorthand School in Boston and former editor of the *American Shorthand Writer*, opposed public school competition that would undoubtedly hurt his business. In 1886, he wrote to the *Phonographic World* to garner support for a debate in Boston from court reporters and students hoping to someday become verbatim reporters. Hickox spoke only about training court reporters, as if they were the only ones learning shorthand. He assured practicing and aspiring reporters that "phonography was no more appropriate in a public school curriculum than architecture, telegraphy or civil engineering," because in the short time that students would study in high school, they could learn very little. To him, teaching students a "little shorthand is almost worthless," because "the object of learning shorthand is to be able to report verbatim, and anything short of that is practically a failure." In other words, he extended the harangue against bogus teaching to a more threatening competitor, the public schools, with the same mantra: learning shorthand could not be rushed. His initial article drew support from law reporters and teachers, who argued that public school teaching of stenography would create more competition and lower wages.[57]

In contrast, Jane Passmore, a public school shorthand teacher in Milwaukee, Wisconsin, recognized the benefits of speedy instruction for the working-class business stenographer. For her, the goal of teaching public school shorthand was "to train . . . shorthand amanuenses," not to prepare the "so extremely small . . . number" for "professional reporting." Passmore agreed that the very few verbatim reporters—that is, court and legislative reporters—would need special instruction, while amanuenses could do well even if they did not finish the business courses. Like other proponents of vocational education, Passmore asserted that "many boys and girls who might not otherwise be encouraged, or ever permitted, to attend the high school, are given an opportunity . . . to get . . . an English education above . . . the graded [*sic*] school." Other public school employees who advocated teaching shorthand in the public schools echoed Passmore and the commercial education wing of the vocational education movement's promise to "train and develop the mind," help with memory, "cultivate habits of literary taste and literary accuracy, . . . clearness of thought and brevity of expression," and "provide employment" for those who would not normally attend high school, that is, the working class. While Passmore thought that shorthand training should focus on the far larger numbers of potential amanuenses who required minimal instruction, she agreed with Hickox that court reporters needed special training.[58]

Notwithstanding this accepted distinction between the instruction of verbatim reporters and amanuenses, Hickox's discussion of the ideal preparation of shorthand students exposes how much the two overlapped. He encouraged the public schools to concentrate on providing stenographers with "the most important qualification . . . a good English education," but his definition of "a good English education" is revealing. Hickox admonished the public schools for failing to train students to spell better and mocked the "theoretical educators who are desirous of introducing all the 'ologies' and 'ographies' possible into the public school curriculum at the expense of English." He wanted the public schools to teach practical writing skills and leave the instruction of shorthand to him. His students would learn applied stenography, well enough to write verbatim, even if most of them in reality ended up employed in offices as amanuenses. Hickox's own curriculum for shorthand training did not include theory or any sophisticated content about the structure of the English language. Even when commercial schools offered subjects other than business, they were limited to remedial classes in reading, writing, history, geography, grammar, algebra, spelling, composition, elocution, and mental and written arithmetic, aimed at younger students behind in their studies, not advanced study. As a champion for educating professionals but an instructor of amanuenses as well, Hickox confined preparation to practical education, rather than theory.[59]

Competition to train the growing numbers of business stenographers drove the preparation of all writers, despite the pretentious speech linking shorthand to theories of language, which required advanced education. While some of the early shorthand books devoted long sections to describing the science behind phonography, newer books became shorter and eliminated much of the theory. Moreover, the connection to spelling reform in the 1860s and 1870s, with its commitment to language theory, disappeared in most books and magazines. Even the development in new writing styles demonstrated the shift toward training business stenographers. In the 1880s and 1890s, Benn Pitman's Easy Reporting Style (or Amanuensis Style) removed all but initial and final vowels to increase the speed of writing and teaching. Prospective court reporters were expected to begin with this style but then learn the Brief Reporting Style, which required memorizing the many contractions. Despite this difference, shorthand authors increasingly tried to whittle down the number of contractions in their systems to speed up the education process.[60]

The growing simplification of rules contrasted sharply with trends in the neighboring emerging profession of accounting. As businesses expected bookkeeping to certify the economic health and predict the future of companies, bookkeeping authors developed theoretical tools, that is, greater abstractions that could encompass specifics.[61] These shared theoretical trappings became the basis for expansive educational training. Shorthand had no such abstract goals and theoretical tools, just simplified rules to increase speed.

Since shorthand students, especially potential business stenographers, wanted to reach acceptable speeds quickly enough to find employment, private and public schools maintained shorthand as a labor-saving device, rather than the basis of language theory. Competition fueled their enthusiasm for simplicity and speed in instruction for all stenographers. By promising ease to suit those with the "humblest capacity" and "little leisure," shorthand educators undermined professionalization, which demanded extended education and a more complex body of knowledge to learn. As public schools and promoters of newer shorthand dialects, like Gregg, set their sights on the rapidly growing number of business stenographers, rather than the court reporters who led the movement for professionalization, they increasingly distanced the professionalization of court reporting from other emerging professions. As a result, stenographers chose a more modest path. Even court reporters, especially the older generation from the working class, agreed that requiring a college education went too far. Nonetheless, all agreed that shorthand writers needed a "fairly good English education" and "good sense." This collective belief in some education, whether on their own or formally, formed the basis of the stenographic fraternity.[62]

"Incompetents": Education as a Language of Class

Despite the limited education required for learning shorthand, commercial educators helped reinforce its connections to the middle class by framing debates about the suitability of potential stenographers around the importance of education. While educators encouraged everyone, including women and African Americans, to learn shorthand, their demands for a certain proficiency in spelling and grammar often slid down that slippery slope leading to the castigation of working-class students in general. Some business and court stenographers also conflated education with class to elevate themselves above the so-called incompetents, although they worried more about competition and potential status loss. By contrasting lettered stenographers with incompetents and beginners, the shorthand press and reporters themselves strengthened the bond between shorthand, the middle class, and education. In the process, they again revealed that stenographers were trained, not educated.

Shorthand editors and language and school promoters strongly supported equal access to stenography to attract adherents to their specific dialects, students to their schools, subscribers to their journals, and consumers to their instruction books, as well as to extend their influence within the field. In the 1870s and early 1880s, when women were rare in stenography, editors publicized the advantages of shorthand for women and resisted discrimination against them. By the late 1880s and into the 1890s, when fewer men than women found business shorthand and typing jobs appealing, editors advertised openings especially for men. Periodically, they reported on the accomplishments of the few male African American stenographers.[63]

To shorthand educators, this expression of openness and tolerance meant that all men and women had the chance to become stenographers, but most would fail to meet the necessary standards. Shorthand boosters presented education as both an opportunity and a bar. While they praised their students as intelligent and educated, they also named, described, and demonized as "incompetents" those who did not meet middle-class measures of knowledge. They reproached young, poorly trained beginners for asking too little for their services, exhibiting poor skills that devalued shorthand, and depressing wages. The press and educators agreed that "incompetents" displayed "bad spelling, bad grammar, . . . faulty punctuation[, and] . . . failure [*sic*] to understand the simplest principles of business." They could not write proper business forms, take notes, and/or type at sufficient speed, nor could they avoid making frequent undisguised erasures.[64] The pages of shorthand magazines were plastered with proof of their poorly written letters, such as the one that follows.

> Dear Sir Yours of the 28 Feb has just come to hand. In replying to the same would say I think I am qual-fied [*sic*] to fill the position. I can write about 125 words per minute and transcribe them at the rate of 40 to 50 words per minute. My age is 41. I have had a common school Education am strictly temprate [*sic*] in every sense of the word. I am married. the [*sic*] only office work done by me was to give out and receive work after it.[65]

Article after article complained about incompetents who could not spell or punctuate correctly and who transcribed "main use" instead of "menus" and "launch his bed on the seat of eternity" instead of "launch his boat on the sea of eternity," because they did not know middle-class cultural expressions and metaphors.[66]

Court reporters and other male stenographers joined in to lament how "so-called business" colleges had turned out lots of "incompetents" who "degraded" their "profession." While court reporters worried that less-skilled business stenographers undermined their status, all groups within the shorthand fraternity who wrote to the stenographic magazines complained that "incompetents" did not satisfy the vague requirement of a "general education," a benchmark that only the middle class likely met. For example, a presumptuous eighteen year old, recently retained by the Schenectady Locomotive Works, explained that his "experienced" predecessors "did not fail because of their insufficient knowledge of shorthand or typewriting, but because of their lack of a good general education." This young stenographer parroted the words of stenography educators who explained that an "incompetent" might know shorthand but did not possess a middle-class "general education," often meaning some schooling.[67]

Shorthand educators and supporters went beyond blaming poor education. Despite their repeated statements that good teaching and hard work enabled anyone to meet the educational standards necessary for shorthand writing, they led the stenographic community in asserting that some people could never meet those benchmarks because of natural deficiencies. A shorthand magazine editor lambasted "cheap evening lessons . . . [for] those of moderate means" as a waste of time because many of the students "are totally unfitted for the profession" and would do better "in almost any other vocation . . . which should call for and demand less mental acuteness and education." Stenographer William Shaw likened teaching such a person phonography to trying "to make a Handel out of a street organ grinder, or a Shakespeare out of a bookseller," because carpenters, mechanics, and other artisans were not "sufficiently educated" and were "over-reaching their capacity." Benn Pitman insisted that leading shorthand writers came equipped with the correct "heredity." The most quoted line reprinted from the *Boston Herald* said it all: "stenographers, like poets, are 'born, not made.'"[68]

The shorthand community supported common views about race and gender, so that some stenographers could not escape their biology or caste, like "lady stenographers," "colored stenographers," or "Jewesses," even though shorthand boosters seemed to welcome all of these groups. Indeed, an upwardly mobile Irish steersman in G. Shankland Walworth's short story "A Grotesque Stenographer: A Quaint and Curious Tale of a Quaint and Curious Pupil," who through hard work becomes a shorthand writer, cannot elude the presumed core Gallic traits of drinking and good humor. These attempts to distinguish white native-born stenographers from immigrants seem similar to the minstrel shows performed by stenographers and salesclerks to separate themselves from African Americans. Such naturalizing of traits fit with social Darwinist exaggeration of intrinsic physiological differences.[69]

However, critics rarely explicitly named incompetents as working-class. Instead, they delineated them by features that the middle class regularly employed to malign the working class, such as their etiquette, demeanor, and intemperance, all cultural symbols of lack of respectability (chapter 5 discusses the critique of women's respectability). Even so, the criticism centered on education, such as promoter and editor Scott-Browne's comparison of "the best-educated . . . who took up the study of shorthand . . . fifteen years ago" as "the opposite from the class who are taking it up to-day." Another writer, probably an educator, boldly differentiated "the competent, honest, sober, and industrious stenographers" from "a large 'floating population,' . . . who are *certainly not competent.*" To distinguish further, he described applicants for a railroad stenographic job as "not the right kind of 'timbre,'" who drank too much and were fired from previous positions. Although a "prominent railroad official" admitted that these men performed "satisfactory work . . . so far as their shorthand and typewriting are concerned," the writer concluded that "hardly anything else favorable can be said of them." The railroad finally hired a twenty-year-old man with requisite middle-class characteristics: "son of a school principal well known in the community for over ten years; graduate of public school and Duff's Business College."[70]

This focus on uneducated "incompetents" may help explain working-class silence to these attacks. Education united the "respectable" working and middle classes who lined up against the incompetents, the undereducated stenographers. Yet lack of education symbolized the range of attributes that the middle class identified and condemned in the working class, such as smoking, cursing, drinking, loud talk, gaudy attire, spitting, sneezing, and other displays of bodily functions in public. The respectable white working class also held up schooling as a sign of their own refinement and their superiority to those below them. They used education along with sobriety, industriousness, demeanor, and attire to define respectability and demarcate themselves from immigrants, African Americans, and the "rowdy" working class.[71] Since assaults on the working class blended with criticism of their undereducation and since stenographers of all classes valued learning, working-class stenographers could not easily defend themselves.

Commercial educators and others in the shorthand community had identified stenographers as educated and intelligent by constructing the incompetent as uneducated and unsuitable to practice shorthand. In doing so, they reinforced the court reporters' and even some amanuenses' positions as professionals in the middle class. They employed an intermediate educational standard that required good grammar, punctuation, and especially knowledge of common phrases (the kinds that the middle class grew up hearing), but they stopped short of a college degree. However, this middling educational standard also enabled the inclusion of the educated working-class and allowed those with middle-class skills to name themselves as experts.

ENDURANCE: MENTAL WORK AS PHYSICAL LABOR

With such slippery meanings of intellect and education for stenographers, court reporters needed to maintain the definition of shorthand as mental work by refashioning a defense of mental work itself. Stenography sponsors and court reporters turned to another pair of oppositions, endurance and weakness, to distinguish experts from beginners and elevate reporters above the masses of women stenographers and typewriters. This manly definition of expertise worked well for mental workers lacking advanced education.

As the growing population of sedentary office men in the late nineteenth century revitalized concerns about their virility, stenography promoters and court reporters sought to portray court reporting and sometimes business stenography as mental work that needed physical endurance. Late nineteenth-century advice writers continued to blur mental and physical labor, justifying deskbound work by depicting brain and brawn as mutually reinforcing. A sound body was necessary for intellectual ability. Now, however, the cultural arbitrators claimed physicality as middle-class but reduced it to "pluck" and "grit," which emphasized decisiveness and aggressiveness. As a result, according to historian Judy Hilkey, stamina and endurance became the necessary proof of the manly muscular body and the means for reinforcing the identity of male court reporters as men of intellect.[72]

Since the 1820s and 1830s, when growing mechanization prompted debates about industrial work, middle-class writers worried about the deteriorating effects of the separation of mental and manual labor. While they complained about the ill effects of limited mental content and physical exhaustion for workers engaged only in mechanical labor, they also bemoaned that too much brain work strained the body and led to disease. Popular solutions encouraged exercise, especially interspersing physical with cerebral endeavors. Proponents of the manual labor school movement urged students to avoid the dangers of stationary life by working in the fields or performing other active tasks for part of the day.[73]

At the turn of the century, a newer style of manhood, dubbed "strenuous masculinity" by Theodore Roosevelt in 1899, refashioned the antebellum middle-class concerns about sedentary life. "Strenuous masculinity" replaced the demands for manual labor with action, decisiveness, power, and muscularity. Men were to climb mountains, shoot wild game in Africa, box, pump iron, fight, and conquer distant lands, in a Darwinian contest for racial control. Manly beards, sideburns, and muscular bodies like those of strongman Eugen Sandow and the fictional Tarzan were admired. Masculinity embraced animal instincts and the primitive as middle-class men rebelled against civilization, women, and the home. Under this newer definition of middle-class manhood, sickly men especially symbolized passivity, weakness, femininity, and working-class manhood.[74]

This late nineteenth-century shift to a newly fashioned physicality for middle-class manhood posed problems for male business stenographers and court reporters. Beyond the middle-class linkage of consumption and neurasthenia with sedentary work, clerical men had long been associated with illness. Many clerks and stenographers chose office jobs because they were not hardy enough for manual labor. For example, Benjamin A. Strawbridge clerked in a general store because he was not "physically equipped for the hard work of farm and forest." H. K. Saunders expressed relief in finding employment other than manual labor, noting that he was "an invalid during all my early years and . . . physically very frail." Others took up stenography while recuperating. Court reporter Edward F. Underhill played with the trope of frailty by joking that an accident that left him without fingers on his left hand "opened the way for him to become a *shorthand reporter.*" In her 1901 stenographic spoof "Queer!" Alice McKee emasculated men in the office, like "Mr. Weak-eyes," whose "eyes are delicate." Such images of "weak-eyed" male amanuenses reinforced threats to their manhood, as the feminine, dependent masses challenged their claims to independence.[75]

In response to the dangers of an overly feminine shorthand man, the stenographic press found ways to reposition court reporters and stenographers to emphasize middle-class manly strength. For example, Mrs. E. N. Miner, wife of the editor of the *Typewriter and Phonographic World,* wrote the following ditty in 1894, supposedly in response to a letter asking, "Shall I study shorthand?" She answered, "It all depends!" and restricted shorthand to young, healthy, strong men.

If you are old and decrepit, or sickly and weak,
(And so but half of a man);
If you hope to gain knowledge without troubling to seek,
And don't know "I can't" from "I can";
If you always are waiting for some one [*sic*] to "boost,"
Or so wedded to Pleasure that she rules the roost—
You would better eschew it;
You surely will rue it.
It takes lots of brains
And labor and pains
And metal [*sic*] and "sand"
To master shorthand.
But if you are made of the stuff Business uses.
(With plenty of grit and backbone);
If you have all the strength that Dame Nature chooses,
To fashion a king for her throne;
If you're willing to labor for Labor's reward,
Aye! work with a will though the Devil retard—

You better would do it;
You never will rue it.
There is plenty of place
For the strong in the race;
There's a broad place to stand
When you master shorthand.[76]

Shorthand educators and the press also invoked the vocabulary of warfare and the West to symbolize the virility of stenographers and even male typewriters. For instance, on the heels of the Spanish-American War, shorthand educator C. W. Kitt equated weaklings with women and soldiers with men: "The ranks are already too full of weaklings, but there is a crying demand for trained and efficient soldiers strong enough to fight their way to positions of honor in the stenographic profession." Stenographic fiction also periodically depicted shorthand writers with masculine brawn. For example, in one story, Mr. Whalen, the private secretary to the president of a company, was the toughest kid on a ranch ten years prior. One day, Jimmie Whalen even captures a rampaging bull to stop the herd from trampling Mr. Moneygrubs's two-year-old baby. This story of Jimmie's bravery, strength, and quick-thinking action is told by an equally colorful fellow in awe of Jimmie, Sandy Allen, who is six feet tall and "of brown, hardy manhood," with a picturesque vocabulary. If rough riding prepared Theodore Roosevelt for the presidency, it certainly would do the same for a stenographer or secretary.[77] At times, the shorthand press also endowed other office workers with strenuous manhood. In the one story about a male typewriter, Charles Gordon Rogers described his protagonist in this language of manhood, probably to overcome the femininity of typing. The hero speaks of his typewriter in military jargon, as "ammunition" and a "weapon in the battle for existence," as well as of his own "strenuous and unceasing effort."[78]

Court reporters and the shorthand press embraced this speech about toughness and physicality to justify mental labor. Dickinson portrayed courtroom note taking as the "hardest and most confining work," requiring great stamina because hard cerebral work caused mental strain. He continued, "The wear and tear on nerves, brain and vital energies is something which only the strongest men can bear for any length of time." Edward F. Underhill bemoaned the long hours, "often from daylight to midnight." The popular press repeated the stories told by court reporters of men who reached the limit of endurance when "nearly overcome with fatigue" while reporting a forty-day trial or who were "so prostrated with fatigue at the end of the case" that they had "not been

NO HOPE FOR HIM

Asylum Warden (to visitors):—"This, ladies and gentlemen, is the most hopeless case we have."

Visitor:—"What drove him crazy?"

Asylum Warden:—"He was the stenographer in a case where medical experts were called in. Sometimes he fancies he is again reporting the doctors, and he begs a piece of charcoal and covers the walls with his hen-tracks. It seems to ease him for a while. But his intellect is entirely shattered."

FIG. 2. This cartoon from the *Typewriter and Phonographic World*, September 1900, depicts court reporting as intellectual work requiring endurance, linking mind and body. (Courtesy of the New York Public Library.)

able to work since." Such work exposed a man to the middle-class "nervous disease under which he must ultimately break down" (see fig. 2). Only those with a strong constitution could survive the rigors of court reporting and sufficiently concentrate on their work.[79]

This emphasis on virility became another arena to contest the occupation. By appropriating distinctive traits of manual work, the privileging of brawn also provided working-class men with leverage. Since shorthand advocates sometimes celebrated men "hardened and drilled by manual labor," those with working-class roots or limited education who found it necessary to counter some college-educated stenographers' calls for exceptionally high levels of formal education insisted on physical strength as a requirement for court reporting. They asserted that their experience as farm boys, mechanics, and printers elevated them above the flabby office workers. James M. Yerrinton, the son of a printer, reminded his fellow reporters of a need for "a strong physical constitution." Edward F. Underhill, who had attended a private school for two years but also worked on a farm and in a woolen factory, delivered a paper entitled "Stenographers and Their Qualifications" at the 1881 annual meeting of the New York Law Stenographers' Association, where he insisted that reporters "must not be afraid of work and must have the strength and disposition to do it." He assured his audience that there was no room in stenography for "gentlemen of leisure."[80]

Some male court reporters claimed that physiology precluded women from the more prestigious positions. In a heated controversy in 1887 among New York's legal stenographers, William H. Slocum contended that when a woman tried to concentrate "for hours at a time . . . she has suffered the strain to a certain degree, and beyond *which she cannot go,* she becomes tired, and finds that her mind is off wool-gathering." In contrast, only those with stamina to maintain their concentration belonged in the courts. Others insisted that women's smaller, weaker hands and bodies limited their endurance and should restrict their employment to business shorthand or typewriting. Court reporter John B. Carey concluded that a "woman's place is at the typewriter and in the office . . . partly because of [her] small fingers."[81]

However, periodically the shorthand press and women themselves championed feminine stamina. In response to an article about the weakness of the female hand, *Browne's Phonographic Magazine* defended "professional women stenographers who have out-lived two or three men . . . in the sense that they have good health, while the men are broken-down wrecks."[82] Bessie Rogers rebutted those who "say that [women] cannot succeed as court reporters, because it is so hard on the nerves." She boasted, "I think it would be very difficult to find a man that can endure more than I did. I worked seven weeks; every day in the court room from 9 o'clock in the morning until 6 o'clock in the evening; from 7 o'clock in the evening until 12 or one o'clock at night. I should like to see man endure much more than that."[83]

Brute strength became proof of superior mental skills, and mental exertion counted as physical effort. Cerebral work was so debilitating that only the strong could endure it. By making such an argument, the shorthand press and court reporters cemented court reporting's bond to mental labor while defending brain work itself. Court reporters named themselves as experts, whose skill rested on the intellectual fields of science and art, in contrast to mechanical labor or drudgery. In constructing court reporters as such, they asserted a stenographic identity as middle-class male professionals, which shorthand educators, the press, and sometimes business stenographers and typewriters themselves tried to spread throughout their community.

CONCLUSION

Male court reporters and, to some extent, business stenographers found a solution to their desire for a middle-class identity that elevated them above the masses. They joined other middle-class workers in professionalizing their occupations at the end of the century. Like other professionals, they privileged the mental over the mechanical components of their work, by emphasizing their own judgment, creativity, and aestheticism and designating women business stenographers and typewriters as the mechanical workers. While other nascent professions responded to the rising number of educated women who challenged mental labor's inherent manliness by drawing themselves closer to the manly objectivity and coldness of science, male court reporters had to settle for bulking up mental labor by requiring endurance to boost their manhood. They found their new manhood by defining experts as possessing judgment, education, and endurance, in contrast to beginners who resembled incompetents, performing mechanical work and lacking bodily strength. However, by trying to achieve their twin class and gender goals, they left themselves open on all fronts.

Despite some pressure for requiring a college degree or theoretical training, like other professionals were advancing, court reporters developed their own standard. They settled on the vague concept of a "good education," which included the growing numbers attending high school and learning shorthand in formal institutions. "Good education" also took into account court reporters' difficulties in distinguishing their education from business stenographers, who appreciated the simplified and sped-up training provided by rival business colleges and language promoters. Rather than pressing for more extensive higher education, court reporters accepted the shorthand community's insistence on a middle-class education that welcomed the middle class and some of the educated working class, while excluding the uneducated working class.

Despite intending to use education and middle-class benchmarks to exclude, specific guidelines also inadvertently made room for women and working-class men to see themselves as professionals. The expansion of high school education, particularly commercial programs, opened real opportunities for working-class men and women. As commercial training blurred with education, stenographers and typewriters could imagine themselves as educated experts, despite the fuzzy educational requirements necessary for their work. Even their vague definitions of mental labor as based on judgment, creativity, aestheticism, and science, as well as their explanation of endurance as a balance between physical and mental work, cracked open the door for the working class. Moreover, the competition among shorthand schools and trade publications encouraged hope, such as when shorthand enthusiasts reminded their readers about the "opportunities . . . for intellectual, educated, rising young men and women."[84]

This shift to a tough professional manhood seemed to eliminate femininity from its gendered balance. However, chapter 7 in this book, on the performance of professionalism, will explore how professional associations combined this tougher professional manhood with femininity for a professional respectability, a new gender balance. But first, chapter 5 examines the female response to class-based gendered critiques that designed women as unprofessional, and chapter 6 addresses women's creation of a new feminine gender balance for working women as professionals.

CHAPTER 5

Typewriter Girls and Lady Stenographers: The Challenges of Respectability

In 1887, M. Jeannette Ballantyne, a New York court reporter, once again addressed the annual meeting of the New York State Stenographers' Association (NYSSA). Miss Ballantyne had been invited to speak more often than any other female and most male speakers. Frequently, she discussed women court reporters. The year before, she had presented a strong case for the "appropriateness of women as court reporters," linking women's quest to become court reporters to the ideals of Susan B. Anthony and Elizabeth Cady Stanton. This time, when she offered friendly advice to women on professional behavior, recommending that they prepare themselves and behave like men in the office, her speech, "Why Some Women Fail of [*sic*] Success in Court Reporters' or Business Offices," provoked an intense debate over female qualifications for court reporting and emboldened critics of their presence in the courts.[1]

Immediately after the talk, William H. Slocum, a well-known official court reporter from Buffalo, remarked that "women were not . . . capable as court reporters; that they lacked concentration of mind upon their work." He advised women to find "other fields for work" (presumably business stenography). Mrs. Eliza Burnz, a venerated stenographer, shorthand teacher, and phonetic reformer, responded that Mrs. Clara E. Brockway, a member of the association, "had been for years filling the position of court reporter . . . to the utmost satisfaction of all concerned." George Bishop jumped into the fray to applaud Mrs. Brockway's skills. Mr. A. P. Little suggested women might actually surpass men in reporting skills, if given a chance. The audience, filled with a strong female presence, cheered his call to "let the ladies have a chance." At that point, Colonel

Edward B. Dickinson, the soon-to-be-president of the NYSSA, interjected that women did not take their work seriously because they intended to marry and quit work. Bishop tendered a compromise, first by praising women for their promptness and steady attendance compared to men's and then by distinguishing elite women court reporters from incompetent ones. He conceded, "As to the first-rate stenographers, of course that was not what he was talking about." The president agreed, and the *Phonographic World* reported the topic closed.[2]

But the matter did not die. Two months later, in the November 1887 issue of the *Phonographic World*, Slocum reiterated his conference statements that women lose concentration. In the same breath, however, he abandoned his gender-defined pronouncements by noting that "many men fail of [*sic*] success for precisely the same reason." His assistant Mrs. R. F. Alle, a court reporter for six years, added her support by criticizing female court reporters, not for their lack of concentration or perseverance, but for unladylike behavior. "There is no true woman," she noted, "but would be embarrassed when reporting cases." She related how witnesses "hesitate[d]" to tell the truth in front of women court reporters. Alle applauded the foundation of female modesty, contrasting "all women of true modesty" who "safeguard" the "nation's morality" with those who engage in "familiarity of intercourse" with their coworkers, and she called for men and women to maintain this "barrier" between the sexes. Although this particular exchange concluded with Mrs. Alle's comments, these issues and positions returned repeatedly without resolution.[3]

This altercation illustrates how some male court reporters challenged women's professionalism, undoubtedly to boost theirs. They questioned women's work ethic by critiquing women's intent to marry, expectation of etiquette and modesty, lack of endurance, and concern notably about their attire. Fashion as a metaphor for women's lack of professionalism reveals the sexual and class dynamics of nineteenth-century clerical work and the Achilles' heel of women stenographers. During this controversy at the NYSSA's annual meeting, Colonel Edward B. Dickinson recounted an anecdote to prove that women did not take their work seriously. In this story, a typewriter operator sauntered into work at noon after her boss explicitly admonished her to be on time because of the day's exceptionally heavy workload. On arriving, she announced, "I wanted to buy a new bonnet, and don't you think it is pretty?" Immediately, Mrs. Behrends assailed the story's veracity, insisting that in her four years as a court reporter, she had never heard of such a story as this, nor could she imagine such an event happening. And if it did, the woman most surely would be discharged immediately. The angry women stenographers let the debate drop when

George Bishop praised them and reminded the convention that "the first-rate stenographers" were not the problem. By shifting the conversation to merit and skills, Bishop explicitly acknowledged the professionalism of some women, while implicitly recognizing class distinctions among women stenographers.[4]

Six years later, in 1893, another encoded anecdote revealed the same criticism of women's professionalism. During another controversy over women's place in the courts, John B. Carey also denounced women court reporters for their inappropriate attention to attire and appearance, when he told the story of a stenographer who interrupted a court proceeding to ask if her hat was on straight. Official court reporter Helen L. Hinckle blasted Carey's "opinion of lady stenographers . . . that their ideas do not rise above their personal appearance and that the matter of dress impresses them more than their work." She insisted that a woman court reporter was too busy for "posing" and "hardly knows whether she has a hat on or not."[5] As in the Ballantyne episode, Hinckle saved her sharpest words for the hat anecdote because it attacked women's professionalism by portraying them as frivolous, undisciplined, and lacking in industry.

To women stenographers, these particular allegations symbolized an even more disturbing indictment. Men used fashion anecdotes to lob cheap shots at their female competitors. Such attacks on what was assumed to be women's nature accused female court reporters of behaving like the stereotyped working-class woman. The clichéd charges indicted women for immodesty, wastefulness, frivolity, manhunting, and coquettishness, code words for lacking the prized middle-class trait of discipline and, of course, professionalism. By assigning class-specific traits to all women, rather than to the unrespectable alone, these male court reporters belittled and conflated all women. Female court reporters resented men's failure to consistently recognize class distinctions among women and direct their unmitigated scorn only at unrefined, incompetent, working-class women. They identified with men along a class axis, even the same men who employed the working-girl discourse to lambast them.

As women and men came to share similar, if not identical, jobs, some men sought to exaggerate gender differences by blurring respectable middle-class women with images of unseemly working-class women. With the treasury courtesan scandals still echoing at the end of the century, court reporters, stenographers, and typewriters also faced accusations of their unsuitability for serious professional work. This time, the image of working-class women as frivolous blossomed into a working-girl discourse that used the markers of the gold digger (without directly naming women as such) and challenged all female court reporters', stenographers', and typewriters' professionalism. Just as the image of the treasury courtesan heightened the necessity of protecting women's virtue, the frivolous gold digger reconciled the new site of employment with middle-class status by reframing office and court employment as respectable. Respectability, however, had its own contradictions. It enabled women to hold a particular job, but it challenged their commitment as well. Women wanted the advantages of respectability, especially its tendency to separate and elevate middle-class women. However, they could not contain its gendered negative representations that damned the work ethic of women, especially those from the working class, and exposed women's differences from male clerical workers, giving men ammunition against their female rivals.

THE WORKING-GIRL DISCOURSE

Changes in late nineteenth-century employment blurred class lines between working-class and middle-class women. As single middle-class women joined the workforce in mounting numbers, gainful employment no longer belonged so dominantly to the working class. On the one hand, middle-class women's presence in the workforce raised the status of working women by elevating the propriety of economic independence. Conversely, the class protection for middle-class women weakened as both classes of single women perused not only the idea of paid work but the same jobs. In the last two or three decades of the nineteenth century, working-class women invaded middle-class jobs, such as nursing, teaching, and office work. Stenography and typing exemplified this class blurring by attracting a growing working-class population as well as large numbers of the middle class. Among Boston stenographers in 1900, 26.9 percent were daughters of professionals, business executives, small businessmen, clerical workers, or salesmen.[6] With middle- and working-class single women holding not just jobs but similar ones at that, some male court reporters could use the working-girl discourse to blur and condemn all women workers, distancing themselves from their female coworkers.

One component of the working-girl discourse rested on contemporary negative views about fashion. Fashion had a long history of symbolizing female failings, serving as a useful target to mock all women or subgroups. Since the eighteenth century, fashion was often deployed to malign women for exhibiting aristocratic tendencies, luxury, tasteless ostentation, artificiality and insincerity, vapidness, self-centeredness, and vanity. In 1869, Virginia Penny characterized the minds of "fashionable women," a code for elite women, as being as "destitute of stability as froth, as unstable as water, and . . . like the mountain mist."

She averred, "They lack strength and discipline." At the end of the century, showy hats symbolized feminine frivolity, extravagance, and self-centeredness. Popular gags told of women wearing hats so big as to block the view of theatergoers seated behind. Husbands and jokesters complained about wives' excessive clothing expenditures.[7]

Male stenographers understood the symbolic meanings of feminine fashion and knew to target it when they wanted to disparage women. A report on the National Association of Women Stenographers spoofed clerical women's interests in clothes, alleging that "typewriter girls" asked, "Should a typewriter girl wear red or black when transcribing a legal brief?"[8] The *Typewriter and Phonographic World* parodied its own column "The Fem-Sten's Retreat" with "The Men-Sten's Retreat" to lampoon women's advice about female office fashion, concluding that only "mama's boys" cared about fashion.

> The pants affected by young men stenographers are of two kinds, the visible [symbols for sounds, like phonography] and the audible [sounds only]. The first range in length all the way from the knee-pant worn by a number of our readers who should be attached to their mamas' apronstrings [*sic*]. . . . The correct length of this nether garment for the adult stenographer is just below the instep in front and just above where the heel joins the shoe in the rear. This is visible pants. The audible kind will never be indulged in by the properly educated, properly qualified amanuensis.[9]

Women readily joined the cultural critique of fashion when applied to others. Those from the rural areas in antebellum years took aim at the frivolity of their city sisters. Working-class women criticized the rich for wearing clothes that they did not earn themselves, and the middle class used fashion to denounce both the upper and working classes for frivolity. Novels portrayed unflattering wealthy women frivolously gossiping and discussing fashion, as slavish adherents to the latest styles, rather than engaged in useful labor, such as charity. Villainesses dressed in fashionable clothes that exposed their vanity, selfishness, and moral weakness.[10] In the late nineteenth century, Jewish immigrants and black women policed themselves to deflect criticism. The more prosperous German Jewish immigrants accused the "ghetto girl," the new Eastern European Jewish immigrants, of engaging in showy dress, especially by wearing jewelry. African American colleges advised their female students to avoid "overdressing" in colorful attire, again in contrast to their poorer sisters.[11]

Middle-class women and men especially aimed sharp barbs at the working class as unrespectable working girls. They developed a discourse that lampooned working-class and lower middle-class women's lack of taste for wearing ostentatious dress that was inappropriate for work and above their station. In his short stories, O. Henry drew from his own experience as clerk, bookkeeper, and bank teller to poke fun at working-class women's flamboyant styles. An anonymous stenographer in "The Romance of a Busy Broker" radiates tacky consumerism with "a high-rolled fringe of golden hair under a nodding canopy of velvet and ostrich tips, and imitation sealskin sacque and a string of beads as large as hickory nuts, ending near the floor with a silver heart." In contrast, the working-girl heroine projects the apotheosis of decorum for avoiding "the alluring pompadour . . . , chains, bracelets, or lockets." A few short stories written by both men and women for stenography magazines portrayed unacceptable female employees in similar attire. Author Hattie Witherington Sutton's protagonist wants the boss to hire "a lady . . . , [o]ne who does not wear bangle bracelets . . . mock ostrich plumes and low-neck dresses."[12]

Working-class women did wear clothes that exaggerated middle-class styles. Historian Christine Stansell describes the antebellum Bowery fashions that accented the bosom, waist, hips, and thighs; they featured "startling combinations of colors" and included ornate hats that exposed women's faces. Historian Nan Enstad depicts distinctive styles that emphasized femininity among early twentieth-century factory and shop women as well, like decorated "three story hats," silk petticoats, and three-inch French heels. They also mixed colors, especially bright ones.[13]

To middle-class critics, these styles confirmed working-class women's waste and lack of economic restraint. Throughout the century, the middle-class denounced domestics for trying to keep up with clothing trends. Since the early years of mill employment, middle-class commentators accused workers of actually seeking paid employment merely to purchase extras, especially clothes. The supposed pin-money workers, according to their detractors, unfairly competed against other working women and depressed wages by working for extras rather than subsistence.[14]

This middle-class condemnation exemplified a broader critique of working-class consumption patterns as wasteful and undisciplined. The middle class blamed working-class men for wasting their earnings on drink and smoke. Didactic authors like Horatio Alger charged that men who squandered money on trivial goods like alcohol, cigars, and gambling failed, while those who saved and avoided drink climbed upward. At the end of the century, government-designed ideal budgets for working-class households faulted men's drinking and smoking for their families' inability to save money. Working-class women were also condemned for munching on caramels and pies and chewing tutti-frutti gum, instead of exercising discipline and consuming more wholesome foods. The *Phonographic World* published Kate Field's characterization of typewriter girls and cashiers as "disagreeable [and] self-assertive" women who "eat pie for their luncheon." Another piece mocked a "typewriter girl" who chose "ice cream on berry pie" as lunch. She lacked forethought and judgment and would later feel the "pangs of hunger and remorse [t]o rack her by and by" for throwing away her money by "purchasing galore." This condemnation of wasted earnings shifted the blame for poverty to workers themselves and assured employers that their employees did not have the self-control to save money and would merely foolishly spend any increases in earnings. Moreover, moralists worried that women who purchased stylish attire that they could not afford might have to turn to casual prostitution to supplement their wages.[15]

Critics especially disapproved of ostrich plumes and large strings of beads for attracting undue attention, like the streetwalker on the prowl for male admirers. Wearing loud colors or "low-neck dresses" implied a sexual cash nexus and an intent to manipulate physical attractiveness and sexuality to snatch a husband. Immodest clothes, along with beauty and flirting, became part of the coded language of the gold digger, a working-class social climber, who cared more about the social atmosphere at work than doing a good job.

According to cultural studies scholar Robert C. Allen, the gold digger appeared in popular culture at the end of the century, sometimes as a lighthearted version of the earlier predatory treasury courtesan. The archetypal gold digger worked as a chorus-line actress or a salesclerk, as in O. Henry's "The Trimmed Lamp," a critique of working-class women's futile social aspirations. In his story, Nancy prefers to work in a shop for $8 a week—rather than as a piecework ironer in a hand laundry earning $18.50 like her friend Lou—because she enjoys being "surround[ed] by beautiful things that breathed of taste and refinement." Even though Lou teases Nancy about her "uplifted nose" and "put[ting] on airs," Nancy boasts about aping her "betters," even copying a handshake and clothing styles of a wealthy customer. While Lou wears a "badly fitting purple dress, and . . . hat plume . . . four inches too long." Nancy has "the high-ratted pompadour and the exaggerated straight-front." Nancy pretentiously imitates wealthy women to boost her chances of marrying above her station. The "other girls" kid her. "'Here comes your millionaire, Nancy,' they would call her whenever any man who looked the role approached her counter." With his characteristic irony, O. Henry foils Nancy's gold digging by marrying her to Dan, a suitable electrician with pluck and seriousness "who had escaped the city's brand of frivolity." Her friend Lou marries a millionaire but ends up sobbing in the street. In another O. Henry story, "A Lickpenny Lover," Masie sells "gents' gloves" as a strategy for finding a man who will spend money on her. But she fails to recognize a millionaire when she meets one. Masie rejects a proposal of marriage from Irving Carter, "painter, millionaire, traveler, poet, automobilist," after he describes an idyllic honeymoon touring the world. She thinks he's too cheap—poor Masie assumes Carter plans to take her to Coney Island for their wedding trip. Nancy, Lou, and Masie, according to O. Henry, rightfully belong with men of their own class.[16]

Working-class language patterns also reflected the folly of such pretensions. Typical of the realist school of writers, O. Henry's working-class characters spoke in dialect using slang and faulty grammar, such as "Oh, cheese it," "aint," "nit," and "gee." Such improper language struck at the heart of successful social mobility. Nancy and Masie plotted to move to the upper class, but their hopes for mobility were foolish and doomed.[17]

O. Henry's exaggerated working-class gold diggers rarely made it into stenography magazines, since the editors wanted to appeal to women readers. Only one story directly portrayed a gold digger, but he was a man. One that came close was Ellis Wood's tale of a typewriter who has her eye on the boss's son but undoubtedly will end up with the bookkeeper.[18] In another instance, a reprinted article transforms a typewriter into a gold digger when a news reporter asks "one of the most bewitching of these ladies" if she has designs on the male lawyers. Although the typewriter carefully chooses her words to escape a manhunter label, the journalists' editorializing sabotages her plan: "I assure you," she says, pinning the reporter to the wall with a glance and then tantalizing him with the dazzle of her eyes, "I have never given the matter a thought, but if I had, I shouldn't own it. So you see my statement doesn't do you much good either way."[19] Other than these few direct accusations of gold digging, shorthand magazines, the popular press, and early movies portrayed more subtly coded messages of stenographers and typewriters as marriage hounds and coquettes. Still, these depictions brought court and office women dangerously close to the dreaded image of gold digger, as women court reporters and business stenographers well understood.[20]

The more subtle working-girl discourse disparaged working-class women's rush to marriage, ultimately tarring all working women. Supposedly, working-class women wanted to find a husband so badly that they neglected their work. Reformer Grace Dodge complained about their preoccupation with "thoughts of marriage . . . and meeting with men and boys." More typically, critics upbraided office women in general. Journalist Joe Howard Jr. grumbled that women became useless in the office after age twenty-three. In his hypothetical story, "Susie has met George around the corner, and thinks only of 4 o'clock in the afternoon, watching the dial from hour to hour with feverish anxiety to get away." Howard accused women of disrupting the office by wasting time at work washing their hands only as "subterfuge for the purpose of . . . look[ing] in the mirror" or pining after men. Shorthand magazines reprinted articles from the mainstream press that criticized such behavior, including indicting women for leaving work for marriage too soon after training and experience qualified them for their salaries. "Finally," says one critic, "I got my present girl—excellent girl and good all 'round. She's a bright, intelligent woman, with an ordinary common-school education, a perfect little lady." But then, he laments, she got married.[21]

The office advice literature by both men and women blamed women's romantic desires for coquetry and for sexually charging the work environment. Shorthand magazines reprinted articles that ridiculed and denounced women as flirts. For example, an article from *Exchange* joked that women do not flirt if "flirting mean[s] pretending to be in love." Rather, for the typewriter girl, "it is the *genuine feeling* which animates her." Advisers berated women for "start[ing] out wrong" as pals rather than ladies. A supposed clerical woman lamented her efforts to "be on friendly, sociable terms with men in the office": "They treat me in a familiar, slap-you-on-the-back kind of way that humiliates me constantly. . . . I am fairly degraded in my own eyes, and I can't help it, because I've started out wrong." Even a female stenographer who wrote to complain about a previous article and accused men of harassing her at work also condemned the victims: "In my opinion, if an employer ever asks his stenographer to dinner, the girl is somewhat to blame, as a gentleman certainly would not ask such a thing were he not encouraged in some way by the girl herself. I do not blame the man. . . . [I]t is a man's permission to ask and a woman's to refuse." Women were expected to hold the line and keep romance out of the workplace.[22]

The popular characterization of office women as attractive contributed to the accusations of them as temptresses. Beginning in the late 1880s, popular magazines and newspapers published poems, jokes, and essays all at the expense of the so-called typewriter girl. Male writers sometimes portrayed her as stupid, aloof, or frivolous and silly, but she was always pretty—the "pretty typewriter," a farcical caricature. Robert Barr referred to the heroine of one of his stenographic short stories in the same stereotypical manner. "Miss Gale was pretty, of course—all typewriter girls are." The working-girl discourse blamed women's beauty, dress, and sexuality for tempting men and wasting their time at work.[23]

Ellis Wood, who frequently contributed short stories to the *Typewriter and Phonographic World,* warned of the dangers of the beauty in the office. In "Two Men and a Maid," two young lawyers hire a stenographer, even though they do not have enough work for her to do, because this "demure creature in a picture hat floated in and fixed a magnetic eye upon us" (see fig. 3). Soon, they both fall in love with her, but "Love and Law make a curious mixture; for Love is a jealous mistress, and Law a cruel one, and serving them both is a rocky road." Each lawyer begins making up work to spend more time with Ada Brannen. When she is injured in a streetcar accident, they take on her case, neglecting their work and growing poorer by the day. Eventually, Ada settles the case after falling in love with the superintendent of the Tramway company. The two lawyers learn their lesson that a "demure" woman with a "Cupid's bow mouth," puckered lips "so red and tempting," is risky for business. Wood cautioned men to beware of beautiful female stenographers, who tempt and even seduce: she "thrust herself upon them" with a witty and "audacious" tongue, saucy manner, and "magnetic eye." Her beauty enhances the danger: "If beauty is the stamp of goodness, as moralists tell us, then Miss Brannen was a saint. Yet I sometimes caught a look in the corner of her eye that never belonged to a saint."[24]

Perceived as injecting romance into the office, women were also blamed for hanky-panky in the office that disrupted marriages. Humorous stories, poems, and cartoons portrayed the supposed clash between the coquettish typewriter and the boss's wronged wife. Although the discussions about the potential of divorce remained light and humorous, sympathy for the wronged wife further reinforced the image of the stenographer or typewriter as a coquette.[25] The following poem presents what a wronged wife might have said.

"You can decorate your office
        With a thousand gilded signs,
And have upholstered furniture
        in quaint antique designs;
Have the latest patent telephone,
        Where you can yell Hello!
But," said she, "I just made up my mind
        That typewriter must go.

You can stay down at the office.
    As you have done after hours;
And, if you're partial to bouquets,
    I'll furnish you with flowers.
You can spring the old club story
    When you come home late, you know;
But, remember I've made up my mind
    That typewriter must go.

[*sic*] You can let your book-keepers lay off
    And see a game of ball;
The office boy can leave at noon
    Or not show up at all.
There—What is this upon your coat?
    It isn't mine, I know.
I think I know a thing or two—
    That typewriter shall go."[26]

This critique of flirtatious women extended from the middle-class view that unrespectable women from the working class lacked modesty. Wearing low-neck dresses or allowing men to give them a slap on the back demonstrated their lack of reserve and self-control. To critics, exposed private bodily functions like coughing, eating, smoking, spitting tobacco, eating caramels, or chewing gum proved a lack of restraint. Kathryn Chatoid, columnist for "The Fem-Sten's Retreat" in the *Typewriter and Phonographic World*, remarked, "Gum-chewing is not a ladylike habit. The girl who chews gum invariable uses slang, moves about the office noisily, slams doors, etc." This behavior was presented as unlike that of the quiet, modest, and proper lady.[27]

Such attacks on working women reflected the growing concern that the expansion of urban pleasures enabled more public courtship and sexuality that threatened morality. The rise of "pleasure clubs" allowing drinking, smoking, and dancing followed by commercial dance clubs permitted unchaperoned public courtship. Moralists disapproved of the new commercialized dance clubs and amusement parks that encouraged sexualized public contact between working-class young men and women. Some tried to legislate and use the courts to regulate such behavior.[28]

When male court reporters told hat stories, they encoded their critiques of

FIG. 3. "A Demure Creature in a Picture Hat Floated In." This illustration from Ellis Wood's "Two Men and a Maid," published in the *Typewriter and Phonographic World* in February 1902, reflects a common theme of fiction in shorthand magazines: that women's beauty and bodies disrupt business. (Courtesy of the New York Public Library.)

women court reporters in a class-based attack couched in the gendered language of the working-girl discourse. Buying hats meant that women cared more about looking attractive and finding a man than taking good dictation. Coquetry and flashy clothes proved their immodesty, gold-digging motives, and lack of discipline, all negative stereotypes of working-class women. Such class-based gendered codes of the overly familiar, pretty flirt, who allowed men to slap her on the back and wore low-neck dresses to catch a husband, maligned women stenographers' respectability, disparaging their professionalism and asserting men's.

RESPECTABILITY AND ITS DRAWBACKS FOR THE "WOMANLY WOMAN"

Since respectability had long since been used to justify women's employment, varying groups within the stenographic community had interests in portraying women stenographers and typewriters as respectable.[29] In doing so, they employed some of the older arguments used in the 1860s and 1870s. While these propriety narratives provided economic opportunities for women, they also exposed gender differences between men and women, disclosing the limits of respectability.[30] The failure to contain the contradictions between women's employment and respectability undermined the claim that women could serve as well as men in the office and courts.

The shorthand press and educators sought to portray women stenographers and typewriters as ladies. Editors of shorthand publications and shorthand and typing educators advertised the respectability of women stenographers and typewriters to attract a readership and greater enrollment for their schools. The shorthand press advocated proper business behavior in original articles and reprinted texts from mainstream publications, sometimes editorializing on them.[31] Educators also wrote to counsel young women (and men) about appropriate conduct.[32] Women business teachers may have defended women stenographers both to attract more students and to enhance their own reputations.

Some women stenographers and typewriters themselves rendered advice, which championed their own respectability. Harriet Louise Husted, who ran a typewriting business in Boston before her 1901 marriage, furnished practical recommendations in the *Phonographic World*, ranging from methods for double-checking one's work to relations with clients. She advised women to wear "neat, simple gowns" and decline "invitation[s] to lunch, . . . matinée tickets,

[and] expensive flowers." Husted, like stenography magazine publishers, editors, and other women stenographers and typewriters, stood to benefit by linking women stenographers and typewriters with respectability.[33]

The rhetoric that the stenographic community used for reconciling respectability and employment in the late 1880s and 1890s in some ways mirrored that of the defenders from the 1860s and 1870s. Promoters of women's employment slowly, but inconsistently, began to label female clerical workers as "ladies" to mark them as upright. Since midcentury, women office workers referred to themselves and were referred to as "women" and "ladies" and sometimes even "females." In 1875, when Mary Clemmer Ames wrote about female government clerks in *Ten Years in Washington: Life and Scenes in the National Capital as a Woman Sees Them,* she mostly identified them as ladies but still also often referred to them as women. At first, stenography periodicals avoided naming women stenographers as ladies. Since its founding in 1875, *Browne's Phonographic Monthly* favored the word *woman* in editorials, columns, reported speeches, and letters to the editor. After 1879, however, with a rise in the number of women entering stenography, *lady* began to supplant *woman* in the stenographic press, at the same time that references to lady telegraph operators, saleswomen, and even chambermaids proliferated elsewhere.[34]

Beyond adopting the term *lady,* female stenographers were repeatedly described as True Women. *Browne's Phonographic Monthly-Weekly* characterized Miss Kate Duffey as a woman "of modest manners and gentle bearing" and Mrs. J. R. Palmer as "one of the most modest and ladylike little women in the world," adding, "everybody likes her." A reprinted article complemented Jennie Gage for her "modesty and sweetness" as well as "all her graces and true and beautiful womanhood," identifying her as a "model type of woman and a stenographer who is an ornament to the profession."[35]

Shorthand periodicals and women stenographers and typewriters themselves continued to remind readers of the social equality between stenographers and middle-class ladies who did not hold jobs. When possible, stenographers and especially court reporters were also described in relationship to prominent relatives, like Miss Jennie A. Gage, "sister of Judge C. H. Gage." Periodically, the shorthand magazines still portrayed shorthand as a refinement for ladies who did not work. A reprinted article supposedly from a businessman agreed that "each of our stenographers earns more money than my wife requires . . . and moves in good society." He added, "If I had a thousand daughters not one of them should teach school nor stand behind a counter. I would make everyone of them stenographers." Shorthand periodicals also insisted that a "lady of fine sensibilities" could both earn money in an office and retain her social status, because her mere presence elevated the job's status and purified the "moral atmosphere" of a public arena. If a woman held on to her ladylike traits of grace, modesty, and purity, she could even reform her male coworkers and transform a work environment. An unknown woman stenographer insisted in the *Phonographic World* that upright working women ought to receive the same deference accorded to ladies. She maintained that "a woman who has five times the education, and every bit as much refinement as the average cultivated woman who does not work, should . . . meet the same respect and courtesy . . . which the lady meets."[36]

The popular press, which occasionally advocated for female stenographers, and women themselves sometimes framed women's search for work in narratives of respectability by focusing on their economic dependence and needs. They blamed market forces and paternal failure for victimizing ladies who would not normally have sought employment and driving them into the workforce. Sometimes, proponents of female stenographers portrayed them as "young women fit for the most exclusive society . . . cultivated, clever, and in many instances better educated than the persons for whom they work . . . [whose] reverses in family fortunes, death, . . . prompt[ed] [them] . . . to seek . . . an honorable and independent livelihood." A male critic of female stenographic salaries published letters supposedly written by women applying for jobs, which impersonated the lady-in-distress prose of government clerks from 1860 to 1900: "It is absolutely necessary for me to seek employment, as I have a mother who is dependent on me." Everyone understood that an application would not seem genuine without the distress narrative. Pauline Roe wrote about a woman pretending to apply for a job as a hoax, naturally following the standard format: "I fear I am but one among many applicants, but it is so important that I must have work. . . . I have met with severe losses in friends and means, but I will not inflict upon you my sad personal history. It is sufficient to say that circumstances make it necessary for me to support myself or become dependent on charity."[37]

The Lady Disqualifies Women for Work

These various traditional defenses of female employment as admirable provided grist for both women workers and their opponents. Etiquette set standards that men and women could use to their advantage, enabling women to translate their moral influence into limited office power.[38] However, etiquette and respectability in general also underscored differences between the sexes, undermining attempts to defend feminine suitability for the office or the courts and providing fodder for critics who imagined ladies in parlors, not offices.

Women stenographers, typewriters, and their supporters recognized respectability as a tool of feminine power to demand respectful treatment. For example, E.L.C., a typewriter who resented the ubiquitous typewriter jokes, took offense at an impression that the typewriter's "chief business in life is the consumption of caramels" and that "she is supposed to fill up what time she can spare from this employment by dining with her employer." The disgusted typist continued her retort: "The typewriter girl is not always a creature of smiles, dimples, and fresh gowns, but she is usually wise enough to make herself a skillful and intelligent assistant with fully enough tact and dignity always to insure being treated as a lady." So, too, Mary Ruckman, a federal government clerk, complained that her supervisor "had made 'unmanly insult to respectable women.'" Shorthand magazine fiction even modeled how women could enhance their power in the office by requiring proper etiquette. In one story, by Hattie Witherington Sutton, "Miss Weldon, [a] soft, pretty creature," is moved to tears after receiving an unwarranted rebuke. Confronting her employer for his harsh words, she insists that he act like a gentlemen and constrain his temper. "No lady could stand the manner in which you talk to your stenographers and be a lady!" Her boss retreats, apologizes, and mends his ways. The lady preserved a woman's dignity and conferred power as well. For stenographers and shorthand magazine promoters, such treatment was not tantamount to special favors; it was merely civility: "Whether man or woman, you may demand the treatment due a lady or gentleman. . . . This is your right . . . to demand and receive the common courtesies—the civilities of life." Proper etiquette gave women a weapon, while proving their respectability.[39]

Male critics, however, argued that the very assumption of etiquette disqualified ladies from the office. By expecting that men should behave in a gentlemanly fashion, women were demanding special treatment, insisting on the courtesies and niceties of the parlor, which were inappropriate in the world of business. A "Mr. A" complained, "Our typewriters expect the other clerks in the office to wait upon them, and then they trade upon their headaches and backaches to get a great many hours off." As seen in chapter 3, in a number of short stories written by men, gentlemanly employers could not fire a woman, which meant that women ran the office. One fictional employer made such statements as "She's the boss here, instead of me!" and "I wish every mother's daughter of 'em would get married and settle down, and let business alone." Women's use of the lady to level the playing field with their bosses and fellow workers had backfired.[40]

Even women stenographers and their proponents sometimes disapproved of women who employed the etiquette card, although they merely wanted women to act differently, not leave the office. Court reporter Jeanette Ballantyne publically chastised women for "over-sensitiveness, or expecting the same little delicate attention from a gentleman during business hours as you are accustomed to receive in the parlor."[41] Women like Miss Ballantyne worried that demands for appropriate etiquette standards challenged their suitability for the court or office. By continuing to identify with the lady, women's usefulness remained suspect and drove them even further from equality with men.

Other elements of women's respectability also drew criticism and provided ammunition for critics. The image of the physically fragile, modest, and ornamental woman, guided by the rules of etiquette and the expectation of achieving her real calling of marriage, threatened her fitness for the office. A fragile constitution, inherent to the lady's gentility, clashed with the ordeals of work. She became an easy target for those opposing female competitors, like male court reporters who insisted that women could not withstand the daily physical rigors of reporting at top speed in the courtroom, as discussed in chapter 4. Modesty also easily became a liability. An 1883 article in *Browne's Phonographic Monthly* blamed women's meekness for their low wages, concluding that they needed instead the "good judgment and business disposition" that men possessed. Others made the argument that a lady's decency unsuited her for the courts, similar to the antisuffrage arguments that politics or jury service would expose women to unseemly horrors. For instance, court reporter John B. Carey insisted, "Court reporting is work for men and for men exclusively. The court room is an unfit place for a decent, self-respecting girl . . . , [any] . . . modest, decent girl—and thank God I know of none other in the profession." Such a self-respecting girl's "cheeks would burn and her hands tremble at the thought of her degrading and loathsome position, . . . where men were dishing up the foulest of bestiality and corruption!" Even the ornamental dimension of the lady image also threatened to undermine her right to employment and her usefulness once in the workforce. Did she pull her fair share of the workload, or did she expect to be put on a pedestal? Women's propriety implied gender differences that damned the lady office worker as lacking in appropriate work habits.[42]

The assumptions of gender etiquette embedded in respectability not only jeopardized women's utility and competitiveness in the office; it also sharpened gender differences by expecting matrimony to drive men toward greater productivity and competitiveness in order to support their dependents, while women were to quit paid work for the higher duties of wife and mother, rightful jobs of a lady. This conceptualization of marriage highlighted women's supposed limited commitment to work, contributing to the working-girl discourse. Men used women's desire for adhering to social conventions to critique them for "car[ing] far more for success in the 'matrimonial business' than in the shorthand business," and they blamed women's devotion to finding a husband for creating situations conducive to spreading gossip and revealing business secrets. The working-girl discourse bludgeoned women for seeking suitable marriages, further distinguishing female from male clerical workers and fueling the critics of women business stenographers and court reporters.[43]

Marriage

Women and men both expected to marry; however, gainful employment created a problem for respectable women, who were supposed to find fulfillment in wedlock, rather than through work. The cultural given assumed that proper women eventually wedded and quit working, even with the growing popularity of the woman's rights activists' denunciation of marriage through the argument that a shortage of men forced women to support themselves. The late nineteenth-century criticism of the institution posed a choice between matrimony and work, especially for professionals. Yet even the many nineteenth-century female doctors and lawyers who married rationalized that their work made them better wives and that marriage improved their prospects of practicing without discrimination.[44]

Instead of presenting matrimony as merely an option, the shorthand press (although not all female stenographers) followed the path of romance dime novels, which made financially secure marriages the ultimate prize for worthy women. Using the popular themes of such novels, the shorthand press touted stenography and typewriting as enabling proper unions and even upward mobility, in a defense against the working-girl discourse. However, they could not resolve the inherent contradictions between respectability and employment: ladies' positions needed to connect to marriage, but the very emphasis on matrimony confirmed their limited job commitment and highlighted the differences between male and female employees.[45]

The expectation that proper women married fueled shorthand magazines' defense against the gold digger: stenography and typewriting facilitated respectable matrimony. Supporters of women argued that a clerical job made a woman into a better wife because she could understand her husband's work, "appreciate his anxieties," and even judge prospects' potential by observing their character at work. In one short story, stenographer Eleanor does not notice Mr. Strong, a clerk in her office, until he rescues her life savings from an investment scam. His actions demonstrate how much he cares for Eleanor, as well as his determination, initiative, risk taking, and foresight, all signs of a man who will succeed. In another story, rich and spoiled Stella poses as a stenographer's replacement in her fiancé's office after her father maintains that she only observes Frank's parlor manners, not his business behavior. Stella discovers that her father is right. Frank is grouchy and ill-tempered, keeps pictures of New York actresses, and has borrowed money from a seedy-looking Jew with the promise of huge returns upon their marriage. The office venue supplies Eleanor and Stella with evidence to assess better their potential husbands' true nature.[46]

Shorthand magazines as well as the popular press touted office work as a site for courtship. According to the *New York Sun*, it "is said that the type-writer stands a better chance to get married than any other working woman." In the 1890s, the *Phonographic World* began regularly publishing engagement and wedding announcements like the following: "Miss Gertrude W. Morse, formerly bookkeeper and stenographer for the Hard Manufacturing Co., Oneida N.Y. was married in that city on the 4th of last month to Mr. Arthur F. Bender, formerly of Utica." Short stories, too, reinforced an image of office romance. Nearly half of the forty-four short stories about women published between 1887 and 1907 in the renamed *Typewriter and Phonographic World* told tales of love, all but one stemming from an office romance. Respectable women with good work habits and morals found marriage partners as either reward for or a relief from work, common themes in sensational romance dime novels.[47]

It was not enough, however, to suggest that jobs in offices and courts provided women with favorable circumstances for finding prospective husbands. Respectable women needed access to economically secure men, especially since many sought employment because of their fathers' deaths or indebtedness. Dime novel heroines also sought financial security by choosing successful men for spouses. This economic motive narrowed the line between gold digging and respectable marriage.[48]

The *Phonographic World*'s wedding announcements frequently noted the man's wealth or status, as in the following example: "Miss Rosa Wald, formerly employed at a salary of $150 a month as stenographer to Mr. Clarence Jones, secretary of the Drummond Tobacco Co., St. Louis, Missouri, was recently wedded to that gentleman. . . . Mr. Jones draws a salary of $10,000 a year, and owns 100 shares of stock in the company." Other articles disclosed the groom's status as a "prominent businessman," "well-to-do-printer," "grandson of Governor Clinton," or reputed millionaire. Stenography editors like D. L. Scott-Browne reiterated, "Marrying the boss, or employer is a frequent occurrence. We have had several cases in this city, recently . . . , where ladies . . . have married into as high as half a million dollars, . . . with love as the foundation."[49]

The vast majority of shorthand magazine fiction repeatedly depicted successful men marrying their stenographers. For instance, when protagonist Marion Orner leaves to study in Europe, her employer gives "her a diamond ring, receiving in return her promise to become, some day his wife." In another story, Evelyn Harvey yearns for romance but is shocked when her married boss shows untoward attention. She tenders her resignation, only to learn that her boss has left his bachelor twin brother in charge while he snuck off on a vacation. "Of course," the story goes, "you know the rest—probably you saw the advertisement for a [replacement] stenographer that Sharp & Co. printed in the *Herald*."[50]

The popular press mirrored the style of fictional narratives' marriages between well-heeled bosses and their typewriters or stenographers. The *St. Louis Republic* reported, "Colonel Luther McGilvray, the well-known iron broker, and Miss Clara Fleschert, formerly a typewriter for the Missouri State Sunday School Association, were united in marriage." After falling in love with "the prepossessing face of Miss Fleschert as she diligently pounded her typewriter," but afraid to ask for her hand, the colonel "resorted to the old comedy of dictating his own proposal to her, leaving out the name of the person to whom it was addressed." Yet there was "not enough romance in that to suit her, and she rejected him," after which "he proposed with pen and ink." She eventually accepted. Again office work provided a means for upward mobility, even if the bosses were romantically challenged.[51]

These gleeful reports of upward mobility tread mighty close to the narrative of the gold digger. To protect women from accusations of gold digging, the shorthand press mirrored romance dime novels that rejected loveless marriages based on money. The shorthand magazines carefully reminded readers of "love as the foundation," since partners in a good marriage wedded for love, that mysterious, protective force. By constructing good marriages, shorthand magazine fiction softened female stenographers' marital ambitions and still allowed for honorable upward mobility. For example, fictional attorney-at-law John

Grant and his stenographer, Grace Brown, finally acknowledge "the one thing needful to their happiness, the knowledge of their love for each other." To prove love as their motive, heroines reject fortune hunting or parental involvement. In "Old Peter Murray's Millions: A Game That Two Could Play At, and—the Stenographer Won," Thomasine Jadwin refuses to wed young Peter Murray, despite eight proposals and her mother's entreaties to snare him for his money. Instead, Thomasine ends up securing her fortune by tying the knot with the man she loves, Peter's older uncle, who controls the family fortune. Love protected women from accusations of gold digging. Popular fiction between 1860 and 1920 depicted similar portraits of stenographers and other clerical women marrying their bosses for love, like Margaret Howth in Rebecca Harding Davis's 1862 novel by the same name, O. Henry's Miss Leslie in "The Romance of a Busy Broker," and Una Goldin in Sinclair Lewis's 1917 *The Job*.[52]

A good marriage also required that the man initiate the relationship and pursue the woman. While dime novels made sure the heroine did not chase her beloved and God ordained love, in shorthand magazine fiction, men hired attractive women as stenographers who later became their wives. One fictional boss even arranges for a woman's firing so he can retain her services. As already seen, many fictional employers write love letters to their surprised stenographers and typewriters, and sometimes the boss proposes by utilizing the old dictation ruse. In a variation of this narrative, independent businessman John Burton, formerly a stenographer himself, offers to let Gertrude Langley, a typewriter operator next door, use his machine, on which he leaves a letter written to her, beginning "My Darling Wife." Assuming incorrectly that he is married, Gertrude avoids John, until a bolt of lightning knocks her unconscious. In despair that he has lost her, John reveals his pent-up feelings of love. The story of John and Grace illustrates the limited acceptable level of women's assertiveness. After John gives roses to his employee Grace on her last day at work, she realizes that something is amiss. She asks him what is wrong a few times until he finally blurts out his love for her. Without his declaration, the relationship would go nowhere. By reminding their readers that romantic love initiated by men defined a good marriage, authors of shorthand fiction hoped to erect a safe harbor for women stenographers' and typewriters' own dreams of marital mobility.[53]

Nonetheless, the line protecting women from accusations of gold digging remained thin. Shorthand magazines' blatant discussion of marital prospects to men of means exposed the economics of matrimony for both middle-class and working-class women. David Graham Phillips's 1911 novel *The Grain of Dust* presented the ambiguity of the stenographers' position by deliberately masking the intentions of Dorothy Hallowell. Neither the hero nor the reader can discern if she is a gold digger or a virtuous woman in a bind.[54] This uncertainty limited female stenographers' and typewriters' ability to distance themselves from the negative stereotypes of working-class women. Moreover, the marriage defense itself still acknowledged wedlock as the ultimate goal, strengthening the criticism that these social goals distracted women from their work.

The limitations of respectability for working women meant that shorthand editors, educators, the popular press, and women stenographers themselves struggled to promote the respectability that came with marriage, while presenting women as dedicated to their work. Editors and educators who had a financial stake in encouraging an image of women as suitable employees also pressed them to seek shorthand positions for marriage opportunities and to please their employers. While editor Scott-Browne denounced an article he reprinted from the *Boston Globe* as "one-sided" for maintaining that female stenographers should become wives, he quoted from a letter to the editor that jokingly encouraged male stenographers to "marry the girl . . . to save the 'profesh.'"[55]

The inconsistencies even appeared in a single article. In a piece from the *New York Truth,* a levelheaded but pretty typewriter, who at first ignores the "fellows" who "flutter round her desk, like wasps round a peach," ends up falling in love with a "big, honest working bee" and "then discovering that a woman's sphere is in her home." The editor of *Browne's Phonographic Monthly-Weekly,* who reprinted the piece, tried to have it both ways. On the one hand, he reported that the "number of ladies . . . [who have] walked into the hearts of their employers . . . [is in the] millions." At the same time, he insisted that shorthand and typing should not be any different from any other professional occupation, "since there is little sentiment in the business of writing shorthand and pounding the typewriter."[56]

Women stenographers themselves also gave contradictory responses. Some asserted that work fostered marriage. A fifty-year-old court reporter wrote about meeting her husband "thro [*sic*] my profession" when "I was reporting in court and he was on the jury." She boasted about her happy marriage but did not want to "lose" her shorthand, so she sometimes took "an important case." Others repeated the canard that shorthand makes "a woman capable of making her own living, and transacting business for herself, [and] will make a better wife and mother . . . than . . . those inane helpless creatures." In contrast to those who emphasized the benefits of stenography for marriage, others insisted that their work did not suffer because they would not want to marry their coworkers. Official reporter Kate Armstrong asserted that "it is preferable to work and earn one's own living rather than to marry the average young man with all his degeneracy." She then added, "Besides, the young men do not wish to marry. They prefer to be free to carouse as they like." Obviously, she was conflicted, particularly since she brought up marriage in a debate about women's suitability for shorthand when no one else had broached this topic. Other women went even further by contending that they did not need to marry. In an article in a shorthand magazine, B.C. wrote, "And I should like to know why . . . [women] should *want* to get married, for in the majority of cases the woman who is accused of this fearful design *makes twice as much* as the average man, and could buy and sell him several times over."[57]

The contradictions between marriage and work for respectable women were not easily resolved, even among their advocates and themselves. Female stenographers and typewriters needed matrimony to prove their respectability. However, by claiming that these jobs promoted marriage and by borrowing the dime novel conceit of work as an acceptable arena for public courtship, the shorthand and popular presses and some female stenographers actually strengthened the criticism that wedlock remained women's goal and undermined their commitment to work. In the process, they helped develop the stock character of the office gold digger that doggedly plagued working women. As long as female respectability required marriage and as long as the contemporary discourse acknowledged that imperative, women could not be equal to men. (Chapter 6 looks at alternative discourses that emphasized gender equality.)

The "Plain Jane" Defense: Sexuality, Bodies, and Fashion

Sexuality, bodies, and fashion exposed other contradictions of respectability. To avoid the charge of gold digging, advocates of women stenographers and typewriters also tried to prove that women played no role in instigating romance or encouraging sexuality in the office. Shorthand editors, educators, and women themselves named men as the sexual initiators and characterized women as asexual by de-emphasizing their physical beauty and pressing for plain attire. However, attractiveness and fashionable dress proved so appealing for social standing that women succumbed and could not contain the attendant negative class-based stereotypes. By failing to resolve the contradictions of respectability, they again undermined attempts to distance office and court women from the image of gold digger.

Proponents of female stenographers turned the tables on the accusers by blaming men for injecting sexuality into the office, much like the defenders of treasury courtesans had done. Martha Ellsbeth's short story "For the Sake of the Office" charges Miss Middleton's employer with misinterpreting her innocent wave to a baby as a flirtatious gesture to a nearby man because his own desire for her clouds his judgment. Presumably other men's attraction to women office workers explained their mistaken conclusions about women as flirts. An anonymous woman (probably a teacher) reminded readers of *Browne's Phonographic Monthly,* during one of the long debates about female stenographers, that "no woman . . . can flirt alone" and that men "will never become earnest thoughtful capitalists, or energetic heads of business houses if they will allow the lady stenographer to . . . stop . . . him in the midst of an abstruse letter and ask . . . if he likes the cut of her dress." Even more blatantly, a "Frisco girl" answered an 1895 article in the *Phonographic World* that "I have in every office . . . been repeatedly told how golden was my hair, or how blue my eyes, until it became a source of greatest annoyance to me; and when I at last found courage to resent it to my employer, he seemed quite taken by surprise, and insinuatingly asked whether I was a TYPEWRITER [the woman] or a type-writer [the machine]." In another example of indicting men, Eliza Boardman Burnz, the well-known elder shorthand teacher and advocate of spelling reform, who favored bloomers and trousers, complained, "Often our Employment Bureau receives, with the request for a stenographer, 'Send a good-looking girl'; and, when several are sent, instead of giving each a trial, the selection for the place is made solely from the personal appearance."[58]

While holding men responsible for the sexualized office made logical sense, the strategy could not succeed unless women were entirely innocent. To that end, some advice writers portrayed female stenographers as asexual by de-emphasizing their appearance and repudiating their beauty. For example, according to a reprinted article by a woman, "the pretty girl is not generally the lady that her plainer sister seems to be, and for that reason does not hold the admiration . . . of the practical business man." She observed, "The ideal working woman would not be beautiful except morally—because hard work is not conducive to beauty, and beauty plays the very mischief with hard work." Another reprinted piece by a female writer explicitly denounced "the beauty, the belle, the dressy girl," insisting, "This is the day of the homely girl . . . , because although men prefer the pretty ones, their wives wanted plain Janes." In a reprinted short story, a young manager, Mr. Bidlington, interviews four women for a stenographer-typewriter position. The first, Miss Faber, is "a very pretty young lady" who "falter[s] . . . in her note-taking" and is dismissed. The next applicant, "not so pretty as Miss Faber, but . . . [not] at all ill-looking," also does not do "well enough." Bidlington is again disappointed when the third candidate, "a lady of distinguished appearance, tall and graceful figure, and brilliant and aristocratic beauty," who is "dressed simply but elegantly," also fails. The final applicant, Miss Stubbs, is "as plain a girl as the crier on his round would be likely to encounter in an hour's march. Cross-eyed a little, too." But Miss Stubbs knows about office work, taking notes rapidly and without error. Naturally, Bidlington hires her, but he mourns the loss of the beauties, exhibiting "a faint tremor, as of pent-up tears, in his voice."[59] Female authors of stenography magazine fiction also tried to de-emphasize appearance by choosing their words carefully in describing their heroines' looks. Some actually avoided mentioning physical traits and focused instead on character. Writer Martha Ellsbeth described her heroine Miss Middleton as "not pretty" but with "an air of earnestness and vivacity . . . and . . . that quality known as 'style.' "[60]

However, the stenography press did not jettison beauty altogether. An announcement of a marriage referred to the bride as "a pronounced blond" and "an exceedingly pretty young lady, of modest manners and gentle bearing." Educator S. S. Packard, who accepted that some women were naturally beautiful, conceded, "It is not necessary that she should be either plain or untidy, to keep people at a proper distance. She may even be good looking." Packard also wrote, "There is no objection to your being pretty—if you can't help it." Like others, Packard demanded that they control their attire as the compromise. A woman must "dress becomingly . . . appropriately to her business," that is, "dress in taste."[61]

Advisers and didactic fiction encouraged women stenographers and typewriters to resolve the beauty conundrum by wearing respectable clothes that denoted sincerity, naturalness, and simplicity, in contrast to fashionable attire. Simplicity had long been the solution to fashion's problems. Plain clothes enhanced a woman's beauty without spotlighting her sexuality. Heroines in popular novels dressed neatly and unostentatiously, but beautifully enough to catch the eye of the hero.[62] O. Henry described a stenographer in a "gray and plain" dress that fit "her figure with fidelity and discretion," although he still remarked that "she was beautiful in a way that was decidedly unstenographic." Shorthand magazines also advised women to dress simply by choosing clothes that were "severely plain, and of good material, without ornament or frills" and to wear "little or no jewelry," "soft shade gloves" and "modest, and healthful," attire.[63]

However, these attempts to contain the negative working-class gold digger by desexualizing women stenographers and typewriters stumbled on the same contradictions of respectability. Looking beautiful and wearing stylish clothing benefited women by representing the wealth and status of the lady and acted as the practical means to attract potential suitors. Beauty also affirmed a woman's goodness, the "natural disposition of woman," but left her open to accusations that she was vapid, was unfit for work, and sexualized the office.[64] Even when authors of shorthand magazine fiction tried to downplay beauty, they found it difficult to escape from its snare.

Authors' attempts to present asexual heroines in their short stories faltered when the women's attractiveness seeped through. Miss Hamilton's "pretty lip curled a trifle." Heroine Dolly Weyland, "tall and slender, with dark and almost tragic face," so sways Dick Desmuth that he arranges to have her fired from her current job, so he could hire her. In "The One Thing Needful," Miss Brown "made a pretty picture as she stood there with her furs and roses." The strong bond between the lady and beauty, as well as the cultural practice of describing women in terms of their physical attributes, sabotaged these efforts to use the language of the lady to keep sensuality at bay.[65]

Even a sympathetic short story by Ethyl B. Palmer could not avoid a lady's need for beauty and fashion to attract a husband. In "Brown's Amanuensis," Madge Russell, the newly hired amanuensis, intrigues the men in the office by her mere presence. She avoids all of them until Ralph Dexter, a clerk, helps capture the thief who snatches her purse. The boss, Mr. Brown, also tries to cultivate a romantic relationship with her, eventually confessing his love in a moment of unrestrained passion. Madge reacts with shock at his effrontery but worries that she may not be able to continue in her position at the office. When Mr. Brown apologizes but tries to remove his rival by promoting Ralph to a department head in another city at double his existing salary, Ralph asks Madge for her hand in marriage, and she accepts.[66]

Throughout this story, the author recounts Madge's respectability, beginning with her education in a convent and fit for a "life of luxury." When "changed circumstances" force her to find employment, Brown hires her for her "brains," and she quickly wins "a reputation for accuracy and alertness." Despite her seeming independence, Madge still lives with her mother in a "very tastefully furnished . . . quite genteel part of the city." She even refuses to testify against the thief, presumably because a lady does not belong in court.[67]

Author Ethyl Palmer struggled to balance respectability and beauty, but ultimately, Madge's body and clothes become central to the story. Her "pale, clear complexion" and "small . . . stature, with dainty hands and feet," testify to her gentility. At first, the author describes Madge as "almost plain" with "irregular features," not a beauty who allures men. However, Palmer relents and completes the same sentence with "but this was offset by a piquancy of expression that rendered her face attractive." Ralph Dexter and another clerk judge Madge "a winner," clearly swayed by her attractiveness. Although Palmer also insists that Madge wears appropriately refined clothes, "models of taste and elegance," the story turns on Madge's attire, which arouses Mr. Brown's fateful declaration of love: "She made a charming picture as she stood there, a small, black toque surrounded her head, a fur boa around her throat. . . . That gentleman, for the first time in his life, lost his head completely." Even if Palmer intended to warn competent and demure female employees of the dangers of beauty and fashionable apparel, she made them indispensable to Madge's respectability and eventual marriage, devoting eleven lines in this four-page story to her height, hands, feet, eyes, and complexion.[68]

The contradictions in fiction mirrored the cultural complexity of beauty, fashion, and sexuality. Women worried about and loved fashion at the same time. Harriet Louise Husted (Lynch), who owned a typing business in Boston, penned four novels under the French pseudonym Marie St. Felix. In her steamy morality tale, *A Little Game with Destiny,* about a party girl whose flirtations with married men, drinking, and gambling lead to her ruin, Husted reveals this love-hate relationship with fashion. Her doomed heroine devotes too much space in her diary to describing clothes and jewels, beginning with a "moonstone pin encircled with pearls," a gift from her mother for her sixteenth birthday. Husted plays with the morality of clothes when an English actress and a Chicago beauty form "The Fire Brigade" club, for which they plan to "wear broad brimmed hats trimmed with flaming red cambric" and as much "scarlet as possible." While these frequent descriptions of clothing prove the unnamed heroine's obsession with clothes as one of her many faults, Husted clearly enjoys tracing the clothes in such loving detail, from the "creme colored crepe de chine," "yellow tulle gown," and "garnet velvet dress" to the "pale pink silk frock." She often devotes a line or two to such features as the "pale blue [frock] with sprays of embroidered daisies, and a huge bunch of Marguerites." Husted relished describing the clothes as much as their cultural dangers, despite her advice elsewhere to typewriters to wear simple styles.[69]

Husted's ambivalence about fashion derived from its muddled associations with femininity and respectability. Nineteenth-century Americans, who often ignored that men's styles also marked class and gender, assumed that fashion reflected a natural, biological difference between the sexes. For example, when the *Phonographic World* sought to appeal to a female audience in the 1890s, the

FIG. 4. This fashionable clothing style for the office was recommended in the *Typewriter and Phonographic World,* March 1900. (Courtesy of the New York Public Library.)

THE

TYPEWRITER

AND

PHONOGRAPHIC WORLD

Devoted to the Interests of Shorthand and Typewriting

VOL. XV—NO. 10 NEW YORK, JUNE, 1900 WHOLE NUMBER 178

This department is conducted for the benefit of the feminine readers of THE WORLD who desire information on subjects that are of particular interest to the women of the profession. I extend a cordial invitation to all women stenographers to become members of the "Retreat."

Communications intended for this department must contain full names and addresses, and should be addressed to its conductor, Kathryn Chatoid, care of THE WORLD. Inquiries received too late for reply in this issue will be answered in the next number.

Costly thy habit as thy purse can buy,
But not expressed in fancy;. rich, not gaudy:
For the apparel oft proclaims the (wo)man.
—*Shakespeare.*

THE subject of dress is one of importance to every man and woman and requires careful thought and consideration. We owe it to our fellow creatures that we make ourselves agreeable in appearance as well as in conduct. The self-respecting person is never slovenly dressed; the person whose garments are neat and tasteful commands the respect of others. There are certain standards of style which must be followed each year, but they will bear modification in many respects, often to advantage, without altering the fundamental principles.

The average business woman, with her characteristic good taste, knows how to dress suitably on all occasions: her gowns are neat, the material is well chosen, the style is appropriate, and the colors are harmonious. The true business woman is always modest in her attire—she never wears anything, no matter how fashionable, that robs her of her womanliness.

On one of our busy streets not long ago I saw a young woman dressed in derby hat, habit-back skirt and automobile coat! She strode along like a Wall Street broker during "Change" hours. She was mannish in every particular, and it was amusing to see the expression of contempt on the faces of those she passed. I felt certain she was not a fem-sten.

The sensible business woman never buys gay or showy clothes that will attract especial attention; shirtwaists of wall paper design she eschews. In fact the eccentric and frivolous Mrs. Fashion never completely controls her, and when Mme. de Style goes to extremes or indulges in ridiculous fancies, that lady is severely snubbed.

If a law should be passed enforcing the wearing of certain garments and restricting the use of others, we would feel that our rights were maliciously interferred with and our indignation would know no bounds. And yet here is an unseen female despot, named Fashion, often laying down tyrannical rules, to whom many obsequiously bow; but our good business woman is not one of her devotees. Dame Fashion almost outshone Solomon recently when she commanded that ankle-length skirts should be worn, but the dear woman has already changed her mind and her followers now have a street sweeping attachment to their garments—a train on a business suit is about as appropriate as fur trimming on a dimity gown.

The question of wearing birds or feathers in one's hats must be settled by each individual for herself, but if the Audubonites ever succeed in inducing our Lady of Modes (and Moods) to per-

FIG. 5. "The Fem-Sten's Retreat" was a regular column in the *Typewriter and Phonographic World.* The logo at the head of the column in this June 1900 issue portrays women in feminine styles and is followed by an article critical of both fashionable and mannish styles of dress. (Courtesy of the New York Public Library.)

editors included fashion tips along with drawings of women's clothes (see fig. 4). This positive view of fashion reached across class lines, as the clothing discourses emphasized individual identity and expressiveness for all women.[70] Working-class women also embraced clothing trends to show their dignity as workers and ladies, according to historian Nan Enstad. Stylish shoes proved that they earned enough to spend their own money on themselves. For immigrants, fashion attested to their status as Americans. Now, they wore modern clothes, rather than the shawls of their mothers' generation. For middle-class women workers, fashion confirmed their middle-class status. Women lawyers, for example, debated among themselves whether they could be both professional and respectable without wearing a hat in the courtroom.[71]

As a result, all women dressed to take advantage of fashion as a purveyor of status, beauty, and self-expression. They donned the latest designs, even if they scoffed at the demands of fashion and its devotees. Clerical workers pictured in the shorthand magazines also dressed in the latest attire. Even one from Ottumwa, Iowa, kept up with the newest trends. Emma Anderson, a stenographer and bookkeeper promoted to cashier of the State Bank, was pictured wearing the popular leg-o'-mutton sleeves, a beaded bodice, and a stiff and straight high-neck collar. She wore her hair coiffured without bangs, short, waved, and with a knot above the crown. The most glaring contradiction between advice and images appeared on the logo of "The Fem-Sten's Retreat" column of the *Phonographic World,* devoted to women stenographers and typewriters. The six New Women in the drawing appeared with accessories ranging from a parasol, a fan, a jacket with a fur collar, a bow tie, and hats with feathers and flowers (see fig. 5). While simplicity might be in the eye of the beholder and while a woman with too little adornment looked like a country bumpkin or a "greener" fresh off the boat, these accoutrements were neither simple nor appropriate for the workplace. Instead, they reaffirmed critics' views about the wearers as self-indulgent, frivolous, and immodest women who did not exercise the judgment needed for the office or court.[72]

CONCLUSION

Fashion and beauty exposed the underlying assumptions of the hat debates, the internal contradictions and limits of respectability, and the working woman's Achilles' heel of class. To encourage female employment, shorthand promoters and women reframed respectability to justify their employment. The more they accentuated respectability, the more they underscored differences between the sexes, enabling men to transform its benefits for women into liabilities. They charged women as unfit for work because gender complicated behavior, whether rooted in feminine frailty, modesty, or courting and marriage plans. Although the cultural assumptions of feminine weakness armed men with ammunition to mark women as incompetents, unsuitable for court reporting and sometimes even for the business office, class became women's great vulnerability.

The middle-class construction of negative images of working-class women in the form of the working-class discourse gave male court reporters license for its use. Stenography editors, educators, fiction writers in shorthand magazines, the popular press, and, as we shall see in chapter 6, some women stenographers themselves agreed that some female stenographers and typewriters were frivolous, tasteless, wasteful, and immodest gold diggers. Male court reporters thus found it easy to apply the working-girl discourse to middle-class women to attack women's work ethic and elevate men's professionalism. Their choice of fashion targeted women as undisciplined, self-absorbed coquettes, marking them as outsiders to the professional world of the court and even the office.

Women stenographers considered these negative working-class characterizations as insulting when directed at themselves. In their view, men confused femininity and class, tarring all women with the same brush, the brush of frivolity. By ascribing these traits to all women, men threatened to reduce their respectability. Women court reporters would not tolerate that but could not contain the working-girl discourse, because they cared about and benefited from wearing fashionable dress, looking beautiful, and marrying men of means. Respectability limited women's attempts to depict themselves as competent office and court workers and instead relegated them to the image of flawed office worker or court reporter. In response, women turned to a feminine version of the self-made man, the New Woman, to shift the balance closer to manliness and the male work ethic.

CHAPTER 6

"My Fondest Hopes Will Have Been Realized": Independence, Ambition, and the New Woman

After reading the poem "The Typewriter Girl" in the *Boston Courier* in 1896, Helen L. Hinckle, an official court reporter in Sullivan, Indiana, sent it to the *Phonographic World*, for republication.

The click of the keys, as her fingers fly,
And the ring of the silvery bell,
I hardly hear, though I sit quite near,
Enchained by her magic spell.

Her hands are as dimpled, and white, and soft,
As a baby's tender fist,
Entrancingly fair is her soft brown hair,
By a lingering sunbeam kissed.

Oh I love her so, with her bright, young face,
And her winsome, witching way!
What bliss it would be if she cared for me;
I would make her my wife to-day!

But my passion I have never dared to tell,
And my trouble may never come;
Just the look of surprise in her clear gray eyes
In an instant would strike me dumb.

So, to her of my love I shall never speak,
'Twould be vain I can clearly see
Why, she gets sixteen dollars a week.
And what does she want of me?[1]

To Hinckle, who had carried on a spirited defense of women's right to work in the courts in 1893, this poem asserted the potential of office and court work for self-support, a true alternative to marriage.[2] For her and others at the close of the nineteenth century, stenography offered opportunities for women by claiming a feminine version of independence under the banner of the New Woman. This womanly independence offered a potential alternative to the problems of maintaining respectability for working women, as discussed in chapter 5, by refashioning the feminine True Woman to incorporate masculine independence. Instead of highlighting women's difference from men, female stenographers became New Women proclaiming equality with men. But this was not entirely new.

Throughout the nineteenth century, middle-class women balanced two sets of values: domesticity, with its connection to family and implied dependence; and the more masculine-identified value of independence, with its companion tenets of initiative, resourcefulness, and agency. As seen in chapter 2, until the 1870s, women reframed independence to fit within the framework of conventional femininity, despite the growing support for something new. The new generation in the 1880s and 1890s, known as the New Women, embraced independence as a generational divide by magnifying differences between their mothers' contemporaries and their own. They reinvented their mothers' generation as housebound, dependent, and blind adherents to traditional womanly standards, meanwhile overlooking their own bonds to convention and refashioning themselves as new and unique symbols of ambition, initiative, independence, and agency, through their involvement in the public sphere. Even though middle-class women's actual involvement in the public arena was not new at all and their own activities remained contained within a safely gendered pattern, women coming of age in the last two decades of the century portrayed themselves as pioneers who broke out of traditional roles. Long-standing behaviors, such as leaving home and working before marriage in emergencies, took on new meanings of independence and agency. Signs of the generational divide included joining a club; supporting new forms of charity work, such as settlement houses; participating in the suffrage movement; studying independently or attending high school, a woman's college, or a coeducational university; new leisure bike riding; and supporting companionate marriage. Although New Women appeared to set new norms, they mostly reinvented long-standing nineteenth-century middle-class values of personal independence as the self-made woman, without abandoning many of the traits of orthodox womanhood.[3]

The New Woman, however, did privilege economic independence and ambition, emphasizing similarities to the self-made man, at least until marriage. Leading the way were women who attended college; founded settlement houses; entered male fields, like medicine, law, or college teaching; labored in new jobs, like trained nursing; or worked with men in telegraph and clerical work. Shorthand promoters and female stenographers themselves championed women stenographers and typewriters as symbols of this self-made woman. As ambitious women, they appeared as agents of their own destiny, rather than helpless victims adrift in the dangerous labor market. By embracing these values of economic autonomy, both working-class and middle-class women could shed the image of degraded workers by reaffirming clerical work as middle-class.[4]

The stenographic establishment, its media and schools, as well as woman's rights supporters and the popular press privileged this representation of stenographers as New Women by refashioning them as independent and ambitious, that is, just like men. Women seemed autonomous when living apart from their families and described, in the language of the self-made man, as plucky, self-reliant, self-supporting, and ambitious enough to prepare for positions that could enable a career-ladder climb. However, by conforming to male types, women faced accusations that they were unwomanly. In response, the stenographic press, educators, and women themselves tried to construct a more feminine "businesswoman," the professional woman. She combined traditional femininity with the self-made man, a new gender balance for the working woman.

FROM TRUE WOMEN ADRIFT TO INDEPENDENT AND AMBITIOUS NEW WOMEN

Despite the New Woman's assertion of a radical break with the past, True Womanhood's features, including the victimized working women, still persisted. Fiction continued to describe heroines as nursing the sick, excelling in domestic skills, and having natural affinities for children.[5] The shorthand press published victim narratives of the struggling but respectable woman adrift, typical of working-girl fiction. Despite these remnants of the victimized working woman, she was rejected as an image for female stenographers.

Since dependence characterized nineteenth-century women's relationships with their families, women living alone, either by choice or "unfortunate circumstances," were viewed as independent women. Such autonomy could be interpreted as either dangerous or liberating. Late nineteenth-century middle-class reformers took the former route and worried about the safety of young unmarried women living on their own, especially those new to the city. Historian Joanne Meyerowitz construes late nineteenth-century working-girl romance novels as highlighting the danger to women's morality, their resultant despair, and their need for rescue. From her view, the childlike heroines in this adrift fiction deserved pity.[6]

In short stories about female stenographers and typewriters written for the *Typewriter and Phonographic World,* a few passive heroines sacrificed for their families. As good daughters, they supported their sisters or widowed mothers, toiling until marriage saved them. For example, hardworking Eleanor in a short story by Mrs. Elizabeth Colberg Washabaugh worries that her mother's "helpless dependence on her made her responsibility heavier." She nearly loses her life savings by unwisely investing in a scam, until her coworker saves the money. In another story, Miss Lawrence works long hours supporting an invalid sister until rescued by a chance encounter with a junior partner.[7]

At times, fiction about stenographers borrowed the trope of the helpless woman adrift to reinforce their criticism of women's low wages and tedious working conditions. Willice Wharton detailed the horrors of women who earned small salaries and scrimped by living in unrespectable sections of town, "walk[ing] several miles to economize on car fare," "do[ing] their own washing and mending at night," and "eat[ing] a slice of bread and butter, and an apple, washed down by a draught of lake water, for luncheon." Heroine Marion Orner worries, "How was a girl with herself to support, to do it on this pittance?" Overworked Miss Helen Cartwright rejects a suggestion to hire an assistant, because she would then have to give up several dollars from her salary that are needed for her "three motherless" siblings. In these two stories, both suffering heroines ultimately win a husband and presumably quit working.[8] Use of the woman adrift as a symbol of victimized working women, along with other features of the conventional femininity of the True Woman, continued well into the era of the New Woman, despite the assertion of a radical break with the past.

Unlike these few victim narratives, most fiction in stenography magazines portrayed working women as New Women and rejected the dangers of independence propounded by fearful middle-class reformers. The majority of shorthand magazine fiction corresponds with the working-girl fiction that Meyerowitz sees developing in the 1910s and taking hold in the 1920s but that historians Michael Denning and Nan Enstad find depicted earlier. These interpretations show the dignity of women's work and the virtue, physicality, and strength of their heroines, features appreciated by their working-class female readers.[9] Most of this fiction turned the woman adrift on her head by portraying family separation and isolation from female friends as a characteristic of the New Woman's independence, much as it had been a characteristic of the independence of antebellum clerks, as discussed in chapter 1. Like most working-girl romances, shorthand magazine stories rarely mentioned women's families.

In stenography magazine fiction, families burdened women. Instead of providing a safe harbor in the city, they dragged women down by necessitating support. Separation and breaking free from parental interference proved women's self-sufficiency. The few examples of clerical women adrift discussed earlier affirm the weight of caring for widowed mothers and younger siblings. One unusual story ridicules a working-class mother and father for interfering in their daughter's work life by visiting the boss even before the daughter begins her job and then by spending hours watching her at work.[10]

Families were also criticized for interfering with unfettered marital choice. Although nineteenth-century men and women chose their spouses without parental interference, stenography magazine fiction still featured marital choice as a symbol of feminine autonomy, similar to the dime novel romances. In Mrs. C. H. Brake's story "One Way: How a Plucky Girl Stenographer Demanded and Obtained a First-Class Situation," Beth strikes out on her own rather than "enter[ing] into the schemes of her ambitious aunt to capture for herself a rich husband." In another story, discussed in chapter 5, Tomasina spoils her mother's attempt to maneuver a marriage to a rich young man; instead, she marries his even wealthier uncle, whom she loves. In the many love stories, women meet their husbands at work or after work, but always on their own, without parental involvement.[11]

Just as marital choice proved the autonomy of fictional heroines in stenographic magazines, their physical separation from family meant opportunity and an "independent air," not helplessness and danger.[12] Some, like Lou in "Women and Their Work: Lesson of a Young Woman Stenographer's Career," yearn "to be free." At age twenty, "two years out of a convent" and "weary of idle dreams and dependence," Lou "had learned stenography and typewriting, not because she must work, but because she wished to make her own way."[13] In a previously mentioned story, the heroine accepts her need to work and delights in the opportunity it brought her. Independent Beth "wished to earn for herself a place in the world."[14] In these stories, living away from parents represented welcomed emancipation, not dangerous isolation. Fictional females seek freedom from the obligations and controls of their birth family.

To reinforce that independence, the shorthand press refashioned the stenographer to conform to the parlance of the self-made man. Traits of self-reliance, pluckiness, resourcefulness, and ingeniousness became hallmarks of the New Woman and the woman stenographer and typewriter. As early as 1876, *Browne's Phonographic Monthly* applauded a Scott-Browne alumnus, official reporter Mrs. J. R. Palmer, for "the pluck to go forth and win laurels in her profession." Court Reporter Edward F. Underhill spoke before the New York State Law Stenographers' Association in 1878 about the "true dignity" of a woman "as . . . beautiful, cultivated, independent and self-reliant." He explained that shorthand "gives her opportunity to show what she can do."[15]

By the end of the century, shorthand magazine fiction also portrayed women with ingenuity, pluck, self-reliance, and resourcefulness. In "Testing Her Speed," heroine Miss Carter works for a man who prides himself in his ability to speak more fluently and quickly than stenographers can write. When Mr. Truelove fails to fluster Miss Carter, he and his "confidential clerk" (personal secretary), Mr. Noble, hatch a plan to humiliate her. They prepare a long letter, which Mr. Truelove will then dictate to her at lightning speed, since he will not have to think as he speaks. Upon overhearing the scheme through the thin walls, Miss Carter eavesdrops and takes notes on the letter as Mr. Truelove dictates it to Mr. Noble. When Mr. Truelove recites the rigged letter to her, she outsmarts her tormenter by pretending to take notes and taunts him for not speaking quickly enough. A second story depicting female ingenuity, Leander G. Bowers's "The Typewriter Telegram: How a Plucky Girl Operator in Colorado Prevented a Terrible Catastrophe," was modeled on the dime novel genre. Upon learning that a band of robbers has wrecked a railroad track, the telegraph agent's sister, Alice Clark, prepares to telegraph a message, until one of the gang members grabs her and holds her hostage. When one of her captors asks how a typewriter works, Alice demonstrates by tapping an emergency message on it in the cadence of Morse code. Alice's quick thinking saves the train and its cargo of gold bullion. In each case, these women demonstrate traits associated with the New Woman, although their personal initiative and independent action still mirror the characteristics of their long-forgotten midcentury fictional counterparts.[16]

The stenography press and even real women applied the discourse and forms of the story of the self-made man to women by zeroing in on pluck as a defining feature of the self-made woman. For example, Miss Alma Sawtelle, a stenographer in a "leading wholesale grocery house," demonstrated "denominated pluck" when, during her vacation, she volunteered to help the overworked secretary of the convention of the International Association of Ticket Agents while on a train and then again at the association's convention in Los Angeles. At the convention, "Miss Sawtelle was summoned from the audience, and with the quiet dignity which is one of her chief charms, she took her place on the platform and reported the proceedings of that important meeting, . . . from 11 A.M. until 5 P.M." She then worked for the editor of the *Ticket Agent* on her return trip. Before reaching home, she was "unanimously elected as official stenographer for the next annual convention."[17] Another woman, Sue Shelton White, overcame her fear that studying stenography in the South in the early 1900s would challenge her "status as a 'lady.'" She decided to become a court reporter when her employer, who had encouraged an office boy to "learn the business," lectured her on women's "proper" place and insisted that she "was not there to learn the business but to type things." She proudly recalled that when she talked about going to law school, "they called me impractical and visionary."[18]

Such common themes of women choosing their own husbands without parental involvement, living apart from their families, and deploying the language of the self-made man served as signs of independence. Although some stenography magazine fiction embraced elements of the nineteenth-century narrative of the woman adrift, with marriage rescuing the heroines from office tedium and family responsibilities, most protagonists proved themselves ready for marriage by selecting their own spouses and making their way in the world as single women. These stories mostly assumed women's detachment from their families as narratives of emancipation—until marriage, when the tales ended. The more women appeared on their own, breaking from their families, the more they seemed autonomous and unlike the characterization of the helpless woman adrift.

Opportunity for Ambitious Women: Earnings for Self-Supporting Women

Employment conditions, especially wages, contributed to the image of stenography as an occupation for independent women. However, women's earnings could elicit varied interpretations, confirming either dependence or independence to contemporaries. Declining overall wages might have signaled clerical women's failure to support themselves. Conversely, the generally higher pay of clerical jobs in comparison to other female positions and especially the narrowing differential between male and female stenographers' wage rates had the potential to bolster the opposite impression of economic opportunities for women and reinforce the discourse of the New Woman. The latter complemented the overblown rhetoric of business school promotions and the shorthand press, providing an image of stenography as an occupation for ambitious women who earned more than other women and on par with men. Here was opportunity for self-supporting work, a crucial sign of independence.

At times, clerical work, with its general declining wage rates during the late nineteenth century, looked like another low-wage job for helpless, dependent women adrift. Female clerical workers, like their male coworkers, suffered from the repeated depressions in the late nineteenth century. As discussed in chapter 3, when the economy recovered from the devastating depression of the 1870s, earnings rose somewhat but were then held down by a recession in the mid-1880s. Writing under the initials "XYZ" in 1881, one stenographer warned that Boston's salaries for amanuenses "are small and the inducements . . . to learn the art . . . are very meager." Two years later, another writer reproached the editor of *Browne's Phonographic Monthly and Reporters' Journal* for exaggerating financial opportunities. In the late 1880s, income stabilized, even improving with deflation. However, a jolting economic collapse in the early 1890s obliterated the previous gains, sending salaries plummeting once again. As the economy revived in the second half of the 1890s, wage rates inched upward but generally failed to reach the peak good wages of the late 1880s. Not surprisingly, data compiled for northeastern states by the U.S. Commissioner of Labor confirms that women's earnings fell during bad times but improved by the end of the century. For example, female stenographers' wage rates tumbled from $1.83 per day in 1885–89 to $1.29 in 1890–94, inching back up to $1.66 in 1895–99. Even in constant dollars, which accounted for deflation, wage rates had fallen by seventeen cents between 1885–89 and 1895–99. While salaries picked up during upswings, the frequent economic downturns pushed them downward (see appendix, table D1).[19]

Despite the sliding salaries and the popular discourse about the six-dollar-a-week stenographer, discussed in chapter 3, wage rates could be and were used to fuel an image of opportunity. Female office workers in general earned relatively high salaries in comparison to other female workers, sometimes for shorter workdays. Even the wages of low-paid office staff in 1884 compared favorably with other women's wage rates. In 1884, a study in Boston reported copyists making $6.78, bookkeepers at $6.55, and clerks at $5.28 per week. In contrast, saleswomen averaged $5.75 and seamstresses $6.18, while dressmakers garnered higher wages at $7.42 and milliners at $7.97 but worked longer days and faced more unemployment. Twenty years later, clerical women's salaries surpassed those of most women's jobs, averaging between eight and ten dollars per week; moreover, the growing numbers who enjoyed yearly vacations enhanced the attractiveness of office jobs. This trend continued into the twentieth century, when secretaries earned the highest women's office wage, followed by experienced stenographers.[20]

Women employed in government offices especially earned more than other women, despite securing less than their male counterparts. They received consistently high salaries, ranging from $540 to $1,400 per year depending on the year, length of service, and the job itself. Whether among office staff of the Treasury Department and Department of the Interior in Washington, D.C., or Boston's postal clerks, salaries climbed upward. For example, the mean of Boston's female postal clerks steadily advanced from $559 per year in 1879 to $686 in 1889 and $885 in 1901, almost triple the amount earned by the six-dollar stenographer (see appendix, table D2). The salaries of these elite female clerical workers exceeded those in the best-paid women's jobs. From 1881 to 1895, new Boston teachers drew payments of $456, while beginning U.S. Treasury Department clerks made $600 per year. These choice office positions afforded women opportunities rarely found elsewhere. Alice Flagg Simons confessed in 1889 how much easier life would have been "if only I had a government office [appointment]." By surpassing the best-paid women's jobs, female government clerks' pay schedules reinforced that image of opportunity for office workers, even though most women did not earn such high incomes.[21]

Women's earnings in business stenography did not come close to those in government, but shorthand still appeared to offer women more opportunity than most office positions. In the study of northeastern states discussed in chapter 3, female stenographers earned consistently higher daily rates than female bookkeepers and typewriters, at $1.40 in 1895–99, compared to $1.27 and $1.19 in constant dollars, respectively (see appendix, table D1). Moreover, business college proprietors and the shorthand press published glowing reports of high stenographic and typing salaries, a glass half full, rather than half empty. For example, the journals exaggerated income of business stenographers: "The smallest paid is $15 per week, . . . up to $60 and in special cases . . . $100 per week." They also regularly reported court reporters' earnings of two thousand to twenty-five hundred dollars per year, six to eight times the amount of the six-dollar stenographer. The popular press filtered these reports through the

New Woman discourse of opportunity and passed them on to a more general audience. The publicity reinforced an impression of a general upward trend when wage rates rose after the devastating early 1890s. The positive depictions of incomes may well have convinced women to seek clerical training, since few could actually remember long-term shifts in salaries, because they seldom worked for more than ten years.[22]

Favorable comparisons to men's earning may have also helped sustain this rosy image of shorthand as self-supporting for ambitious women. As women monopolized typing and moved solidly into shorthand, their shorthand wage rates caught up with men's, as seen in chapter 3 (see appendix, table D1). Moreover, female stenographers generally compared better economically to men in their field than did women clerks and bookkeepers. For example, economist Albert W. Niemi Jr. found that in 1880, women shorthand writers in positions with a majority of females earned 70.6 percent of what men made, while women clerks brought in 67.4 percent and women bookkeepers only 62.3 percent of their male counterparts' earnings. Ten years later, female stenographers increased their lead to 75.6 percent, while both female clerks and bookkeepers dropped further behind, to 61.3 percent and 57.3 percent, respectively. Stenography's narrowing salary differential gave women an opportunity to "keep pace with men," the ultimate proof of the New Woman. Highly paid court reporter Bessie A. Rogers knew she had succeeded when she earned one hundred dollars per week and matched male salaries: "I told the Judge that my prayer was answered, . . . get[ting] just as much money for the same amount of work as a man." Rogers linked success to parity with men's pay, women's rights, and the New Woman: "If my efforts and example shall have contributed to the enlargement of the limited circle of woman's employment, my fondest hopes will have been realized." The same journal later hailed Rogers as a role model who studied stenography on her own at home then "left . . . [for] Chicago" to practice court reporting.[23]

Despite long-term declining wage rates that might have limited options for self-support and that appeared at times to reinforce the stereotype of the six-dollar stenographer, clerical salaries, especially stenographers', actually bolstered the image of independence and opportunity for ambitious women. Supporters of the New Woman could embrace the material conditions that portrayed stenography as such. The modest financial success of clerical work for women seemed significant thanks to its higher wage rates over other female jobs, a narrowed wage gap with male stenographers, and the relentless publicity about high-earning women, mostly court reporters and government workers. This optimism about opportunities occurred within the context of the New Woman. Clerical women, especially stenographers, could view themselves as ambitious and independent workers in men's positions now open to women.

CONSTRUCTING THE AMBITIOUS WOMAN

Nineteenth-century gendered discourses about social mobility defined the New Woman and female stenographer. By the last decades of the century, the self-made man's marker of ambition came to stand for the New Woman, with stenography and typewriting as symbols for the masses. The shorthand community endorsed the trope of social mobility by adopting the New Woman's use of male aspirational language. Despite this refashioning of womanhood to encompass a more masculine self, the feminine meaning of ambition remained fuzzy, ranging from respectable employment to actual advancement on a career ladder, even if limited.

Midcentury sentimental fiction portrayed working-class women's initiative through the trope of class mobility. It depicted working-class heroines with innate goodness who change, *Pygmalion*-like, into middle-class ladies, like Maria Susanna Cummins's Gertrude (Gerty) Flint in *The Lamplighter*. In the opening pages of that novel, the eight-year-old orphaned Gerty appears dirty, ugly, mistreated, "fierce, untamed," "impetuous," "passion[ate]," and "obstina[te]." As she becomes a lady, she begins to transform physically, from an unattractive child with "thin and sharp" features, a "sallow complexion," and "not a single attraction," to a "slight and delicate" woman with "handsome eyes" and a rose-hued complexion "that flushes her cheeks." She gradually gains one of those faces "sanctified by the divine presence."[24]

Dime novels espoused upward class mobility even more boldly as an alternative to poverty during the last four decades of the century. Heroines enter and compete well in society, eventually achieving independence by inheriting wealth and then marrying millionaires. Although, according to historian Nan Enstad, the path to advancement for working-class heroines unfolds differently in dime novels than in middle-class fiction, still they end up leaving their class via inheritance and marriage. Often their early lives begin in comfort but succumb to poverty before they achieve their rightful place at the end of the story, like some Horatio Alger characters. While Alger's characters move to the middle class, female dime novel heroines rise to the upper class.[25]

Despite such upward mobility, authors only began to name their female protagonists as ambitious in the postwar years. Fiction from the early 1860s, such as Rebecca Harding Davis's *Margaret Howth: A Story of To-day* (1862) and *Life in the Iron Mills* (1861) and Elizabeth Stuart Phelps's *Men, Women, and Ghosts* (1864), never mentions women's ambition. More frequent and favorable usage appeared in the late 1860s and most apparently in *Little Women* (1869). Louisa May Alcott repeatedly refers to tomboy Jo's "great plans [for an economic future that] fermented in her busy brain and ambitious mind," employing the masculine language of economic independence. Even though Jo outgrows her tomboyishness, Alcott treated her desire for independence with respect, explaining the difficulty "for a restless, ambitious girl . . . to give up her own hopes, plans, and desires, and cheerfully live for others."[26] Alcott's language of ambition flowered at the end of the century, becoming the hallmark of the New Woman.

By the close of the century, mobility to white-collar jobs signaled drive. Middle-class writers portrayed working-class women who became stenographers or typewriters as acceptably enterprising social movers. In William Dean Howells's 1885 novel, *The Rise of Silas Lapham,* a minor Irish female character rises from abject poverty to become a "typewriter," the working woman's savior. Twenty years later, in 1914, Theodore Dreiser still presented such class mobility when he described the daughter of "foreign parents . . . with her fine, lithe body, her good taste in dress, her skill in stenography, bookkeeping, and business details," who "blossomed forth into something exceptional."[27] The *Phonographic World* identified the working-class roots of Blanche Hard, a machinist's daughter from Lowell, Massachusetts, intimating that after graduating from high school, taking shorthand lessons, and working for a year, she was now prepared to launch a general shorthand and typing business in 1889. This rare discussion of female class mobility in the shorthand press differed from the biographical sketches of men. More typically, the shorthand press turned to the popular definitions of advancement that could appeal to both middle- and working-class students and readers.[28]

One such favored definition of ambition applauded women who exhibited the effort expected of the self-made man to achieve class mobility. Preparation for shorthand positions signaled an ascent. For example, Dorothy Richardson's impoverished middle-class heroine in her 1905 muckraking fictionalized autobiography, *The Long Day,* climbs from the depths of despair as a struggling woman adrift to a decent job as a demonstrator in a department store. By studying nights to "brush up" on spelling and grammar and to acquire the requisite skills and speed, she achieves a good-paying and respectable job as a stenographer, eventually working for a publisher.[29]

For middle-class fiction writers, however, female ambition could merely mean embracing employment itself. Increasingly, novels portrayed women choosing between marriage and respectable careers as doctors, teachers, and even telegraph operators. Although conservatives dominated in the 1870s, leading characters to choose wedlock, the mere discussion illustrates a change in thinking. By the 1880s, some female protagonists prefer careers or at least appreciate work, their skills, and independence. From the 1870s through the 1890s, Harriet Beecher Stowe, Mark Twain and Charles Dudley Warner, William Dean Howells, Sarah Orne Jewett, Louisa May Alcott, Elizabeth Stuart Phelps, and Hamlin Garland portrayed central characters who decide between marriage and a pursuit in medicine. While the male writers' protagonists opt for matrimony, the female writers' heroines more likely continue their careers. In her 1897 autobiography, author Elizabeth Stuart Phelps boasted, "I am proud to say . . . that I have always been a working woman" and that "I could take care of myself."[30]

In contrast to middle-class fiction's representation of ambition as the choice of work over marriage, at least one stenographer labeled women compelled to find employment as enterprising. In a letter in the *Phonographic World,* B.C. explained that many women did not work out of choice, but she claimed that "some . . . are just as much interested in making a name for themselves as any man ever was," in contrast to "the Oriental woman . . . [who has] no ambition, no desire to be anything." She pleaded "for a woman to be allowed to make her living without being talked about," but she limited her aspirations to economic concerns. B.C. consoled her conservative readers that "I would not vote if I could, for it does not pay men to be politicians, sometimes, and it would never pay a woman to go into politics." For B.C., ambition meant securing middle-class positions.[31]

For many, employment in white-collar jobs alone connoted ambition, but the shorthand press, like the mass media and middle-class writers in general, confused aspirations with middle-class positions and jobholders. They repeatedly portrayed stenography and typewriting as situations held by middle-class women, implying that those who reached such posts would naturally join their sisters in the middle class, proving that they had ambition. Some shorthand magazine vignettes about women advertised advanced education, such as that about Mary Rowe, a clergyman's daughter educated in French, Latin, and Greek, who could read Virgil's *Aeneid* and translate parts of the Greek New Testament into English by age thirteen and became a chief stenographer with two assistants in the early 1880s. While biographical sketches mostly left out fathers' occupations, they did point out prominent middle-class relatives as proof of middle-class respectability. Biographical narratives on Alice B. Sanger, the first woman to hold the position as presidential stenographer (for President Benjamin Harrison), played up her relationship to General N. P. Banks and Elias Howe.[32]

However, promoters of stenography and typing schools promised more than mere entrance to middle-class positions. They linked shorthand to career prospects by exploiting the vocabulary of opportunity to hawk their programs. They spoke in vague generalities about each woman "profiting by her new opportunities." At times, they more specifically portrayed shorthand as a stepping-stone to law or "independent business offices" for women, like a rung on a career ladder for the self-made man. In 1889, the *Phonographic World* republished an article from the *Business Woman's Journal* that made the same point: "We know of nothing better for a young woman to do, who anticipates taking up the study of law, than to learn either stenography or typewriting, if possible, both—and then obtaining a position for a part of the day in a law office, leaving a few hours for attendance in the law school." Ellis Wood, a frequent critic of female stenographers, wrote a didactic story that advised women to develop "commercial values" so they could recognize "opportunity [when it] knocks." Advice such as this reinforced an image of stenographers and typewriters as New Women—ambitious, independent, and looking for opportunities—rather than passive victims.[33]

The stenography press also exaggerated employment prospects for women and men to become legal stenographers and court reporters. They kept track of the small, but growing, number of women who reached the pinnacle of stenography as official court reporters. The press published biographical pieces of solo reporters, partners in existing stenographic firms, and official court reporters. For instance, Cora Elisabeth Burbank, daughter of a country merchant, first taught in the public schools, then ran a private commercial school, and later opened her own shorthand company, before becoming a well-known official stenographer of the Massachusetts Superior Court. *Browne's Phonographic Monthly* reported Alice C. Nute's career as a junior member of the Chicago stenography firm Bennett, Scates, Davison, and Edwards. When the firm dissolved, she became a junior partner of Scates and Nute, which succeeded, according to the shorthand press, because of "her diligent application to her profession, her business ability, tact and prepossessing manners."[34] The press also quoted women reporters like Helen Hinckle, who made it clear that "energetic and ambitious" women preferred court reporting rather than work as "mere" amanuenses.[35]

The shorthand press told of intrepid and ambitious women starting their own businesses. Some articles advertised reports of a surge in demand in the 1880s and 1890s for independent typing and stenographic contractors, who put out their shingles in hotels to sell their services to traveling businessmen. The shorthand press covered women who launched stenography and typewriting firms as independent proprietors, some of whom hired staffs of employees to contract out work. For example, in 1891, the *Phonographic Magazine* featured the "indomitable" and plucky Mrs. Edna I. Tyler, who "trained her left hand to write ordinary longhand" after losing the "use of her right hand." In 1883, Tyler and her mother, Annie L. Smith, launched the first typewiter and general stenographic office in Worcester, Massachusetts. The *Phonographic World* wrote two puff pieces in the 1890s about the rise to independent proprietorship of the Rosenfield sisters of New York City. After studying shorthand, Zerlina Rosenfield entered into a three-month contract to take charge of a copying office in exchange for a salary and a share of the profits. She next contracted for desk room at a law firm, "securing their work and privileges of outside business," so that "by the end of the year she had many customers, and was then employing two stenographers." The following year, Zerlina and her two sisters, Laura and Alice, who she had trained, opened a typewriting, stenography, and translating office. They eventually owned six offices, with over thirty typewriting operators. The *Phonographic World* attributed the sisters' success to "pluck, energy, perseverance, and hard work" and reported their faith in the standard maxim of the ambitious that "there is plenty of room at the top, and that success can only be achieved by perseverance and close application to business."[36]

Stenography periodicals gave shorthand and typing teachers the most attention because their commercial school sponsors sought to convince prospective students of the competence of their personnel. Biographical sketches of faculty and managers of business schools again publicized employment positions for ambitious women. Alice W. Baker, for instance, opened a stenographic office after completing her studies. Within a year, she returned to school to earn a teacher's certificate at the Phonographic Institute and taught there. Another woman, Mary E. Pearce, graduated to an assistant at Hickox's shorthand school, after finishing her training. Three years later, she launched a public stenographic business, while continuing to furnish private lessons. Since teaching absorbed so much of her time, Pearce founded her own "thriving" shorthand school in "one of the finest buildings" in Boston.[37]

The stenography press vignettes also included tales of women who used shorthand or typing as a stepping-stone to managerial, administrative, editorial, and legal positions in the private and public sectors. In 1886, Elizabeth W. Walter, daughter of a music teacher and composer, secured a position with the Metropolitan Life Insurance Company in New York, where she oversaw type-writing operators. By 1891, she had three assistants and 140 operators under her jurisdiction. Mina Minton Dyke, a young woman from Massachusetts, worked part-time for the New York City building commissioner before becoming his private secretary. She studied at night, graduated from a law school for women (possibly New York University's Women's Law Class), and advanced to a "sort of assistant commissioner," with her own stenographer. A report on Rachel C. Brown praised her "rapid rise" between 1895, when she took a civil service exam, and November of 1896. She began typing in the Department of the Interior, then assisting the clerk of the superintendent of Indian schools, switching to the U.S. Patent Office, where she still typed; she then became a stenographer to the assistant chief of the Assignment Division and, in 1896, was placed in charge of the clerical staff in the office of the superintendent of Indian schools. Netta McLaughlin "began her independent career as a school teacher," but after learning shorthand, she progressed from an enrolling clerk for the Kansas legislature to chief enrolling clerk, then to commissioner for the U.S. Court of Claims, and finally to an editor of a weekly medical journal in 1897. Mary F. Seymour edited the *Business Woman's Journal* and served as principal of the Union School of Stenography and Typewriting in New York.[38]

These examples, of course, also reveal that real women did find opportunities from typewriting and shorthand. Some female stenographers parlayed their experiences in law offices as an entrée into the legal profession as lawyers. Others moved in the reverse direction, learning shorthand to supplement their law practices, especially if they lived in areas with few court reporters. Lelia Josephine Robinson applied the shorthand that she had learned for "reference work" while building her practice in Seattle. In a letter to other women lawyers in the Equity Club, she advised female law students to study shorthand as "invaluable in getting . . . clerkship opportunities, and if . . . practic[ing in the] west, [for] filling in empty hours by reporting testimony in court." Laura A. W. LeValley also found shorthand advantageous. After she and her husband graduated from the University of Michigan Law School and he opened a law office, she assisted him with stenography and general office work, while establishing her practice. These women viewed shorthand as a skill for improving their career prospects.[39]

Despite the options for such educated women and the relentless publicity of unlimited occupational mobility, most remained in low-level office positions. At times, even business schools, the shorthand press, and stenographers themselves acknowledged the expectation that women could only rise to a certain level. Philadelphia's Peirce School encouraged women to improve their skills and speed, while men were expected to earn real promotions, according to historian Jerome P. Bjelopera. As early as 1888, Frances Fox of San Francisco complained to the press, "A man of ambition . . . is given a chance for promotion, and ultimate independence, if he will but apply himself. . . . A woman may go so far, and no farther. Her ladder has but one rung." Fox suggested that women become discouraged with low wages and marry for relief. Over twenty-five years later, a 1915 stenography publicity circular for Gregg Publishing Company entitled *Shorthand, the Open Door to Opportunity* replayed the familiar theme. This booklet summarized short biographies of prominent men who practiced stenography, including President Woodrow Wilson, senators, congressmen, judges, lawyers, business executives, railway officials, authors, and financiers. In contrast, the section on women revealed that the vast majority moved up to higher-level clerical or management jobs but that most nevertheless remained in offices as private secretaries. A few other women rounded out the list: a tribulation actress, a theatrical broker and producer, a lawyer, a real estate broker, a high official of a corporation, a director of the Remington Typewriting Company, and the wife of the governor of Illinois. The handful outside of the office did not compare in stature and in diversity to the achievements of men who wrote shorthand. Such catalogues of women's accomplishments exposed their limitations.[40]

Despite such periodic admissions of limitations, stenography (and sometimes typing) earned a reputation for offering New Women opportunities for economic independence through social mobility. While popular fiction reminded readers of clerical work's potential for class mobility, the stenographic press encouraged a depiction of social mobility that could speak to all classes of women—the self-made woman: she prepared for an occupation, demonstrated middle-class values of hard work and pluck, and made small gains, all of which proved that she had ambition for a career. The shorthand press affirmed an image of stenography and typing as a means for the masses of women to achieve financial independence. This picture of economic opportunity through shorthand and typing provided an alternative to the helpless woman adrift.

CONSTRUCTING THE COMPETENT FEMALE STENOGRAPHER

While both employers and female stenographers could appreciate the New Woman's drive and spunk, female office workers still faced the problem of respectability. As discussed in chapter 5, propriety both justified middle-class women's employment and challenged it. To resolve this paradox, female stenographers and typewriters joined with commercial educators and the shorthand press in refashioning a new definition of middle-class respectability for employed women. Some of the participants periodically restricted incompetency to working-class women, while they all stressed similarities between male and female shorthand writers. They did this by refashioning female stenographers and typewriters as professionals through the new concept of the businesswoman. When that concept proved problematic, they merged professionalism with conventional femininity.

Narrowing Incompetents to Working-Class Women

A reaction to an 1888 didactic article written for the *Phonographic World* by S. S. Packard, owner of a string of business colleges, discloses the strategy of isolating incompetency as a characteristic of working-class women. Packard addressed his remarks to a "seventeen year old girl who has dropped her croquet mallet and tennis racquet, and taken up her fountain pen." He patronizingly reminded her, "Firstly, dear girl, do you understand what it is to be necessary to somebody—not as a friend, or a possible wife, but as a helper—a co-worker?" Concerned that she remain a lady, he counseled her to dress appropriately, not expect favors if she is pretty, and "be helpful, . . . not unpleasantly aggressive, nor . . . over-anxious and fidgety." He recommended quiet, helpfulness, and sweetness: "The presence of the girl amanuensis should be felt rather than observed; and when . . . she is absent from her post, those whom she serves should miss her, not from the greater quiet . . . but from realizing that something sweet and pleasant has dropped out of their routine, that the office is more gloomy and less attractive, and that some how things don't get on as they should."[41] Packard's condescending tone struck a responsive cord with an unexpected audience. Immediately after reading the above commentary, Geraldine Hussey fired off a letter to the *Phonographic World* because the Packard article "reminded me of an amusing incident which happened to me not long ago." Hussey remembered temporarily teaching a night class of twenty stenography students "all older than myself" and "mostly shopgirls," until a regular teacher could be hired. Hussey deemed them inherently unfit on their first day of school, criticizing their slang and castigating the classroom as a "Dante's Inferno." She assured her readers, "For the honor of our profession, . . . I do not think . . . many of these girls will stand the test." While Packard envisioned young middle-class women as his audience, Hussey identified not with Packard's gender pronouncements but with his patronizing middle-class assumptions. She ignored or did not see that his column was directed to women like her or her younger sisters. Instead, she redirected it at working-class women, unwavering in her approval of women's involvement in "public life" and of "the . . . business woman."[42]

Working-class women may well have recognized middle-class women's scorn, although their voices rarely rose above the middle-class din. One of Miss Hussey's students threatened that "she would leave, if the teacher was not of the masculine gender." This student may have preferred a male teacher because she understood women's limited status in society as well as in the world of stenography. She most likely also used gender to undermine the authority of her arrogant teacher, who believed in her own class superiority.[43]

This exchange reveals a resolution to the class and gender tensions discussed in chapter 5. While some men portrayed women—even young middle-class women—as unfit, female shorthand teachers constructed working-class women as the sole incompetents in a class-based feminine version of ineptitude aimed at women they deemed unrespectable. Writers to the stenographic press shared Geraldine Hussey's disdain and belittled working-class women's aspirations to learn shorthand, lambasting them as incapable. Educator Mrs. Doherty called them "servant girls of no education whatsoever," while teacher Minnie Pratt pronounced them "cheap girls," "illiterate, ill-bred girls," and "shiftless student[s]." Grace Lincoln Hall (probably also a teacher) scorned a "lady" who wanted her daughter to become a stenographer although "she has a taste for" millinery and "isn't quick enough at figuring to make a successful clerk." Hall continued her rebuke, "Poor, deluded soul, she honestly thought that although her daughter didn't have brains enough to be a good mathematician, she could without any trouble, master shorthand!"[44]

The shorthand press also took shots at working-class female stenographers' competence, corresponding to the critiques of teachers. Of course, female teachers may have chosen this direct assault on working-class women to deflect accusations that they failed to educate female stenographers and bore responsibility for their incompetence, as well as to differentiate themselves from their working-class students. Female writers of short stories had no such motivation, but as employed middle-class women, they may have recognized the advantages of demonizing working-class women. At least one shorthand short story, "Laura's Mother" by Emily Ruth Calvin, similarly portrayed a working-class female stenographer in an unflattering description. Calvin told of a longshoreman's daughter who is hopelessly ill-equipped to work as a shorthand writer. Although her family has saved for two years to pay for training at a business college, Laura Denman is incapable of taking even the simplest dictation at a reasonable pace and never seems to improve. She even looks incompetent, "tall and angular," with a "thin forehead (a sign of limited intelligence)" and "coarse and uninteresting" features. The story's tone grew exceedingly condescending, clucking that Laura has the nerve to ask for a raise even though she actually deserves to be fired. Obviously, the implication of the story was that women like Laura did not belong in the office.[45]

By locating all of the negative feminine traits in women they deemed objectionable and accusing them of improper work habits, female commercial educators and the shorthand press helped define the competent female stenographer and typewriter as middle-class and respectable. Since upwardly mobile working-class women could hardly recognize themselves in these crude representations of incompetents and since the capable clerical worker rested on values open to anyone, they could easily identify themselves as respectable, competent stenographers. By distinguishing themselves from the incompetent, it would now be easier for them to equate middle-class women with men of their class as professionals.

The Competent Woman Stenographer: The Businesswoman

As seen in chapter 5, respectability fell short of proving women's proficiency for work. The image of the lady pointed up differences between men and women and similarities between women. Since this universalizing of women made them vulnerable to the negative images of the working-class woman, female stenographers and typewriters, commercial educators, and the shorthand press fashioned an image of the competent female clerical worker modeled after male stenographers and based on middle-class solidarity and equality of the sexes.

As women increasingly tread on male spheres of education, politics, the courts, and the office, they often likened themselves to men. For example, Hattie A. Shinn drew on an equality model to rebut jokes about typewriter girls: "We are tired of it. We are working for the same reason a young man works—because necessity compels us." In 1896, stenographer and suffragist S. Louise Patteson rejected differences between men and women—in this case, the idea of women's superiority—and opted for equality. A woman "is not so very much better or more capable than the average man, as some of the sisters would have you believe," she argued, "but . . . just as good and . . . capable; and she demands equal pay for equal work."[46]

Female stenographers counseled each other to follow a masculine work ethic. In her 1887 speech "Why Some Women Fail of [*sic*] Success in Court Reporters' or Business Offices," given before the New York State Stenographers' Association and provoking one of the hat controversies discussed in chapter 5, Jeannette Ballantyne recommended that women prepare themselves through study, develop an interest in their work, and separate business from social life. She also warned women to be prompt, diligent in their accounts, and less sensitive. Women should conduct themselves similarly to men, rather than "expecting the same little delicate attention from . . . gentlem[e]n during business hours as . . . accustomed . . . in the parlor." She advised, "Do not put on a *horrified* air should one of the male persuasion approach you in the office with hat on head, at the same time indulging in his favorite Havana." Ballantyne's commitment to equity in the courts and offices extended to her support for women's suffrage, which she believed would expand job opportunities for women.[47]

As a means of achieving equality between male and female coworkers in offices and courts, the stenographic community appropriated a popular late nineteenth-century icon. Despite women's longtime involvement in business, it was associated with manliness and considered inappropriate for women. Mid-century novels portrayed women in business unflatteringly, whether in male occupations, like farming, or female trades, like millinery and dressmaking. Men repeatedly attacked women competitors as "unbusinesslike" in telegraph work in the 1860s and in millinery from the 1860s to the turn of the century. According to historian Wendy Gamber, men in the wholesale millinery trade accused women of carelessness, irrationality, indecisiveness, and frivolity, as evidence of their unbusinesslike behavior. In response to the critique, some women embraced the term *business*. In 1857, Jane Bragg Pitman, Benn's wife, enthusiastically wrote to her sister, "I am now quite a business woman, spending all my time in the office and happy indeed . . . to help . . . Benn." Clerical work helped women gain a more positive connection to business. From its early days, shorthand, typewriting, and commercial education were associated with commerce. When women moved into office stenography and typewriting, commercial words were used. Shorthand and typing boosters regularly referred to women in shorthand and typewriting as "businesswomen." Even the popular press called typing a business in the early 1880s. The language of commercialism complimented women and offered them rhetorical access to a class-based equality with men in the world of work.[48]

This image of the businesswoman, in contrast to the lady, played up women's work ethic to encourage their employment. A lady could not work as a railroad stenographer, because travel overnight on trains with her employer was "unladylike," but a businesswoman could. In response to objections that a lady could not handle the job of office boy, "copy papers among a lot of men" at the county clerk's office, "go into court and report" "at a moment's notice, and be gone all day," or deal with an irrational and "crazy" employer, an advocate of female employment asserted that women could do anything because "a business woman does the same things in business that a business man does." Businesswomen were even permitted to eat lunch with their employers without damaging their reputations.[49]

A businesswoman's image also offered a possible solution to problems of the sexually charged office. The shorthand community, including female stenographers, borrowed from the iconic businessman to portray businesswomen as unemotional and too serious to withstand distractions of nonbusiness concerns. In one didactic story, a female shorthand writer incorporated her boss's compliment "What very pretty hair you have" in her typed letter. The stenographer did not recognize her employer's indiscretion, because she was absorbed in her work. Like other representations of businesswomen, she insisted that business, not "sentiment," belonged in the workplace, squashing any chance of amative relationships. A reprinted article from the *Boston Journal* reported a stenographer who bristled at a sexual image of office women, reiterating an appropriate work ethic. "I am here for *business*," she asserted, "and not to be told that I have fine eyes or a white hand." She related how such talk first "disgusted" her and sometimes made her angry. "Now I simply let them talk," she concluded, "and charge time that they occupy." Helen L. Hinckle, the feisty challenger to one of the hat stories and the woman who submitted the poem at the opening of this chapter, announcing the independence of female typewriters, summed up women's preference for identifying themselves as businesswomen by reminding critics that women work too hard to become involved in workplace romances. A shorthand story that characterized the businesswoman type as "decidedly not a girl" explained, "Neither is she a young lady, nor even a girl bachelor. She is just a 'business woman,' that being much more dignified than any of the other appellations."[50]

The businesswoman represented the modern independent woman, the New Woman who appreciated her work, rather than working only out of necessity.[51] She took her work seriously, leaving no time for frivolity. This modern independent woman made room for all classes of women but elevated the middle class. The businesswoman image reasserted a middle-class identity while aligning women with men. It held sway because it appeared to offer clerical women protection that the lady missed, by constructing a competent female stenographer similar to the professional man.

Problems of the Businesswoman

The vocabulary of business, while offering a better way to promote middle-class women's position in the office and courts, posed new perils for office women. Unlike the lady rooted in female imagery, the businesswoman trope appeared neutral but maintained a masculine center. When fictional women were portrayed as businesswomen, they often looked cold and hard.[52] To avoid that negative representation and maintain a feminine identity, women in the stenographic community defined the businesswoman in a way that reclaimed business from a masculine construction.

At times, the promotion of the businesswoman moved increasingly close to embracing a masculine definition of business. In an earlier speech on the "appropriateness of women as court reporters," given before the New York State Stenographers' Association's annual meeting in August 1886, Jeannette Ballantyne championed "strong-minded" women. Eliza Boardman Burnz, the prominent stenographer and spelling reformer, went even further in 1890 when she advocated a costume for businesswomen modeled after styles worn by George Sand, the well-known French author who dressed in men's clothing. The outfit consisted of a matching waistcoat and trousers, a replica of the office man's uniform, and was even more manly than the bloomers that Burnz had worn during the midcentury heyday of woman's rights activists' dress reform.[53]

Not surprisingly, women repudiated such a blatant masculine style. Like the vast majority of nineteenth-century women, female stenographers and columnists rejected nineteenth-century dress reform that advocated their wearing anything resembling pants, including bloomers. Stenographer S. Louise Patteson immediately, but diplomatically, objected to Burnz's cross-dressing design and instead suggested that women dress in skirts. Kathryn Chatoid, editor of the column "The Fem-Sten's Retreat" in the *Typewriter and Phonographic World,* told a story of a "mannish"-dressed woman, outfitted in a "derby hat, habit-black skirt and automobile coat!" who earned "contempt on the faces of those she passed." Although no one dared chastise the well-respected Mrs.

Burnz, they understood the dangers of crossing the line to an overtly masculine look and spurned it.[54]

Instead of making females into masculine clones, women in the shorthand community tried to redefine business as inclusive by maintaining a feminine demeanor in their characterization of the businesswoman. Typical was Mary McCalla's advice in an 1882 letter to the editor.

> [N]ine times out of ten men object to [women stenographers] on account of the "masculine manner" of some. . . . A woman who swings herself into an office and talks loud, thrusting her opinions right and left, is hardly a pleasing companion for women of opposite characteristics; and . . . [makes] herself obnoxious to some legal men by her "mannish ways." There is no reason why a woman of business should lose the gentleness of nature and the unpretending manner which go to make up every true woman . . . but [she should] preserve all the fine edges of womanly nature.[55]

Sixteen years later, women in the "business world" received the same advice: "If she endeavors to be a man, she will be a signal failure." This same article listed admired feminine traits necessary for business: "1. Be modest. 2. Be dignified, but not *prudish.* 3. Be neat. 4. Be thorough. 5. Be prompt. 6. Be obliging."[56]

To soften the businesswoman, women stenographers and their supporters embraced her as a lady. For example, one writer angered by one of many snide articles about typewriter girls rejoined that "the 'type-writer girl' . . . is modest, lady-like, business-like and worthy of all high esteem in the minds of good men and women, but . . . business men as a class, are respectful, dignified, and gentlemanly in their treatment of her. . . . [I]t comes down to a simple matter of business." Jeannette Ballantyne, a frequent speaker at conventions of court reporters, expected the businesswoman to incorporate femininity. She claimed that women "have demonstrated to the world that modesty, gentleness, dignity, and sweet womanliness are not incompatible with a successful reporter's career." In fact, she argued that "women who have been successful at reporting are without exception, essentially feminine," and she said of the businesswoman that "she's a lady." For her and others, businesswomen were ladies, a feminine middle-class definition of business.[57]

As a result, the symbols of the ideal businesswoman's costume resembled the styles of the middle-class lady. Both should be simple, modest, and neat. The clothing, however, took on a new meaning for the businesswoman when she emulated the simple lines of the uncluttered modern design. By avoiding "gay or showy clothes that will attract special attention; shirtwaists of wall paper design . . . eccentric and frivolous [dress]," she could contribute to the image of the office as a place for serious business. By rejecting traditional femininity and working-class fashion, she moved closer to middle-class men, even mirroring the masculine shirt uniform and its black-and-white color scheme. The businesswoman and lady coexisted because one represented equality, the other difference, two conflicting nineteenth- and twentieth-century gender values. By performing as businesswomen, stenographers and typewriters of any class could imagine themselves as serious workers and professionals rather than frivolous typewriter girls. Now, they fit in the middle-class domain.[58]

The Competent Woman Stenographer: The Professional

Since the businesswoman often stood for the professionalism of the office, the words *businesswoman* and *professional* were used interchangeably, though they carried distinct connotations. Speaking before the International Congress of Shorthand Writers in 1882, even before the explosion of women stenographers, Helen T. Pierson mixed terms while articulating the dilemma that women faced: either women were assumed to lack "business capacity," or "they go to the other extreme, and become unwomanly in their efforts to become business-like." Pierson insisted that a woman "takes great pride in her work" and will make fewer errors than men, and she concluded that "I have never met a professional lady who was unfeminine," because such women "are satisfied with being women and good stenographers." She explained, "We admire our stenographic brethren very much . . . but we don't admire them enough to imitate them." Pierson's desire to use the "professional lady" to soften the hard edges of the businesswoman sounds very similar to the blurring of the lady and the businesswoman. However, professionalism offered something different from the businesswoman. The professional value of expertise was refashioned to explain women's new business training; moreover, professional efficiency and service slid easily into traditional feminine qualities of neatness and caring. By situating professionalism within these conventional womanly attributes, the shorthand and popular presses, commercial educators, and female stenographers created a feminine version of the competent stenographer that redefined professional values of expertise, efficiency, and service as respectable. This same softening named women as natural professionals in a way that businesswomen could not.[59]

Slippery ranks and honorific designations, like "expert stenographer" and "expert typewriter," spread easily to women. The term *expert* was used so casually that even a twenty-year-old shorthand writer who had become a teacher was described as such. Like commercial educators and the shorthand press who encouraged this lack of precision, women and men rushed to call themselves experts as soon as they dared. Moreover, men were willing to label women expert typewriter operators, which undoubtedly made it more difficult to limit the term to court reporters.[60]

The increasing involvement of women in formal shorthand training near the end of the century provided a simple means to prove their expertise. Like "trained nurses," formal preparation gave female stenographers an added cache. By 1890, women comprised 60 percent of students in amanuenses courses in business colleges, especially dominating in the cities. For example, the Metropolitan Business College in Chicago reported twenty female and only three male students. The feminization of stenographic education added to an image of women as experts and therefore professionals.[61]

The loose definition of the basic professional criteria of efficiency also made room for women as natural professionals. The characteristic womanly qualities of neatness and orderliness afforded a feminine definition of efficiency. Since respectable women were expected to naturally maintain neat, orderly, and clean homes, the shorthand press often employed the metaphor of office housekeeping to take advantage of these presumed feminine traits, just like female reformers did. In one didactic story, the first woman stenographer in an office with "worn and faded carpet, and the desks strewn with books and papers, dusty and disorderly," brings "order, neatness, efficiency and comfort" to her new workplace. The new amanuensis begins to "clear her desk . . . , dusts . . . tidies the sample table . . . [with] water and a sponge . . . , [put] fresh pens . . . in the holders"; even "the ink stands were washed." The boss, who notices her handiwork, "appreciated order, though like many men, he had no facility for keeping it." The storyteller remarks, "There was now a place for everything."[62]

Teachers, advice columnists, and women stenographers and typewriters themselves embraced female cleanliness, neatness, and order as signs of a superior work ethnic. In a one-sentence paragraph from a symposium on teaching shorthand, Carrie A. Clarke mentioned neatness twice as a requirement for a competent stenographer: "neat typewriting" and "keeping desk, machine and self neat." In another instance, typing gratified typewriting entrepreneur Harriet L. Husted if she completed it without smudges. She loved the order that comes from cleanliness: "Each year I find typewriting more fascinating. I can never get over that glad little thrill of pride which creeps over me, as I put away completed, a neatly written brief, specification or other document, and note its orderly artistic arrangement and clean pages." As early as 1900, advisers encouraged methodically organized practices. "The Fem-Sten's Retreat" in the *Typewriter and Phonographic World,* counseled women on how to "be systematic," for example, by addressing all of the envelopes first, laying out the "circulars" so that "while employed in doing this work of folding and enclosing, [you] will make the fewest movements possible—thus saving time and labor." While such advice culminated in scientific management for the office in the late 1910s and the 1920s, for these women, advice reinforced their professionalism, not the routinization that it would become. Maintaining cleanliness, neatness, and even quiet in the office proved one's capability, a skill that domesticity provided any respectable woman. Even men who challenged women's shorthand abilities accepted their neatness and cleanliness. This feminized efficiency thawed the image of the cold, heartless, and efficient businesswoman, while guaranteeing women's natural professionalism.[63]

The concept of public service provided the most useful means to soften the businesswoman. As early as midcentury, male shorthand promoters and court reporters joined with other professionals in adopting public service as a criterion for professionalism. Benn Pitman's 1855 *Manual of Phonography* touted its preservation and diffusion of knowledge and progress for language and communication, while court reporters continued to boast of their service to the court and humanity. In the 1890s and 1900s, the stenographic and popular press used women's service ethic of caring to feminize the businesswoman as well as portray her as naturally professional. The female ethic of caring, which stemmed from the selfless, nurturing, and domestic woman, transformed the traditionally expected loyalty of the clerk into a feminine sign of business professionalism. As service to large corporations became a new standard, this feminized professional ethic of service tempered women's ambition by balancing equality and independence with respectability.[64]

Business heroines in short stories retained the customary feminine ethic of caring. Nurturance softened an enterprising heroine. In A.H.'s supposed true story "Women and Their Work: Lesson of a Young Woman Stenographer's Career," industrious, ambitious, curious, and self-willed Lou "began to look more and more often into the future" as an employee in Mrs. Sedgwick's copying business. Lou's business skills push her upward. When other employees turn down work because they are too busy, Lou offers to take the jobs if the clients pay hefty overtime costs. Eventually, she becomes a partner and then sole owner of the company. However, the author redefines Lou's triumph as proof of her maternal qualities: "Her profits are now between three and four thousand a year; but it is not by this that she measures her success"; instead, Lou judges her accomplishments by the training of "a hundred girls scattered throughout the city who came to her office ignorant, immature, utterly lacking, and have left it, after an apprenticeship with her, to take good positions, and fill them well." To highlight Lou's nurturing, the author explains that she "has learned how to serve [the world] and cajole it." She proves her femininity as well as her professionalism through service.[65]

To draw credit for women's achievements, stenography magazine fiction carefully merged the vocabulary of business with the feminine ethic of caring. In an Ellis Wood story, three stenographers refuse an overworked bookkeeper's request for assistance, feigning ignorance of "figures" to curtail their employer's unlimited demands. Unlike her coworkers, Miss Houghton, "engineered by her sense of commercial values," agrees to do the extra work, ultimately leading to a promotion. Wood's use of "commercial values" as the key to Miss Houghton's feats, however, masks his real explanation for her willingness "to help." Miss Houghton demonstrates her femininity by exhibiting compassion, selflessness, and helpfulness, unlike her selfish coworkers in their mistaken defense of workers' rights. Again, the author modernized the selfless true woman by couching his advice in the language of commerce.[66]

Service rooted in caring and commercial values also explains other fictional women's successes in the business world. In "The Too Obliging Miss Blake: An Investment That Brought the Amanuensis Rich Returns," Miss Blake also defies her coworkers' advice to limit her work hours. Instead, she spends extra hours, including lunchtime, helping a doddering old woman with her business affairs. When the old woman dies, she leaves thirty thousand dollars to Miss Blake, enough for her to retire from the workforce. Again, the heroine acts on her own for the good of the company, like an antebellum fictional male clerk would have done, except after receiving her well-deserved reward, she quits rather than invest her inheritance in a new business venture. Moreover, the author attributes Miss Blake's success to feminine qualities of compassion and selflessness, not inventiveness, assertiveness, or skill. Even her office critics, who only regard the old woman as "an insufferable bore," recognize Miss Blake as "the kindest, most obliging girl living," who felt "sorry for the poor old thing."[67]

The shorthand press also characterized women stenographers and typewriters who assisted men in subservient positions in the court or office hierarchy as symbols of this new service ethic. E. K. Stevens's heroine in "The Little Typist" assumes the role of helper when she informs her employer, a young and eligible lawyer, "My ambition does not soar to court practice . . . but it would be very nice to join with somebody else, and look up the cases for him to plead." In this case, the ethic of caring limited women to the position of amanuenses. In a piece entitled "An Iowa Girl's Opinion of Female Stenographers" in *Browne's Phonographic Monthly*, G. insisted that "man certainly possesses a better executive ability than woman, and woman's work should in the main, be supplementary." The press often reported about wives and daughters of leading male court reporters who learned from their fathers or husbands and served as their aides: for instance, Martha C. Underhill and Ida Pankhurst assisted their fathers; Eveline T. Underhill, Marion A. Driffil, and Mrs. Wevelt, their husbands. Abbie Pulsifer, who, along with three of her siblings, studied under her father, became a "pioneer lady stenographer" herself.[68] Care and service went hand in hand. Like nurses and teachers, stenographers could be professional and caring women who provided service. Thus, by nurturing employers and customers, women in shorthand distinguished themselves from their male counterparts and prepared for marriage as well.[69]

The shorthand press's definition of service by selfless and caring assistants blended business and respectability for women. This feminine definition of service contrasted female office workers with the frivolous and self-absorbed working girl, while safeguarding the businesswoman from edging too close to mannishness. This version of service also trumpeted the businesswoman as the ideal loyal, even subservient, employee. Like men, women's work benefited their employers, commerce, and the nation. But their service, like their efficiency, came naturally, which furnished proof of women's special, even superior, professionalism. By reframing the professional values of service, efficiency, and expertise in line with respectability, the shorthand press, teachers, and stenographers and typewriters themselves created a feminine professional. The same traits that men used to exclude women now became a means for their inclusion.[70]

CONCLUSION

To justify respectable female work, women stenographers in business and the courts, the shorthand press, and educators extended the long-standing middle-class appreciation of female independence in the personal arena to the economic sphere as central to the New Woman. At the end of the nineteenth century, the stenographic community constructed shorthand and typing as examples of economic opportunity for ambitious women. Female stenographers and typewriters appeared autonomous from their families, supporting themselves, and possessed economic aspirations for a job or a career.

Once employed, these ambitious women would need to prove their competence. To narrow the definition of incompetence, female educators especially tried to restrict the negative characteristics of the incompetents to working-class women, instead of all women. For respectable women, the shorthand community supplemented the discourse of the lady with the masculine terminology of the businesswoman to announce women's equality to men and reinforce the middle-class image of the clerical woman. However, the more women appeared like men, the more they seemed cold, unemotional, and manly. Hence, the stenographic community, especially female teachers, stenographers, and typewriters, blended the businesswoman and the lady, claiming professionalism for women. Now, they blurred professionalism with conventional femininity. Service became feminine caring, efficiency became neatness, and expertise became training, all of which made professionalism the new balance for working women. Performing professionalism, however, affirmed this equilibrium, as chapter 7 will explore.

CHAPTER 7

Performances of Professionalism

In early August 1892, the Indiana State Stenographers' Association met for its fourth annual meeting in the "parlors of the Denison House." Despite the absence of many of the "most active members," numerous local stenographers attended. The first day began with a welcome address from Professor L. H. Jones, superintendent of the city schools, followed by a response from Miss Jennie T. Masson. The president of the association, W. S. Garber, delivered an annual talk critiquing the use of the phonograph by court reporters as well as discussing the shorthand notes in Samuel Pepys's diary. As usual, letters were read from prominent stenographers not in attendance. The evening session also followed a common practice of interspersing professional papers with entertainment, beginning with the "Clayton's Grand March" performed by the Coplan Brothers, then an essay entitled "What Constitutes a Successful Stenographer," followed by a violin and piano duet by Mr. J. N. Coplan and Miss A. Marks. Two whistling solos and a vocal solo flanked commentaries by W. E. McDermut on "outlines of words" and Jennie Masson's "Essay on Man."[1]

A major theme of the conference appeared the next day, when J. D. Strachan proposed establishing a national organization, after which a committee was appointed to draw up resolutions on the World's Fair Congress for the next year. Letters and papers from Dan Brown and George B. Lockwood on the same topic generated lots of discussion again. The afternoon was devoted to socializing, as everyone rode the electric cars to Armstrong's Park for boating and other activities, paid for by the typewriter agents and official reporters of the city. The convention wound down after an "elegant lunch" at the hotel at five o'clock. When the participants realized that many of the members could not return the next day, they conducted the business of electing officers (W. S. Garber as president, W. E. McDermut as vice president, George B. Lockwood as secretary, Jennie T. Masson as treasurer) and adjourned the convention.[2]

Professional meetings, like this one in Indiana, became popular among male and female court reporters and amanuenses in the 1880s and 1890s. Along with a handful of unions, they addressed grievances about salaries, competition, and bogus schools. They made efforts to lift members above the crowd by baring and marginalizing their competition (incompetents) and promoting mutuality. However, court reporters and stenographers in general rejected unions and instead preferred associations that reinforced an identity as middle-class professionals whose activities centered around studying, practicing, socializing, and protecting their interests. Despite these similarities, the associations' aims and styles differed. Court reporters, most of whom were men, sought to validate their middle-class identity, elevating themselves above ordinary stenographers by institutionalizing a meritocracy based on middle-class values of the expert. Newer stenographers, many of whom were women, pursued the professional associations for skill and job advancement. Even with these differences, professionalism legitimized their work ethic and marked them all as competent and ambitious.

All of the professional organizations provided a middle-class identity for their members through new gendered balances by acting out respectability in the context of professionalism. By performing professionalism, men could retain the more feminine refinement associated with the middle and upper classes while confirming their masculine expertise and elevating themselves above the masses. Since both men and women participated in these performances at clubhouses and annual meetings, the femininity of respectability opened another avenue to professionalism for women, while containing women's participation to traditional gendered practices. Through professional associations, women could enact the refashioned middle-class working woman, the professional who blended the manly businesswoman with conventional femininity.

UNIONS

Beginning in the late 1870s, with the rise of the Knights of Labor, unions seemed a likely choice for protecting stenographic interests. Small numbers of shorthand writers and typewriters organized unions, some affiliated with the

Knights of Labor, others associated with the American Federation of Labor, and still others operating on their own. Male stenographers hoped to redress their grievances by excluding the least skilled and institutionalizing themselves at the top of a hierarchy. However, court reporters who wrote to the shorthand press disapproved of unions, which symbolized confrontation in the 1880s and 1890s between working-class labor and capital, a condition that middle-class stenographers deplored.

From the 1870s on, some writers of shorthand and then typewriters engaged in limited union activity. During the heyday of the Knights of Labor, small groups of stenographers joined with them at least twice. Even more union activity appeared in the mid-1880s and especially in the early 1890s. In 1886, A. B. Reid of Chicago issued a pamphlet calling for a National Union of Stenographers, and on 7 May 1890, in Cincinnati, Ohio, the Order of Railway and Transportation Stenographers (OR&TS) inaugurated its charter for stenographers employed with the railroad, mail, or steamboat lines. In the midst of the crushing 1890s depression, on 9 November 1894, twenty-five men and ten women met in St. Joseph, Missouri, to form the National American Union of Stenographers and Typewriters. Two years later, the Local Stenographers' Protective Union No. 6456 reorganized its American Federation of Labor charter. Women also organized the Women's Stenographers' and Typewriters' Union of New York and Its Vicinity in 1891.[3]

Although historians know very little about these nineteenth-century shorthand and typewriter unions, we do know that they expressed many of stenographers' and typewriters' common concerns, especially about maintaining salaries. An 1875 union organized like a guild to keep income up. In 1890 OR&TS, like other unions, tried to "establish and maintain a proper scale of salaries." In 1886, the National Union of Stenographers (NUS) also planned to establish uniform wage rates and an eight-hour workday, with double time for Sunday or overtime work, similar to the goals of organized railway clerks. NUS's manual of rules and regulations set a scale of prices of one hundred dollars per month for senior male stenographers and seventy-five dollars for senior females; seventy-five dollars for junior male stenographers and fifty dollars for junior females as well as expert typewriters; and fifty dollars for male apprentice stenographers and forty dollars for females.[4]

These unions also dealt with another common complaint voiced by shorthand writers. They sought to minimize competition and maximize the number of jobs. The OR&TS forbade members to "teach the art of stenography to any person without permission, in writing, from the chief Stenographer of the division, and the consent of the Grand Chief Stenographer." Members must disavow any connection "with any instrument or invention . . . for the purpose of taking or recording dictation." To limit the number of apprentices and still promote shorthand education, the NUS critiqued "bogus professors" and called for boycotts of "scab" schools that it did not certify.[5]

Other than attempting to redress these typical union grievances, these unions also offered mutual assistance and fellowship for the shorthand community. Stenographic unions embraced the language of fraternal associations and trade unions. Union members signed letters with "Fraternally Yours" and referred to "scabs," "rats," "fair rate of wages," "boycott," "arbitration," and an "eight-hour day." At times, some spoke like members of craft unions, encouraging "that fraternal feeling" and willingness to "extend a helping hand, to a brother." The NUS's call for hiring halls recognized shorthand writers' interest in establishing places where members could congregate and find employment. Modeled after fraternal associations and Knights of Labor practices, the OR&TS chose passwords for visiting members and designed emblems and insignias: officers wore a badge of white silk ribbon with the logo "OR&TS," the symbols of a pen and a locomotive, and "Grand Division, Cincinnati, Ohio" stamped in gold; local members' insignia were trimmed in silver; grand officers donned "helmets . . . with the initiation of their office in gold."[6]

Women in New York City organized a single-sex union that was affiliated with the American Federation of Labor and that shared the typical concerns about salaries, shady schools, self-help, and fellowship. On 22 April 1891, about seventy-five women met "to discuss the present unsatisfactory condition of the progression of stenography and type-writing and to devise measures for the betterment of the women employed as amanuenses." Edward F. Underhill, an official stenographer and president of the Metropolitan Stenographers' Association of New York City, "urged the women to organize like workingmen to raise the standard of the profession." At the meeting, the gathered women formed the Women's Stenographers' and Typewriters' Union of New York and Its Vicinity, where they criticized "bogus" professors and proposed a trade union for "bread and butter unionism," especially improved salaries, along with a mutual aid society for self-improvement. Underhill may have encouraged these women to form a union as a means to raise their salaries, since men worried that low female wages undercut their own. Their next meeting convened at rooms of the American Federation of Labor where they had invited Samuel Gompers to speak.[7]

Most union goals should have appealed principally to the elite legal stenographers and court reporters. The unions balanced an appearance of inclusion while still privileging the most experienced. For example, the OR&TS's charter specifically extended membership to "ladies" but restricted it by age, race, experience, and examination. Membership was open to those seventeen years or older, white, and "actually employed as a stenographer" for one or more years with one of the railroad, mail, or steamboat lines. Members had to pass an examination of at least one hundred words per minute or win approval by the grand secretary and treasurer. The OR&TS's clause excluding nonwhites may have been copied from railroad unions concerned about the Chinese and African Americans, since nowhere else did stenographers mention race as a criterion. Speed provisos appealed to the goal of barring incompetents. The NUS also established an open-door policy but with an elitist bias. The union welcomed all "practical stenographers and machine experts (male and female), known to be competent workers and of good character."[8] But it also intended to license stenographers and typewriters, which would institutionalize rankings within the occupations by dividing them into three classes based on experience and would set salaries accordingly; first-class female stenographers would receive 25 percent less than equally skilled men. A seemingly open door actually fixed hierarchies, marginalizing women and the less experienced.[9]

Stenographers and typewriters would have appreciated these union goals of raising salaries, limiting competitors, licensing schools, and providing fellowship. They certainly must have approved of the periodic use of the language of professionalization, like the NUS's repeated references to its members' "profession."[10] Even outspoken critics of unions acknowledged their support of "associations of stenographers . . . for legitimate purposes" and borrowed union language, like the phrase "in union there is strength" and the salutation "Fraternally Yours." Nonetheless, unions drew very little support among stenographers in the nineteenth century. For stenographers, the working-class identity of unions undermined their appeal.[11]

Unions' willingness to confront employers, despite efforts to avoid strikes, drove stenographers away. The OR&TS, like other Knights of Labor unions, discouraged work stoppages and prohibited sympathy strikes. In their bylaws, the NUS promised to "protect . . . just and honorable employers" and pledged "no strike or boycott . . . until arbitration has failed" and "after secret ballot votes." Even with these provisions to avert strikes, the NUS still prepared for inevitable conflict by drafting a system of strike assessments and benefits. The NUS planned to establish a "Lodge" for every group of six or more workers in a city, with a "Chairman," to "adjust . . . differences that may arise between employer and employes [*sic*]." For each company, the union members would choose an office chief, similar to a union representative, in expectation of a confrontation with employers.[12]

This fundamental strategy of confrontation for addressing complaints lost stenographers' support. Court reporters especially disapproved because they still controlled much of their work environment, determining their own hours and even hiring their own staff. As a result, they worried less about employers than about competitors for their jobs and sought to influence legislatures to increase their payment, as seen in chapter 3. Male amanuenses also identified with employers, expecting advancement. J. S. Rogers complained to the *Phonographic World* about the NUS, "How many of us would like to have our employer think that we . . . , his right-hand and mouth-piece—. . . on whom he relies is likely at any time to 'strike' and perhaps assist in 'boycotting' him?"[13] Even those approving of union organizing insisted on nonconfrontational associations. One called for "an inoffensive trade union," while lambasting the failure of strikes.[14] Another warned stenographers to "organize quietly," without the knowledge of businessmen, and to "quietly withdraw" when employers resist wage requests, with no demands, no mediation, no confrontation.[15]

Stenographers also shared middle-class fears of proletarianization. They perceived of strikes and unions as working-class activities that undermined their hard-fought respectability. J. S. Rogers admonished, "Whoever heard of a first-class stenographer 'striking,' or who in the profession would want such a thing. . . . Perish the thought . . . that the term 'Union Stenographer,' 'Scab Stenographer' . . . maybe applied." The New York State Stenographers' Association (NYSSA) denounced as an "insult" the NUS belief that trade unionism could be applied to them. Some shorthand writers objected to the NUS provision that allowed them to "act in concert with other trade organizations." Arkansas court reporter G. E. Rider registered his disgust that stenographers "descend to the level of tailors, plumbers, barbers, hod carriers." He asked, "When hod carriers go on strike, are we going to strike, too, out of sympathy?" Despite his own interest in organizing, Rider pleaded with the "more respectable" members of the profession, "in the name of decency," to stop these people from "forming . . . associations on the trades-union basis" or "change the name of their calling."[16]

Stenographers were not alone among the new middle class in privileging a professional identity over unionization. Retail salesclerks, telegraphers, telephone operators, and railway clerks shared similar views, but more joined unions. Retail clerks also identified with employers, preferred professional associations, and feared that unions undermined their respectability. Despite struggling to attract members, 5 to 10 percent of retail clerks still managed to organize. Salesclerks for department stores, telegraphers, telephone operators, and railway clerks may have found it easier to organize at fewer locations than the multiple sites for other salesclerks and stenographers. Still, at times, even salesclerks in disparate establishments unionized through consumer boycotts, especially in the early 1890s and 1900s. They also may have joined unions more readily because they all worked in a single business sector, unlike male stenographers dispersed in positions with railroads, insurance companies, industry, professionals, and government and expecting to leave shorthand if they did not become reporters.[17]

Without such conditions promoting shorthand trade unionization, male stenographers and the shorthand press, with its self-employed editors, fell back on common middle-class values about laissez-faire and upward mobility in their criticism of unions. The *Phonographic World* which had in the past maligned shorthand unions, specifically lambasted the NUS for its stand on uniform wage rates. Connecticut stenographer William H. Browne accused unions of false "attempt[s] to restrict or impede the natural order of things." He insisted that "the price of labor cannot be regulated . . . other . . . than by the law of supply and demand." With absolute faith in merit, individualism, upward mobility, and survival of the fittest, he asserted, "The really competent man will always receive good pay . . . while the great majority will never rise above mediocrity. . . . The best will rise to the top." The editor concurred, "We have never yet known a good stenographer who was not abundantly able to protect himself."[18]

Although some nineteenth-century stenographers wished to address their grievances in unison, they generally disapproved of using trade unions for that form of collective action. Business stenographers had difficulty organizing and did not want to confront employers, with whom they identified. Moreover, the more independent court reporters preferred to concentrate on limiting competition and lobbying state legislatures. Unions surely reminded all shorthand writers of the growing Irish radical labor activity in the 1880s, which coincided with the rising Irish population in the offices. Unionization, they feared, would lead to exactly the process they feared, proletarianization.[19]

MULTIPLE PERFORMANCES OF PROFESSIONALISM

Instead of aligning with unions and their implicit working-class solidarity and protest, court reporters and business stenographers affiliated with middle-class professional associations. They formed professional organizations that differed in class orientation and strategies and also promised to deliver middle-class respect. While unions generally stood up to employers in solidarity with "plumbers" and "hod carriers," professional associations presumed fellowship with doctors and lawyers as well as employers, who evoked the autonomy, power, and respect characteristic of the iconic antebellum self-made man. Instead of challenging employers, professionals sought to maintain salaries and limit competition through government regulation and self-policing and to provide fellowship. The professional organization appeared a promising means to achieve economic goals and institutionalize a middle-class representation of an occupation, at the same time that unions were losing power to the growing corporations and the professionalization mania infected diverse occupations, like engineers, historians, and nurses.[20]

Stenographers and typewriters mirrored the professional drives of other late nineteenth-century occupations by joining together at local, state, regional, national, and international levels. Their early societies began in the 1870s and flourished in the 1880s and 1890s. As early as 1873, the Law Stenographers' Association of the City of New York was founded. Then, in 1876, the New York State Law Stenographers' Association began, becoming the NYSSA in 1876, which continued with name changes to today. By 1889, many others had built local organizations in cities—including Council Bluffs, Iowa; Omaha, Nebraska; Wichita, Kansas; Cleveland, Ohio; Portland, Oregon; Syracuse, New York; Boston, Philadelphia, and New York City—while Nebraska, Indiana, Missouri, Ohio, New York, and other states housed their own societies. New Englanders erected regional organizations, the New England Shorthand Writers' Association in 1883 and the New England Shorthand Reporters' Association (NESRA) in 1890, although some of the societies had difficulty remaining in tact in the 1890s. Attempts to sustain international associations, like the World Congress of Stenographers, floundered, while women, African Americans, students, and alumni launched their own organizations. In 1899, professionalization culminated in a national stenographic organization, the National Shorthand Reporters' Association, predecessor to the National Court Reporters Association.[21]

Historians and sociologists studying professionalization have often stressed the elitism of self-policing and licensing designed to exclude competitors who did not meet self-defined educational or training requirements. They have shown how professional self-definition grew from tensions between related occupations, such as accountants' efforts to distinguish themselves from bookkeepers, as well as contentions between competing emerging professionals, like mechanical and civil engineers. Scholarship on nursing exposes a split between elite nurses and nursing educators who wanted to professionalize, on the one hand, and the resisting rank and file, on the other—a conflict not so different from the amanuenses' periodic resentment of court reporters. However, even among those performing similar work, different approaches could develop. Rival accounting organizations emerged in response to different understandings of expertise and varying strategies for professionalization between education, state certification, and self-regulation. Like other professionalizing occupations, court reporters experimented with and at times disagreed about approaches for professionalization, but unlike other callings, the lower-ranked amanuenses also formed professional associations. Together, stenographers reveal more varied meanings of professionalism.[22]

In some ways, court reporters' professionalization came close to duplicating that of other occupations. Large proportions of official court reporters and private legal stenographers organized small, exclusive organizations by states, regions, and nation-states and even internationally. Moreover, their goals and tactics conformed to the typical professional model, seeking to regulate, limit, and contain the less skilled stenographers, especially the working class and women.

In contrast to this standard model of professionalization, business stenographers also joined local associations. These organizations of mainstream shorthand writers centered in cities, such as New York's four local groups. Some attracted hundreds, like the Chicago Stenographers' Association, with 307 members. Unlike the court reporters' associations, these organizations concentrated more on self-improvement and employment opportunities, welcoming, more than excluding, potential members. Some seemed similar to the working girls' clubs organized by middle-class women reformers, even naming themselves clubs, rather than associations; however, others behaved more like elite organizations by limiting membership. Most accepted male dominance of their public face. Because of the varied styles of professional organizations, they attracted a wide range of stenographers, all of whom sought respect through professionalization.[23]

Marking Competent Stenographers

While court reporters and business stenographers organized differently, they shared similar approaches about gendered leadership. Court reporters behaved like other middle-class professionals by self-policing, lobbying for state regulation, and encouraging class and gender exclusivity, although disagreeing about strategies. In contrast, the more mainstream stenographic professional associations set lower standards and accepted a wider range of members. Although the numbers and participation of women grew in all organizations, their involvement centered more on the private, rather than the public, face of the organizations.

Court reporters and legal stenographers led the drive for professionalization through organizational self-policing and state regulation. They set their own pay schedules and lobbied for state approval. The NYSSA's, for example, specified salary gradations "where compensation is not fixed by statute," such as "notetaking and transcription at 25 cents per folio . . . attendance—no notes $5 per day." By drafting legislation and testifying at government hearings, they turned to the government to enforce their preferred pay schedules. They also set rigid criteria for members and then lobbied legislatures for licenses to limit the number of court stenographers to those who met certain skill specifications, marking the experts and excluding the incompetents.[24]

Legal stenographers pressured courts to adopt uniform exams to test the abilities of potential court reporters, although they disagreed on whether lawyers, phonography professors, reporters, or associations should do the testing and whether shorthand writers other than court reporters should also be ranked. As early as 1873, California required testing of 140 words per minute for reporters. NYSSA president Edward B. Dickinson, the status-anxious court reporter discussed in chapter 3, led the charge by presenting a bill before the New York State Legislature to require exams for all new court reporters and to distinguish between the amanuensis and the expert. The *Phonographic World* called for license renewal every two years for court reporters and official stenographers of committees and professional organizations.[25]

In 1898, Massachusetts instituted an extensive assessment of court reporters, when a vacancy became available and the judge found it difficult to appoint a successor. A judge and two official court reporters, Frank H. Burt and Cora Elisabeth Burbank, evaluated candidates over a period of three evenings. On the first night, the judge tested applicants at 125 words per minute, which required transcription. That same night, two more examinations were given: one employed medical terminology and required a typed transcript; another entailed reading back sections of a third, five-minute exam. Day two consisted of a battery of tests in spelling, punctuation, composition, writing, testimony, definition of legal words, general knowledge, and culture. On the third evening, candidates took a half hour of testimony and then transcription, which were compared to Burt's notes. Such state regulation of competition mirrored practices in other contemporary professions.[26]

Professional organizations also sought to police themselves and certify competent stenographers. They all expected to bar incompetents but disagreed about whom they should include. Should they only organize expert stenographers, like the American Federation of Labor's representation of craft workers? Or should they adopt a more inclusive policy, like industrial unions or the Knights of Labor, to pressure amanuenses to demand higher standards?[27]

An example of the debate over the two strategies occurred in 1893, at a meeting of the newly founded Universal Association of Stenographers. Secretary J. Gale Needham took visitor Colonel Dickinson to task for his "supercilious spirit in referring to the amanuenses and their connection with the Association, and especially [for] slurr[ing] the fair members of the profession, whom he grouped as a class of incompetents." Members blamed Dickinson's attitude for "the failure to take . . . [amanuenses] in as co-operators in the work." Dickinson insisted that "he had the greatest . . . respect for the office workers, but that he did not consider that the reporters . . . would join with them in this work."[28]

The "Universalists" wanted "a national association . . . of stenographers, phonographers, typewriter operators, typewritists, and all worthy members of the profession." They distinguished among their members, requiring 175 words per minute for "reporters" and 125 words per minute for "all other practicing stenographers." However, when they could not draw enough participants, they temporarily suspended some requirements. Others shared the Universalist's approach. A writer to *Browne's Phonographic Weekly* proposed a three-tiered system of pupils, associates, and full-fledged members, each taking more difficult tests and needing more extensive educational training, culminating in a B.A. diploma or equivalent examination.[29] This plan would reify the leadership of the middle-class stenographers in the profession by keeping out the "pretenders and illiterates," raising the status of the "well-trained responsible stenographer," and "placing . . . our calling where it righteously belongs, with . . . the 'learned professions.'"[30]

Despite these differences in strategies, the more geographically broad associations remained the most selective. When the National Shorthand Reporters' Association (NSRA) formed in 1899, it embraced exclusivity to "advanc[e] the interests of the deserving stenographers, and elevat[e] as a whole the common profession." The NSRA imposed rigorous membership standards, inviting only official court reporters or legislative reporters with three years' experience in law reporting or those who could maintain a speed of 150 words per minute for five consecutive minutes on a test. In other words, only a few of the most expert business stenographers were welcome and joined. Of the 147 charter members, nearly 70 percent of the men and 44 percent of the women worked as legal or legislative reporters, with many of the others as teachers (see appendix, table E1).[31]

Like the NSRA, state and regional elite associations also primarily attracted court reporters and legal stenographers who policed their members and lobbied for favorable legislation. Of the fifty-one members of the New England Shorthand Reporters' Association (NESRA) in 1900, two-thirds were current or former official court reporters or law stenographers, nearly identical to the NSRA founders (see appendix, table E1). Others were stenography teachers, authors, and editors. Like the NSRA, they adopted speed tests to bar novices and slower stenographers and elevate experienced shorthand writers. The Chicago Law Stenographers' Association went even further to defend its members' interests and ward off others. In pursuit of "mutual protection," the fifteen members agreed to submit to an examination and transfer work only to each other. This exclusivity did not differ much from the desires of shorthand unions to limit apprentices or neophytes.[32]

Besides these elite organizations, there were other, more mainstream and often local professional associations, usually with less-restrictive membership provisions. New York shorthand writers could choose from five organizations, including one in an outlying borough and one at the state level: the Stenographers' Association of the City of New York (1890), the Metropolitan Stenographers' Association of New York City (1885), the Brooklyn Stenographers' Association (1890), the Harlem Stenographic Association, and the NYSSA. Except for the last, these organizations were much more likely to attract business stenographers. While the statewide NYSSA (originally known as the New York State Law Stenographers' Association) imposed a speed test of 150 words per minute, the local Metropolitan Stenographers' Association was open to anyone. Other local groups of rookies welcomed all writers of shorthand, in St. Paul, Minnesota; Trenton, New Jersey; and Queen City, Cincinnati.[33]

Some mainstream organizations did establish minimum criteria, while still attracting beginners and business stenographers. For example, the Stenographers Club of Chicago invited stenographers with six months' experience to become active members and those merely interested in shorthand to join as associates. The Boston Shorthand Club, formed in 1893, divided its participants into active, associate, and honorary. Active members needed either six months' employment experience or passage of a speed test of "ninety words per minute for five consecutive minutes and correctly transcribing the same." The New Orleans Phonographic Association prescribed a speed test of one hundred words per minute or "employment as a stenographer for six consecutive months" for new members.[34]

The membership requirements of these mainstream professional associations resembled those of the working girls' clubs, founded by middle-class women to help employed women. One of the working girls' clubs, the New Century Club of Working Women (also known as the New Century Guild of Working Women), which targeted women in the higher-skilled and better-paid positions, gave birth to a stenographic association in October 1888. Like the mainstream shorthand professional associations, this offshoot of the New Century Club aimed at the average stenographer. The association expected full members to "write at least eighty words per minute," while associate members "need have only a knowledge of shorthand." These provisions echoed the many local professional associations that either established no speed standards at all or set them between 90 and 100 words per minute, in contrast to the elite National Shorthand Reporters' Association's stipulation of 150 words per minute for enrollment. Both working girls' clubs and local associations tried to institute professional standards, while remaining inclusive. The New Century Club's low provision of eighty words per minute reflected its membership of typical business stenographers, as did its depressed base salary demands of "no less than $8 per week" to "keep prices up," a guideline that fit well within common wage rates, especially for novices.[35]

In addition to technical provisos, all professional associations shared a middle-class bias: class and gender composition differed between the elite and mainstream organizations. Many organizations inserted into their bylaws a boilerplate clause calling for "good character." These laws were meant to assert the respectability of the participants and exclude incompetents, similar to the bylaws of the National Union of Stenographers. Even more significantly, but not surprisingly, the prestigious associations admitted fewer people with Irish, German, or Russian surnames than the mainstream organizations. For example, the NESRA, whose many court reporters met rigorous skill specifications for membership, included only 11 percent with Irish or German names among its 52 members in 1900. Conversely, 20 percent of the 157 members of the more open Chicago Stenographers' Association had ethnic surnames in 1889. These organizations did attract different groups of stenographers, but both were limited to a narrow sector of the clerical population, a more middle-class segment.

If the Chicago Stenographers' Association reflected the proportion of first- and second-generation clerical workers in the city, 68 percent, not 20 percent, of the women's names would have been ethnic. Even the more accessible organizations, like the Chicago Stenographers' Association or the Brooklyn Stenographers' Association, attracted a relatively privileged enrollment.[36]

In all of the organizations, women's numbers and acceptance grew over time. The earliest were all-male clubs. At an 1879 meeting of the Chicago Stenographers' Association at which all twenty-two participants were male, one speaker reminisced, to the laughter of the audience, about a celebrated fellow stenographer who in 1868 "ogled the pretty girls." Another member referred to "the ladies" as "an enigma, a puzzle," then recounted Eve's fall in Eden because "she invested in fruit; fruit suddenly went down, and . . . [she] was [left] without a cent in her pocket," concluding, "If she had remained in her proper sphere as wife and mother, and let business alone, I truly believe there would not today be a single sin, sorrow or Jew clothing house in this world." Ultimately, M. H. Dement confessed, "I do not like the idea of woman adopting our profession," nor probably Jews either. As late as 1889, the newly founded NESRA chose all male officers but began to acknowledge women's presence in the occupation. When the incoming president, James M. W. Yerrinton, repeatedly addressed the audience as "Gentlemen," he caught himself by saying, "When I say 'man,' I include his sister woman." By their second annual meeting in 1892, two women (possibly wives) were listed in attendance and a third as a member. Only eight years later, at the turn of the century, women made up over one-third of the membership. At an 1899 meeting, W. L. Haskell corrected Frank H. Burt's reference to the "men" behind the different shorthand systems by adding, "And the women!"[37]

By the late 1880s, all of the organizations officially welcomed women, while some treated them as less than equal to the men. Many charged women reduced fees to encourage their membership since low rates, in general, did spur female participation. The NYSSA's half-off discount fees for women, at six dollars per year for residents and three dollars for nonresidents, corresponded with its two-thirds female membership, as did the Trenton Stenographers' Association's much lower fee of ten cents per month plus a low twenty-five-cent initiation fee. Although the membership and fee structures may have encouraged women's involvement, they also declared women as inferiors.[38]

Despite women's growing presence in all organizations, fewer belonged in the elite associations. Their participation thinned as the organizations grew more geographically disparate. Men held all forty-one offices and executive committee posts representing each state at the founding of the National Shorthand Reporters' Association (NSRA) in 1899. Women made up only 11.9 percent of its 176 charter members, about their share of court reporters, dropping to 8.6 percent in 1904. Conversely, they comprised 36.5 percent of the regional New England Shorthand Reporters' Association in 1900 and even more of the local associations: 57 percent of the Chicago Stenographers' Association in 1889 and 65 percent of the NYSSA in 1890.[39]

Contributing to the gender imbalance in the elite organizations were membership policies that privileged elite men. Two- or three-tiered plans, with associates and regular members, often distinguished notable court reporters and legal stenographers from the others. For example, while the NESRA expected all members to write at "150 words per minute for five consecutive minutes and read the same correctly," the rules were waived for those of "known ability and standing," the eminent men. There would be no embarrassment for the leading men in the field, some of whom no longer practiced shorthand but taught or edited periodicals. Moreover, men, unlike women, were invited to attend conferences from outside their state; 36 percent of men at the NYSSA annual meeting in 1887 came from out of state.[40]

Despite these differing membership profiles, men monopolized the public face in both elite and mainstream organizations, while women participated more in private functions. A typical pattern took place in 1889, when fifty or more stenographers met in New Orleans, at the request of two women and three men, to form a professional association. At the meeting, a fourth man temporarily chaired the meeting and proposed that another man take his place. After he refused, a different man assumed the chair. No woman ever received the nod, despite the musical chairs and women's leadership in organizing the association. However, women were not ignored but instead nominated to the constitution committee. The two female cofounders became the only women considered for the seven elected positions, Miss Edith Brown as first vice president and Miss Breeden as assistant secretary. In many organizations, few women held elective offices, except for librarian, the lower-level offices, or sometimes second vice president. Periodically, they also organized social activities.[41]

At their annual conventions, where elite organizations paraded their public face, men overwhelmingly overshadowed women. Men gave the speeches and toasts and were treated as the real audience. The few women speakers talked about either female stenographers or their specialized area of interest; for example, Eliza Boardman Burnz advocated spelling reform. The NYSSA and its successor, the New York State Shorthand Reporters' Association, invited only ten different women out of 104 presenters for their annual conventions from 1876 to 1912, even though women stenographers comprised 25 percent of the attendees as early as 1886. Of those women lecturers, eight spoke only once; two of these discussed women stenographers. Burnz addressed the association seven times, at least on four occasions about spelling reform. Jeannette Ballantyne spoke eleven times, with four of her early talks being primarily about women. After establishing herself, she moved on to other topics. When Burnz died in 1903 and Ballantyne quit speaking in 1906, nine years before her death, conferences frequently did not hear from any female speakers.[42]

Women's public face in the more mainstream associations was more mixed. They more frequently held public leadership positions. Some organizations chose women presidents, like the Cooperstown Shorthand Writers' League in Pennsylvania in 1891. Women dominated major positions in a few others, like the Oakland Stenographic Club, whose president, ex-president, vice president, secretary, and treasurer in 1886 were all female. However, even in the mainstream associations with large female membership, men eclipsed women as the public face of the profession. For example, in 1891, men occupied the most visible posts of president, vice president, and secretary in the Trenton Stenographers' Association, even though thirty-seven of the fifty-three members, over two-thirds, were women. Trenton women served many posts—as corresponding secretary, recording secretary, and treasurer—and dominated the membership committee and the auditing committee, but not the leading assignments. In another public ritual of leadership, when a delegation from the Metropolitan Stenographers' Association, an organization with many women, formally met with Philadelphia stenographers, all fifteen of the New Yorkers were men.[43]

All of the associations favored the mostly male members of the shorthand community, like prominent court reporters, legal stenographers, and business school proprietors. The many inside jokes, toasts at conferences, poems, stories, and hagiographies in the trade journals attest to the renown of some local and national figures. One stenographer wrote a love story with names of Chicago's high-profile reporters. All types of organizations featured court reporters, legal stenographers, and business school proprietors as keynote speakers and honored guests. The Brooklyn Stenographers' Association invited over three hundred of the "most prominent members of the 'profesh'" in the city to their 1892 annual meeting. A year later, they proudly printed complementary letters from court reporters with national reputations. Even at local meetings of the mainstream organizations, male court reporters took center stage. The Metropolitan Stenographers' Association of New York City touted its benefits by boasting of "the reading of papers by such well-known stenographers as George R. Bishop, Edward B. Dickinson, Edward F. Underhill, John R. Potts." Not surprisingly, no women's names graced this august crowd. Undoubtedly, women, too, gave papers at the local meetings, but only men merited advertising.[44]

The attitudes and motivations of the male leadership suggests some of this masculine bias. Some male leaders in the mainstream organizations shared similar views with the elite court reporters, encouraging young stenographers to join to raise the salaries of amanuenses.[45] Moreover, a president of the Brooklyn association revealed his paternalism for the rank and file by referring to them as "toilers" in need of "recreation and diversion." President W. P. Charles hoped their new clubhouse would give the "advantages of home" to those who left the "paternal home."[46]

The elitism of these officers reflects not only the variations within and between stenography associations but also some of their shared goals and practices. The prestigious state, regional, and national organizations focused more on safeguarding the occupation by limiting access through weeding out and segregating members with lower skill levels. These elite professional associations lobbied governments and restricted and ranked membership, unlike the mainstream associations, with their more inclusive policies. However, both types of organizations shared an interest in raising salaries and marginalizing the incompetents, often the working class and especially women, by privileging male court reporters' leadership and authority as the public face of the profession.

Making Competent Stenographers

The degree of inclusiveness reveals the agenda of the professional associations. Elite organizations primarily emphasized the elevation of the profession. Mainstream societies sometimes borrowed the same language but mostly sought to prepare individuals for employment and advancement, through self-improvement and access to information about job opportunities.

Like accountants' groups, the elite shorthand organizations were more likely than mainstream associations to use the language of late nineteenth-century professionalism in their bylaws. For example, the NESRA sought "to secure the maintenance of a proper standard of efficiency" as an objective in its constitution. Other constitutions, like those of the National Shorthand Reporters' Association and New York State Law Stenographers' Association (eventually the NYSSA), used similar language. However, even the middling Stenographers' Association of Western Pennsylvania called for the "recognition [of shorthand] as a scientific profession." So did the Colored Stenographers' League of Baltimore City, which sought to promote the "science of stenography and typewriting."[47]

While, at times, mainstream organizations of stenographers also called for elevating the profession, they joined together primarily for self-improvement and self-help. The Boston Shorthand Writers Association was founded in 1883 for "mutual benefit in shorthand dictation and practice." The Boston Shorthand Club's 1893 preamble called for "mutual improvement, sociability, unity, and harmony of feeling, with a view to combine our efforts for the practical maintenance of proficiency in the stenographic profession." Twenty shorthand writers formed the Oakland Stenographic Club in 1886 to increase their speed and accuracy by devoting their time to dictating and reading notes. The Metropolitan Stenographers' Association of New York City wanted a "common meeting place" to hone their skills, arguing that "those whose daily work calls for only a restricted vocabulary, and perhaps, a slow rate of speed, need opportunities for familiarizing themselves with new outlines, and acquiring greater rapidity in writing." With this as their goal, they set aside rooms for drilling every evening. This practice set them apart from the professionalism of court reporters and the theoretical works of accountants who sought to train and an elite cadre in the 1880s and 1890s. At times, they went beyond teaching speed, instead holding meetings for self-improvement where well-known stenographers read professional papers. Some locals, such as in Omaha and Chicago, met once per week; others, such as in Boston, convened monthly; state associations assembled yearly. The Metropolitan Stenographers' Association of New York City also held weekly literary society meetings. By attending the meetings, beginners might pick up professional tips from the more experienced members. The societies also housed libraries with shorthand reference materials, books, and periodicals. Stenographers believed that all of these resources prepared novices for more challenging and better-paying jobs. Organizations, like the Metropolitan Association of New York City, often served as employment agencies. In 1891, the National Association of Women Stenographers provided both employment services and sick and death benefits. Members paid a monthly fee of twenty-five cents, fifty cents, or one dollar, entitling them to $3.50, $7.00, or $15.00 per week, respectively, in sick payments.[48]

These associations—especially those, like the Brooklyn Stenographers' Association, devoted to the "young stenographer"—were similar to clubs formed by students to practice their newly acquired skill. The advanced class of an evening high school in Boston, probably made up of working-class men and especially women, formed an organization to "study the art of phonography," acquire periodicals, and learn about different shorthand languages. Business colleges encouraged their students and alumni to organize such clubs. They may have been similar to the ones that John Robert Gregg founded to promote his non-Pitmanic language. Limited to Gregg writers who wrote at seventy-five words per minute, the first club met in Chicago in January 1896 for weekly dictation practice.[49]

The few African American stenographers also created segregated professional organizations for self-improvement and mutual protection. We know very little about their associations, but the National Organization of Colored Stenographers first met in Chicago in October 1895. Miss Pearl B. Jones, a bookkeeper and cashier and an "official stenographer" to R. M. Mitchell, supreme grand chancellor of the colored Knights of Pythias, there called for a society with a goal of "mutual benefit and protection." She estimated that there were twelve hundred "colored stenographers" in the United States and more than one hundred in Chicago, adding that "more colored girls are learning." Like the mainstream white organizations, this association planned to provide "lectures by experts," "exercises to practice for speed," and an employment agency. In 1903, male and female stenographers and typewriters also formed an African American association in Baltimore. The one notable exception to the segregated professional societies is Charles W. Chesnutt, lawyer, legal reporter, and prominent African American novelist. Even before his major works were published, Chesnutt had been elected president of the Ohio State Stenographers' Association. A stenography magazine sketch on him did not mention his race, unlike other articles on African Americans.[50] Whether integrated or segregated, mainstream black and white organizations sought to assist stenographers in improving their job prospects through practice and providing employment connections, while the elite associations primarily deployed the language of professionalism and sought to exclude members.

Fellowship and Sociability

In support of their professional goals, all stenographic professional associations sought fellowship, just like the shorthand unions. Stenographers joined organizations partially to meet with people who shared their interests. Nearly every society included a clause about fellowship. In its 1900 annual meeting, the newly formed National Shorthand Reporters' Association invited "every reputable," "right-minded," and "deserving" stenographer to participate in "the spirit of comradeship and fraternity." In 1890, the mainstream Boston Stenographers' Association proclaimed its goals: "to promote sociability, assist members in obtaining positions, and elevate the standard of the profession." The New Orleans Phonographic Association's statement of purpose called for "the promotion of feelings of fraternity through social intercourse."[51]

To encourage fellowship, professional organizations sponsored social activities. The layout of the Metropolitan Stenographers' Association—including a parlor, various rooms with "easy chairs," a large smoking room, and a pool table—was designed to encourage conversation and camaraderie. The fall and winter dances and the monthly receptions were also "a means of promoting sociability and good-fellowship," as was the "annual reception held in some public hall." Dances, a combination billiard and pool table, and games like checkers, whist, and chess supplemented the "business features" at the Brooklyn Stenographers' Association. Various associations sponsored dramatic, cycling, and camping clubs. Gregg's clubs devoted much attention to social activities, like a themed "lynching bee" dance. Even members of the elite New York State Stenographers' Association expanded their "social intercourse," when, in 1911, a local offshoot began meeting monthly just for dinner. At the annual conferences, speakers' readings of papers on professional topics were interspersed with leisure activities, such as balls with musical entertainment and tours or outings to the river, all to further friendship and community identity.[52]

Like religious institutions, fraternal organizations, and the Knights of Labor, shorthand professional associations developed insignia and badges to foster companionship, self-identity, and pride. In the 1880s and 1890s, stenographers periodically lobbied among themselves for a badge to "distinguish us from the 'maddening crowd.'" In 1891, Charles A. Brockway called for a badge with the name of the stenographer's hometown, the word *phonography,* and the inscription "To Save Time Is to Lengthen Life." Two years later, a badge emerged, "a triangle and the '*In hoc signo vinces*' [In this sign victory]," with a stickpin for women and a clasp pin for men. The exact wording or pictures on the badge seemed to matter less to proponents than announcing their competency and legitimacy to each other and outsiders, although, ironically, the triangle design mirrored the most popular Knights of Labor lapel buttons.[53]

At least one typewriter made fun of the multitude of rules and badges of the associations. Harriet Louise Husted (Lynch), proprietor of a public typewriting business in Boston from 1886 to the 1890s, parodied clubs whose sole purpose was socializing. In her torrid melodrama *A Little Game with Destiny,* discussed in chapter 5, the protagonist and her wild girlfriends form the Dispensation Club for "the promotion of sociability and good fellowship . . . to contribute to . . . the long-hoped-for millennium, when all mankind shall love each other." To that end, members are to avoid "unnecessary formality and ceremoniousness." Husted pokes fun at their crest as well as the many useless committees and the specificity of rules, such as the distinctions between the "stated meeting" and additional meetings, known as "adjourned or occasional meetings," which were exceptions when the president or vice president were too busy to meet. Despite Husted's lampoon, men and women enthusiastically joined these organizations.[54]

Organization members appreciated professionalism, even if they disagreed on its meaning. The elite organizations stressed self-policing, exclusion, containment, and legislative regulation, in contrast to the mainstream associations' promotion of self-help activities to aid their members' advancement. Both types of professional organizations shared with unions concern over the important workplace issues of salaries and availability of jobs. Like some of the unions, the elite professional associations engaged in self-policing, although the professionals turned to the state for licensing, while the unions expected confrontation with employers. All types of professional societies as well as unions shared a commitment to fellowship and mutuality, but professionals demonstrated middle-class ambition through effort to elevate the profession or themselves. Despite the variations, these differences between unions and professional organizations explain the latter's appeal.

Men and women expected membership in professional organizations to elevate them above the masses. For men, emphasis on expertise proved their manly professional status in the middle class. For women, their presence in any association, especially elite ones, marked them as competent and ambitious professionals who demonstrated a male work ethic. Men were careful to note that the women in their organizations were, of course, competent. For example, during the battle between male and female court reporters at the NYSSA annual meeting in 1887, discussed in chapter 5, even men who criticized females as ill-suited for court work acknowledged that the women at the meeting were, of course, the exception.[55] The associations' performances of professionalism reinforced a middle-class identity that elevated their members above the masses—a desire shared by all stenographers, male and female.

PROFESSIONAL ASSOCIATIONS PERFORMING MIDDLE-CLASS RESPECTABILITY

Whether stenographers joined professional societies primarily to exclude others, to raise salaries, or for self-improvement, they all expected the organizations to affirm their middle-class status by marking them as respectable. Performing middle-class respectability in the associations helped women balance the ambition and independence of manhood with their femininity. Men, too, could strike a new gendered balance. By creating spaces suitable for wives and daughters, they performed an enactment of propriety that protected them from appearing like the popular images of the crude working class, yet without seeming effeminate.

Young stenographers at the turn of the twentieth century had the opportunity to participate in the disreputable, new commercial leisure, if they lived in the "furnished district." Unlike antebellum urban neighborhoods, such districts attracted both male and female sales and office clerks. Historian Jerome P. Bjelopera found that Philadelphia's salesclerks and business college graduates who lived in gender-integrated housing sometimes caroused at "booze" parties, dances, and other gender-integrated leisure that threatened their reputations. Like their antebellum predecessors, Philadelphia's clerks could also choose more proper leisure activities. Some participated in Peirce Alumni Association's dances and cycling clubs, whose primary functions were social.[56]

Stenographers, instead, could join professional organizations, which paraded refinement by combining middle-class professionalism with leisure. Shorthand men and women endowed professional associations with standards that mirrored the gentility of the wealthy, standing beyond the reach of the working class. Taste in clothing, housing, food, and cleanliness demanded sufficient purchasing power and knowledge of middle-class styles. Respectability required the execution of etiquette, with its appropriate gendered versions of values like self-control. These could be demonstrated in proper eating, leisure, and carriage of one's body.[57]

Following genteel practices meant constructing feminine spaces, which symbolized respectability. If men could bring their wives, then the locations met middle-class standards. Stenographers shaped their professional organizations to perform middle-class propriety by domesticating their professional spaces. Clubhouse designs were modeled after middle-class homes, and annual conventions featured suitable social activities along with professional papers. Domesticated clubhouses and annual conventions reinforced a middle-class identity by legitimizing deserving professionals.[58]

The most corporeal symbol of the associations was the clubhouse, where the basic activities of meetings, practice sessions, employment connections, and socializing took place. Whether organizations rented or purchased their clubhouses, they modeled them after the middle-class home. The Stenographers' Association of the City of New York referred to its meetinghouse as having "an air of refinement . . . which only the touch of woman's hand can produce."[59] The clubhouse of the Metropolitan Stenographers' Association of New York City featured a parlor "with easy chairs" and a reading room with "good and useful books" (see fig. 6). The Metropolitan designated "a large smoking room—the only place in the building where cigars are allowed." In 1891, when the neighborhood grew "increasing undesirable . . . , especially to the lady members," they leased a new building, complete with a seven-hundred-foot parlor, large enough for dancing in the fall and winter, "gilded chandeliers of rich design, and an elaborately carved mantelpiece, above which is an immense French plate glass mirror." The Brooklyn Stenographers' Association described their meetinghouse in a souvenir program as "a neat and cozy clubhouse, centrally located, in a charming neighborhood, and combining the efforts of home with the pleasures of club life." Clubhouses featuring parlors, libraries, smoking rooms, and French decor and located in charming neighborhoods modeled a professional world after the middle-class home.[60]

The professional orientation of stenography associations' yearly conferences also documented their middle-class sensibility. Beyond a business meeting, members and prominent invited speakers within the shorthand community delivered professional papers to further mutual improvement and reflection. At the NYSSA's annual convention in 1887, for example, the program listed talks entitled "The Future Shorthand—Can It be Done by Machinery," "Professional Stenography: To What Extent Should It Be Regarded as a Learned Profession," "Policy and Propriety of Stenographers' Advertising from a Professional or Business Point of View," and "Why Some Women Fail of [*sic*] Success in the Court-Reporters or Office." Such trade talks marked organizations' middle-class professionalism, more so than practice sessions at the clubhouses.[61]

Social activities at annual conferences glowed with an aura of respectability. Some organizations announced their programs in extravagant brochures. For its third annual entertainment event, the Brooklyn Stenographers' Association printed a souvenir program of thirty pages filled with advertisements, readings, photos, and letters, "on highly calendared paper in brown ink, with a chaste white cover on it in gold lettering."[62] New mainstream associations without much of a treasury assembled in gatherings at local halls, like the Stenographers Club of Chicago's first meeting at the Hall of the Patriotic Order of Sons. Statewide and national organizations met at scenic resorts or hotels; for example, the California State Stenographers' Association held its 1900 conference at the Marble Room Palace Hotel. Some organizations, like the NSRA, timed their

FIG. 6. Parlor of the Metropolitan Stenographers' Association's clubhouse, 1891. From the *Annual Announcement of the Metropolitan Stenographers' Association of New York City* (New York, 1891). (Courtesy of the New York Public Library.)

conferences to coincide with the "vacation season," as clerks, insurance agents, stenographers, and other white-collar workers began to take vacations regularly, leaving the city during the heat of the summer. The column "The Fem-Sten's Retreat" in the *Typewriter and Phonographic World* described August as "vacation month," where "we long to get away from the noisy city into the green fields, . . . where we are lost in the sublimity of our surroundings and willingly yield ourselves to the 'perfect whole.'" The NSRA's annual report described the location of their August 1900 convention at Put-in-Bay, Ohio, as a place "where lovely scenery gratifies the eye and cool breezes banish half the ills of midsummer season." Only the most well-paid stenographers could afford the housing, at $2 to $4.50 per day or $10 to $25 per week.[63]

Annual conferences devoted considerable time to leisure activities, appropriate for wives and daughters. Many followed the middle-class custom of touring, an activity increasingly common among working-class families as well.

At the 1903 NSRA's convention in Cincinnati, stenographers took excursions every afternoon: a trolley car ride, a river outing to Coney Island, and trips to the U.S. military post at Fort Thomas, Kentucky, and the zoo. Socializing and outings took up a large chunk of the conference time, with one night passed in mingling and another at a banquet. Their four-day meeting in Boston in 1902 had nothing but socializing after 2:00 p.m. At their 1887 convention, the NYSSA arranged for sailing around the islands of the St. Lawrence River, suitable for the nine members (24 percent in attendance) who brought along their wives.[64]

At the stenography conferences, sporting activities reinforced middle-class respectability, even as the middle class engaged in more vigorous activity common to working-class leisure. Sports like croquet, tennis, baseball, and bicycling became particularly popular. Some conventions devoted an entire day to physical activity. The meeting of the Metropolitan Stenographers' Association at Highland Beach, New Jersey, on 2 September 1889 included dancing, boating, fishing, bathing, and baseball. The Iowa State Stenographers spent an afternoon sailing, rowing, fishing, swimming, and playing tennis and croquet. These vigorous activities, however, maintained a middle-class tone, compared to the Knights of Labor baseball games and other sports that often degenerated into fistfights. Moreover, they encouraged more gender integration than the races and the football and baseball games of Philadelphia's salesclerks.[65] Shorthand writers also sometimes portrayed the exercise as beneficial, rather than just for fun, a typical distinction between middle- and working-class reaction to leisure. For example, shorthand writers' bicycle clubs advocated cleaner streets. One stenographer touted the bicycle, which "refreshed" his "brain and nerve force," as "a relief to an overworked brain." The *Phonographic World* even initiated a "Wheelman's Department" to discuss issues of interest to stenographic cyclists, similar to cycle clubs organized by Philadelphia's Peirce College alumni.[66] Compared to the more raucous activities of the telegraph unions, strolling, "light amusement," and dancing seemed sedate.[67]

Stenography conference banquets also featured a genteel dining style. The Boston Shorthand Club's convention boasted an "elaborate menu" for its forty members.[68] At the fall meeting of the NESRA in 1899, dinner reported in the published menu included Little Neck Clams on Shell, Mock Turtles, Fillet of Turbot with Hollandaise Sauce, Victoria Potatoes, Chicken in Casses Toulouse, Peaches Imperial with Claret Sauce, Spring Lamb with Currant Jelly and French Peas, Charlotte Russe, and more. Drinks reflected a middle-class temperance menu of coffee without any alcoholic beverages, although dessert included a fruit-wine jelly. Typically, some of the dishes were written in French, like tomato soup aux croutons, served at the fall meeting of the same organization. These grand dinners with many courses reinforced the sense of plenty and the opportunity for the guests to exercise appropriate middle-class restraint and propriety. Older associations entertained in an outmoded masculine genteel style. At their 1896 convention, the NYSSA served different liquors and wines (sherry, sauterne, and claret) with each course and ended the meal with cigars.[69]

Banquet entertainment underscored the middle-class aura of professional associations. Sometimes, stenographic associations' entertainment moved to the newer style of performance that highlighted composers rather than performers and split culture into lowbrow and highbrow. Programs announced the composers as well as the "artists," as in the 23 April 1891 Beethoven concert sponsored by the Brooklyn Stenographers' Association, which boasted "a high class entertaining performance." However, shorthand conferences mostly modeled entertainment after the popular middle-class vaudeville and variety shows that displayed an eclectic combination of musical and literary styles, rather than risqué entertainment geared for all-male audiences. For example, the 1894 annual meeting of the Indiana State Stenographers' Association, recounted at the beginning of this chapter, mixed a speech, a violin and piano duet, and a whistling solo. The 1895 Fifth Annual Meeting of the Brooklyn Stenographers' Association best illustrates the variety show concoction of types of entertainment. It began with an overture, then a violin recital, followed by banjo, mandolin, and guitar selections. Next, comedienne Sylvia Denton performed "Little Alabama Coon" and a "humorous, musical monologue." The second half of the program began with a vocal soloist, followed by a polka and Hugh J. Emmett's ventriloquism, and ending with Shakespeare's *Othello,* act 3, scene 3. Denton's performance of "Little Alabama Coon" echoes the minstrel shows put on by Philadelphia's salesclerks. Such activities reassured attendees of their middle-class whiteness.[70]

Performances of respectability at the stenographers' annual conventions differed from some working-class unions' annual meetings, although elements of refinement appeared in working-class activities at times. The *Proceedings of the American Federation of Labor* mentioned one carriage ride and a yearly banquet but did not acknowledge entertainment or food, just speeches and toasts. The Brotherhood of Carpenters and Joiners of America met in major cities like Cincinnati, Buffalo, Detroit, Chicago, St. Louis, Indianapolis, Cleveland, and New York, close to their urban populations, instead of taking summer retreats. Although they, too, convened in August, they spent long days discussing union business, regularly beginning at 8:00 a.m., breaking for an hour and a half for lunch and dinner and finishing at 10:00 p.m. The Knights of Labor, however, which contained both middle- and working-class members, sponsored picnics, socials, and dances that both contrasted and mirrored stenographic leisure. A Knights of Labor local in Massachusetts renovated a local opera house for a meeting hall, a far cry from the homelike stenographic clubhouses, though in the 1910s and 1920s, several unions bought clubhouses, too. Despite these differences, one New York local printed a sixteen-page booklet for a special event, which included the familiar style of entertainment of "four soloists, three story readers, a musical club, and an actor recreating 'humorous selections.'" Late nineteenth-century women's trade unions and working girls' clubs also engaged in staid leisure, like recitations and singing, aimed at encouraging boyfriends to behave more courtly.[71]

While stenographers pursued middle-class leisure, the working-class roots of some of its members periodically shone through. The Brooklyn Stenographers' Association, with its "cozy clubhouse," elaborate souvenir program, and concern about refinement, still managed to include a pool and billiard table for clubhouse recreation. By the 1870s, pool and billiards had become popular among working-class and lower middle-class bachelors. While middle-class reformers critiqued these working-class watering holes as dens of dissipation, elite men playing billiards in clubs received no such condemnation. Hence, billiards and pool in a shorthand club might have seemed perfectly acceptable for men, though less so for women. Other social events mixed working- and middle-class styles. Affairs often lasted until the "wee sma' hours" or the "milkman's call," yet partygoers danced the genteel waltzes, quadrilles, and lancers and proceeded in a traditional grand march. Despite periodic displays of their working-class origins, clubhouses and convention announcements, leisure, banquets, and entertainment together announced the middle-class character of professional organizations by broadcasting stenographers' propriety. Professional associations spoke to a middle-class sensibility within clerical work, even among those who came from the working class.[72]

Since performing professionalism meant acting out respectability, stenographers' professional associations took on the unquestionably refined character of feminine private space. Instead of dark walls, spittoons, and universal smoking, the clubhouses looked like homes, with parlors, libraries, ballrooms for dancing, and secluded male spaces for smoking. These middle-class feminized spaces were one reason why professional associations and professionalism in general attracted women. The cultured ambiance of libraries for book reading, parlors, balls, and genteel leisure provided safe and comfortable spaces that welcomed women seeking respectable environments. But these feminized spaces did not just appear on their own. Women planned some of the social life of gender-integrated associations, as in the announcement from the Stenographers' Association of the City of New York that "the ladies took possession of the parlors." Women also nurtured self-improvement and fellowship, rather than merely addressing grievances. Female professionalism incorporated middle-class domesticity. For example, Mary Arnold saw the Stenographers Club of Chicago as a "family together like a home." Socializing in genteel spaces and styles made shorthand professional organizations dignified. Performing professionalism proved both male and female stenographers' respectability.[73]

CONCLUSION

Although unions and professional associations acknowledged similar concerns, the middle-class sensibility and aura of professionalism won over late nineteenth-century stenographers. To some degree, union troubles and the general rise in professional organizations explain stenographers' preferences. More important, however, stenographers rejected unions' working-class identification and overwhelmingly embraced the associations as the best way to institutionalize a middle-class identity.

The two types of professional organizations enlarged the reach of professionalism to deliver respectability, by speaking to each group's different concerns. The elite sought to gain greater esteem and solidify their position in the middle class by containing competitors. So, too, the mainstream stenographers sought admiration and a middle-class identity, but for them, improving competence proved their professionalism most effectively.

Although gender distribution varied between the two styles of professional association, neither segregated rigidly by gender. Both provided different advantages for male and female shorthand writers, while also exposing the instability of gender and class. For many men, professional associations forged a middle-class identity based on checking the competition, especially women. These associations sanctioned middle-class men's hopes of success for the deserving, expressed and relieved their anxieties about working-class encroachment on their turf, and enshrined middle-class respectability in its newest form. Professionalism provided the means to secure economic aims, while also refashioning the individualistic self-made man to a position above the masses and more in line with the modern office, a site for the mass production of information and services. However, men's performance of middle-class standards relied on women—their domesticity of the clubhouses and genteel leisure at the annual meetings. Women made men's respectability happen, both literally and symbolically.

Women joined these organizations to improve their skills and prove their competency, marking themselves as practitioners of an acceptable male work ethic. While professionalism acknowledged women's businesslike, male work ethic, it could not shake the image of the cold, manly businesswoman, despite efforts to inject femininity. However, the performance of professionalism, by building institutions that followed respectable practices, made room for women and enabled them to appear feminine and domestic, at least in the context of professional associations.

Epilogue

The discourses that developed at the end of the nineteenth century among court reporters and business stenographers continued even into the twenty-first century, despite changes in both the courts and offices. Court reporting retained its gender balance of manly professionalism well into the twentieth century. Business stenographers struggled to maintain the professional feminine balance and replicated the same divisions between the typewriter girls and professionals throughout the twentieth century, even when replaced by secretaries and administrative assistants.

COURT REPORTERS

Court reporters succeeded in preserving opportunities for men, despite the difficulties of building a national professional organization. Even mechanization sustained their autonomy, enabling court reporting to remain a male occupation until the 1970s. While demographic and social changes ultimately led to women's dominance, men and women clung to their balanced version of gendered professionalism.

Building a professional infrastructure required more than forming a national organization. In the 1910s, the National Shorthand Reporters' Association (NSRA) struggled to draw members because most reporters preferred local organizations for socializing and lobbying of the more immediate state legislatures. For example, while two-thirds of the members of the Pennsylvania Shorthand Reporters belonged to the NSRA in 1916, less than one-third of their

New York counterparts participated.[1] By 1940, the NSRA attracted only around one thousand members, compared with over twenty-two thousand today.[2] The lack of commitment hurt dues collection and led to repeated discussions in the 1910s and 1920s about arranging with locals for automatic affiliations, as well as organizing amanuenses.[3]

Nonetheless, the NSRA forged ahead to force national uniformity, but with less success than they expected. Their standardization movement tried to develop a single Pitmanic system but failed to pass a resolution naming it as the standard in 1910 and petered out after publishing the *Phrase Book of Pitmanic Shorthand* in the early 1930s.[4] Challenges from Gregg, a non-Pitmanic system based on light-line phonography, and later the stenotype sapped their motivation.[5] Gregg's method captured business shorthand through the use of modern advertising techniques, despite court reporters' continued preference for Pitmanic systems. Among NSRA court reporters, 85 percent worked in Pitman in 1923 and 60 percent in 1942, after which the stenotype surpassed them both.[6]

Despite the initial difficulties at the national level, reporters at the state level continued to prod their legislators to pass favorable statutes on appointments, duties, compensation, assistants and temporary replacements, and pensions, although laws varied dramatically by state. By 1913, 58 percent of the forty states with official reporters paid salaries, at a median of two thousand dollars, while the remainder compensated per diem, mostly between ten and fifteen cents per folio for transcriptions. New York led the way with the creation of the Certified Shorthand Reporter (CSR) certification, which required four years of high school and speed and accuracy testing. Despite grandfathering of practicing official court reporters, few were anxious to be certified. Other states were slow to pass similar legislation; by 1960, only eight had done so. Instead, the NSRA switched to a national strategy, lobbying for the passage of a federal bill. When President Franklin Roosevelt vetoed a bill in 1936, the NSRA created its own Certificate of Proficiency in 1937, which eventually became the Registered Professional Reporter (RPR) certification. By 1995, certification was required in twenty-seven states for official reporters and in nineteen for freelance reporters.[7]

Court reporting still continued to draw well-educated men, even some with law licenses. Young men who came of age at the end of the nineteenth-century turmoil remained in the courts. William C. Booth, born in 1873, who graduated from City College of New York and then law school in 1889, stayed a stenographer in the district courts. Claude W. Myrose, born in 1885, studied law for one year before leaving for court reporting in 1906. John H. Nodes, born in 1898, graduated from Ohio State University in engineering in the 1920s but turned to court reporting when disillusioned with his initial career.[8]

Through the twenties, court reporting still symbolized upward mobility. J. L. McAttee began as a railroad amanuensis and became a court reporter in Waco, Texas, in 1920. Norman E. Metcalf, born in 1894, served as secretary to a former senator before joining his father's firm as an official reporter. Some still moved into the middle class via shorthand, like Charles Lee Swem, who had "only a grammar school education" and worked at a mill when studying Gregg shorthand. He eventually became a competitive champion stenographer and court reporter.[9]

Private reporting firms persisted in attracting young men, even as 72 percent of the NSRA's membership identified themselves as official reporters in 1942.[10] Three generations of Burts demonstrate the continued potential for reporting firms. In 1924, Philip Burt, a graduate of Amherst College, formed a partnership with his father, venerated court reporter Frank H. Burt. They covered conventions, hearings, depositions, political speeches, sermons, special Supreme Court cases, and more. Philip's son, Lawrence, joined his father as an alumni of Amherst College in 1949 and then in his office, which employed four shorthand writers and four stenographer-typists as of 1964. In 1975–76, Lawrence presided over the NSRA.[11]

As partners in reporting firms, court reporters saw themselves as businessmen. When scientific management captivated American offices, the *National Shorthand Reporter* in 1913 advised reporters how to keep modern business records. In the 1920s, an NSRA president talked about "clients," "profit," and a convention theme of "selling Shorthand Reporting Service." After World War II, in 1947, the NSRA arranged for group insurance, and in the 1950s, it endorsed legislation for "self-employed reporters tax relief and retirement security."[12]

Even mechanization did not undermine reporters' autonomy. Despite repeated concerns, mechanization was slow to invade the courts. Not until the 1950s did the stenotype challenge manual shorthand. In 1942, only 10 percent of members of the NSRA used it, compared to 43 percent in 1956 and 86.5 percent in 1976. The stenotype finally separated the training of court reporters from business stenographers, as it precluded the latter from studying a shorthand language. Nonetheless, even in the 1990s, some women may have learned shorthand before turning to the stenotype. While two-thirds of female court reporters held secretarial, clerical, or transcribing positions before becoming reporters, only 26 percent of men did. Reporters' procedures did not change until the 1980s, when computer-aided transcription enabled court reporters to eliminate the need for dictation. Even this technological change bolstered their autonomy, since they no longer needed transcribers. After 1991, the NSRA (now known as the National Court Reporters Association) actually encouraged the adoption of computers, in order to forestall replacement by electronic audio recordings. Although recent attempts to supplant court reporters with electronic recording again threaten to reduce their work, they have thus far not weakened reporters' autonomy and only slightly scaled down relatively high salaries. This survival may stem from reporters' transition from primarily courtroom employees to providing transcription services for the deaf, other captioning, and video recording.[13]

The maintenance of a relatively high income, autonomy, and professionalized manliness preserved court reporting's male dominance until second-wave feminism of the 1970s. Despite the anxiety about women in the 1880s and 1890s, not much changed in the following decades. Women like Miss R. Eva Byers at the 1913 NSRA annual conference continued to call for equal opportunities in the courts, echoing Jeannette Ballantyne's pleas from twenty-five years before. Even by 1942, women made up only 26 percent of members of the NSRA, barely rising to 30 percent in 1968. While few court reporters were female, even fewer women participated in the national and state organizations, with the exception of the Indiana contingent, where women like Helen Hinckle reigned in the 1890s.[14]

The gender-balanced professional language continued throughout the teens and twenties. While the NSRA still held elaborate yearly conferences that performed domesticated professionalism, men continued to insist on manly intellectual qualities. A 1913 article in the *National Shorthand Reporter,* the official organ of the NSRA, protested that reporters had to work like machines, but its author especially resented when a judge saw himself as an "intellectual superior."[15] A speech in 1916 discussed shorthand as an "exact science" that "takes brains to know what to leave out as well as what to leave in."[16] The presidential speech made on the occasion of the NSRA's twentieth anniversary praised the competent court reporter's notes for the potential to rescue women clients from incompetent counsel.[17]

Male reporters continued their muscular language in the 1910s and 1920s. They boastfully complained that they worked harder than their predecessors, that contemporary speakers talked 30 percent faster than in the past and included immigrant accents, making "court reporters' labors . . . more onerous and unenviable."[18] They insisted that their work demanded "muscles in condition to respond instantly to a slight direction of the brain, . . . [from a] body radiating energy," and they excluded those with "weak eyes," "frequent headaches" or "stomach troubles" who get "nervous and . . . 'rattled.'"[19]

Moreover, court reporters' language still assumed a male audience. From the teens to the thirties, reporters referred to themselves as the "boys." As late as 1965, the *National Shorthand Reporter* saw women as "others," as in an article on "vivacious Hazel Lewis," a secretary studying stenotyping who worked weekends as a Tahitian dancer. A photograph accompanying the article showed the costumed "blue-eyed miss" sprawled in front of a stenotype machine, with her breasts as the focal point.[20]

Despite these efforts at maintaining manly professionalism, court reporters never succeeded in shaking the public view equating business and court stenographers, and they continued to bemoan their social standing. In 1913, the *National Shorthand Reporter* reiterated the frequent complaint that the "ordinary man . . . cannot distinguish between" the beginner and "one who has been actively engaged in reporting for twenty years." Again in 1946, Lawrence Orr acknowledged that "professional shorthand reporters resent the failure of the public to distinguish between the expert reporter and the thousands of stenographers who 'take dictation' at slow speeds on perfectly familiar matter." A 1967 sociology study explained that court reporters avoided calling themselves stenographers among colleagues because of the continued association with stenographers-secretaries. The failure to separate court reporting from secretarial work may well have contributed to the quick domination of women in the 1970s.[21]

Until then, women's numbers remained small. Many women who planned to marry may not have wanted to devote so much time preparing for an occupation that required years to perfect. However, as more married women sought employment, their numbers climbed in the NSRA.[22] By 1964, 70 percent of the twenty-seven women who did belong to the NSRA were married (or used a married title), compared to only 19 percent in 1931–32. With the new burst of feminism and the recession of 1973 that spurred the upsurge of married women in the workforce, the membership of the NSRA finally changed. Reporting offered these women a high-paying occupation that appeared accessible to women, especially with the mounting proportion of freelance work that enabled part-time and at-home transcription. By 1975, women made up 55 percent of the NSRA membership, climbing to 86 percent in 1992.[23]

Despite women's growing footprints in reporting, elements of the older discourses remained. Columns, book reviews, and vocabulary-building exercises in the *Journal of Court Reporting* still emphasized reporters' skill with language. A 1988 issue on verbatim reporting included pieces on linguistics and the judicial consequences of edited testimony. Women announced their own professionalism repeatedly, while still incorporating feminine twists. A biography on veteran court reporter Stella Butterfield noted her children's graduation from college and her "love of words," not her skill with words, yet also complimented her "uncompromising demand for professionalism." For contemporary women reporters, professionalism may mean running their own businesses, using computer technology, travel, and belonging to a professional association.[24]

Even after the feminization of court reporting, men also continued to borrow elements of the balanced manly professional developed at the end of the nineteenth century. A 2000 *New York Times* article on the dangers of audio recorders for court reporters reminded readers of the proximity between male reporters and womanhood by referring to them in feminine language as "soft-spoken," speaking "with a sigh," and performing "typing" that "is not just drudgery" in this "unsung profession." To recruit young men, a spokeswoman for the National Court Reporters Association touted opportunities to "broadcast captions for local football games." The male court reporters themselves deployed a familiar balanced language of manly professionalism. Fifty-one-year-old David Teich, a Brooklyn Supreme Court reporter, insisted that the work "serves a very important purpose" and can "even be lofty." Teich vouched for reporters' judgment to recognize the "complexities of human speech" and "interrupt the proceedings" for clarification, in contrast to machines. Reporters still valued their "attention to language." Bill Cohen, a fifty-year veteran of New York's courtrooms, commented that "ideally the reporter is someone with a curiosity about words, . . . scholarly, superior in English, and always working to be better." The *New York Times* journalist described Teich's apartment as "crammed with dictionaries, thesauruses and books of obscure slang [for] 'a little extra edge [when] . . . someone uses some very esoteric or fancy language.'" Even tamer variations of muscular expressions survived. Teich bragged that New York reporters need to write especially quickly because the "average rate of speech" is about 60 percent faster than elsewhere and is complicated by more "diversity of people and accents," echoing remarks from the 1910s. A few years later, in 2006, a baby boomer referred to the "mental toughness [necessary] to keep concentrating." Despite these continuities, of course, new gender and class discourses would influence recent balanced masculine discourses. Teich referred to reporting as "like zen," softening the masculine prose. The few male reporters may be using computerspeak as their new manly language. In 2006, both members of the NCRA's Tech Evaluation Committee and the editor of the *National Court Reporter*'s Ask Mr. Modern column were male, though men comprised only one-third of the National Court Reporters Association's committees and none of its officers.[25]

Throughout the twentieth century, older discourses of the middle-class manly professional continued in men's attempts to maintain a balanced gendered language, despite the eventual mechanization and feminization of court reporting. Women, too, continued to employ a gendered professionalism to affirm their middle-class womanhood.

BUSINESS STENOGRAPHERS

While male and female court reporters hung on to elements of their gender balances from the end of the nineteenth century, business stenographers could not easily shake the working-girl discourse of the typewriter girl and continued to embrace the feminine professionalism developed in the nineteenth century. Changes in the office that had begun in the nineteenth century meant that the stock character of the typewriter girl persisted in plaguing the stenographer and her successor, the secretary, as she, too, struggled to find a feminine professional balance. Rather than the dictating machinery being the prime cause of change for business shorthand, the tension between the working-girl discourse and feminine professionalism explains the shift from the stenographer to the secretary.

The division of labor and mechanization of the office grew in the twentieth century. As historian Sharon Strom and others establish, scientific management extended the division of labor in the early 1910s and 1920s, although businesses never achieved their desired routinization. Dictating machines affected stenographers most, until personal computers in the 1980s eliminated nearly all shorthand needs. First invented in 1877, dictating machines had the potential to eliminate stenographers by enabling businessmen to dictate directly to the typist who listened to the recorded dictation. Although some companies replaced stenographers with Dictaphones and typists, many resisted investing in this new technology. Businessmen found dictating to a machine difficult. They could not remember their train of thought or include all of the punctuation without prodding from the stenographer. As late as 1967, a study found that only one-third transcribed from dictation machines. Despite the failure of dictating machines to become ubiquitous, they illustrate the continued perception of business stenographers as machinelike workers who provided no input into the dictation process.[26]

Male stenographers did not immediately disappear from the office, although they declined to less than 6 percent of all stenographers by 1920 (see appendix, table C2). They and male secretaries also continued to confront the feminine working-class image of the nineteenth century. In 1920, advice for male secretarial students sounded like tips for the typewriter girl's brother. They were reminded to refrain from wearing "gaudy yellows, greens, reds" or "loud plaid suits" and to remove stains.[27] They should also avoid "glaring faults of education that indicate slovenliness or indifference," such as "double negatives," "confusion of pronouns," "[un]clear enunciation, like 'did ja' or 'would ja,'" and "incorrect use of don't with a singular pronoun." Ultimately, they must act like gentlemen in the office and "rise when [a] lady approaches." To counter this male working-class image, schools trying to attract male secretarial students continued to portray men as executives, emphasizing the nineteenth-century values of self-interest and "responsibility." Moreover, corporations expanded their definition of the career ladder in the 1920s, according to historian Clark Davis. Now, they could truly see themselves as corporate salesmen and ambassadors.[28]

For women in the 1910s through the 1930s, the routinized stenographer and professional secretary replicated the nineteenth-century split between mental labor and unthinking, mechanical work. The stenographer came to appear more like the typewriter girl of the 1890s, while the ambitious secretary looked like the court-reporting professionals.[29] Women employed in offices continued to find a gender balance that took into account this divide, even with new job titles.

Management experts, educators, and films acknowledged this distinction between the presumably middle-class professional secretary and the ordinary stenographer. The father of modern office management, William Henry Leffingwell, who had worked as a stenographer in the nineties, expected secretaries to use "good judgment" in constructing correspondence, in contrast with the mechanical work suitable for working-class women trained in his techniques. Speaking for Syracuse University's "secretarial science" program, Dean Edward Wiest distinguished between the "great army of stenographers and clerk[s who] can be trained at the high-school level . . . [and the] secretarial positions that require a cultural background, initiative, poise, and managerial ability . . . only . . . acquired through . . . extended education." George Cukor's 1938 film, *You Can't Take It With You,* also divided shorthand women into the same binaries: an elitist, wealthy banker referred to Alice Sycamore as a stenographer when he wished to denounce his son's romantic interest in her, while the son called her his secretary.[30]

In the 1920s and 1930s, the professional secretary appeared even more individualistic. According to sociologist Margery Davies, the secretary demonstrated the older values of initiative, judgment, and responsibility. She wrote letters for her employer, fixed his mistakes, and understood the business well enough to establish the office routine. Edward McNamara's secretarial training course defined her as a "craftsman, proud of the work," accurate, and artistic in typewriting. She was "more conscientious and careful about the work she has to do" than the stenographer. Moreover, because she knew what to do—"what forms are correct," "what is right and what is wrong,"and the "mechanics of the letter"—she had confidence in her work. Every decision in writing a letter reflected a mixture of individuality and artistry. McNamara modeled six differ ent ways to write the date on a letter but explained that the secretary's choice, "which offers a little touch of individuality," should "harmonize" with the letterhead. The same combination of individuality and artistry was to influence the secretary's arrangement of the introductory address. Her artistry softened her superiority, as did her womanly touch.[31]

At times, film and fiction, including plays by the Gregg Shorthand Institute, still distinguished between the good and bad stenographer, and popular films generally portrayed the stenographer as a respectable young middle-class woman, yet stock characters modeled on the typewriter girls still pervaded fiction and film. Sinclair Lewis describes "stenographer Rita Simons [as] . . . pretty as a picture" in *Main Street* and Miss Theresa McGoun as "the swift and rather pretty stenographer" in *Babbitt.* A stenographer turns into the prototypical flapper in Anita Loos's 1925 *Gentleman Prefer Blonds:* the dippy working-class gold digger Lorelei Lee stays at a "business college" only a week before a lecherous employer plucks her out of the class for her looks. Lee joined the list of literary or film gold-digging stenographers, like Joan Crawford's scheming Flaemmchen in *Grand Hotel* and Jean Harlow's Lil Andrews in *Red-Headed Woman,* both films released in 1932.[32]

Female office workers understood the implications of the dichotomy between the stenographer and secretary. Stenographers sought to distinguish themselves from the working-class image. Josephine Lehmann insisted that she snagged a job because she wrote on the application that she did not chew gum. Historian Sharon Strom reports interviews by the Bureau of Vocational Information in 1925 of women who delineated between the "stenographer as a 'dictating machine'" and secretarial "self-expression." One specifically acknowledged that the "gum chewing stenographer of newspaper jokes and cartoons" led "many people [to] look down upon stenographers." Some admitted that they worked as stenographers with secretarial titles. One interviewee claimed no difference between the two occupations but said that the secretary had a "high sounding name which some stenographers assume."[33]

As a result, the secretary began to replace the stenographer in popular jargon. In Los Angeles, women who would have reported their occupations as stenographers on their marriage licenses in 1900s called themselves secretaries in the 1920s. Stenographer Josephine Lehmann's experience reveals this transition. She referred to a job advertisement for a "stenosock" (slang for stenographer-secretary) but said that when her hometown paper wanted to report on her success, they named her a "private secretary."[34]

As the line between secretaries and stenographers blurred like that between court reporters and business stenographers in the previous century, the older stock characters continued to plague the secretary and the female court reporter.[35] In the 1936 film *Wife vs. Secretary,* Jean Harlow portrays a competent and efficient secretary whose beauty alone convinces the gossips, her boss's mother, and eventually his lovely wife that she and the boss are having an affair. Only through extraordinary womanly compassion and self-sacrifice does the secretary reunite her boss and his wife.[36] In the 1960s, secretaries and, periodically, even women court reporters again faced these images. A 1966 advertisement referred to the "pretty . . . secretary," and a cartoon in the *National Shorthand Reporter* pictured a buxom woman reporter theatrically reading a transcript to the somber judge.[37]

New discourses modified the secretary's attempts to find a balanced gendered discourse as a feminine professional. In the 1910s and 1920s, when the psychological language of personality provided a scientific justification for demanding gendered qualities in the office, personality became a new tool for discussing the feminine component of the gendered balance. Now, the secretary should have a "courteous, gentle, cheerful, tactful, sunny, courageous, optimistic personality."[38]

The changing usage of the term *office wife* reveals how far into the twentieth century the working-girl discourse survived, but also the subtle shifts misread by scholars. From the late 1920s through World War II, the dominant view of the office wife represented the secretary as a woman who wanted to or did marry her boss. When Hollywood produced Faith Baldwin's book *Office Wife* as a film in 1930, the term took on popular usage, in which a secretary manipulated her business relationship to the boss into marriage.[39] While some were gold diggers, most recapitulated the romantic love stories from the end of the nineteenth century.[40] Secretaries resented this version of the office wife and the attendant expectations, especially the implication that they "must anticipate" their bosses' every desire.[41] They lambasted male employers for injecting their personal wants in the business offices: "No, indeed it is not a part of their duties to see that Mr. X. doesn't forget his rubbers . . . [nor] . . . to keep his necktie trimly knotted. . . . If he can't remember to send flowers to his wife on his wedding anniversary the United States government is sorry, but it is none of the concern of its employees."[42]

While scholars have explained well this indignation over the expectation that secretaries foresee their bosses' needs, they have missed its roots in the tension between the language of the efficient professional and that of the gold digger. Women begrudged the popularization of the office wife because involvement in the personal affairs of their bosses, as well as romantic attractions, undermined their professionalism. As a result, supportive articles reminded readers of secretaries' place as models of "efficiency" rather than as "winners of beauty contests," similar to articles about women court reporters in the 1890s.[43]

Like the character of the pretty typewriter girl of years past, that of the office wife also developed a more bland usage, sometimes equivalent to the working woman or the working wife. One 1930s article used the image of the office wife to criticize employed married women, a common theme during the Depression. Once she gave up her job, the ex–"office wife" now became a supportive wife in a happier, "successful marriage." Another woman asked for advice on how to lose weight, signing herself "Office Wife."[44]

After World War II, through the 1960s, the office wife who married the boss did not entirely disappear as a type, but the secretary who catered to the boss's every want now appeared more often. In the late forties, members of "the southeastern section of the National Secretaries Association" accepted that they should "anticipate" the bosses' wishes. Newspaper columnists even advised wives to emulate the office wife and place their husbands' desires first, at least for a while, to blunt the close relationship with their secretaries. Obviously, the threat of sexual competition had not completely disappeared. One writer said that she took up golf and joined a group of lawyers' wives to share more of her husband's interests, when she realized that he turned to his efficient secretary for choosing office carpets and furniture and other decisions she thought belonged in her realm. Although she never feared losing her husband to the secretary who was subconsciously in love with him, she felt the imposition on her role. Moreover, married men seemed comfortable openly referring to their secretary as their office wife, to the consternation of their wives who complained to Dear Abby.[45] With second-wave feminism in the 1970s, the office wife became what scholars had assumed for the early years: the pitied, misused, gofer who served coffee for her boss and tended to his whims, rather than the consummate professional.[46] These images of the office wife disclose not only the long arm of the image of the typewriter girl but its repositioning as well. At midcentury, with the sexualization of popular culture, the working-class typewriter girl had become the bosomy secretary sitting on her boss's lap.[47]

In opposition to these stock characters, from World War II to today, secretaries have struggled to find an acceptable image for the professional woman. In 1942, the National Secretaries Association (NSA) was formed, and in 1951, it first administered the Certified Professional Secretaries Examination. Within a year of beginning certification testing, the NSA encouraged the celebration of National Secretaries Week. Although organized secretaries emphasized their competence, they could not ignore the cultural expectation that bosses recognize their work by giving feminine gifts of candy and flowers. A 1963 advertisement for filing folders shows a secretary wearing a mink stole that she received as an "unusual" gift from her boss because the product had improved her performance. Moreover, in 1961, the NSA's officers wore prom dresses and corsages for a formal picture, while comfortably referring to themselves as "career women" in "the field of secretarial science."[48]

When second-wave feminism nudged the gender balance slightly from the feminine, office secretaries strengthened their drive to shed remnants of the image of the typewriter girl and demanded to be called administrative assistants. The NSA changed its name to Professional Secretaries International in 1981 and then to International Association of Administrative Professionals in 1998, and it changed National Secretaries Day to Professional Secretaries Week in 1981 and then Administrative Professionals Week in 2000. Now, the organization's Web site calls for "professional development" speakers and seminars and "encourage[s] study for and attainment of professional certification," rather than the flowers and candy offerings listed on the many Web sites mentioning National Secretaries Day.[49]

The computer revolution of the 1980s and 1990s diminished the need for shorthand but re-created the divide between the routine work of data entry or word processing and the autonomous secretary or administrative assistant. In a November 2006 essay for National Public Radio's series *This I Believe,* executive assistant Yolanda O'Bannon illustrated how educated secretaries still struggle to reconcile service-oriented work with the feminist rejection of traditional woman's work by emphasizing their masculine autonomy. She countered the "stereotypes" of secretaries as "nice . . . but not smart," by touting her ability as a former programmer, her role as founder of a nonprofit organization, her educational accomplishment of a master's degree in English, and the fact that she was independent enough to travel solo in New Zealand, Japan, Africa, and India. She stressed her work skills of organization, multitasking, untangling finances, and remembering everything, like the fast-talking staff of the popular television show *West Wing.* O'Bannon strained, though, to reconcile the office wife's task of serving food with her reconfigured image. Although rejecting food service as "humiliating," she borrowed another, more masculine discourse to portray her housewifery task: now, when required to serve food, she thought about Tibetan views of food service as a form of respect and imagined serving Tibetan monks. Like the female court reporters, she stressed her independence and skills and her similarity to male workers, moving as far from the feminine "stereotypes" as possible.[50]

Recent studies of secretaries find a modest recentering. Cathleen Armstead's 1990s ethnography of three Orange County, California, offices of white working-class women revealed that secretaries demanded their own professional dress code of middle-class feminine dresses, nylons, and heels to match their "professional touches" on documents and reports, balanced by a wariness of career women who fail to keep their "family perspective." Scholar Ivy Kennelly's more racially diverse secretaries of 1997 and 1998 appreciated their work as "service-oriented" and "people-oriented." In other words, the ethic of caring continued in their definition of feminine professionalism.[51]

Older discourses lasted well past the nineteenth century. Women continued to battle and avoid the image of the typewriter girl and sustain a feminine professionalism, even as newer discourses modified the older. Men struggled to maintain a manly professionalism. By searching for gendered balances that would name them as middle-class, men and women influenced the shape of twentieth-century offices and courts.

Notes

INTRODUCTION

1. A. B. Wrighter, "The Trafton Tragedy," *TPW* 27 (April 1906): 212.

2. Ibid., 210.

3. Wrighter, "The Trafton Tragedy," *TPW* 27 (May 1906): 284.

4. Ibid., 279.

5. Wrighter, "Trafton Tragedy" (April 1906): 211.

6. Wrighter, "Trafton Tragedy" (May 1906): 278. Quote on "quick-witted": Wrighter, "Trafton Tragedy" (April 1906): 211.

7. "'Wanted—a Stenographer' and This Law Firm Still Requires One; Do You Want The Job," *TPW* 28 (November 1906): 344.

8. Ibid., 345.

9. For examples of many possible contemporary understandings of class: *Richard L. Bushman, The Refinement of America: Persons, Houses, Cities* (New York: Alfred A. Knopf, 1992); John F. Kasson, *Rudeness and Civility: Manners in Nineteenth-Century Urban America* (New York: Hill & Wang, 1990); Stuart M. Blumin, *The Emergence of the Middle Class: Social Experience in the American City, 1760–1900* (Cambridge: Cambridge University Press, 1989); Stephen P. Rice, *Minding the Machine: Languages of Class in Early Industrial America* (Berkeley: University of California Press, 2004).

10. Scholars have also shown gender standing for class: Amy Schrader Lang, *The Syntax of Class: Writing Inequality in Nineteenth-Century America* (Princeton: Princeton University Press, 2003), 6–12; Kathryn Kish Sklar, "The Historical Foundations of Woman's Power in the Creation of the American Welfare State," in *Mothers of a New World: Maternalist Politics and the Origins of Welfare States,* ed. Seth Koven and Sonya Michel (New York: Routledge, 1993), 43–93; Daniel E. Bender, *Sweated Work, Weak Bodies: Anti-Sweatshop Campaigns and Languages of Labor* (New Brunswick: Rutgers University Press, 2004); Thomas Winter, *Making Men, Making Class: The YMCA and Workingmen, 1877–1920* (Chicago: University of Chicago Press, 2002); On shifting between womanhood and manhood to improve class standing: Daniel. J. Walkowitz, *Working with Class: Social Workers and the Politics of Middle-Class Identity* (Chapel Hill: University of North Carolina Press, 1999).

11. Authors of popular narratives written for the working class portrayed upper-class men and women as brutish and too masculine. Ex-slave Frederick Douglass did so as well, possibly to balance his own image as especially physical and protect himself from accusations of brutishness, as Douglass could justify beating up the vicious slave breaker Covey because of Covey's own horrendous brutality: *Narrative of the Life of Frederick Douglass: An American Slave,* 2nd ed. (1845; reprint, New York: Dover, 1989), 61–98;

Michael Denning, *Mechanic Accents: Dime Novels and Working-Class Culture in America* (London: Verso, 1987), 97, 193; Bruce Dorsey, *Reforming Men and Women: Gender in the Antebellum City* (Ithaca: Cornell University Press, 2002), 191.

12. Bender examines the relationship between workers and reformers in *Sweated Work, Weak Bodies.*

13. On scholarly debates over the extent of and relationships between mechanization, routinization, the demography of workers, and feminization: Sharon Hartman Strom, *Beyond the Typewriter: Gender, Class, and the Origins of Modern American Office Work, 1900–1930* (Urbana: University of Illinois Press, 1992), 172–226; Cindy Sondik Aron, *Ladies and Gentlemen of the Civil Service: Middle-Class Workers in Victorian America* (New York: Oxford University Press, 1987), 65–95; Elyce J. Rotella, *From Home to Office: U.S. Women at Work, 1870–1930,* Studies in American History and Culture, no. 25 (Ann Arbor: UMI Research Press, 1981); Carole Srole, "'A Position That God Has Not Particularly Assigned to Men': The Feminization of Clerical Work, Boston, 1860–1915" (Ph.D. diss., University of California, Los Angeles, 1984); Lisa M. Fine, *The Souls of the Skyscraper: Female Clerical Workers in Chicago, 1870–1930* (Philadelphia: Temple University Press, 1990); Margery W. Davies, *Woman's Place Is at the Typewriter: Office Work and Office Workers, 1870–1930* (Philadelphia: Temple University Press, 1982).

14. In contrast, accountants successfully separated themselves from bookkeepers: Charles W. Wooton and Barbara E. Kemmerer, "The Emergence of Mechanical Accounting in the U.S., 1880–1930," *Accounting Historians Journal* 34 (June 2007): 89–124; idem, "The Changing Genderization of the Accounting Workforce in the U.S., 1930–90," *Accounting, Business & Financial History* 10 (July 2000): 175.

15. New shorthand periodicals listed in the New York Public Library Shorthand Collection display this peak (in 1870–79 there were only eleven in the United States, tripling to thirty-four between 1880 and 1889 and jumping to fifty-six between 1890 and 1899; in the next decade, they dropped to nine): Daniel C. Haskell, comp., *The Shorthand Collection in the New York Public Library* (New York: New York Public Library, 1935), 1–644; "The 'World' in Clubs in Schools," *PW* 25 (January 1905): 9; Decreasing magazine prices improved accessibility (in 1878 *Browne's Phonographic Monthly* charged two dollars per year; the more popular *Phonographic World* cost ten cents per issue or one dollar per year in 1885; by 1891, national circulation of the major stenographic magazines totaled 23,500): George P. Rowell's *American Newspaper Directory* (New York: Printer's Ink Publishing, 1891); Some readers borrowed from subscribers or read copies at business colleges or clubhouses.

16. At least twenty-eight editors also published shorthand or typing texts. Of the twenty-four located, one-quarter had already published a book before becoming editor, suggesting that they used their journals to spur book sales. Slightly over one-half became editor within a year or two after publishing a book, again demonstrating the expectation that the two publication types would feed each other. Another fifth published books years after attempts at editing, although at least two of them already owned a school. One of these, Daniel L. Scott-Browne, whose periodical survived for eighteen years until his death, publicized his school in the first issue. A few rose from the ranks of journalists who had learned shorthand to report speeches. Some, like Andrew Jackson Graham, Benn Pitman, and John Robert Gregg, promoted their own systems. Among

those, quite a few, like James Munson and Charles Currier Beale, continued practicing court reporting and advancing their variations of Isaac Pitman's phonography. S. S. Packard, W. E. Packard, and Benn Pitman headed schools.

17. "Wanted—a Stenographer," 345.

18. Jerome P. Bjelopera points out that shorthand schools portrayed women as competent, but he misses the elements of professionalism in these stories and especially in other stenography writings: *City of Clerks: Office and Sales Workers in Philadelphia, 1870–1920* (Urbana: University of Illinois Press, 2005), 35.

19. Historians have defined respectability as a synonym for middle-class and whiteness, but it is a fungible category that others have used for their benefit; Richard L. Bushman shows its spread throughout the middle class: *The Refinement of America: Persons, Houses, Cities* (New York: Knopf, 1992); Paul Michel Taillon discusses a working-class version in "'What We Want Is Good, Sober Men': Masculinity, Respectability, and Temperance in the Railroad Brotherhoods," *Journal of Social History* 36 (Winter 2002): 319–38.

20. For an example of gender blurring that matched female consumerism with expertise: Mary Ann Clawson, "Masculinity, Consumption, and the Transformation of Scottish Rite Freemasonry in the Turn-of-the-Century United States," *Gender & History* 19 (April 2007): 115–16.

21. For examples of men of the same class using gender to distinguish themselves: Kristen L. Hoganson, *Fighting for American Manhood: How Gender Politics Provoked the Spanish-American and Philippine-American Wars* (New Haven: Yale University Press, 1998); On gender across races and classes: Gail Bederman, *Manliness and Civilization: A Cultural History of Gender and Race in the United States, 1880–1917* (Chicago: University of Chicago Press, 1995); Louise Michelle Newman, *White Women's Rights: The Racial Origins of Feminism in the United States* (New York: Oxford University Press, 1999), 22–85; Barbara Young Welke, *Recasting American Liberty: Gender, Race, Law, and the Railroad Revolution, 1865–1920* (New York: Cambridge University Press, 2001).

22. Shahpar Modarresi, Dianna L. Newman, and Mitchel Y. Abolafia explain sociological approaches to professionalism: "Academic Evaluators versus Practitioners: Alternative Experiences of Professionalism," *Evaluation and Program Planning* 24 (February 2001): 1–11; For examples of the spread beyond traditional professionals: Wendy Gamber, "'Reduced to Science': Gender, Technology, and Power in the American Dressmaking Trade, 1860–1910," *Technology & Culture* 36 (July 1995): 455–82; Angel Kwollek-Folland, *Engendering Business: Men and Women in the Corporate Office, 1870–1920* (Baltimore: Johns Hopkins University Press, 1994), 72–76; For examples of middle-class identity and professionalism: Burton J. Bledstein, *The Culture of Professionalism: The Middle Class and the Development of Higher Education in America* (New York: Norton, 1976); Bruce A. Kimball, *The "True Professional Ideal" in America: A History* (Cambridge, MA: Blackwell, 1992); Rice, *Minding the Machine,* 115–45; For recent works on gender and professionalism: Walkowitz, *Working with Class;* Winter, *Making Men, Making Class;* Ruth Oldenziel, *Making Technology Masculine: Men, Women, and Modern Machines in America, 1870–1945* (Amsterdam: Amsterdam University Press, 1999); Jeffrey M. Hornstein, *A Nation of Realtors: A Cultural History of the Twentieth-Century American Middle Class* (Durham: Duke University Press, 2005).

CHAPTER 1

1. English-speaking countries that adopted Pitman's shorthand include Canada, Australia, South Africa, Ireland, and the United States; other countries developed other shorthand languages as well as versions of Pitman's; there are a few master's theses and educational dissertations on shorthand history, mostly as a business subject; practitioners published most articles on the subject, even academic ones, like Harry M. Scharf's "The Court Reporter," *Journal of Legal History* 10, no. 2 (1989): 191–227; For dissertations on shorthand in the United States: Roger B. Landroth, "The History and Development of Pitmanic Shorthand in the United States, 1843–1976" (Ed.D. diss., New York University, 1977), 46–49; John Allen Rider, "The History of the Male Stenographer in the United States" (Ed.D. diss., University of Nebraska, 1966), 31–43; "Shorthand," *LoveToKnow Classic Encyclopedia* (based on the 1911 edition of *Encyclopaedia Britannica*), http://www.1911encyclopedia.org/shorthand.

2. This concept of a "middle ground . . . between learnedness and moral authority" as the basis for middle-class manly morality among antebellum clerks is based on Thomas Augst's *The Clerk's Tale: Young Men and Moral Life in Nineteenth-Century America* (Chicago: University of Chicago Press, 2003), 191.

3. Vincent J. Bertolini, "Fireside Chastity: The Erotics of Sentimental Bachelorhood in the 1850s," in *Sentimental Men: Masculinity and the Politics of Affect in American Culture*, ed. Mary Chapman and Glenn Hendler (Berkeley: University of California Press, 1999), 21.

4. For excellent discussions on the weakening of apprenticeship and retail clerking work: Brian P. Luskey, "The Marginal Men: Merchants' Clerks and Society in the Northeastern United States, 1790–1860" (Ph.D. diss., Emory University, 2004), 121–36, 147–70; idem, "'What Is My Prospects? The Contours of Mercantile Apprenticeship, Ambition, and Advancement in the Early American Economy," *Business History Review* 78 (Winter 2004), 665–702; Allan Stanley Horlick, *Country Boys and Merchant Princes: The Social Control of Young Men in New York* (Lewisburg and London: Bucknell University Press and Associated University Presses, 1975), 73–79, 110–12; Stuart M. Blumin, *The Emergence of the Middle Class: Social Experience in the American City, 1760–1900* (Cambridge: Cambridge University Press, 1989), 77; Mary P. Ryan, *Cradle of the Middle Class: The Family in Oneida County, New York, 1790–1865* (Cambridge: Cambridge University Press, 1981), 29–31, 168–72; George K. Stoddard, "Shorthand in the Railroad Office," *Shorthand Review* 2 (February 1890): 58–59; Cindy Sondik Aron, *Ladies and Gentlemen of the Civil Service: Middle-Class Workers in Victorian America* (New York: Oxford University Press, 1987), 123–24, 132; For examples of continued family connections: Walter Barrett [Joseph Alfred Scoville], *The Old Merchants of New York City*, vol. 1 (New York: John W. Lovell, 1885), 17, 128.

5. Brian P. Luskey, "Jumping Counters in White Collars: Manliness, Respectability, and Work in the Antebellum City," *Journal of the Early Republic* 26 (Summer 2006): 173–219.

6. See the appendix for procedures followed; Boston City Directory, 1821, 1834; Aron, *Ladies and Gentlemen of the Civil Service*, 15, 22–23, 31, 35, 97–99.

7. Aron, *Ladies and Gentlemen of the Civil Service*, 19, 25–39; Edward J. Balleisen, *Nav-*

igating Failure: Bankruptcy and Commercial Society in Antebellum America (Chapel Hill: University of North Carolina Press, 2001), 212–24; On ages when men began permanent positions: Joseph F. Kett, *Rites of Passage: Adolescence in America, 1790 to the Present* (New York: Basic Books, 1977), 31–33; Blumin, *Emergence of the Middle Class*, 77; Under one-third of clerks were thirty or older in Poughkeepsie, New York, from 1850 to 1880: Clyde Griffen and Sally Griffen, *Natives and Newcomers: The Ordering of Opportunity in Mid-Nineteenth-Century Poughkeepsie* (Cambridge: Harvard University Press, 1978), 18, 134; Among male clerks over forty-one, high in-migration to New York City dropped to 5.1 percent in 1850 and 6.6 percent in 1855: Calculated from Luskey, "Marginal Men," 393.

8. Horlick, *Country Boys and Merchant Princes*, 69, 106, 122, 126–30; Aron, *Ladies and Gentlemen of the Civil Service*, 35.

9. For examples of the extensive literature on independence, republicanism, and work: Sean Willenz, *Chants Democratic: New York City and the Rise of the American Working Class, 1788–1850* (New York: Oxford University Press, 1984), 91–93; Gary J. Kornblith, "Becoming Joseph T. Buckingham: The Struggle for Artisanal Independence in Early-Nineteenth-Century Boston," in *American Artisans: Crafting Social Identity, 1750–1850*, ed. Howard B. Rock, Paul A. Gilje, and Robert Asher (Baltimore: Johns Hopkins University Press), 128–32; David Montgomery, *The Fall of the House of Labor: The Workplace, the State, and American Labor Activism, 1865–1925* (New York: Cambridge University Press, 1987), 10–44; Lawrence B. Glickman, *A Living Wage: American Workers and the Making of Consumer Society* (Ithaca: Cornell University Press, 1997), 43; Blumin, *Emergence of the Middle Class*, 64–65, 68, 74–78.

10. On the self-made man, from eighteenth-century roots to iconic type: C. Dallett Hemphill, *Bowing to Necessities: A History of Manners in America, 1620–1860* (New York: Oxford University Press, 1999), 67; Richard Weiss, *The American Myth of Success: From Horatio Alger to Norman Vincent Peale* (New York: Basic Books, 1969), 29–63; Ronald Preston Byars, "The Making of the Self-Made Man: The Development of Masculine Roles and Images in Ante-Bellum America" (Ph.D. diss., Michigan State University, 1979), 34, 74–75; John G. Cawelti, *Apostles of the Self-Made Man* (Chicago: University of Chicago Press, 1965); Ryan, *Cradle of the Middle Class*, 145–48; Irwin Wyllie, *The Self-Made Man in America: The Myth of Rags to Riches* (New Brunswick: Rutgers University Press, 1954); Karen Halttunen, *Confidence Men and Painted Women: A Study of Middle-Class Culture in America, 1830–1870* (New Haven: Yale University Press, 1982), 25–32; Paulette D. Kilmer, *The Fear of Sinking: The American Success Formula in the Gilded Age* (Knoxville: University of Tennessee Press, 1996), 61–62, 108–11, 149; Judy Hilkey, *Character Is Capital: Success Manuals and Manhood in Gilded Age America* (Chapel Hill: University of North Carolina Press, 1997); Rodney Hessinger, *Seduced, Abandoned, and Reborn: Visions of Youth in Middle-Class America, 1780–1850* (Philadelphia: University of Pennsylvania Press, 2005); On masculinity and independence: E. Anthony Rotundo, *American Manhood: Transformations in Masculinity from the Revolution to the Modern Era* (New York: Basic Books, 1993), 18–20.

11. Household heads who were clerks grew from 98 in 1821 to 288 in 1834, and Boston's population rose from 61,392 in 1830 to 93,383 in 1840 to 136,881 in 1850, excluding the suburbs later incorporated into the city: Massachusetts Bureau of Statistics of Labor, *The Census of Massachusetts, 1885: Population and Social Statistics*, vol. 1, pt. 1 (Boston: Wright

& Potter, 1887), 68–69; Peter R. Knights, *The Plain People of Boston, 1830–1860: A Study in City Growth* (New York: Oxford University Press, 1971), 20, 23, 84; Between 1800 and 1830, the population grew slightly to over 3 percent per year; between 1830 and 1850, the annual growth rate jumped to 4 percent: Matthew Edel, Elliott D. Sclar, and Daniel Luria, *Shaky Palaces: Homeownership and Social Mobility in Boston's Suburbanization* (New York: Columbia University Press, 1984), 40–46.

12. Although both banking and government employment continued to expand, their clerking staffs barely kept up with Boston's growing population (the number of banks almost quadrupled from eight to thirty, but their staffs of clerks and bookkeepers only doubled from 18 to 39; government clerks doubled from 20 to 40; conversely, those not identified in a specific sector of the economy multiplied sixfold, from 26 to 159, from one-fourth to over one-half of all clerical workers): see appendix, table A1; This expansion of Boston's clerking jobs as merchant apprentices continued in the next ten years following 1835 (rising from 288 in 1834 to 389 in 1840, with almost two-thirds in nonspecific industries); this rise of unspecific clerking did not merely reflect a decline in precision, since the city directory's staff members did not misrecord banking, insurance, and government employees listed elsewhere: Boston City Directory, 1821, 207, 269, 273, 277, 279–81; From the 1830s on, mercantile clerking became the most common experience and most discussed: Horlick, *Country Boys and Merchant Princes,* 107–24, 147–69; Weiss, *American Myth of Success,* 38, 41–42; "Familiar Scenes in the Life of a Clerk," *Hunt's Merchants' Magazine* 5 (1841): 536–40.

13. Horlick, *Country Boys and Merchant Princes,* 69, 106, 122, 126–30; Paul E. Johnson, *A Shopkeeper's Millennium: Society and Revivals in Rochester, New York, 1815–1837* (New York: Hill & Wang, 1978), 123; Blumin, *Emergence of the Middle Class,* 77.

14. Auctioneers, booksellers, druggists, peddlers, and others in mercantile trades besides bookkeepers, accountants, and clerks increased from 970 to 5,352, 5.5 times: Secretary of the Commonwealth, *Abstract of the Census of the Commonwealth of Massachusetts* (Boston: W. W. White, 1857), 173; Knights, *Plain People of Boston,* 84, 43; Horlick, *Country Boys and Merchant Princes,* 107–24, 165, 168–69; Ryan, *Cradle of the Middle Class,* 129, 153, 254; Griffen and Griffen, *Natives and Newcomers,* 60; *Hunt's Merchants' Magazine* 33 (1855): 394, quoted in Blumin, *Emergence of the Middle Class,* 78; For earlier criticisms: Michael Zakim, *Ready-Made Democracy: A History of Men's Dress in the American Republic, 1760–1860* (Chicago: University of Chicago Press, 2003), 116–17; On clerks' boredom: Augst, *Clerk's Tale,* 207–15; Scott A. Sandage, *Born Losers: A History of Failure in America* (Cambridge: Harvard University Press, 2005), 62; Quotes on weary and unnatured brain: Nathaniel Hawthorne, *The Scarlet Letter* (New York: Dell, 1960), 47–48, 67.

15. On clerks living with masters or relatives: Blumin, *Emergence of the Middle Class,* 212, 239–40; Two-thirds in an 1850 sample of sales and office clerks lived in the central business district of Philadelphia, and only one-half lived at home: Jerome P. Bjelopera, *City of Clerks: Office and Sales Workers in Philadelphia, 1870–1920* (Urbana: University of Illinois Press, 2005), 146, 149; Almost 60 percent of clerks in New York boarded in houses, hotels, or businesses: Luskey, "Marginal Men," 235, 394; On clerk's boarding, boardinghouses in general, and urban excitement: Rotundo, *American Manhood,* 57–58; Augst, *Clerk's Tale,* 175–76; Mark Peel, "On the Margins: Lodgers and Boarders in Boston, 1860–1900," *Journal of American History* 72 (March 1986): 826–31; Wendy Gamber, *The*

Boardinghouse in Nineteenth-Century America (Baltimore: Johns Hopkins University, 2007); Patricia Cline Cohen, *The Murder of Helen Jewett: The Life and Death of a Prostitute in Nineteenth-Century New York* (New York: Knopf, 1998), 208, 27, 127; Brian Roberts, *American Alchemy: The California Gold Rush and Middle-Class Culture* (Chapel Hill: University of North Carolina, 2000), 27–28; Robert C. Allen, *Horrible Prettiness: Burlesque and American Culture* (Chapel Hill: University of North Carolina Press, 1991), 68–69; Christine Stansell, *City of Women: Sex and Class in New York, 1789–1860* (New York: Knopf, 1986), 91–92, 203–9; Carol Nackenoff, *The Fictional Republic: Horatio Alger and American Political Discourse* (New York: Oxford University Press, 1994) 53–92; Horatio Alger, *Ragged Dick; or, Street Life in New York with the Boot Blacks,* with an introduction by Alan Trachtenberg (1867–68; reprint, New York: Signet, 1990), 30–43; Timothy J. Gilfoyle, *City of Eros, New York City, Prostitution, and the Commercialization of Sex, 1790–1920* (New York: Norton, 1992), 103, 107, 109, 112, 230.

16. Horlick, *Country Boys and Merchant Princes,* 108; Robert McCoskry Graham diary, NYHS; Edward N. Tailer diary, NYHS; Andrea Stulman Dennett, *Weird and Wonderful: The Dime Museum in America* (New York: New York University Press, 1997).

17. Quoted in Horlick, *Country Boys and Merchant Princes,* 78, see also 125, 131, 136.

18. Augst, *Clerk's Tale,* 176.

19. Henry A. Patterson diary, NYHS; Tailer diary; Luskey, "Marginal Men," 263–67; On living in working class districts and with the working class: Bjelopera, *City of Clerks,* 144, 148; Luskey, "Marginal Men," 237; On leisure: Richard B. Sott, *Workers in the Metropolis: Class, Ethnicity, and Youth in Antebellum New York City* (Ithaca: Cornell University Press, 1990), 204, 243, 245, 251, 273; On drinking, gambling, whoring, and other working-class leisure: Rotundo, *American Manhood,* 71–72; Michael Kaplan, "New York City Tavern Violence and the Creation of a Working-Class Male Identity," *Journal of the Early Republic* 15 (Winter 1995): 591–617; Helen Lefkowitz Horowitz, *Rereading Sex: Battles over Sexual Knowledge and Suppression in Nineteenth-Century America* (New York: Knopf, 2002), 360, 125–43; On civic cross-class contact: Olivier Zunz, *Making America Corporate, 1870–1920* (Chicago: University of Chicago Press, 1990), 132; Mary P. Ryan, *Civic Wars: Democracy and Public Life in the American City during the Nineteenth Century* (Berkeley: University of California Press, 1997), 38–57; Bruce Dorsey, *Reforming Men and Women: Gender in the Antebellum City* (Ithaca: Cornell University Press, 2002), 107; On fire companies: Amy Greenberg, *Cause for Alarm: The Volunteer Fire Department in the Nineteenth-Century City* (Princeton: Princeton University Press, 1998), 50–70, 80–108; On plays and theater: Richard Butsch, "Bowery B'hoys and Matinee Ladies: The Re-Gendering of Nineteenth-Century American Theater Audiences," *American Quarterly* 46 (September 1994): 381; Benjamin A. Baker, *Glance at New York,* in *On Stage, America: A Selection of Distinctly American Plays,* ed. Walter J. Meserve (New York: Feedback Theaterbooks & Prospero Press, 1996), 165–96; Allen, *Horrible Prettiness,* 54–57, 64.

20. Horowitz, *Rereading Sex,* 159–71; Gilfoyle, *City of Eros,* 96, 102, 106; Cohen, *Murder of Helen Jewett;* Aron, *Ladies and Gentlemen of the Civil Service,* 151; Rotundo, *American Manhood,* 58–74; Howard P. Chudacoff, *The Age of the Bachelor: Creating an American Subculture* (Princeton: Princeton University Press, 1999), 108, 131–35; Allen, *Horrible Prettiness,* 64, 94–96, 127, 133; Luskey, "Marginal Men," 296.

21. Patterson diary.

22. On anxiety about leaving home: Rotundo, *American Manhood,* 58; On slumming: Roberts, *American Alchemy,* 220; John F. Kasson, *Rudeness and Civility: Manners in Nineteenth-Century Urban America* (New York: Hill & Wang, 1990), 78; On working-class culture as masculine and middle-class culture as feminine: Sott, *Workers in the Metropolis,* 270–76; The tough working-class culture may have appealed to clerks because injuries and illness, signs of weakness and femininity, often drew men to clerking: see the discussion of illness in chapter 4 and Roberts, *American Alchemy,* 198–99; Alger, *Ragged Dick,* 107.

23. Byars, "Making of the Self-Made Man," 81–89; Ann Fabian, *Card Sharps, Dream Books, and Bucket Shops: Gambling in 19th-Century America* (Ithaca: Cornell University Press, 1990), 39, 55, 65; Horowitz, *Rereading Sex,* 139–43, 152–53, 360; Rotundo, *American Manhood,* 73.

24. Cohen, *Murder of Helen Jewett,* 65, 287; Laurel Thatcher Ulrich, *The Age of Homespun: Objects and Stories in the Creation of an American Myth* (New York: Knopf, 2001), 385–86.

25. Hemphill, *Bowing to Necessities,* 89, 91, 132, 162–63, 177–78.

26. Rotundo, *American Manhood,* 72–73; Nina Baym, *Woman's Fiction: A Guide to Novels by and about Women in America, 1820–1870* (Ithaca: Cornell University Press, 1978); Jane P. Tompkins, *Sensational Designs: The Cultural Work of American Fiction, 1790–1860* (New York: Oxford University Press, 1985); Horowitz, *Rereading Sex,* 151–53; Hemphill, *Bowing to Necessities,* 67–68, 82, 146, 216; Horlick, *Country Boys and Merchant Princes,* 98–104, 165; Freeman Hunt, *Worth and Wealth: A Collection of Maxims, Morals, and Miscellanes* [*sic*] *or Merchants and Men of Business* (New York: Stringer & Townsend, 1856), 315, 199; Jürgen Kocka says German employers criticized clerks' wanderings, but American merchants accepted this as normal: *White Collar Workers in America, 1890–1940: A Social-Political History in International Perspective,* trans. Maura Kealey (London: Sage, 1980); Patricia Cline Cohen, "Unregulated Youth: Masculinity and Murder in the 1830s," *Radical History Review* 52 (Winter 1992): 33–52; John B. Ellis [James Towner], *The Sights and Secrets of the National Capital: A Work Descriptive of Washington City in All Its Various Phases* (New York: U.S. Publishing, 1869), 383–87; T. S. Arthur, *The Way to Prosper; or, In Union There Is Strength, and Other Tales* (Boston: L. Crown, 1853), 7–8; Alger, *Ragged Dick,* 41–43, 77–80; T. S. Arthur, *True Riches, and Other Tales* (Philadelphia: J. W. Bradley, 1859); 55–57, 73, 183–90; idem, *Nothing but Money* (New York: Carleton, 1865); idem, *Making Haste to Be Rich; or, The Temptation and Fall* (New York: Collins & Brother, 1847).

27. Allen, *Horrible Prettiness,* 82; David Grimsted, *Melodrama Unveiled: American Theater and Culture, 1800–1850* (Chicago: University of Chicago Press, 1968), chap. 9; Wyllie, *Self-Made Man,* 32, 34; Horlick, *Country Boys and Merchant Princes,* 157–207; Hunt, *Worth and Wealth,* 316; On speakers: Augst, *Clerk's Tale,* 144–57; Kocka found this pattern of tension between salesclerks and their German employers but misses how the fiction framed the U.S. discussion: *White Collar Workers in America,* 80–81; T. S. Arthur, *Sparing to Spend; or, The Loftons and Pinkertons* (New York: Scribner, 1853).

28. Kornblith, "Becoming Joseph T. Buckingham," 134; Augst, *Clerk's Tale,* 55.

29. Ryan, *Cradle of the Middle Class,* 146–55; T. S. Arthur, *True Riches; or, Wealth without Wings* (Philadelphia: L. Crown, 1852); Hilkey, *Character Is Capital,* 89–92, 127–29.

30. Augst, *Clerk's Tale,* 82; Hoffman quoted in Horlick, *Country Boys and Merchant Princes,* 111; see also Kett, *Rites of Passage,* 96–102.

31. Blumin, *Emergence of the Middle Class,* 239–40.

32. Dorsey, *Reforming Men and Women,* 111.

33. Horlick, *Country Boys and Merchant Princes,* 231–43; Horowitz, *Rereading Sex,* 360.

34. Dorsey, *Reforming Men and Women,* 110–11, 102–6.

35. For examples on female and male advice: Kathryn Kish Sklar, *Catharine Beecher: A Study in American Domesticity* (New Haven: Yale University Press, 1973); Hessinger, *Seduced, Abandoned, and Reborn;* For examples of the huge literature on women's association with antebellum morality: Dorsey, *Reforming Men and Women,* 38, 83–85; Elizabeth R. Varon, *We Mean to Be Counted: White Women and Politics in Antebellum Virginia* (Chapel Hill: University of North Carolina Press, 1998), chap. 3; Michael D. Pierson, *Free Hearts and Free Homes: Gender and American Antislavery Politics* (Chapel Hill: University of North Carolina Press, 2003): 57–69; Anne M. Boylan, *The Origins of Women's Activism: New York and Boston, 1797–1840* (Chapel Hill: University of North Carolina Press, 2002); On femininity of clergy and piety: Rotundo, *American Manhood,* 169–72; Horlick, *Country Boys and Merchant Princes,* 226–66; On late nineteenth-century uses of the YMCA for manhood construction: Thomas Winter, *Making Men, Making Class: The YMCA and Workingmen, 1877–1920* (Chicago: University of Chicago Press, 2002); On how temperance men masked entering the "feminized realm of religion and reform": Dorsey, *Reforming Men and Women,* 131–35.

36. Luskey, "Marginal Men," 295–96; Patterson diary. For other examples of oscillating: Susan Lee Johnson, "Bulls, Bears, and Dancing Boys: Race, Gender, and Leisure in the California Gold Rush," *Radical History Review* 60 (Fall 1994): 16.

37. Patterson diary.

38. Roberts, *American Alchemy,* 207–9, 212; Dorsey, *Reforming Men and Women,* 123, 147–9, 144.

39. Zakim, *Ready-Made Democracy,* 110–11, 124; Cohen, *Murder of Helen Jewett,* 267.

40. Sandage, *Born Losers,* 124, 94, 131, 146, 152–53. I extend Augst's discussion of character as morality to distinguish between gendered moralities: *Clerk's Tale,* 191.

41. Alger, *Ragged Dick.*

42. Byars, "Making of the Self-Made Man," 109; Johnson, *Shopkeeper's Millennium,* 123; Michael Zuckerman, "The Nursery Tales of Horatio Alger," *American Quarterly* 24 (May 1972): 191–209; Hilkey, *Character Is Capital,* 89; Mary Clemmer Ames, *Victoire* (New York: Carleton, 1864), 40–41; A Working-Woman, "Woman's Work and Wages," *Harper's New Monthly Magazine* 38 (March 1869): 667; Fanny Fern, *Ruth Hall, and Other Writings,* ed. Joyce W. Warren (1855; reprint, New Brunswick: Rutgers University Press, 1986), 107, 103, 108, 93.

43. Herman Melville, "Bartleby," in *The Portable Melville,* ed. Jay Leyda (New York: Viking, 1952); Augst points out the over three-hundred and fifty writings on "Bartleby, the Scrivener": *Clerk's Tale* 208, 218–31, 242–48; Sandage, *Born Losers,* 62–64.

44. Melville, "Bartleby," 5, 6, 8, 10, 11, 13.

45. Ames, *Victoire,* 140–41; Melville, "Bartleby," 11, 45–46; Dorsey, *Reforming Men and Women,* 110; Balleisen suggests that bankrupt proprietors heeded the midcentury advice for patience by embracing the stability of clerkships over risks of borrowing, yet he found that two-fifths of thirty-five New York clerks had become proprietors again within a few years: *Navigating Failure,* 212.

46. George William Curtis, *Prue and I* (New York: Dix, Edwards, 1856), 136, 85.

47. Self-study was not new: Rhys Isaac, "Preachers and Patriots: Popular Culture and the Revolution in Virginia," in *The American Revolution,* ed. Alfred F. Young (DeKalb: Northern Illinois University Press, 1976), 132; Thomas Augst, "The Business of Reading in Nineteenth-Century America: The New York Mercantile Library," *American Quarterly* 50 (June 1998): 284; W. J. Rorabaugh, *The Craft Apprentice: From Franklin to the Machine Age in America* (New York: Oxford University Press, 1986), 33–36; Ryan, *Cradle of the Middle Class,* 170–72.

48. Aron finds that about one-third of those in the Department of the Interior had only a common school education in 1880 and 1900: *Ladies and Gentlemen of the Civil Service,* 198; Joel Perlmann, "After Leaving School: The Jobs of Young People in Providence, R.I., 1880–1915," in *Schools in Cities: Consensus and Conflict in American Educational History,* ed. Ronald K. Goodenow and Diane Ravitch (New York: Holmes & Meier, 1983), 17–204; William J. Reese, *The Origins of the American High School* (New Haven: Yale University Press, 1995), 234; For biographical examples: "Obituary," *S-PV* 1 (October 1863): 33; Thomas C. Quinn, ed., *Massachusetts of To-Day: A Memorial of the State Issued for the World's Columbian Exposition at Chicago* (Boston: Columbia Publishing, 1892), 188, 93; John C. Rand, comp., *One of a Thousand: A Series of Biographical Sketches of One Thousand Representative Men Residents in the Commonwealth of Massachusetts, A.D. 1888–89* (Boston: First National, 1890), 10.

49. Stephen P. Rice, *Minding the Machine: Languages of Class in Early Industrial America* (Berkeley: University of California Press, 2004); 27; Jonathan A. Glickstein, *Concepts of Free Labor in Antebellum America* (New Haven: Yale University Press, 1991), 55–70; Barbara Sicherman, "Reading and Ambition: M. Carey Thomas and Female Heroism," *American Quarterly* 45 (March 1993): 75; On common criticism of novel reading since the American Revolution: Linda K. Kerber, *Women of the Republic: Intellect and Ideology in Revolutionary America* (Chapel Hill: University of North Carolina Press, 1980), 237–52; Louise L. Stevenson, "Prescription and Reality: Reading Advisers and Reading Practice, 1860–1880," *Book Research Quarterly* 4 (Winter 1990–91): 47–54; Edwin G. Knepper, *History of Business Education in United States* (Bowling Green, OH: Edwards Brothers, 1941), 31–32, 37ff.; Despite the common portrait of fiction reading as feminine, Augst shows advisors recommending fiction as an entrée to serious reading: *Clerk's Tale,* 191–203; On similarities of men's and women's reading interests: Ronald J. Zboray and Mary Saracino Zboray, "'Have You Read . . . ?': Real Readers and Their Responses in Antebellum Boston and Its Region," *Nineteenth-Century Literature* 52 (September 1992): 153; Ronald J. Zboray, *A Fictive People: Antebellum Economic Development and the American Reading Public* (New York: Oxford University Press, 1993), 164–67.

50. T. S. Arthur, *Advice to Young Men on Their Duties and Conduct in Life* (Boston: Phillips, Sampson, 1853), 45, 178, 53, 44, 60–61; Hunt, *Worth and Wealth,* 199.

51. Alger, *Ragged Dick,* 109; Morse quoted in Augst, *Clerk's Tale,* 82.

52. Augst, *Clerk's Tale,* 35, 39, 42–49.

53. Ronald J. Zboray, "Literary Enterprise and the Mass Market Publishers and Business Innovation in Antebellum America," *Studies in Economic and Business History* 10 (1992): 168–82; idem, *Fictive People,* 123–24; My tabulation from H. R. Hatfield and A. C. Littleton's "A Check-List of Early Bookkeeping Texts" shows an upsurge in European texts at the end of the eighteenth century, but nowhere as high as the antebellum American expansion: *Accounting Review* 7 (September 1932): 194–206; Henry George, *The Life of Henry George* (Garden City, NY: Doubleday, 1911), 47.

54. Patterson diary; On judging others: Sandage, *Born Losers,* 123.

55. *Hunt's* quoted in Blumin, *Emergence of the Middle Class,* 215; Augst, "Business of Reading," 271, 274; idem, *Clerk's Tale,* 161, 167–68.

56. Augst, *Clerk's Tale,* 88–90, 176–77, 183, 200.

57. Benjamin R. Haynes and Harry P. Jackson, *A History of Business Education in the United States* (Cincinnati: South-Western, 1935), 9, 10, 20–22, 27, 33; Emit Duncan Grizzell, *Origin and Development of the High School in New England before 1865* (New York: Macmillan, 1923), 42–43, 86–87, 290–91; Janice Harriet Weiss, "Educating for Clerical Work: A History of Commercial Education in the United States Since 1850" (Ed.D. diss., Harvard University, 1978).

58. Haynes and Jackson, *History of Business Education,* x, 23, 28–29; Horlick, *Country Boys and Merchant Princes,* 176–77, "Comer's Commercial College, at Boston, Mass.," *PW* 6 (July 1891): 371; "The Bryant Stratton Commercial School," *PW* 15 (May 1900): 536; May Allinson, comp., *The Public Schools and Women in Office Service,* Studies in Economic Relations of Women (Boston: Women's Educational and Industrial Union, 1914), 5, 7; Boston's business colleges grew from six in 1840–70 to thirteen in 1876–88 and eleven in 1889–95: Massachusetts Bureau of Statistics of Labor, *Census of the Commonwealth of Massachusetts, 1895: Population and Social Statistics,* vol. 3 (Boston: Wright & Potter, 1896), 215; Boston School Committee, *Annual Report 1865–66* (Boston, 1867), 133–35; U.S., Department of the Interior, Bureau of Education, cited in Knepper, *History of Business Education,* 67–68; Boston School Committee, *Annual Report* (Boston, 1869), 177–78; idem, *Annual Report* (Boston, 1876), 206–8; Ileen A. DeVault, *Sons and Daughters of Labor: Class and Clerical Work in Turn-of-the-Century Pittsburgh* (Ithaca: Cornell University Press, 1990), 28–35; Anita J. Rapone, "Clerical Labor Formation: The Office Woman in Albany, 1870–1930" (Ph.D. diss., New York University, 1981), 118; Lisa M. Fine, *The Souls of the Skyscraper: Female Clerical Workers in Chicago, 1870–1930* (Philadelphia: Temple University Press, 1990), 120–27.

59. Joyce Appleby, *Inheriting the Revolution: The First Generation of Americans* (Cambridge: Harvard University Press, Belknap, 2000), 104.

60. T. J. Griffin, "Oliver Dyer," *PM* 8 (1 February 1894): 54; "The Writing and Spelling Reform: Spelling Reform," *Propagandist* 1 (6 November 1850): 5; "Disadvantages of Common Spelling; Advantages of Phonetics," *UP* 3 (1854): 42; Otis B. Goodall, "Augustus French Boyle," *PM* 7 (1 October 1893): 262–64; "Both Sides of the Question: Stenography vs. Phonography," *Propagandist* 1 (18 December 1850): 1 [*Daily Albany Argus*].

61. "Our Name," *Propagandist* 1 (6 November 1850): 4; Quote: "Prospectus," *A-S* 1 (1 June 1850): n.p. [4].

62. "The Present Condition of the Reform," *A-S* 1 (1 June 1850): n.p. [1]; "The Phonographic Correspondence," *A-S* 1 (1 June 1850): n.p. [1].

63. "Mrs. Eliza Boardman Burnz," *PM* 7 (1 May 1893): 164–66; Landroth, "History and Development of Pitmanic Shorthand," 42, 216–17.

64. On generational faith in progress: Appleby, *Inheriting the Revolution,* 56–89; *Dictionary of the History of Ideas,* 1973 ed., s.v. "Perfectability of Man" and "Progress in the Modern Era"; Edward F. Underhill, "Biographical Sketch of Theron C. Leland," *PM* 6 (September 1892): 361–62.

65. "Stephen Pearl Andrews," *PM* 7 (February 1893): 24–27.

66. Helen Lefkowitz Horowitz, "Victoria Woodhull, Anthony Comstock, and Conflict over Sex in the United States in the 1870s," *Journal of American History* 87 (September 2000): 412–13; Griffin, "Oliver Dyer," 52–57; "Mr. Oliver Dyer," *PW* 4 (May 1888): 190; "Shorthand Authors," *BPM* 4 (November 1879): 225; letter to the editor, *Propagandist* 1 (6 November 1850): 6; Elizabeth Cady Stanton, "Seneca Falls Declaration of Sentiments," http://www.senecafalls.com/history/sentiments.php; *UP* 2 (May 1853): 97–100.

67. "Prospectus," *Propagandist* 1 (6 November 1850): 1; Quote: "Prospectus," *A-S* 1 (1 June 1850): n.p. [1]; "Book Reviews," *BPM* 3 (June 1878): 119.

68. On popularity of dime museums: Dennett, *Weird and Wonderful;* "Presidents of the State Stenographers' Associations," *PM* 8 (15 October 1894): 301 [*New York World;* "Shorthand Writing in Washington," *PM* 2 (August 1888): 172 [*New York World*]; "Dr. Wm. H. Samuel," *PM* 8 (1 November 1894): 363–64; Quote on attention: "Personal," *BPMRJ* 14 (October 1889): 307–8; "Personal—Biographical Sketch of Mr. and Mrs. Chas. T. Brown," *BPM* 10 (November 1885): 292–93; Quote on show window: "Presidents of the Stenography Associations," *PM* 5 (November 1891): 344, 342; "Stephen P. Corboy," *PM* 14 (July 1890): 204; H.T.O., "Experiences," *BPM* 2 (June 1877): 97–98; "Biographical Portraits and Sketches," *BPM-W* 14 (6 January 1889): 6–7; "Personal," *BPM* 10 (September 1885): 221–22; "Personal," *BPM* 8 (April 1883): 95; "Charles C. Weller," *PM* 5 (October 1891): 311; "Personal—Biographical Sketch of S. W. Goodalf, Pioneer of the Art in Michigan," *BPM* 7 (May 1882): 123–24; "Henry J. Gensler," *PM* 11 (15 February 1897): 57–59; "Dan Brown," *PM* 8 (1 May 1894): 132.

69. "Personal—Theodore F. Shuey, the Old Phonography," *BPM* 3 (October 1878): 188–89.

70. "Col. Edward B. Dickinson," *PM* 4 (April 1890): 77; David Wolfe Brown, "How Long?—a Symposium—Concluded," *PM* 9 (1 August 1895): 228–32; "The 'World's' Pictures of Popular American Stenographers—No. 2," *PW* 3 (July 1888): 236; "Biographical Sketch of O. W. Whittlesey of Missouri Valley, Iowa," *BPM* 9 (December 1884): 337; "Presidents of the State Stenographers' Associations," *PM* 6 (October 1892): 407, 409; "Shorthand and the Law: A Distinguished Trio," *PM* 7 (15 July 1893): 263; Andrews: "Prospectus," *Propagandist* 1 (6 November 1850): 1.

71. "Stenographers Who Have Risen," *PW* 3 (May 1888): 189.

72. "Mr. Truman J. Ellinwood," *PW* 4 (May 1888): 191; "Presidents of the State Stenographers' Associations," *PM* 8 (15 October 1894): 301–2; Some used stenography to hide secrets of inappropriate behavior in their diaries: Johnson, "Bulls, Bears, and Dancing Boys," 17–18.

73. Landroth, "History and Development of Pitmanic Shorthand," 77; F.A.N., "How I

Learnt Shorthand," *American Short-hand Writer* 2 (October 1882): 5–6; On journalist apprentices: "Presidents of the Stenography Associations," *PM* 5 (November 1891): 344, 342; "Stephen O'Meara," *PM* 7 (1 December 1893): 445–46; "Personals," *BPM* 7 (December 1882): 331–35.

74. "To Lawyers," *Propagandist* 1 (6 November 1850): 5; "Shorthand and the Law," 5–8; "Personal—Biographical Sketch of J. G. Pomerene," *BPM* 7 (July 1882): 175; "Dr. William H. Samuel," *PM* 8 (1 November 1894): 363–64; "Hon. Charles A. Sumner," *PW* 3 (May 1888): 192; "Presidents of the State Stenographers' Associations," *PM* 8 (15 October 1894): 300.

75. "Office of Osgoodby & Gilbert, Stenographers and Law Reporters," 1 October 1868, O'Keefe Collection, box 15, NYPL; "Louis Feeser, Buffalo New York, Phonographic Law Reporter," O'Keefe Collection, box 15, NYPL; Philander Deming, *The Story of a Pathfinder* (1907; reprint, Freeport, NY: Books for Libraries Press, 1970), 24–42.

76. "Portraits and Sketches of Graduates of Scott-Browne's College of Phonography," *BPM* 8 (December 1883): 328.

77. "Personal," *BPM* 6 (March 1881): 47.

78. "Stenographers Who Have Risen," 190.

79. "'World's' Pictures of Popular American Stenographers," 235; "Charles A. Sumner," 192; Charles T. Dunwell, "Personal—Biographical Sketch of Edward F. Underhill," *BPM* 2 (September 1877): 145; "H. W. Thorne," *PM* 10 (1 May 1896): 275–76, "Shorthand and the Law," 5; "Personal—Brief Biographical Sketch of John J. McElhone," *BPM* 4 (April 1879): 67; "Reporters Ahoy!" *Propagandist* 1 (6 November 1850): 4; *Propagandist* 1 (4 December 1850): 4.

80. "William Dawson Bridge, A.M.," *IPW* 9 (May 1894): 296; "Personal," *BPM* 8 (April 1883): 95; "Shorthand Authors," 222; "Autobiographic Sketch of Thomas Towndrow," *PM* 8 (1 June 1894): 163–65; "Personals," *BPM* 7 (December 1882): 331–33, 348; Griffin, "Oliver Dyer," 56; Advertisement: *PM* (1856): n.p.; W. I. Pratt, ed., "A History of American Shorthand Journalism," *PW* 8 (June 1893): 282–83, 8 (July 1893): 300–302, 8 (August 1893): 320; "Shorthand and the Law," 5–8; Landroth, "History and Development of Pitmanic Shorthand," 63–65; Zboray, *Fictive People,* 145; On sporting weeklies' price: Horowitz, *Rereading Sex,* 159.

81. "Certified Teachers—Jay Thomas," *PM* 8 (15 April 1894): 123; On Fazel: "Presidents of the Stenography Associations," *PM* 5 (November 1891): 345.

82. "Personals," *BPM* 7 (December 1882): 336–37; "Personal," *BPM* 7 (January 1882): 8; Quote in Brown, "How Long?" 228–32; "Personal," *BPM* 2 (November 1877): 181–83.

83. "Presidents of the State Stenographers' Associations," *PM* 7 (15 October 1893): 385; "Presidents of the State Stenographers' Associations," *PM* 8 (15 October 1894): 302; "Stenographers Who Have Risen," 189; "Personal," *BPM* 8 (April 1883): 95.

84. "Intelligence, etc.," *PM* (October 1860): n.p.; Benn Pitman, *Manual of Phonography* (Cincinnati: Phonographic Institute, 1855), 16; Elias Longley, *American Manual of Phonography: Being a Complete Guide to the Acquisition of Pitman's Phonetic Shorthand* (Cincinnati: Longley, 1864), vi–viii.

85. Catherine Allgor, *Parlor Politics: In Which the Ladies of Washington Help Build a City and a Government* (Charlottesville: University Press of Virginia, 2000), 109.

86. "Personal," *BPM* 7 (December 1886): 313–14.

87. Rider, "History of the Male Stenographer," 4, 9–11, 20, 71; Dunwell, "Sketch of Edward F. Underhill," 145; On flitting between jobs early in the century: Appleby, *Inheriting the Revolution,* 60; "Personal," *BPM* 2 (November 1877): 181–83; "'World's' Pictures of Popular American Stenographers," 235; "American Court Reporters and What Systems of Shorthand They Write," *PW* 8 (July 1893): 296; On state constitutional conventions: B. Rowland Berthoff, "Conventional Mentality: Free Blacks, Women, and Business Persons, 1820–1870," *Journal of American History* 76 (December 1989): 754–55.

CHAPTER 2

1. John B. Ellis [James Towner], *The Sights and Secrets of the National Capital: A Work Descriptive of Washington, City in All Its Various Phases* (New York: U.S. Publishing, 1869), 383; I thank Jesse Battan for these citations about Ellis's pseudonym, utopian activism, and conflicts with free lovers: Molly McGarry, "Spectral Sexualities: Nineteenth-Century Spiritualism, Moral Panics, and the Making of U.S. Obscenity Law," *Journal of Women's History* (Summer 2000): 25; Spencer C. Olin Jr., "The Oneida Community and the Instability of Charismatic Authority," *Journal of American History* 67 (September 1980): 2:285–300.

2. On separate spheres and women as dependents: Linda K. Kerber, "Female Worlds, Woman's Place: The Rhetoric of Women's History," *Journal of American History* 75 (June 1988): 14–39; Barbara Welter, "The Cult of True Womanhood," in *Dimity Convictions: The American Woman in the Nineteenth Century* (Athens: Ohio University Press, 1976); Christine Stansell, *City of Women: Sex and Class in New York, 1789–1860* (New York: Knopf, 1986), 22–30, 46–53; Lee Virginia Chambers-Schiller, *Liberty, a Better Husband: Single Women in America; The Generations of 1780–1840* (New Haven: Yale University Press, 1984), 48–53; Jeanne Boydston, *Home and Work: Housework, Wages, and the Ideology of Labor in the Early Republic* (New York: Oxford University Press, 1990), chaps. 5–7.

3. For other studies on domesticity: Kathryn Kish Sklar, *Catharine Beecher: A Study in American Domesticity* (New Haven: Yale University Press, 1973); Nancy F. Cott, *The Bonds of Womanhood: "Woman's Sphere" in New England, 1780–1835* (New Haven: Yale University Press, 1977); Mary P. Ryan, *Cradle of the Middle Class: The Family in Oneida County, New York, 1790–1865* (Cambridge: Cambridge University Press), 1981; Karen Halttunen, *Confidence Men and Painted Women: A Study of Middle-Class Culture in America, 1830–1870* (New Haven: Yale University Press, 1982); Wendy Gamber, *The Boardinghouse in Nineteenth-Century America* (Baltimore: Johns Hopkins University Press, 2007); Literary criticism on domesticity: Nina Baym, *Woman's Fiction: A Guide to Novels by and about Women in America, 1820–1870* (Ithaca: Cornell University Press, 1978); Jane P. Tompkins, *Sensational Designs: The Cultural Work of American Fiction, 1790–1860* (New York: Oxford University Press, 1985); Mary Kelley, *Private Woman, Public Stage: Literary Domesticity in Nineteenth-Century America* (New York: Oxford University Press, 1984); Frances B. Cogan, *All-American Girl: The Ideal of Real Womanhood in Mid-Nineteenth-Century America* (Athens: University of Georgia Press, 1989), 33–55; Janice Hume, "Defining the Historic American Heroine: Changing Characteristics of Heroic Women in Nineteenth-Century Media," *Journal of Popular Culture* 32 (Summer 1997): 4–7; Fanny Fern, *Ruth Hall, and Other Writings,* ed. Joyce W.

Warren (1855; reprint, New Brunswick: Rutgers University Press, 1986), 40, 53, 69, 167–72; Fern's criticism of her family made her work controversial: Ronald J. Zboray and Mary Saracino Zboray, "'Have You Read . . . ?': Real Readers and Their Responses in Antebellum Boston and Its Region," *Nineteenth-Century Literature* 52 (September 1992): 155.

4. In 1860, nearly half of clerical women living in Boston alone or with a family member other than parents came from outside of Massachusetts, usually Maine, New Hampshire, or Connecticut, whereas very few of the third-generation or more women living with both parents were born out of Massachusetts; middle-class women were more likely to be native-born of native-born parents: Carole Srole, "'A Position that God has not Particularly Assigned to Men: The Feminization of Clerical Work, Boston, 1960–1915" (Ph.D. diss., University of California, Los Angeles, 1984), Appendix, B10; On family crisis: idem, "'Beyond One's Control': Life Course and the Tragedy of Class, Boston, 1880 to 1900," *Journal of Family History* 11, no. 1 (1986): 43–54; In 1870, triple the percentage of immigrant and second-generation clerical women lived with fathers (30 percent) in comparison to those without fathers (10.7 percent), suggesting that the working class needed to work despite their fathers' presence; more women lived with unemployed fathers, 6.7 percent compared to only 1.4 percent of the men, although numbers are small: see appendix, table C3.

5. Amal Amireh, *The Factory Girl and the Seamstress: Imagining Gender and Class in Nineteenth Century American Fiction,* (New York: Garland, 2000), 19, 21–24; Wendy Gamber, *The Female Economy: The Millinery and Dressmaking Trades, 1860–1930* (Urbana: University of Illinois Press, 1997), 15–19, 161–68; Cogan, *All-American Girl,* 206–7, 211–12, 216, 237; Lee Virginia Chambers-Schiller described the difficulties for women who did have ambition: *Liberty: Better Husband,* 175–81; On lampooning ambitious women: Scott A. Santage, *Born Losers: A History of Failure in America* (Cambridge: Harvard University Press, 2005), 85.

6. Cogan, *All-American Girl,* 209, 213; Hume, "Defining the Historic American Heroine," 10; Amy Gilman, "'Cogs to the Wheels': The Ideology of Women's Work in Mid-19th-Century Fiction," in *Hidden Aspects of Women's Work,* ed. Christine Rose et al (New York: Praeger, 1987), 121, 129; Barbara Sicherman, "Reading *Little Women:* The Many Lives of a Text," in *U.S. History as Women's History: New Feminist Essays,* ed. Linda K. Kerber, Alice Kessler-Harris, and Kathryn Kish Sklar (Chapel Hill: University of North Carolina Press, 1995), 256–60, 264; Maria Susanna Cummins, *The Lamplighter,* ed. Nina Baym (1854; reprint, New Brunswick: Rutgers University Press, 1988), 140.

7. Susan Warner, *The Wide, Wide World* (1850; reprint, New York: Feminist Press, 1987), 9, 140–41; Fern, *Ruth Hall,* xvii, 79–82, 114–22, 125–27.

8. Cummins, *Lamplighter,* 218.

9. Michael D. Pierson, *Free Hearts and Free Homes: Gender and American Antislavery Politics* (Chapel Hill: University of North Carolina Press, 2003), 76–77.

10. Women who never married looked for a religious or artistic "calling" to give meaning to their lives: Chambers-Schiller, *Liberty, a Better Husband,* 84–97, 67–82; Quoted in Pierson, *Free Hearts and Free Homes,* 160–61, 87–88, 90.

11. D. C. Bloomer, *Life and Writings of Amelia Bloomer* (New York: Schocken, 1975), 152–53, 62–63, 165; Blanche Glassman Hersh, *The Slavery of Sex: Feminist-Abolitionists in*

America (Urbana: University of Illinois Press, 1978), 49–50, 88; For some recent examples of this literature: Nancy Isenberg, *Sex, Citizenship in Antebellum America* (Chapel Hill: University of North Carolina Press, 1998), 175; Sylvia D. Hoffert, *When Hens Crow: The Woman's Rights Movement in Antebellum America* (Bloomington: University of Indiana Press, 1995): 32–52; Judith Wellman, *The Road to Seneca Falls: Elizabeth Cady Stanton and the First Woman's Rights Convention* (Urbana: University of Illinois Press, 2004): 91–159.

12. Brian P. Luskey, "Jumping Counters in White Collars: Manliness, Respectability, and Work in the Antebellum City," *Journal of the Early Republic* 26 (Summer 2006): 207, 211; idem, "The Marginal Men: Merchants' Clerks and Society in the Northeastern United States, 1790–1860," (Ph.D. diss., Emory University, 2004), 217–19; *Godey's Lady's Book* quoted in Edwin Gabler, *The American Telegrapher: A Social History, 1860–1900* (New Brunswick: Rutgers University Press, 1988), 125; Pierson, *Free Hearts and Free Homes,* 104; "Phonography—for the Ladies," *PM* (January 1858), n.p.; "A Secretary Wanted," *PM* (October 1859), n.p.

13. Lyde Cullen Sizer, *The Political Work of Northern Women Writers and the Civil War, 1850–1872* (Chapel Hill: University of North Carolina Press, 2000), 176.

14. A Working-Woman, "Woman's Work and Wages," *Harper's New Monthly Magazine* 38 (March 1869): 667; Alice Fahs, "The Feminized Civil War: Gender, Northern Popular Literature, and the Memory of the War, 1861–1900," *Journal of American History* 85 (March 1999): 1476–78; "Women as Government Clerks," *New York Times,* 18 February 1869, 2; Ann Russo and Cheris Kramarae, eds., *The Radical Women's Press of the 1850s,* 2nd ed. (London: Routledge, 2001), 2:95–123.

15. Quoted on "sentimental victims": Amireh, *Factory Girl,* 137, see also 65–73; Elizabeth Stuart Phelps, *The Silent Partner, a Novel, and "The Tenth of January," a Short Story,* with an afterword by Mari Jo Buhle and Florence Howe (1868; reprint, Old Westbury, NY: Feminist Press, 1983), 50, 52, 79, 81, 86, 89, 77, 291–92, 319, 348; Gilman, "'Cogs to the Wheels,'" 121, 129; Michael Denning, *Mechanic Accents: Dime Novels and Working-Class Culture in America* (London: Verso, 1987), 187, 195–96; Virginia Penny, *Think and Act: A Series of Articles Pertaining to Men and Women, Work and Wages* (1869; reprint, New York: Arno and *New York Times,* 1971), 128–29, 65.

16. A Working-Woman, "Woman's Work and Wages," 665–70; Cummins, *Lamplighter,* 218; Most of Chambers-Schiller's unmarried authors calling for financial independence wrote in the 1860s and 1870s: *Liberty, a Better Husband,* 67–72.

17. Felicia Luz Carr, "All for Love: Gender, Class, and the Woman's Dime Novel in Nineteenth-Century America" (Ph.D. diss, George Mason University, 2003), 23–37, 152–218; Henry Nash Smith, *Virgin Land: The American West as Symbol and Myth* (Cambridge: Harvard University Press, 1950; reprint, New York: Random House, Vintage, 1970), 112–14; Denning, *Mechanic Accents,* 185–86, 193–95; Amireh, *Factory Girl,* 55; Nan Enstad, *Ladies of Labor, Girls of Adventure: Working Women, Popular Culture, and Labor Politics at the Turn of the Twentieth Century* (New York: Columbia University Press, 1999), 74–75; Dorothy S. Pam, "Exploitation, Independence, and Solidarity: The Changing Role of American Working Women as Reflected in the Working-Girl Melodrama, 1870–1910" (Ph.D. diss., State University of New York, 1980), 58, 65, 151–53.

18. Michael Zakim, "The Business Clerk as Social Revolutionary; or, A Labor History of the Non-Producing Classes," *Journal of the Early Republic* 26 (Winter 2006): 14–21; On

store and office clerks: Luskey, "Marginal Men," 146–53; Lemuel Shattuck, *Report to the Committee of the City Council Appointed to Obtain the Census of Boston for the Year 1845* (Boston: John H. Eastburn, 1846); The 1860 U.S. Manuscript Census on Boston recorded only nine male copyists.

19. Zakim, "Business Clerk," 21.

20. Kenneth W. Dobyns, *The Patent Office Pony: A History of the Early Patent Offices* (Newville, PA: Sergeant Kirklands Museum, 1997), 78–86; JoAnne Yates, *Control through Communication: The Rise of System in American Management* (Baltimore: Johns Hopkins University Press, 1989), 28; In 1860, the census reported male copyists as the poorest of all clerks—while 32.4 percent of Boston's clerical men over age twenty-five owned some personal property, only one of nine male copyists held any: U.S. Manuscript Census, 1860.

21. Jonathan A. Glickstein, *Concepts of Free Labor in Antebellum America* (New Haven: Yale University Press, 1991), 95–96, 101, 123–25, 189–219; Hawthorne quoted in Amireh, *Factory Girl,* 80–81; Herman Melville, "The Paradise of Bachelors and the Tartarus of Maids," in *The Heath Anthology of American Literature,* vol. 1 (Lexington, MA: D. C. Heath, 1990), 2458.

22. Tamara Plakins Thornton, *Handwriting in America: A Cultural History* (New Haven: Yale University Press, 1996), 62, 56–58, 73; Charles Dickens, *David Copperfield,* with a foreword by May Lamberton Becker (1850; reprint, New York: Dodd, Mead, 1943), chaps. 36, 5.

23. Thomas Dublin, *Transforming Women's Work: New England Lives in the Industrial Revolution* (Ithaca: Cornell University Press, 1994), 21, 59; Dobyns, *Patent Office Pony,* 81, 119, 145; 43; Cindy Sondik Aron, *Ladies and Gentlemen of the Civil Service: Middle-Class Workers in Victorian America* (New York: Oxford University Press, 1987), 67–74, 81–84, 23, 211.

24. Dobyns, *Patent Office Pony,* 81, 119, 142–45, 158; William E. Barton, *The Life of Clara Barton: Founder of the American Red Cross* (Boston: Houghton Mifflin, 1922), 89–100.

25. Janet E. Kaufman, "'Treasury Girls': Working Women of the South," *Civil War Times Illustrated* 25, no. 3 (1986): 32–38; "Women as Government Clerks," 2; Aron, *Ladies and Gentlemen of the Civil Service,* 68–73.

26. U.S. Manuscript Census, Boston, 1870; Massachusetts Bureau of Statistics of Labor, *The Census of Massachusetts, 1875,* vol. 1 (Boston: Albert J. Wright, 1876), 551–53.

27. Rebecca Harding Davis, *Margaret Howth: A Story of To-day* (Boston: Ticknor Fields, 1862; reprint, New York: Feminist Press, 1990), 79, 11, 9–10, 51.

28. Glickstein, *Concepts of Free Labor,* 101, 187–219; idem, *American Exceptionalism, American Anxiety: Wages, Competition, and Degraded Labor in the Antebellum United States* (Charlottesville: University Press of Virginia, 2002), 4; Chicago Stenographers, *The Second Annual Dinner,* 11 January 1879 (Chicago: Blakely, Brown Marsh, 1879), 18.

29. House Select Committee, *Report of the Select Committee to Investigate Certain Charges against the Treasury Department,* 38th Cong., 1st sess., 1864, H. Rep. 140, 21–68; Aron, *Ladies and Gentlemen of the Civil Service,* 164–69; Barton, *Life of Clara Barton,* 91; Lester Ward, *Young Ward's Diary,* ed. Bernard J. Stern (New York: G. P. Putnam's Sons, 1935).

30. Cathy N. Davidson, *Revolution and the Word: The Rise of the Novel in America*

(New York: Oxford University Press, 1986), 110–50; Although Angela Farkas differentiates story papers from dime novels because of their overlap with conventional literature, I will refer to both as dime novels or mass-marketed stories: Angela Farkas, "Sensational Tales and Working-Girl Melodrama: Popular Story Paper Fiction and Its Readers in Late Nineteenth Century America" (Ph.D. diss., University of Pittsburgh, 2003), 6–21; Carr, "All for Love," 115–218; Judith R. Walkowitz, *City of Dreadful Delight: Narratives of Sexual Danger in Late-Victorian London,* with a foreword by Catharine R. Stimpson (Chicago: University of Chicago Press, 1992), 81–120; Denning, *Mechanic Accents,* 93–97, 106, 111; A. I. Cummings, *The Factory Girl; or, Gardez La Coeur* (Lowell: J. E. Short, 1847); 1, 51–52, 58–62; Halttunen, *Confidence Men and Painted Women,* 5–13, 33–40.

31. "The Lady Clerks in the Departments," *New York Times,* 10 November 1865, 4; Ellis, *Sights and Secrets of the National Capital,* 383–87; Aron, *Ladies and Gentlemen of the Civil Service,* 166, 170, 172; Government corruption fiction: María Amparo Ruiz de Burton, *Who Would Have Thought It?* ed. Rosaura Sánchez and Beatrice Pita (1872; reprint, Houston: Arte Público Press, 1995), 11, 58–59; "Women as Government Clerks," 2; Mark W. Summers, "The Press Gang: Corruption and the Independent Press in the Grant Era," *Congress & the Presidency* 17 (March 1990): 29–44.

32. Lewis Vital Bogy, *In Office: A Story of Washington Life and Society* (Chicago: F. J. Schulte, 1891), 5; Enstad, *Ladies of Labor,* 31–42; Carr, "All for Love," 155–74.

33. Carr, "All for Love," 192; Nancy Catherine Enstad, "Compromised Positions: Working-Class Women, Popular Culture, and Labor Politics, 1890–1920" (Ph.D. diss., University of Minnesota, 1993), 62; Bogy, *In Office,* 53, 75–79, 83–95, 127–28, 143–7, 27–28, 160–61, 176–77, 189, 193, 201–2.

34. Quoted from "Lady Clerks in the Departments," 4; Stansell, *City of Women,* 28–29, 83–89, 96–99, 183–84.

35. On dangers from prostitutes: Amanda Anderson, *Tainted Souls and Painted Faces: The Rhetoric of Fallenness in Victorian Culture* (Ithaca: Cornell University Press, 1993), 16; Rodney Hessinger, *Seduced, Abandoned, and Reborn: Visions of Youth in Middle-Class America, 1780–1850* (Philadelphia: University of Pennsylvania Press, 2005), 44–68; Mary P. Ryan, *Women in Public: Between Banners and Ballots, 1825–1880* (Baltimore: Johns Hopkins University Press, 1990), 70–76; Robert C. Allen, *Horrible Prettiness: Burlesque and American Culture* (Chapel Hill: University of North Carolina Press, 1991), 138–42; John F. Kasson, *Rudeness and Civility: Manners in Nineteenth-Century Urban America* (New York: Hill & Wang, 1990), 100, 103; Halttunen, *Murder Most Foul: The Killer and the American Gothic Imagination* (Cambridge: Harvard University Press, 1998), 191–207, 188–90; On blaming: Helen Lefkowitz Horowitz, *Rereading Sex: Battles over Sexual Knowledge and Suppression in Nineteenth-Century America* (New York: Knopf, 2002), 151, 154; On new government clerks: Aron, *Ladies and Gentlemen of the Civil Service,* 165–70; "Women as Government Clerks," 2; Mary Clemmer Ames, *Ten Years in Washington: Life and Scenes in the National Capital as a Woman Sees Them* (Hartford, CT: A. O. Worthington, 1875), 374–75; Ellis, *Sights and Secrets of the National Capital,* 383.

36. Bogy, *In Office,* 23–24, 37–8, 68, 148–50, 160, 168–69; Carr, "All for Love," 177–86.

37. Boydston, *Home and Work,* 142–63; Glenna Matthews, *The Rise of Public Woman: Woman's Power and Woman's Place in the United States* (New York: Oxford University Press, 1992), 106, 119; Alice Kessler-Harris, *Out to Work: A History of Wage-Earning*

Women in the United States (Oxford: Oxford University Press, 1982), 52–58; C. Dallett Hemphill, *Bowing to Necessities: A History of Manners in America, 1620–1860* (New York: Oxford University Press, 1999), 194–97.

38. Laurel Thatcher Ulrich, *Good Wives: Images and Reality in the Lives of Women in Northern New England, 1650–1750* (New York: Oxford University Press), 37–38; Elisabeth Anthony Dexter, *Career Women of America, 1776–1840* (Francestown, NH: Marshall Jones, 1950), 139–62; Women merchants and artisans also kept records: Patricia A. Cleary, "'She Will Be in the Shop': Women's Sphere of Trade in Eighteenth-Century Philadelphia and New York," *Pennsylvania Magazine of History and Biography* 119, no. 3 (1995): 181–202; Margaret A. Nash, "Rethinking Republican Motherhood: Benjamin Rush and the Young Ladies' Academy of Philadelphia," *Journal of the Early Republic* 17 (Summer 1997): 179; Boydston, *Home and Work*, 88 and 186ff., chap. 7; Laurel Thatcher Ulrich, "Martha Ballard and Her Girls: Women's Work in Eighteenth-Century Maine," in *Work and Labor in Early America*, ed. Stephen Innes (Chapel Hill and London: University of North Carolina Press for the Institute of Early American History and Culture, 1988), 101; Louise A. Tilly and Joan W. Scott, *Women, Work, and Family* (New York: Holt, Rinehart & Winston, 1978), 44–51; T. S. Arthur, *Advice to Young Ladies on Their Duties and Conduct of Life* (1847; reprint, Boston: G. W. Cottrell, 1851), cited in Cogan, *All-American Girl*, 87, 211, 212, 235.

39. Nash, "Rethinking Republican Motherhood," 179; French quoted in Ray Nash, *American Penmanship, 1800–1850: A History of Writing and a Bibliography of Copybooks from Jenkins to Spencer* (Worcester: American Antiquarian Society, 1969): 52; Benjamin R. Haynes and Harry P. Jackson, *A History of Business Education in the United States* (Cincinnati: South-Western, 1935), 22.

40. "Women to the Front," *BPM* 3 (December 1878): 220–21; "Mrs. M. V. Longley," *PM* 8 (15 August 1894): 236–37; Dorinda Outram, "Before Objectivity: Wives, Patronage, and Cultural Reproduction in Early Nineteenth-Century French Science," in *Uneasy Careers and Intimate Lives: Women in Science, 1789–1979*, eds. Pnina G. Abir-am and Dorinda Outram, with a foreword by Margaret W. Rossiter (New Brunswick: Rutgers University Press, 1987), 28–30; Ava Baron, "Women and the Making of the American Working Class: A Study of the Proletarianization of Printers," *Review of Radical Political Economics* 14 (Fall 1982): 27.

41. "A Talk with Mrs. Burnz," *PW* 1 (May 1886): 167; *In Memoriam: Eliza Boardman Burnz* (New York: Burnz, 1906), 27.

42. Kessler-Harris, *Out to Work*, 101–4; Stansell, *City of Women*, 125–28; Joanne J. Meyerowitz, *Women Adrift: Independent Wage Earners in Chicago, 1880–1930* (Chicago: University of Chicago Press, 1988), 117–18; Thomas Dublin, ed., *Farm to Factory: Women's Letters, 1830–1860* (New York: Columbia University Press, 1981), 166–81; On the middle-class assumption that men and women would mix but that men would protect women: Hemphill, *Bowing to Necessities*, 91–92; Later on saleswomen: Susan Porter Benson, *Counter Cultures: Saleswomen, Managers, and Customers in American Department Stores, 1890–1940* (Urbana: University of Illinois Press, 1986), 135–36; House Select Committee, *Report to Investigate Certain Charges*, 21–68.

43. Nurses also entered a world of men; saleswomen worked with and sold primarily to other women, but public concern focused on their few male customers: U.S. Indus-

trial Commission, *Report of the Industrial Commission on the Relations and Conditions of Capital and Labor Employed in Manufacturers and General Business,* vol. 2 (Washington, DC, 1901): 695; Aron, *Ladies and Gentlemen of the Civil Service,* 63, 168–69, 70–73; Robert Edward MacKay, "Managing the Clerks: Office Management from the 1870s through the Great Depression," (Ph.D. diss., Boston University, 1985), 12–14; Sarah Eisenstein, *Give Us Bread but Give Us Roses: Working Women's Consciousness in the United States, 1890 to the First World War* (London: Routledge & Kegan Paul, 1983), 82; Kessler-Harris, *Out to Work,* 102; Mary H. Blewett, *Men, Women, and Work: Class, Gender, and Protest in the New England Shoe Industry, 1780–1910* (Urbana: University of Illinois Press, 1988), 14–17, 179–80; Stansell, *City of Women,* 124–25.

44. On clerks' thievery as resistance: Luskey, "Marginal Men," 313–316; idem, "Jumping Counters," 183; "An Alleged Dishonest Railway Clerk," *Police Gazette,* 26 January 1867, 1, 3; "Confession of A. H. Lee, the Absconding Treasury Clerk," *New York Times,* 15 March 1867, 2. "Life Sketches in the Metropolis: Voices From the Tombs," *Frank Leslie's Illustrated Newspaper,* 3 February 1872, 327; Jerome P. Bjelopera, *City of Clerks: Office and Sales Workers in Philadelphia, 1870–1920* (Urbana: University of Illinois Press, 2005), 125–28.

45. Patricia Cline Cohen, *The Murder of Helen Jewett: The Life and Death of a Prostitute in Nineteenth-Century New York* (New York: Knopf, 1998), 203–17, 19–33, 100; idem, "Unregulated Youth: Masculinity and Murder in the 1830s," *Radical History Review* 52 (Winter 1992): 33–52; Allan Stanley Horlick, *Country Boys and Merchant Princes: The Social Control of Young Men in New York* (Lewisburg and London: Bucknell University Press and Associated University Presses, 1975) 68, 149; "Helen Jewett Murder: A Singular Statement," *New York Times,* 21 August 1855, 3; Horowitz, *Rereading Sex,* 152–53; Ellis, *Sights and Secrets of the National Capital,* 458–61, 452–53; More erotic contact between employees than managers: Aron, *Ladies and Gentlemen of the Civil Service,* 166, 171–72, 84–85; "The Trial of Miss Mary Harris," *New York Times,* 9 July 1865, 8.

46. Denning, *Mechanic Accents,* 191–92; Halttunen, *Confidence Men and Painted Women,* 33–34, 37–41; Bogy, *In Office,* 44–45, 143–44; Stansell, *City of Women,* 125–28; Benita Eisler, ed., *The Lowell Offering: Writings by New England Mill Women, 1840–1845* (New York: Harper, 1977), 187–92; On later concerns about women alone: Meyerowitz, *Women Adrift;* On men raping independent women: Michael Kaplan, "New York City Tavern Violence and the Creation of a Working-Class Male Identity," *Journal of the Early Republic* 15 (Winter 1995): 611–14.

47. On concerns: Patricia Cline Cohen, "Safety and Danger: Women on American Public Transport, 1750–1850," in *Gendered Domains: Rethinking Public and Private in Women's History,* ed. Dorothy O. Helly and Susan M. Reverby (Ithaca: Cornell University Press, 1992), 111, 114; Barbara Young Welke, *Recasting American Liberty: Gender, Race, Law, and the Railroad Revolution, 1865–1920* (Cambridge: Cambridge University Press, 2001), 57; On efforts to make traveling respectable: Amy G. Richter, *Home on the Rails: Women, the Railroad, and the Rise of Public Domesticity* (Chapel Hill: University of North Carolina Press, 2005), 32–47; Meyerowitz, *Women Adrift,* 31; Aron, *Ladies and Gentlemen of the Civil Service,* 56; For Boston's 1880 number (10 of 28): U.S. Manuscript Census, 1880.

48. "The Female Clerks," *New York Times,* 8 May 1864, 3 [*Petersburgh Express*].

49. "Women in Washington," *Winona Daily Republican,* 31 July 1866, 1; Theodore Dreiser, *The Titan* (1914), chap. 39, Project Gutenberg, http://www.gutenberg.org/; Ames, *Ten Years in Washington,* 357–58; Aron, *Ladies and Gentlemen of the Civil Service,* 99, 169.

50. Quotes from J.M.C., "The Female Clerks," *New York Times,* 10 April 1869, 11; "Women as Government Clerks," 2; "Lady Clerks in the Departments," 4.

51. J.M.C., "Female Clerks," 11; "Women as Government Clerks," 2; Ames, *Ten Years in Washington,* 363, 375.

52. J.M.C., "Female Clerks," 11.

53. On scholarly debates over the extent of mechanization, routinization, and demography of workers accounting for the feminization: Sharon Hartman Strom, *Beyond the Typewriter: Gender, Class, and the Origins of Modern American Office Work, 1900–1930* (Urbana: University of Illinois Press, 1992), 172–226; Aron, *Ladies and Gentlemen of the Civil Service,* 65–95; Elyce J. Rotella, *From Home to Office: U.S. Women at Work, 1870–1930,* Studies in American History and Culture, no. 25 (Ann Arbor: UMI Research Press, 1981); Lisa M. Fine, *The Souls of the Skyscraper: Female Clerical Workers in Chicago, 1870–1930* (Philadelphia: Temple University Press, 1990); Margery W. Davies, *Woman's Place Is at the Typewriter: Office Work and Office Workers, 1870–1930* (Philadelphia: Temple University Press, 1982).

54. Alfred D. Chandler Jr., *The Visible Hand: The Managerial Revolution in American Business* (Cambridge: Harvard University Press, Belknap, 1977), 150, 207–35, 249, 287–91, 313, 316–17, 340–44; Glen Porter, *The Rise of Big Business, 1860–1910* (New York: Crowell, 1973); Naomi Lamoreaux, *The Great Merger Movement in American Business, 1895–1904* (New York: Cambridge University Press, 1985); Wesley C. Mitchell, *Business Cycles, The Problem and Its Setting,* National Bureau of Economic Research, no. 10 (New York: National Bureau of Economic Research, 1927), 428; Yates, *Control through Communication,* 66–78, 80–100; Strom, *Beyond the Typewriter,* 184–90; Charles W. Wooton and Carel M. Wolk, "The Evolution and Acceptance of the Loose-Leaf Accounting System, 1885–1935," *Technology & Culture* 41 (January 2000): 80–98.

55. Zunz, *Making America Corporate,* 116; Rotella, *From Home to Office,* 85; Alba M. Edwards, *Population: Comparative Occupation Statistics for the United States, 1870 to 1940* (Washington, DC, 1943), 153; U.S. Department of the Interior, *Ninth Census of the United States, 1870: Statistics of the Population of the United States,* vol. 1 (Washington, DC, 1872), 704–6; U.S. Department of the Interior, Census Office, *Twelfth Census of the United States, 1900: Population,* vol. 2, pt. 2 (Washington, DC, 1901), 505–6, 554.

56. Yates, *Control through Communication,* 43; Carole Srole "'A Blessing to Mankind, and Especially to Womankind': The Typewriter and the Feminization of Clerical Work, Boston, 1860–1920," in *Women, Work, and Technology: Transformations,* ed. Barbara Drygulski Wright et al. (Ann Arbor: University of Michigan Press, 1987), 92–93; "Shorthand in Railroading," *BPMRJ* 10 (November 1885): 281–82; Richard Current, *The Typewriter and the Men Who Made It* (Urbana: University of Illinois Press, 1954).

57. Yates, *Control through Communication,* 31, 33, 36–45; "The Type-Writer Speed Contests," *PM* 2 (September 1888): 200; In 1889, a federal government employee calculated prospective savings of twenty thousand dollars: "Points to Typewriter Operators," *PW* 5 (September 1889): 15; Quotes on mid-1880s: "The Typewriter vs. Saleswomen and

Governesses," *PW* 2 (October 1886): 34 [*New Orleans Daily City*]; "Chicago's Typewriter Operators," *PW* 4 (July 1889): 261 [*Chicago Tribune*]; "Modern Methods of Business Correspondence," *PM* 6 (March 1892): 122–23 [*Springfield Republican*].

58. Quote on breakdowns: E. L. Chambers, "Advice to Amanuenses," *TPW* 17 (April 1901): 149; Quote on wishing for more stenography: K. A. Williams, "Neatness in Typewriter Work," *MS* 1 (20 March 1890): 103.

59. James N. Kimball, "An Average Day," *TPW* 17 (June 1901): 336–37; "Demand for Stenographers in the Navy Yard Branch of the Government Service," *TPW* 19 (May 1902): 264–67; Rotella, *From Home to Office,* 199.

60. U.S. Department of the Interior, *Ninth Census, 1870,* vol. 1, 676, 688; Edwards, *Population,* 153; Rotella, *From Home to Office,* 85; U.S. Department of the Interior, Census Office, *Eleventh Census of the United States, 1890: Report on the Population of the United States,* vol. 1, pt. 2 (Washington, DC, 1897), 638; Massachusetts Bureau of Statistics of Labor, "Sex in Industry," in *Thirty-third Annual Report* (Boston: Wright & Potter, 1902), 140–212; Janice Weiss, "Educating for Clerical Work: The Nineteenth-Century Private Commercial School," *Journal of Social History* 14 (Spring 1981): 410.

61. Janet Hooks, *Women's Occupations through Seven Decades,* U.S. Department of Labor, Women's Bureau, Bulletin 218 (Washington, DC, 1947): 76; Rotella used Alba Edwards's figures for nonagricultural labor force participation, resulting in slightly different percentages (2.5 in 1870, 4.4 in 1880, 19.3 in 1890, 30.2 in 1900, 37.6 in 1910, and 49.2 in 1920): Edwards, *Population,* 91, 100; Rotella, *From Home to Office,* 106.

62. Robert Edward Gleeson, "The Rise of Graduate Management Education in American Universities, 1908–1970" (Ph.D. diss., Carnegie-Mellon University, 1997); W. Ross Yates, *Lehigh University: A History of Education in Engineering, Business, and the Human Condition* (Bethlehem, PA: Lehigh University Press, 1992); Dennis Harlen Day, "The Evolution of Collegiate Accounting Instruction in the United States (1635–1995)" (Ed.D. diss., Northern Illinois University, 1996); Before the Civil War, one-third of all men listed in the *Dictionary of American Biographies* attended college; by 1900, one-half to two-thirds did: Burton J. Bledstein, *The Culture of Professionalism: The Middle Class and the Development of Higher Education in America* (New York: Norton, 1976), 84, 277–78, 297, 124–26, 193; Samuel Haber, *The Quest for Authority and Honor in the American Professions, 1750–1900* (Chicago: University of Chicago Press, 1991), 221–22, 295–96; Of the fifty-three graduates from Boston's English High School in 1888 who went on to college, 60.4 percent entered the professions, while 17 percent chose careers in business: English High School, *Commemorating the Fiftieth Anniversary of the Class of '85, English High School, Boston, Massachusetts* (Boston: n.p., 1935), 65–124; Reed Ueda, *Avenues to Adulthood: The Origins of the High School and Social Mobility in an American Suburb* (Cambridge: Cambridge University Press, 1987), 157; Richard Angelo, "The Students at the University of Pennsylvania and the Temple College, Philadelphia, 1873–1906: Some Notes on Schooling, Class, and Social Mobility in the Late Nineteenth Century," *History of Education Quarterly* 19 (Summer 1979): 188, 191; Burritt B. Bailey, *Professional Distribution of College and University Graduates,* U.S. Department of the Interior, Bureau of Education, Bulletin 19 (Washington, DC, 1912), 145; Joseph F. Kett, *Rites of Passage: Adolescence in America, 1790 to the Present* (New York: Basic Books, 1977), 154.

63. Boston's male foreign-born population as a whole remained relatively stable: Stephen Thernstrom, *The Other Bostonians: Poverty and Progress in the American Metropolis, 1880–1970* (Cambridge: Harvard University Press, 1973), 113; Niles Carpenter, *Immigrants and Their Children, 1920,* U.S. Department of Commerce, Bureau of the Census, census monograph 7 (Washington, DC, 1927), 26–27.

64. There were other signs of a surging working class between 1880 and 1900; slightly more divorcees, wives, and widows joined the clerical workforce, up from 5.4 percent to 7.8 percent; the proportion of single clerical women employed and living with their fathers grew from 35.8 percent to 39.8 percent; Catholic priests officiating at marriages among clerical women that stated who presided also rose from 26.3 percent (26 of 99) to 37.2 percent (383 of 1,028), greater than the growth among the general population, from 40.2 percent (177 of 440) to 44.6 percent (401 of 900); statistics from Carole Srole, "'Position That God Has Not Particularly Assigned to Men', appendix, tables B2 and B4; For a discussion of the relationship between class and demography: Srole, "Position That God Has Not Particularly Assigned to Men," chap. 6; idem, "Beyond One's Control,'" 43–54; Ileen A. DeVault, *Sons and Daughters of Labor: Class and Clerical Work in Turn-of-the-Century Pittsburgh* (Ithaca: Cornell University Press, 1990), 71, 77; Jürgen Kocka, however, found a decline among foreign-born salesclerks from 1880 to 1890–1920: *White Collar Workers in America, 1890–1940: A Social-Political History in International Perspective,* trans. Maura Kealey (London: Sage, 1980), 71; On Philadelphia's slower but similar shift: Bjelopera, *City of Clerks,* 22.

65. Luskey reveals a much higher percentage (43 percent) of foreign-born workers among clerks (most in stores) in midcentury New York: "Jumping Counters," 176.

66. *American Short-hand Writer* 1 (January 1881): 12; William Thorpe, "Correspondence," *BPM* 1 (May 1876): 83; "Editorial Paragraphs," *Munson's* 3 (January 1880): 24; Quote from "The Incompetent Stenographer," *TPW* 13 (July 1898): 492; "News and Things," *Munson's* 5 (March 1886): 145.

67. Marion Mitchell Barr, "A Mistake in Identity: Caused by the Blunders of a Bachelor and a Benedick," *TPW* 26 (October 1905): 203; Elizabeth Colberg Washabaugh, "Eleanor's Investment Which Yielded Better Returns Than Even She Had Hoped For," *TPW* 23 (May 1904): 335; Jennie E. Cook, "True Blue: The Stenographer Was Tried in the Balance and Not Found Wanting," *TPW* 23 (April 1904): 271; Hattie Witherington Sutton, "A Failure! Dorothy's Last Chance—and What She Made of It," *TPW* 25 (May 1905): 342.

68. Glickstein, *Concepts of Free Labor,* 101, 203, 187; Aron, *Ladies and Gentlemen of the Civil Service,* 74, 82.

69. Glickstein, *Concepts of Free Labor,* 101, 187, 203.

CHAPTER 3

1. Ileen A. DeVault, *Sons and Daughters of Labor: Class and Clerical Work in Turn-of-the-Century Pittsburgh* (Ithaca: Cornell University Press, 1990), 157.

2. Stuart Bruchey, ed., *Small Business in American Life* (New York: Columbia University Press, 1980); Mansel G. Blackford, *A History of Small Business in America* (New York: Twayne, 1991), 31–32, 36; U.S. Department of the Interior, *Ninth Census of the*

United States, 1870: Statistics of the Population of the United States, vol. 1 (Washington, DC, 1872), 778; U.S. Department of the Interior, *Tenth Census of the United States, 1880: Statistics on the Population of the United States,* vol. 1 (Washington, DC, 1883), 864; U.S. Department of the Interior, Census Office, *Eleventh Census of the United States, 1890: Report on the Population of the United States,* vol. 1, pt. 2 (Washington, DC, 1897), 638; U.S. Department of the Interior, Census Office, *Twelfth Census of the United States, 1900: Population,* vol. 2, pt. 2 (Washington, DC, 1901), 554; In Boston, proprietor fathers of single women over age fourteen plunged from 20.3 to 13.2 percent, down 35 percent between 1880 and 1900: U.S. Manuscript Census, Boston, 1880 and 1900; Clyde Griffen and Sally Griffen, *Natives and Newcomers: The Ordering of Opportunity in Mid-Nineteenth-Century Poughkeepsie* (Cambridge: Harvard University Press, 1978), 104–5, 127; Massachusetts Bureau of Statistics of Labor, "Changes in Conducting Retail Trade in Boston, since 1874," *Thirtieth Annual Report* (Boston: Wright & Potter, 1899), 2–69; Albert Benedict Wolfe, *The Lodging House Problem in Boston* (Cambridge: Harvard University Press, 1913), 32; U.S. Industrial Commission, *Report of the Industrial Commission on the Relations and Conditions of Capital and Labor Employed in Manufacturers and General Business,* vol. 2 (Washington, DC, 1901): 705–15, 723–24, 731–38; Albert C. Stevens, "The Commercial Death Rate," *Publications of the American Statistical Association* 2 (March 1891): 186–94; Harold C. Livesay, "Lilliputians in Brobdingnag: Small Business in Late-Nineteenth-Century America," in Bruchey, *Small Business in American Life,* 343–44; William Leach, *Land of Desire: Merchants, Power, and the Rise of a New American Culture* (New York: Pantheon, 1993), 26–32.

3. Griffen and Griffen, *Natives and Newcomers,* 60; The proportion of proprietors among lower-wage white-collar workers fell from 77.7 percent (147 of 189) in 1880 to only 56.4 percent (93 of 165) in 1900 among men identified as fathers of single women (fourteen and older) and listed as clerks, salesmen, and proprietors: U.S. Manuscript Census, Boston, 1880 and 1900; In Philadelphia, more younger men worked as clerks between 1890 and 1920: Jerome P. Bjelopera, *City of Clerks: Office and Sales Workers in Philadelphia, 1870–1920* (Urbana: University of Illinois Press, 2005), 41.

4. On saving: Cindy Sondik Aron, *Ladies and Gentlemen of the Civil Service: Middle-Class Workers in Victorian America* (New York: Oxford University Press, 1987), 28–29; On flitting and middle managers: Olivier Zunz, *Making America Corporate, 1870–1920* (Chicago: University of Chicago Press, 1990), 47–49, 129; Angel Kwolek-Folland, *Engendering Business: Men and Women in the Corporate Office, 1870–1930* (Baltimore: Johns Hopkins University Press, 1994), 25, 30; Bjelopera, *City of Clerks,* 40, 75; Clark Davis, *Company Men: White-Collar Life and Corporate Cultures in Los Angeles, 1892–1941* (Baltimore: Johns Hopkins University Press, 2000), 152–60.

5. "Biographical," *BPM-W* 14 (6 January 1889): 6–7; "Presidents of the State Stenographers' Associations," *PM* 5 (November 1891): 344–46; "The Bryant & Stratton Commercial School of Boston," *PW* 5 (July 1890): 355–58; "The Bryant & Stratton Commercial School," *TPW* 15 (May 1900): 536; "Comer's Commercial College, at Boston, Mass.," *PW* 6 (July 1891): 371–73; "A Shorthand School," *PW* 3 (January 1888): 102–4; William E. Hickox, "Shorthand Not for Schools," *IPW* 12 (December 1896): 118; Massachusetts Bureau of Statistics of Labor, *Census of the Commonwealth of Massachusetts, 1895: Population and Social Statistics,* vol. 3 (Boston: Wright & Potter, 1896), 3:215; Julius Ensign Rock-

well, "The Teaching, Practice, and Literature of Shorthand," in U.S. Department of the Interior, Bureau of Education, *Circular of Information of the Bureau of Education,* no. 2 (Washington, DC, 1884), 191.

6. "Notes," *Stenographer* 7 (June 1895): 237; "William O. Wyckoff," *Stenographer* 8 (October 1895): 99.

7. House Committee on the Judiciary, *Stenographers in United States Courts,* 58th Cong., 2nd sess., 30 March 1904, 5–6.

8. "Personal—Frank F. Wood," *BPMRJ* 6 (March 1881): 47; "William O. Wyckoff," *Stenographer* 8 (October 1895): 99.

9. One woman claimed that her employer first brought typewriters to reporting firms in 1875: "A Pioneer in Typewriting," *TPW* 15 (December 1899): 217; "Special Uses of the Typewriter," *BPM-W* 14 (2 December 1889): 364–65; "Frank F. Burt," *TPW* 15 (April 1900): 485–86; F. J. Squibb and I. S. Dement, "Our Courts," *PW* 3 (November 1887): 57.

10. "Henry Oviatt, Attorney-at-Law, Master-in-Chancery, and Stenographic Reporter, Montpelier," 2 October 1878, O'Keefe Collection, box 15, NYPL; "Personal," *BPM* 1 (December 1875): 24; "Personal," *BPM* 1 (June 1876): 95; John Allen Rider, "The History of the Male Stenographer in the United States" (Ed.D. diss., University of Nebraska, 1966), 107.

11. "Extract from the Remarks of Joseph Howard, Jr., before the Association, as Printed by Mr. Howard in the N.Y. 'Press,'" in Stenographers' Association of the City of New York, *Souvenir* (New York, 1891), 21.

12. Quoted in "The Chicago Combine," *BPM-W* 15 (27 January 1890): 53–54; "The Chicago Combine Going to Smash," *BPM-W* 15 (26 May 1890): 308 [*Chicago Times*]; Walter S. Taylor, "Locked Out: Three of the Court Stenographers Are Dismissed," *PM* 9 (1 April 1895): 99 [*Morning Call*].

13. *Proceedings of the New England Shorthand Reporters' Association, 1889–1892* (vol. 1 Boston: George H. Ellis, 1892), 14–15; "Personal," *BPM* 2 (September 1877): 145; Roger B. Landroth, "The History and Development of Pitmanic Shorthand in the United States, 1843–1976" (Ed.D. diss., New York University, 1977); 159–60; Rider, "History of the Male Stenographer," 26–40, 47, 100–103; Squibb and Dement, "Our Courts," 57; Quoted from "Pro and Con of Official Stenographers," *BPMRJ* 10 (November 1885): 276–77; "Frank F. Burt," 485–86.

14. "Massachusetts Law as to Official Stenographers," *Packard's Short-Hand Reporter* 1 (October 1885): 318; Cora Elisabeth Burbank, "Civil Service Examinations for Official Stenographers," in *Proceedings of the New England Shorthand Reporters' Association, 1899–1900,* vol. 4 (Boston, 1900), 28.

15. *The Term End Club,* ca. 1910s, pamphlet, O'Keefe Collection, box 16, NYPL; A chief Senate reporter reaped twenty-five thousand dollars per year, while five House reporters earned five thousand dollars per year plus more per diem: "Shorthand Writing in Washington," *PM* 2 (August 1888): 172 [*New York World*]; Landroth, "History and Development of Pitmanic Shorthand," 130–31; House Committee on the Judiciary, *Stenographers in United States Courts,* 3, 5–6, 18–20.

16. "Notes," 154–55; "Legislative Meddling," *Stenographer* 7 (March 1895): 113; National Shorthand Reporters' Association, comp., *Digest of Statutes and Legal Decisions Relating to Official Stenographers* (New Haven: Mae, 1906), 116, 122, 124; *Proceedings of the New*

England Shorthand Reporters' Association, 1889–1992 (Boston: George Ellis, 1892), 14; quote on Charles D. Gay: Darius Dust, "What about the Shorthand Man?" *NSR* 1 (October 1913): 235; Rider, "History of the Male Stenographer," 26, 40.

17. "Frank F. Burt," 485–86; House Committee on the Judiciary, *Stenographers in United States Courts,* 5–6.

18. "President of the Ohio State Stenographer's Association," *PM* (1 December 1895): 252–58.

19. "H. W. Thorne," *PM* 6 (June 1892): 277.

20. "Notes," 193; "C. I. Daughtry," *TPW* 15 (December 1899): 222; Walter E. Spicer, "Only Wants a Chance," *Stenographer* 8 (July 1895): 11.

21. Arthur Head, "There Are Stenographers and Stenographers," *TPW* 21 (March 1903): 203.

22. "To Court and Law Stenographers," *Stenographer* 7 (February 1895): 63; *Stenographer* 7 (June 1895): 250.

23. "Louis E. Schrader, Official Reporter," *TPW* 15 (January 1900): 285; "The Court and General Reporter—Harold Johnson," *TPW* 15 (December 1899): 219; "Presidents of the State Stenographers' Associations," *PM* 7 (15 October 1893): 387; Frederick J. Warburton, "Appointment of Court Reporters," *PW* 3 (November 1887): 51.

24. Albert W. Niemi Jr., "The Male-Female Earnings Differential: A Historical Overview of the Clerical Occupations from the 1880s to the 1970s," *Social Science History* 7 (Winter 1983): 97–107; Salaries and employment stability, though, remained high enough to attract working-class men: DeVault, *Sons and Daughters of Labor,* 62, 66; Alexander Keyssar, *Out of Work: The First Century of Unemployment in Massachusetts* (Cambridge: Cambridge University Press, 1986), 308–19, 327, 331–39; Massachusetts Bureau of Statistics of Labor, "Testimony of Working Men," in *Tenth Annual Report* (Boston: Wright & Potter, 1879), 130; Stuart M. Blumin, *The Emergence of the Middle Class: Social Experience in the American City, 1760–1900* (Cambridge: Cambridge University Press, 1989), 273–74, 291, 380 n. 40, 384 n. 87; Peter R. Shergold, "Wage Differentials Based on Skill in the United States, 1899–1914: A Case Study," *Labor History* 18 (Fall 1977): 491, 497, 501–3; Daniel D. Luria, "Trends in the Determinants Underlying the Process of Social Stratification: Boston, 1880–1920," *Review of Radical Political Economics* 6 (Summer 1974): 103.

25. U.S. Commissioner of Labor, "A Compilation of Wages in Commercial Countries from Official Sources," in *Fifteenth Annual Report,* 2 vols. (Washington, DC, 1900), 1:148–52, 2:1407–8, 1535; Male bookkeepers earned $8.34 more per week than their female counterparts: Massachusetts Bureau of Statistics of Labor, "Mercantile Wages and Salaries," in *Thirty-third Annual Report* (Boston: Wright & Potter, 1902), 120–22; On rationalization and mechanism of bookkeeping in the 1900s: Sharon Hartman Strom, *Beyond the Typewriter: Gender, Class, and the Origins of Modern American Office Work, 1900–1930* (Urbana: University of Illinois Press, 1992), 185–87.

26. Lisa M. Fine, *The Souls of the Skyscraper: Female Clerical Workers in Chicago, 1870–1930* (Philadelphia: Temple University Press, 1990), 100.

27. U.S. Commissioner of Labor, "Compilation of Wages," 1:148–52, 2:1407–8, 1535; On Boston mercantile wages (ten men earned $12.03; forty-four women, $10.86): Massachusetts Bureau of Statistics of Labor, "Mercantile Wages and Salaries," 120–22.

28. "What Salary Does a Bookkeeper-Stenographer Command?" *BPW* 16 (16 March 1891): 115; "Doing Things Right," *BPW* 17 (31 October 1892): 1; "Conscious and Unconscious Misrepresentation," *BPMRJ* 7 (January 1882): 2–3; Bjawrj Bjh. Bjohrnsohn [*sic*], "Railroad Stenographers and the Men They Work For," *BPMRJ* 11 (June 1886): 134–36; "Intelligence," *PM* 2 (December 1888): 265–66; F. W. Craig, "Intelligence," *PM* 3 (September 1889): 193–4; "Pay of Stenographers in Nebraska," *PM* 9 (1 April 1895): 99–100; Oliver B. Harden, "Cheap Stenographic Labor," *PW* 3 (November 1887): 51; Roy Shoemaker, "Lady Stenographers and Salaries," *IPW* 12 (June 1897): 359; George Lucas, "Lady Stenographers and Salaries," *IPW* 13 (November 1897): 105.

29. On fears that women did not demand a standard of living and replaced men: Lawrence B. Glickman, *A Living Wage: American Workers and the Making of Consumer Society* (Ithaca: Cornell University Press, 1997), 85, 90–91, 51.

30. "Special Uses of Typewriting," *BPM-W* 14 (2 December 1889): 364–65 [*New York Sun*].

31. "Maj. J. D. Pulsifer and the Pulsifer Family," *PM* 7 (15 May 1893): 187–88; "American Court Reporters and What Systems of Shorthand They Write," *PW* 8 (July 1893): 296–99 (In my calculation, I excluded two names that were gender ambiguous); B. F. Faust, "Can Women Legally Hold the Office of Official Stenographer?" *PW* 7 (October 1891): 62.

32. Judy Hilkey, *Character Is Capital: Success Manuals and Manhood in Gilded Age America* (Chapel Hill: University of North Carolina Press, 1997), 157–60; Davis, *Company Men,* 220, 208.

33. On success manuals: Hilkey, *Character Is Capital,* 142–65; John B. Carey, "Reminiscences of a Shorthand Writer: With a Few Odd Ideas as to Speed and Other Things," *PW* 8 (February 1893): 182–84; Alice McKee, "Queer!" *TPW* 17 (September 1901): 21–23; For a 1930s example: Kwolek-Folland, *Engendering Business,* 166–67.

34. Carolyn Kitch, *The Girl on the Magazine Cover: The Origins of Visual Stereotypes in American Mass Media* (Chapel Hill: University of North Carolina Press, 2001), 63–68; Robert Barr, "The Typewritten Letter: A Difficult Bit of Dictation From 'The Face and the Mask,'" *TPW* 26 (November 1905): 267–72; Arthur J. Monro, "'Nick': How a Shrewd Stenographer Saved His Firm a Fat Contract," *TPW* 22 (December 1903): 476.

35. Ellis Wood, "The Revolt of the Abominated: An Interesting Dialogue Overheard in the Quiet of the Office," *TPW* 20 (September 1902): 158; "Made Her Promise: An Ironclad Agreement with a New Typewriter," *TPW* 15 (November 1899): 171 [*Pernin's Monthly Stenographer*].

36. Ellis Wood, "Two Men and a Maid," *TPW* 18 (February 1902): 570–71.

37. Ellis Wood, "The Mighty Atom: 'Where a Woman Will, She Will, and You May Depend on 't——,'" *TPW* 23 (January 1904): 4, 3; The picture adjoining Wood's story, however, presents an overweight, unattractive woman, possibly emphasizing her working-class roots.

38. Bettina Friedl, *On to Victory: Propaganda Plays of the Woman Suffrage Movement* (Boston: Northeastern University Press, 1987), 45–53, 191, 193, 129–33; Aileen S. Kraditor, *Up From the Pedestal: Selected Writings in the History of American Feminism* (Chicago: Quadrangle, 1968), 189–93; Mara Mayor, "Fears and Fantasies of the Anti-Suffragists,"

Connecticut Review 17, no. 7 (1974): 68–69; Jane Jerome Camhi, *Women Against Women: American Anti-Suffragism, 1880–1920* (Brooklyn: Carlson, 1994), 20, 26.

39. Elyce J. Rotella, *From Home to Office: U.S. Women at Work, 1870–1930,* Studies in American History and Culture, no. 25 (Ann Arbor: UMI Research Press, 1981), 199; See appendix, table C2.

40. John B. Carey, *The Oddities of Shorthand; or, The Coroner and His Friends* (New York: Excelsior, 1891), 201, 203, 210; On telegrapher tramps: Edwin Gabler, *The American Telegrapher: A Social History, 1860–1900* (New Brunswick: Rutgers University Press, 1988), 87; On tramps and the middle class: Frank Tobias Higbie, *Indispensable Outcasts: Hobo Workers and Community in the American Midwest, 1880–1930* (Urbana: University of Illinois Press, 2003), 66–94; Todd Depastino, *Citizen Hobo: How a Century of Homelessness Shaped America* (Chicago: University of Chicago Press, 2003), 40–47, 61; On applicants declaring sobriety: Zunz, *Making America Corporate,* 129.

41. Frank Rutherford, "What is the Difference between a Male and a Female Stenographer?" *IPW* 9 (October 1893): 65; Kate Armstrong, "Lady Stenographers and Salaries," *IPW* 12 (August 1897): 463; Ohio, "A Free Lance for Our Brothers and Advice for Our Sisters," *BPW* 15 (7 July 1890): 390–91.

42. Chicago Stenographers, *The Second Annual Dinner,* 11 January 1879 (Chicago: Blakely, Brown & Marsh, 1879), 9.

43. Michael Zakim, *Ready-Made Democracy: A History of Men's Dress in the American Republic, 1760–1860* (Chicago: University of Chicago Press, 2003), 119–26.

44. Rob Schorman, *Selling Style: Clothing and Social Change at the Turn of the Century* (Philadelphia: University of Pennsylvania Press, 2003), 28–31 , 82–83; Carol Turbin, "Collars and Consumers: Changing Images of American Manliness and Business," in *Beauty and Business: Commerce, Gender, and Culture in Modern America,* ed. Philip Scanton (New York: Routledge, 2001), 95; Michael J. Murphy, "Orthopedic Manhood: Detachable Shirt Collars and the Reconstruction of the White Male Body in America, ca. 1880–1910," *Dress* 32 (2005): 75–95; On the dude: Harlen Makemson, "A 'Dude and Pharisee': Cartoon Attacks on *Harper's Weekly* Editor George William Curtis and the Mugwumps in the Presidential Campaign of 1884," *Journalism History* 29 (Winter 2004): 183–85.

45. Bjelopera, *City of Clerks,* 39–40; Depastino, *Citizen Hobo,* 159; Heber [*sic*] Butts, "The Tramp Stenographer: A True Story of How a Knight of the Road Took a Western Office by Surprise," *TPW* 15 (September 1900): 5–7; Christine Photinos, "The Figure of the Tramp in Gilded Age Success Narratives, " *Journal of Popular Culture* 40 (December 2007): 994–1018; "Raymond's Discovery: Many Stenographers Who Read This Should Go and Do Likewise," *TPW* 21 (March 1903): 197.

46. "Raymond's Discovery," 195–97; Bjelopera, *City of Clerks,* 40.

47. Schorman, *Selling Style,* 29, 82–83; "Raymond's Discovery," 197; On refinement: L.C.R. and Editor, "About Lady Amanuenses," *BPMRJ* 7 (October 1882): 261.

48. Scott A. Sandage, "The Gaze of Success: Failed Men and the Sentimental Marketplace, 1873–1893," in *Sentimental Men: Masculinity and the Politics of Affect in American Culture,* ed. Mary Chapman and Glenn Hendler (Berkeley: University of California Press, 1999), 192; Davis, *Company Men,* 40–66, 152–60.

49. "The Prospect for Boys, Common School and Success," *BPW* 15 (30 June 1890): 371; "John T. Michel," *PM* 11 (15 January 1897): 224; see also "Pioneer Stenographers," *BPMRJ* 7 (December 1882): 338; Edward F. Underhill, "Biographical Sketch of Theron C. Leland," *PM* 6 (September 1892): 361–62; Shert-Nerter [*sic*], "Experiences: Where I *Was!* and Where I *Am!*" *BPM* 1 (November 1875): 10.

50. "Henry J. Gensler," *PM* 11 (15 February 1897): 57–60.

51. Richard Weiss, *The American Myth of Success: From Horatio Alger to Norman Vincent Peale* (New York: Basic Books, 1969), 99–101; Hilkey, *Character Is Capital,* 122, 125; "Stenographers Who Have Risen," *PW* 3 (May 1888): 180–81; "Personal—Doings of Stenographers," *BPMRJ* 14 (May 1889): 153; Bernard Rodey, "A Stenographic Feat," *PW* 1 (July 1886): 203; "Shorthandities," *BPMRJ* 12 (December 1887): 371–75; William Harrison, "After Five Years' Desertion of Shorthand," *BPW* 15 (9 June 1890): 325; DeVault, *Sons and Daughters of Labor,* 157; "Association Department—Gossip Bureau: Personal Items of Interest from Our Different Shorthand Schools," *TPW* 14 (March 1899): 311–12; H. L. Andrews, "Give the Young Men a Show!" *PW* 8 (March 1893): 219–20; "Shorthand Considered as a Calling," *BPMRJ* 13 (February 1888): 45–49; "Young Men Wanted," *Business Education* 8 (September 1892): 15; Walter E. Ingersoll, comp., *Shorthand, the Open Door to Opportunity; Some Distinguished Persons Who Write Shorthand* (New York: Gregg Publishing, 1915), 1–19.

52. J. F. M'Clain, "The Qualifications Necessary for Success as a Stenographer and Typewriter Operator," *MS* 1 (20 September 1889): 10 [*Frank Harrison's Shorthand Magazine*]; "Stenographers Who Have Risen," 189.

53. "W. T. Crenshaw, of Atlanta," *PW* 7 (November 1891): 111–12.

54. Monro, "Nick," 475; Emily Stipes Watts, *The Businessman in American Literature* (Athens: University of Georgia Press, 1982), 55–63.

55. Quote cited in Ronald Preston Byars, "The Making of the Self-Made Man: The Development of Masculine Roles and Images in Ante-Bellum America" (Ph.D. diss., Michigan State University, 1979), 79; John F. Kasson, *Houdini, Tarzan, and the Perfect Man: The White Male Body and the Challenge of Modernity in America* (New York: Hill & Wang, 2001), 170, 173, 174; On legitimization of professional authority: Christopher P. Wilson, *White Collar Fictions: Class and Social Representation in American Literature, 1885–1925* (Athens: University of Georgia Press, 1992), 101–29.

56. T. A. Hayes, "Lady Stenographers and Salaries," *IPW* 13 (September 1897), 11; John L. Peer, "Lady Stenographers and Salaries," *IPW* 13 (October 1897): 57.

57. J. B. Reid, "Shorthand in the Public Schools," *PW* 1 (July 1886): 218.

58. Editorial, *PM* 8 (1 February 1894): 34–36; Quote from Dickinson: "The New York State Stenographers' Association," *PW* 4 (September 1888): 5.

59. "New York State Stenographers' Association," *PW* 4:4–5; Quotes from "New York State Stenographers' Association," *PW* 3 (September 1887): 19; House Committee on the Judiciary, *Stenographers in United States Courts,* 6–7, 18–20.

60. "New York State Stenographers' Association," 19; "Col. Edward B. Dickinson," *PM* 4 (April 1890): 77.

61. "New York State Stenographers' Association," *PW* 4:4–5; Andrews, "Give the Young Men a Show!" 219–20; Edward F. Underhill, "Stenographers and Their Qualifications," *BPMRJ* 6 (January 1881): 5–8; Hilkey, *Character Is Capital,* 122, 125.

CHAPTER 4

1. C. C. Herr, "The Scovil System Denounced," *BPM* 3 (July 1878): 128–29.

2. Rosemary O'Day, *The Professions in Early Modern England, 1450–1800: Servants of the Commonwealth* (New York: Longman, 2000); Gianna Pomata, *Contracting a Cure: Patients, Healers, and the Law in Early Modern Bologna* (Baltimore: Johns Hopkins University Press, 1998); Thomas Broman, "Rethinking Professionalization: Theory, Practice, and Professional Ideology in Eighteenth-Century German Medicine," *Journal of Modern History* 67 (January 1995): 835–72.

3. On gendered logic: Nancy F. Cott, *The Bonds of Womanhood: "Woman's Sphere" in New England, 1780–1835* (New Haven: Yale University Press, 1977), 161–62; On discipline: Edwin R. Gardiner, "Phonography," *PM* 6 (November 1892): 452; On elevating: John F. Kasson, *Houdini, Tarzan, and the Perfect Man: The White Male Body and the Challenge of Modernity in America* (New York: Hill & Wang, 2001), 165–83.

4. For examples on the language of professionalism: Bruce A. Kimball, *The "True Professional Ideal" in America: A History* (Cambridge, MA: Blackwell, 1992); Wendy E. Gamber, *The Female Economy: The Millinery and Dressmaking Trades, 1860–1930* (Urbana: University of Illinois Press, 1997), 172–73; For examples on expertise and the desire to surpass the masses: Samuel Haber, *The Quest for Authority and Honor in the American Professions, 1750–1900* (Chicago: University of Chicago Press, 1991), 50, 109, 201–2, 311; Christopher P. Wilson, *White Collar Fictions: Class and Social Representation in American Literature, 1885–1925* (Athens: University of Georgia Press, 1992); On balancing theory and practice: Broman, "Rethinking Professionalization," 835–72; On salesmen: Angel Kwolek-Folland, *Engendering Business: Men and Women in the Corporate Office, 1870–1930* (Baltimore: Johns Hopkins University Press, 1994); On accounting: Sharon Hartman Strom, *Beyond the Typewriter: Gender, Class, and the Origins of Modern American Office Work, 1900–1930* (Urbana: University of Illinois Press, 1992); 82–93.

5. Haber, *Quest for Authority and Honor,* 222–23, 235–36, 296; Burton J. Bledstein, *The Culture of Professionalism: The Middle Class and the Development of Higher Education in America* (New York: Norton, 1976), 189–96; College programs did not keep pace with calls for higher education: Elliot L. Slocum and Alfred R. Roberts, "Warren W. Nissley: A Crusader for Collegiate Education," *Accounting Historians Journal* 23 (June 1996): 89–116.

6. S. C. Rogers, "The Mind of the Profession: Eptracts [*sic*] from the Contributions of Stenographers to Phonographic Literature," *BPMRJ* 8 (July 1883): 170–71; "Betrayed by Voices: Liars Are Unable to Deceive the Stenographer's Ear," *TPW* 20 (September 1902): 183–87 [*New York Sun*]; Bledstein, *Culture of Professionalism,* 87–92; Jürgen Kocka, *White Collar Workers in America, 1890–1940: A Social-Political History in International Perspective* (London: Sage, 1980), 90–91; Kwolek-Folland, *Engendering Business,* 75–93, especially 87; Edwin Gabler, *The American Telegrapher: A Social History, 1860–1900* (New Brunswick: Rutgers University Press, 1988), 89–90.

7. Edward F. Underhill, "Stenographers and Their Qualifications," *BPMRJ* 6 (January 1881): 5–8; Benn Pitman, *Reporter's Companion* (Cincinnati: Phonographic Institute, 1872), 5–7; *Proceedings of the Second Annual Convention of Eastern Gregg Shorthand Association, 26–27 November 1915* (New York: Eastern Gregg Shorthand Association, 1915), 38.

8. Benn Pitman, *Manual of Phonography,* (Cincinnati: Phonographic Institute, 1855),

19; Gardiner, "Phonography," 452; "Some Things an Amaneunsis Should Observe," *PW* 14 (March 1899): 314.

9. Elias Longley, *American Manual of Phonography: Being a Complete Guide to the Acquisition of Pitman's Phonetic Shorthand* (Cincinnati: Longley, 1864), vi–viii; Benn Pitman, *Suggestions for the Practical and Theoretical Completion of Phonography in Respect to Order, Harmony, Simplicity, Brevity, and Legibility* (Cincinnati: Phonographic Institute, [1866]), n.p.; Quotes in Andrew J. Graham, *The Hand-Book of Standard or American Phonography* (New York: Andrew J. Graham, Phonetic Depot., 1886), v; John Robert Gregg also presented his system based on "natural physiological laws": *Light-Line Phonography: The Phonetic Handwriting* (Liverpool: Light-Line Phonography Institute, 1888), 3; David Wolfe Brown, *The Science and Art of Phrase-making* (Washington, DC: Shorthand Publication Bureau, 1902), preface.

10. Even critics of binary gender distinctions in science accept its masculine construction: Arleen Tuchman, "'Only in a Republic Can It Be Proved That Science Has No Sex': Marie Elizabeth Zakrzewska (1829–1902) and the Multiple Meanings of Science in the Nineteenth-Century United States," *Journal of Women's History* 11 (Spring 1999): 122.

11. On antebellum views about manual and mental labor: Jonathan A. Glickstein, *Concepts of Free Labor in Antebellum America* (New Haven: Yale University Press, 1991), 23–25; Stephen P. Rice, *Minding the Machine: Languages of Class in Early Industrial America* (Berkeley: University of California Press, 2004), 42–114; Kimball, "*True Professional Ideal*," 204–5; Keith P. McMillan, "The Science of Accounts: Bookkeeping Rooted in the Ideal of Science," *Accounting Historians Journal* 25 (December 1998): 3–6.

12. "Shorthand and the Law: A Distinguished Trio," *PM* 7 (15 July 1893): 263; Ernest Freeberg, *The Education of Laura Bridgman: First Deaf and Blind Person to Learn Language* (Cambridge: Harvard University Press, 2001), 34; Gardiner, "Phonography," 451–55; Thomas Augst, *The Clerk's Tale: Young Men and Moral Life in Nineteenth-Century America* (Chicago: University of Chicago Press, 2003), 36–39.

13. "Report of Historian," 11, O'Keefe Collection, box 4, NYPL; Discussion of other shorthand practitioners who wrote fiction: Mrs. Marcie E. Reay: "Some Typical Boston Typewriter Girls," *Boston Sunday Post*, 15 June 1902, clipping, Beale Collection, box 16, NYPL; Alexander J. Jones's "Irish Characteristics" and "The Peculiar Irishman": "Obituary," *NSR* 1 (March 1913): 70–71; Charles Lee Swem, mystery writer of the *Wereworth*, published in 1920s, and other stories: "In Memoriam," *NSR* 18 (February 1957): 162–63.

14. Richard Brodhead, ed., *The Journals of Charles W. Chesnutt* (Durham: Duke University Press, 1993), 141–42; "Philander Deming," *NSR* 3 (March 1915): 60–62; Edward F. Underhill [Q. K. Philander Doesticks, pseud.], *The History and Records of the Elephant Club* (New York: Livermore & Rudd, 1856); John B. Carey, *The Oddities of Shorthand; or, The Coroner and His Friends* (New York: Excelsior, 1891).

15. McMillan, "Science of Accounts," 26; O. H. White, "The Stenographer and the Mermaid: A Six Months' Trip in the Depths of the Sea and the Discovery of the North Pole," *TPW* 21 (June 1903): 453–56.

16. Judy Hilkey, *Character Is Capital: Success Manuals and Manhood in Gilded Age America* (Chapel Hill: University of North Carolina Press, 1997), 114; For many years, the popular image of Thomas Edison ignored his team: Wyn Wachhorst, *Thomas Alva Edison: An American Myth* (Cambridge: MIT Press, 1981), 13, 15, 108; Breazie Wrighter, "The

Most Wonderful Stenographer (From the *Typewriter and Phonographic World* October, 1930)," *TPW* 26 (December 1905): 333–37; Scott Reynolds Nelson, *Steel Drivin' Man: John Henry; The Untold Story of an American Legend* (New York: Oxford University Press, 2006).

17. "Autobiographical Sketch of Thomas Towndrow," *IPM* 8 (1 June 1894): 163–64; "Isaac Pitman Knighted!" *PW* 9 (June 1894): 316; Nicholas K. Bromwell, *By the Sweat of the Brow: Literature and Labor in Antebellum America* (Chicago: University of Chicago Press, 1993), 43–58; Joseph Baron, "A Hundred Thousand Dollar Pill: A Stenographer All But Makes a Remarkable Scientific Discovery," *TPW* 21 (January 1903): 3–7.

18. Quotes in order: Harris Dickson, "Stenography and Insanity," *PW* 4 (December 1888): 67; Underhill, "Stenographers and Their Qualifications," 5–8; Gardiner, "Phonography," 451–55.

19. Rice, *Minding the Machine,* 27; Gardiner, "Phonography," 451–55; Colonel Edward B. Dickinson, "Is Stenography a Profession?" *IPW* 9 (January 1894): 170.

20. Quotes in "International Shorthand Writings," *PW* 2 (September 1886): 16–18; see also "Took Dictation Literally," *TPW* 20 (November 1902): 344 [*New York Telegram*]; "Which Shall It Be?" *PW* 1 (June 1886): 184; Telegraphers also discussed judgment: Thomas C. Jepsen, *My Sisters Telegraphic: Women in the Telegraph Office, 1846–1950* (Athens: Ohio University Press, 2000), 124–25.

21. *PW* 4 (January 1889): 94 [*St. Paul Exchange*]; Harry P. Godwin, "'Graphophone' Department," *IPW* 13 (April 1898): 353.

22. "Speed and Respect," *BPMRJ* 10 (November 1885): 275–76; Typing quote: "Stenographers, Shorthand and Typewriters," *BPMRJ* 10 (July 1885): 166–67 [*Phila. Paper*].

23. On intelligence: Underhill, "Stenographers and Their Qualifications," 5–8; editorial, *PM* 8 (1 February 1894): 34–36; On assumed gender and sex differences: Cynthia Eagle Russett, *Sexual Science: The Victorian Construction of Womanhood* (Cambridge: Harvard University Press, 1989), 94–95, 100; Virginia G. Drachman, *Women Lawyers and the Origins of Professional Identity in America: The Letters of the Equity Club, 1887 to 1890* (Ann Arbor: University of Michigan Press, 1993), 28.

24. Charles R. Barrett, "Good Outlook for Women," *TPW* 14 (March 1899): 321–22 [*Chicago News*]; On Seattle stenographer: I. B. M, "Power of Imagination in Boston," *TPW* 14 (April 1899): 382.

25. Oliver B. Harden, "Cheap Stenographic Labor," *PW* 3 (November 1887): 51.

26. B.C., "A Woman Stenographer's Plea for her Rights," *PW* 7 (August 1892): 501–2.

27. John B. Carey, "Reminiscences of a Shorthand Writer: With a Few Odd Ideas as to Speed and Other Things," *PW* 8 (February 1893): 182–84; H. L. Andrews, "Give the Young Men a Show!" *PW* 8 (March 1893): 219–20; Dickinson, "Is Stenography a Profession?" 172.

28. "The 'Dennis Duplex' Typewriter," *PW* 7 (August 1892): 502; "Bill Nye as a Typewritist," *PW* 7 (August 1892): 502; Charles Gordon Rogers, "Number Seven: The Love Tale of a Talisman," *TPW* 25 (April 1905): 262–66; On consumerism and magic: Jackson Lears, *Fables of Abundance: A Cultural History of Advertising in America* (New York: Basic Books, 1994), 41–65.

29. Bledstein, *Culture of Professionalism,* 84–85, 277; Haber, *Quest for Authority and*

Honor, 193–358; On professional education: Kenneth M. Ludmerer, *Time to Heal: American Medical Education from the Turn of the Century to the Era of Managed Care* (New York: Oxford University Press, 1999); Thomas Neville Bonner, *Becoming a Physician: Medical Education in Britain, France, Germany, and the United States* (Baltimore: Johns Hopkins University Press, 2000); Dennis Harlen Day, "The Evolution of Collegiate Accounting Instruction in the United States (1635–1995)" (Ed.D. diss., Northern Illinois University, 1996).

30. Hilkey, *Character Is Capital,* 108–9; Diane Bjorklund, "School as a Waste of Time? Complaints about Schooling in American Autobiographies," *Journal of American Culture* 27 (September 2004): 292–94.

31. Reed Ueda, *Avenues to Adulthood: The Origins of the High School and Social Mobility in an American Suburb* (Cambridge: Cambridge University Press, 1987), 103, 116, 127; Joel Perlmann, "Curriculum and Tracking in the Transformation of the American High School: Providence, R.I., 1880–1930," *Journal of Social History* 19 (Fall 1985): 32–33.

32. Carole Srole, "'A Position That God Has Not Particularly Assigned to Men': The Feminization of Clerical Work, Boston, 1860–1910" (Ph.D. diss., University of California, Los Angeles, 1984), chap. 2; Joel Perlmann, "After Leaving School: The Jobs of Young People in Providence, R.I., 1880–1915," in *Schools in Cities: Consensus and Conflict in American Educational History,* ed. Ronald K. Goodenow and Diane Ravitch (New York: Holmes & Meier, 1983), 11, 24, 28; In a sample of clerical men in Boston in 1880 who had graduated from grammar school, 63 percent attended some high school, surpassing the general population averages: Boston School Committee, *Annual Reports* (Boston, 1870–80); Carl F. Kaestle and Maris A. Vinovskis, "From Fireside to Factory: School Entry and School Leaving in Nineteenth-Century Massachusetts," in *Transitions: The Family and the Life Course in Historical Perspective,* ed. Tamara K. Hareven (New York: Academic Press, 1978), 155, 158; Joseph F. Kett, *Rites of Passage: Adolescence in America, 1790 to the Present* (New York: Basic Books, 1977), 152; Ueda, *Avenues to Adulthood,* 91; Kocka, *White Collar Workers,* 108.

33. "Presidents of the State Stenographers' Associations," *PM* 7 (15 October 1893): 388; "Biographical Sketch of W. C. Martin of San Francisco, Cal.; Stenographer to the Southern Pacific Company," *BPM* 12 (February 1887): 44; Of ten stenographers born in the 1850s or before, four attended some college, one an academy, and one an "excellent private school": "William D. Guthrie," *PM* 9 (15 October 1895): 308–9; "W. A. F. Scott, Carbondale, Pa.," *TPW* 14 (May 1899): 418; "W. N. Tiffany," *TPW* 15 (April 1900): 488; Ileen A. DeVault, *Sons and Daughters of Labor: Class and Clerical Work in Turn-of-the-Century Pittsburgh* (Ithaca: Cornell University Press, 1990), 152; Ueda, *Avenues to Adulthood,* 181–85; "Presidents of the State Stenographers' Associations," *PM* 8 (15 October 1994): 300; "Biographical Sketch of Daniel Lloyd of the United States Senate Corps of Official Reporters," *PM* 11 (1 June 1897): 171–72; "Personal—Biographical Sketch of T. P. Hanbury, Selma, Ala: Stenographer to the East Tennessee, Virginia & Georgia Railroad," *BPMRJ* 8 (September 1883): 233.

34. On grades: Joel Perlmann, "Who Stayed in School? Social Structure and Academic Achievement in the Determination of Enrollment Patterns, Providence, Rhode Island, 1880–1925," *Journal of American History* 72 (December 1985): 599, 593–609; Ueda, *Avenues to Adulthood,* 177, 181; Kocka, *White Collar Workers,* 108–10; DeVault, *Sons and Daughters*

of Labor, 156; Jerome P. Bjelopera, *City of Clerks: Office and Sales Workers in Philadelphia, 1870–1920* (Urbana: University of Illinois Press, 2005), 71–76; Far more stenographers, bookkeepers, typewriters, clerks, and teachers attended and graduated from high school than other working women: Massachusetts Bureau of Statistics of Labor, "Industrial Education of Working Women," in *Thirty-seventh Annual Report* (Washington, DC, 1906), 4–28; In 1900 in Brighton, Massachusetts, a Boston suburb, only half (47.9 percent, or 70 of 146) of employed single women other than clerks had graduated from grammar school, compared to 90 percent (9 of 10) for clerical workers; the ten clerical men averaged 12.4 years in school: U.S. Manuscript Census, Brighton, 1900; Brighton census accidentally recorded education for every resident.

35. Bjorklund, "School as a Waste of Time?" 94–299; "Presidents of the State Stenographers' Associations," *PM* 8 (15 October 1894): 299–301; Charles T. Dunwell, "Personal—Biographical Sketch of Edward F. Underhill," *BPM* 2 (September 1877): 144–45; "Personal—W. A. Cox," *PM* 6 (January 1892): 35; "Presidents of the State Stenographers' Associations," *PM* 5 (November 1891): 344; "Presidents of the State Stenographers' Associations," *PM* 6 (October 1892): 406–8; "Presidents of the State Stenographers' Associations," *PM* 7 (15 October 1893): 385–87; "W. H. Pritchard," *PM* 4 (April 1890): 107.

36. "Comer's Commercial College, at Boston, Massachusetts," *PW* 6 (July 1891): 372; Calculations: Julius Ensign Rockwell, "The Teaching, Practice, and Literature of Shorthand," in U.S. Department of the Interior, Bureau of Education, *Circular of Information of the Bureau of Education*, no. 2 (Washington, DC, 1884), 30–34, 36, 38, 191; A. W. Lowe, "Then and Now," *PM* 6 (May 1892): 204–8; Amanuensis classes grew from 12 percent to 36 percent of all business courses in the 1890s: Janice Weiss, "Educating for Clerical Work: The Nineteenth-Century Private Commercial School," *Journal of Social History* 14 (Spring 1981): 411, 413; Edwin G. Knepper, *History of Business Education in United States* (Bowling Green, OH: Edwards Brothers, 1941), 91, 108, 232.

37. "Presidents of the State Stenographers' Associations," *PM* 8 (15 October 1994): 300; "Biographical Sketch of W. C. Martin," 44; "Louis E. Schrader, Official Reporter," *TPW* 15 (January 1900): 285; Examples of some stenographers born in the 1870s who studied for some time at school: "The Court and General Reporter—Harold Johnson," *PW* 15 (December 1899): 219; "George W. Sanford," *TPW* 15 (April 1900): 493; "J. E. Gill, Quincy, Ill.," *TPW* 14 (August 1899): 540; Kaestle and Vinovskis, "From Fireside to Factory," 152–53; Janice Harriet Weiss, "Educating for Clerical Work: A History of Commercial Education in the United States since 1850" (Ed.D. diss., Harvard University, 1978), 25–27, 43; Weiss, "Educating for Clerical Work," 411–12; Kocka, *White Collar Workers*, 108; On female students: "Gossip Bureau: Personal Items of Interest from Our Different Shorthand Schools," *IPW* 13 (April 1898): 326–28.

38. Herbert M. Kliebard, *The Struggle for American Curriculum, 1893–1958*, 2nd ed. (New York: Routledge, 1995), 5; William J. Reese, *The Origins of the American High School* (New Haven: Yale University Press, 1995), 134–36; DeVault, *Sons and Daughters of Labor*, 24–32; On diplomas: Bryant and Stratton Commercial School, *Annual Catalogue and Prospectus of the Bryant & Stratton Commercial School* (Boston: Gunn & Bliss, 1877), 56; Albany Business College and School of Shorthand, Typewriting, and Telegraphy, *Annual Catalogue of the Albany Business College and School of Shorthand, Typewriting, and Teleg-*

raphy (Albany, NY: Albany Business College and School of Shorthand, Typewriting, and Telegraphy, [1899?], {1900?]), 62.

39. Hilkey, *Character Is Capital,* 107–10; Dickinson, "Is Stenography a Profession?" 170; Thomas S. Lewis, "What It Takes to Make a Reporter," *PM* 4 (October 1890): 247; Nellie M. Milburn, "Shorthand as a Stepping Stone," *PM* 4 (October 1890): 246–47; T. C. Rose, "Stenographic Amanuenses: The Best Mode of Training Them with a View to Value and Efficiency," *PW* 1 (February 1886): 115–16; C. H. Rush, "The World's Congress of Stenographers," *PW* 8 (August 1893): 318; On retail salesclerks also rejecting extensive education: Kocka, *White Collar Workers,* 91–92.

40. Hilkey, *Character Is Capital,* 107–8.

41. Editor, "The Raw Material Necessary for a Stenographer," *BPMRJ* 7 (August 1882): 198–200; On Rose: "Presidents of the State Stenographers' Associations," *PM* 7 (15 October 1893): 385; Mary E. Folsom, "The Competent Stenographer: A Symposium," *IPW* 13 (August 1898): 528–30.

42. *Proceedings of the New England Shorthand Reporters' Association, 1889–1892,* vol. 1 (Boston: George Ellis, 1892), 4–5, 19–21; Hilkey, *Character Is Capital,* 129–31. Retail clerks also distrusted theory and preferred on-the-job learning: Kocka, *White Collar Workers,* 92.

43. A Per Lee Plumb, "Manual vs. Mental Speed," *PW* 5 (April 1890): 233; "Public Speed Records of Isaac S. Dement," *IPW* 13 (March 1898): 277; On Murphy: Frank G. Carpenter, "Shorthand Writing in Washington," *PM* 2 (August 1888): 172 [*New York World*]; Leslie Cowan, *John Robert Gregg: A Biography of the Shorthand Inventor, Educator, Publisher, and Humanitarian Whose Achievements Enriched the Lives of Millions* (Oxford: Pre-Raphaelite Press, 1984), 73–80; Charles Currier Beale, "A Unique Examination," *TPW* 14 (October 1898): 73.

44. Eastman National Business College, *Anniversary* (Poughkeepsie, NY: Eastman Business College, 1892), 10; Pitman, *Manual of Phonography,* 13; *Proceedings of the Second Annual Convention of Eastern Gregg Shorthand Association,* 32, 34–35; On speed and graduation: "Association Department," *IPW* 13 (March 1898): 263.

45. Pitman, *Manual of Phonography,* 20, 32.

46. "Speed and Respect," 275–76; Bjelopera, *City of Clerks,* 66.

47. Eastman National Business College, *Anniversary,* 10; Albany Business College, *Annual Catalogue,* 9; "Three Months' Stenographers," *BPM-W* 15 (24 March 1890): 164; Bjelopera, *City of Clerks,* 33–36; On difficulty evaluating the relative costs of attending a private commercial school rather than staying in public high school: Lewis C. Solomon, "Estimates of the Costs of Schooling in 1880 and 1900," *Explorations in Economic History,* supp. 7 (Summer 1970): 531–58.

48. "Personal—William Milligan," *BPMRJ* 8 (December 1883): 340–41; Gregg, *Light-Line Phonography,* 3–5; Cowan, *John Robert Gregg,* 32; Weiss, "Educating for Clerical Work: The Nineteenth-Century Private Commercial School," 409–10.

49. Roger B. Landroth, "The History and Development of Pitmanic Shorthand in the United States, 1843–1976" (Ed.D. diss., New York University, 1977), 101, 125–28; "His Disposition," *BPMRJ* 8 (February 1883): 31; "Graham and Munson by the Ears," *BPMRJ* 8 (November 1883): 284–87; "A Noble Man," *BPM* 1 (February 1876): 44–45; John Gregg to Charles Currier Beale, 16 May 1902, Beale Collection, NYPL.

50. W. B. Wright, "Boston Shorthand Schools," *PM* 4 (April 1890): 109–10; On middle-class fears and advice: Karen Halttunen, *Confidence Men and Painted Women: A Study of Middle-Class Culture in America, 1830–1870* (New Haven: Yale University Press, 1982), 34; On concerns about male victimization: Rodney Hessinger, *Seduced, Abandoned, and Reborn: Visions of Youth in Middle-Class America, 1780–1850* (Philadelphia: University of Pennsylvania Press, 2005), 23–68; On telegraph "colleges" and respectability: Gabler, *American Telegrapher,* 59, 123, 132, 175; Joanne Meyerowitz, *Women Adrift: Independent Wage Earners in Chicago, 1880–1930* (Chicago: University of Chicago Press, 1988), 48–49; Martha H. Verbrugge, *Able-Bodied Womanhood: Personal Health and Social Change in Nineteenth-Century Boston* (New York: Oxford University Press, 1988), 61; On seducing: G. Whillikins, "Newsey," *BPM* 1 (May 1876): 82; Benjamin R. Boggs, "Stenographers in 30 Days," *PW* 1 (January 1886): 94.

51. Theodore C. Rose, "Girls! Girls! Be Not Deceived," *PW* 7 (December 1891): 171.

52. Whillikins, "Newsey," 82.

53. On taking fifty dollars and "eternity is too short": Carey, "Reminiscences of a Shorthand Writer," 182–84.

54. "Intelligence," *PM* 5 (May 1891): 131 [*The Press*].

55. Graham, *Hand-Book of Standard or American Phonography,* v; "American Court Reporters and What Systems of Shorthand They Write," *PW* 8 (July 1893): 296–99; Benn Pitman and Jerome B. Howard, *The American System of Shorthand: The Manual of Phonography* (Cincinnati: Phonographic Institute, 1902), 2; Brown, *Science and Art of Phrase-making,* 15, 17.

56. "Fac-Simile: Causes of Failures," *BPW* 16 (14 September 1891): 419–20; "What Have They Done?" *BPW* 15 (30 June 1890): 371–72; "Three Months' Stenographers," 164.

57. William E. Hickox, "Shorthand Not for Schools," *IPW* 12 (December 1896): 118; Frances M. Fox, "Stenography in the Public Schools," *PW* 1 (March 1886): 137; J. B. Reid, "Shorthand in the Public Schools," *PW* 1 (July 1886): 218; In the twentieth century, Pitmanites critiqued Gregg shorthand for its inaccuracy because of its simplicity and ease of learning: Arthur Bailey to Robert S. Taylor, 21 February 1935, National Shorthand Reporters' Association Records, NSRA Papers, box 1, NYPL.

58. On Passmore: "In Favor of Shorthand in Schools: Replies from Teachers to the Article 'Shorthand Not for Schools,' in our December Number," *IPW* 12 (February 1897): 190–91; Other advocates' quotes: "Phonography in the Public Schools," *PM* 1 (October 1887): 221; Herbert M. Kliebard, *Schooled to Work: Vocationalism and the American Curriculum, 1876–1946* (New York: Teacher's College Press, 1999).

59. Hickox, "Shorthand Not for Schools,"118; Weiss, "Educating for Clerical Work: A History of Commercial Education in the United States since 1850," 9–10.

60. Landroth, "History and Development of Pitmanic Shorthand," 200–201, 112–15, 196–97, 80, 215–17.

61. McMillan, "Science of Accounts," 1–33.

62. *Proceedings of the New England Shorthand Reporters' Association, 1889–1892,* vol. 1, 21.

63. Frank Harrison, "The Demand for Shorthand Writers," *PM* 1 (April 1887): 77; Editor, "Opportunities for Young Men," *BPW* 18 (20 March 1893): 179; "Colored Stenographers," *PW* 2 (November 1886): 45; "Afro-American Stenographers and Typewriters at Chicago," *PW* 6 (July 1891): 359; "Personal," *BPMRJ* 12 (October 1887): 302–3;

"Certificated Teachers: Govan Darius August," *PM* 9 (1 April 1895): 107; "Personal," *BPMRJ* 10 (September 1885): 220–22; Editors ignored black women, even though Massachusetts recorded fourteen in contrast to only eight male stenographers and typewriters in 1905: Massachusetts Bureau of Statistics of labor, *The Census of Massachusetts: 1905*, vol. 2 (Boston: Wright & Potter, 1910), 146.

64. J. J. Roberts, "Stenographic Incompetency," *PW* 6 (September 1890): 7; Dressmakers also used the term *incompetents:* Wendy Gamber, "'Reduced to Science': Gender, Technology, and Power in the American Dressmaking Trade, 1860–1910," *Technology & Culture* 36 (July 1995): 463; "Learning Shorthand," *BPMRJ* 13 (June 1888): 164–65; Editor, "Stenographers and Stenographers," *BPW* 17 (21 November 1892): 739; On criticisms of women telegraphers' spelling: Jepsen, *Sisters Telegraphic*, 130.

65. "Young Stenographers," *BPMRJ* 9 (March 1884): 57–60.

66. Charles M. Miller, "Time Required to Learn Shorthand," *IPW* 13 (July 1898): 493.

67. "Licensing Stenographers in Courts of Record," *IPW* 11 (October 1895), 51; On Schenectady job: Fred F. Wiley, "A Good General Education Necessary," *TPW* 14 (May 1899): 424; Miller, "Time Required to Learn Shorthand," 493.

68. "We Don't Believe in It," *PW* 1 (January 1886): 95; William A. Shaw, "The Stenographer," *BPMRJ* 14 (February 1889): 45–47; Benn Pitman, "The Choice of a Profession," *PM* 7 (1 September 1893): 325–27; "Well Said!" *PW* 8 (June 1893): 279 [*Boston Herald*]; On natural inequality: Hilkey, *Character Is Capital*, 122; For a similar discussion on dressmakers: Gamber, "Reduced to Science," 462–63.

69. "Personal," *BPMRJ* 12 (April 1887): 120; Charles Currier Beale, "The Colored Man as Stenographer," *IPW* 9 (May 1898): 409; G. Shankland Walworth, "A Grotesque Stenographer: A Quaint and Curious Tale of a Quaint and Curious Pupil," *TPW* 21 (March 1903): 222–24; Russett, *Sexual Science*, 6–7, 22–24, 150, 201–2; Halttunen, *Confidence Men and Painted Women*, 40–50; Bjelopera, *City of Clerks*, 131–40.

70. On telegraphers', bookkeepers', and salesmen's superior attitude: Gabler, *American Telegrapher*, 99–100, 103–4; Scott-Browne quote in "Sorting Students of Shorthand," *BPW* 16 (2 November 1891): 531; On railroad applicants: "Another Phase of the 'Incompetent' Stenographer," *TPW* 14 (October 1898): 60–62; see also "Learning Shorthand," 164–65.

71. On native-born skilled workers' views about industrial education for immigrants: DeVault, *Sons and Daughters of Labor*, 121–27; On varied class views on "bad" habits: John C. Burnham, *Bad Habits: Drinking, Smoking, Taking Drugs, Gambling, Sexual Misbehavior, and Swearing in American History* (New York: New York University Press, 1993); John F. Kasson, *Rudeness and Civility: Manners in Nineteenth-Century America* (New York: Hill & Wang, 1990), 117–32, 195–210; David Brundage, "The Producing Classes and the Saloon: Denver in the 1880s," *Labor History* 26 (Winter 1985): 29–52; Minnie C. Pratt, "The Shiftless Student, the Poor Stenographer," *IPW* 12 (July 1897): 407.

72. E. Anthony Rotundo, *American Manhood: Transformations in Masculinity from the Revolution to the Modern Era* (New York: Basic Books, 1993), 222–46; Hilkey, *Character Is Capital*, 118–19.

73. Rice, *Minding the Machine*, 23–28, 73–95; "Phonographic Teachers," *Universal Phonographer* 1 (1852): 91.

74. Rotundo, *American Manhood*, 222–46; Gail Bederman, *Manliness and Civiliza-*

tion: A Cultural History of Gender and Race in the United States, 1880–1917 (Chicago: University of Chicago Press, 1995), 184–96; Howard P. Chudacoff, *The Age of the Bachelor: Creating an American Subculture* (Princeton: Princeton University Press, 1999), 227; On strong bodies: Kasson, *Houdini, Tarzan, and the Perfect Man,* 8; Joan Severa, *Dressed for the Photographer: Ordinary Americans and Fashion, 1840–1900* (Kent: Kent State University Press, 1995), 411, 398, 447; On English beards: Michael Kimmel, *Manhood in America: A Cultural History* (New York: Free Press, 1996), 384n; On male garment workers as frail and weak: Daniel E. Bender, *Sweated Work, Weak Bodies: Anti-Sweatshop Campaigns and Languages of Labor* (New Brunswick: Rutgers University Press, 2004), 54–55.

75. "Benjamin A. Strawbridge," *PM* 9 (1 November 1895): 323; On Saunders: "Presidents of the State Stenographers' Associations," *PM* 8 (15 October 1894): 300; Dunwell, "Sketch of Edward F. Underhill," 144–45; Alice McKee, "Queer!" *TPW* 17 (September 1901): 21–23; "Certificated Teachers," *PM* 10 (1 January 1896): 10; "Personal," *BPMRJ* 8 (December 1883), 345; "Personal," *BPMRJ* 12 (July 1887): 202–4; F. G. Gosling, *Before Freud, Neurasthenia and the American Medical Community, 1870–1910* (Urbana: University of Illinois Press, 1987), 79–80, 32, 86, 6, 46, 144–63; Tom Lutz, *American Nervousness, 1903: An Anecdotal History* (Ithaca: Cornell University Press, 1991), 29.

76. E. N. Miner and Mrs. E. N. Miner, "Shall I Study Shorthand?" *IPW* 10 (September 1894): 15.

77. C. W. Kitt, "Pointers for Students," *TPW* 15 (September 1899): 12–14; Foeng, "The Rise of Jimmie Whalen," *TPW* 17 (August 1901): 533.

78. Rogers, "Number Seven," 179–85.

79. Edward Dickinson, "The New York Stenographers' Association," *PW* 4 (September 1888): 5; Underhill, "Stenographers and Their Qualifications," 5–8; On various popular culture quotes about fatigue: "Stenographers in New York," *BPMRJ* 12 (October 1887): 297–98 [*St. Louis Globe-Democrat*]; On other occupations' justifications: Ava Baron, "Contested Terrain Revisited: Technology and Gender Definitions of Work in the Printing Industry, 1850–1920," in *Women, Work, and Technology: Transformations,* ed. Barbara Drygulski Wright et al. (Ann Arbor: University of Michigan Press, 1987), 70–72; Drachman, *Women Lawyers,* 22, 32, 34; Jepsen, *Sisters Telegraphic,* 126.

80. First quote: William Brinkerhoff, "Personals," *BPMRJ* 7 (December 1882): 329–31; Hilkey, *Character Is Capital,* 112; On Yerrinton: *Proceedings of the New England Shorthand Reporters' Association, 1889–1892,* vol. 1, 4–5, 18–19; Underhill: "Eighth Annual Dinner of the Law Stenographers' Assoc'n of the City of New-York [*sic*]," *BPMRJ* 6 (January 1881): 7; see also Dunwell, "Sketch of Edward F. Underhill," 144–45.

81. "Why Some Women Fail of [*sic*] Success in the Court Reporter's Office," *PW* 3 (November 1887): 53; Carey, "Reminiscences of a Shorthand Writer," 182–84.

82. "Curious Shorthand Information," *BPMRJ* 14 (August 1889): 232–33.

83. Bessie A. Rogers, "Correspondence," *SJ* 6 (March 1877): 7.

84. "Shorthand Considered as a Calling," *BPMRJ* 13 (February 1888): 45–49.

CHAPTER 5

1. Between 1876 and 1912, Ballantyne spoke eight times, more than any of the other nine female speakers, and was surpassed by only three of the ninety-four male speakers:

New York State Shorthand Reporters' Association, *An Author List of the Papers Read at the Convention of the New York State Shorthand Stenographers' Association, 1876 to 1912* (New York, 1912), NYPL; Fred Irland, "New York State Stenographers' Association," *PW* 2 (September 1887): 16–18; M. Jeanette Ballantyne, "Woman Stenographers," *PM* 10 (1 May 1896): 131 [*Rochester Post-Express*].

2. Female stenographers and family members comprised 25 and 23.7 percent of attendees, respectively, in 1888: Irland, "New York State Stenographers' Association," 14–22, especially 17.

3. "Why Some Women Fail of [*sic*] Success in the Court Reporter's Office," *PW* 3 (November 1887): 53.

4. Irland, "New York State Stenographers' Association," 17; "Why Some Women Fail," 53.

5. John B. Carey, "Reminiscences of a Shorthand Writer: With a Few Odd Ideas as to Speed and Other Things," *PW* 8 (February 1893): 182–84; Helen L. Hinckle, "The Lady Court Stenographer," *PW* 8 (March 1893): 254.

6. Alice Kessler-Harris, *Out to Work: A History of Wage-Earning Women in the United States* (Oxford: Oxford University Press, 1982), 113–16; Susan M. Reverby, *Ordered to Care: The Dilemma of American Nursing, 1850–1945* (Cambridge: Cambridge University Press, 1987), 79, 87–90; See appendix, tables C3 and C5.

7. Kate Haulman, "Fashion and the Culture Wars of Revolutionary Philadelphia," *William and Mary Quarterly* 62 (October 2005): 625–62; Catherine E. Kelly, *In the New England Fashion: Reshaping Women's Lives in the Nineteenth Century* (Ithaca: Cornell University Press, 1999), 219–28; Wendy E. Gamber, *The Female Economy: The Millinery and Dressmaking Trades, 1860–1930* (Urbana: University of Illinois Press, 1997), 120–22; Patricia Marks, *Bicycles, Bangs, and Bloomers: The New Woman in the Popular Press* (Lexington: University of Kentucky Press, 1990), 151; Charlotte Perkins Gilman, *Herland*, with an introduction by Ann J. Lane (New York: Pantheon, 1979), 50; Virginia Penny, *Think and Act: A Series of Articles Pertaining to Men and Women, Work and Wages* (1869; reprint, New York: Arno and *New York Times*, 1971), 236; Benita Eisler, ed., *The Lowell Offering: Writings by New England Mill Women, 1840–1845* (New York: Harper, 1977), 186; Lois W. Banner, *American Beauty* (Chicago: University of Chicago Press, 1983), 156–58; Marilyn Elkins, "Fashion," in *The Oxford Companion to Women's Writing in the United States*, ed. Cathy N. Davidson, Linda Wagner-Martin, Elizabeth Ammons, et al. (New York: Oxford University Press, 1995), 303; Karen Halttunen, *Confidence Men and Painted Women: A Study of Middle-Class Culture in America, 1830–1870* (New Haven: Yale University Press, 1982), 63–70; Maria Susanna Cummins, *The Lamplighter*, ed. Nina Baym (1854; reprint, New Brunswick: Rutgers University Press, 1988), xxiv, 188, 190, 219, 286; Jenna Weissman Joselit, *A Perfect Fit: Clothes, Character, and the Promise of America* (New York: Metropolitan Books, 2001) , 125, 177–79; On contemporaries also waxing eloquently about the benefits of fashion: Rob Schorman, *Selling Style: Clothing and Social Change at the Turn of the Century* (Philadelphia: University of Pennsylvania Press, 2003), 73–74.

8. Charles H. Seem, "National Association of Women Stenographers," *IPW* 12 (January 1897): 156.

9. Willie Regardus, "The Men-Sten's Retreat," *TPW* 16 (December 1900): 205.

10. Kelly, *New England Fashion*, 219–28; Robert C. Toll, *Blacking Up: The Minstrel Show in Nineteenth-Century America* (London: Oxford University Press, 1974), 69; Bruce Dorsey, *Reforming Men and Women: Gender in the Antebellum City* (Ithaca: Cornell University Press, 2002), 32; On fictional villains: Harriet Beecher Stowe, *Uncle Tom's Cabin* (New York: Signet Classics, 1966), 169–71; Cumins, *Lamplighter*, 194; María Amparo Ruiz de Burton, *Who Would Have Thought It?* ed. Rosaura Sánchez and Beatrice Pita (1872; reprint, Houston: Arte Público Press, 1995), 232; Cheryl Lynn Cavanaugh, "Fashion, Class, and Labor: Clothing in American Women's Fiction, 1840–1913" (Ph.D. diss., University of Illinois, 1998).

11. Joselit, *Perfect Fit*, 179–86, especially 180.

12. Nan Enstad, *Ladies of Labor, Girls of Adventure: Working Women, Popular Culture, and Labor Politics at the Turn of the Twentieth Century* (New York: Columbia University Press, 1999), 31–42, 26–29; Priscilla Murolo, *The Common Ground of Womanhood: Class, Gender, and Working Girls' Clubs, 1884–1928* (Urbana: University of Illinois Press, 1997), 42; Christopher P. Wilson, *White Collar Fictions: Class and Social Representation in American Literature, 1885–1925* (Athens: University of Georgia Press, 1992), 35–37; Schorman, *Selling Style*, 69; O. Henry, "The Romance of a Busy Broker," in *The Complete Works of O. Henry*, with a foreword by Harry Hanson (1899; reprint, Garden City, NY: Doubleday, 1953), 87, 86; Hattie Witherington Sutton, "A Failure! Dorothy's Last Chance—and What She Made of It," *TPW* 25 (May 1905): 347; A number of pictures showed overdressed women, such as in Foeng, "Why Tommy Went to Manila," *TPW* 18 (September 1901): 2.

13. Christine Stansell, *City of Women: Sex and Class in New York, 1789–1860* (New York: Knopf, 1986), 94, 164–65; Enstad, *Ladies of Labor*, 78–81; In contrast, costume historian Joan L. Severa's examination of material culture points to working-class women wearing styles in tune with general fashion trends: *Dressed for the Photographer: Ordinary Americans and Fashion, 1840–1900* (Kent: Kent State University Press, 1995).

14. Eisler, *Lowell Offering*, 184–87; Stansell, *City of Women*, 194; "'Pin-money' Girls Crowding Out Breadwinners," *IPW* 8 (November 1894): 69; Women telegraphers also wanted to distance themselves from "extravagant" and "foolish" factory workers: Edwin Gabler, *The American Telegrapher: A Social History, 1860–1900* (New Brunswick: Rutgers University Press, 1988), 129.

15. On male wastefulness: Horatio Alger, *Ragged Dick; or, Street Life in New York with the Boot Blacks*, with an introduction by Alan Trachtenberg (1867–68; reprint, New York: Signet, 1990), 7–8, 89; T. S. Arthur, *Sparing to Spend; or, The Loftons and Pinkertons* (New York: Scribner, 1853); idem, *The Way to Prosper; or, In Union There Is Strength, and Other Tales* (Boston: L. Crown, 1853); Daniel Horowitz, *The Morality of Spending: Attitudes Toward the Consumer Society in America, 1875–1940* (Baltimore: Johns Hopkins University Press, 1985), 16–18, 21, 27, 38–47; Senate Committee on Education and Labor, *Report on the Commission of the Senate upon the Relations between Labor and Capital* (Washington, DC, 1885); O. Henry, "A Lickpenny Lover," in *Complete Works*, 1262; On typewriter girls' pie: William Dean Howells, *The Rise of Silas Lapham*, ed. Edwin H. Cady (1885; reprint, Boston: Houghton Mifflin, 1957), 841; Murolo, *Common Ground of Womanhood*, 25; Kate Field and editor's reply, "Ought a Woman to Earn Her Living?" *PW* 7 (January 1892): 237

[*Kate Field's Washington*]: the editor rebuked Field for only describing the behavior of "incompetents"; On berry pie: Myra C. Hole, "The Typewriter Girl," *TPW* 15 (October 1899): 78; idem, "The Typewriter Girl," *TPW* 15 (November 1899): 149; "The Typewriter Girl," *TPW* 15 (December 1899): 212; On workers fault: Enstad, *Ladies of Labor,* 85, 105; On labor's view of women's failure as a consumer: Lawrence Glickman, *A Living Wage: American Workers and the Making of Consumer Society* (Ithaca: Cornell University, 1997), 90; On work and casual prostitution: Susan Porter Benson, *Counter Cultures: Saleswomen, Managers, and Customers in American Department Stores, 1890–1940* (Urbana: University of Illinois Press, 1986), 135–36; Joanne J. Meyerowitz, *Women Adrift: Independent Wage Earners in Chicago, 1880–1930* (Chicago: University of Chicago Press, 1988), 101–6.

16. Robert C. Allen, *Horrible Prettiness: Burlesque and American Culture* (Chapel Hill: University of North Carolina Press, 1991), 201–2, 206–21; Susan A. Glenn, *Female Spectacle: The Theatrical Roots of Modern Feminism* (Cambridge: Harvard University Press, 2000), 187–202; Laura Hapke, *Labor's Text: The Worker in American Fiction* (New Brunswick: Rutgers University Press, 2001), 88; Meyerowitz, *Women Adrift,* 126–33; Until the 1920s, novelists, the popular press, and shorthand periodicals rarely described stenographers and typewriters as outright gold diggers; O. Henry, "The Trimmed Lamp," in *Complete Works,* 1368, 1369, "Lickpenny Lover," 1261, 1262–66; Joselit, *Perfect Fit,* 171–72; To Wilson, Lou's marriage to a millionaire proved her ascendancy but minimized Lou's unhappiness at the end and ignored an explanation of Protestant moralism that the "poor are truly happy," but this story was about place and identity, not poverty; Masie found a respectable working-class man, perfect for her: *White Collar Fictions,* 52–53.

17. O. Henry, "Trimmed Lamp," 1366; idem, "Lickpenny Lover," 1263–64; idem, "The Ferry of Unfulfilment," in *Complete Works,* 1472; Female telegraphers and women in working girls' clubs worried about slang and poor grammar as well: Gabler, *American Telegrapher,* 129; Kathy Peiss, *Cheap Amusements: Working Women and Leisure in Turn-of-the-Century New York* (Philadelphia: Temple University Press, 1986), 170; Murolo, *Common Ground of Womanhood,* 163–64.

18. Florence Calvert, "Love versus Business: The Tale of a Match, a Machine, and a Masking Maid," *TPW* 26 (September 1905): 141–46; Ellis Wood, "The Revolt of the Abominated: An Interesting Dialogue Overheard in the Quiet of the Office," *TPW* 20 (September 1902): 157–59.

19. "Women as Typewriters," *PW* 3 (October 1887): 36 [*Chicago Herald*].

20. Lisa M. Fine, *The Souls of the Skyscraper: Female Clerical Workers in Chicago, 1870–1930* (Philadelphia: Temple University Press, 1990), 71–73.

21. On reformers like Dodge: Murolo, *Common Ground of Womanhood,* 65–66; Peiss, *Cheap Amusements,* 171; On reasons immigrant women married young: Randy D. McBee, *Dance Hall Days: Intimacy and Leisure among Working-Class Immigrants in the United States* (New York: New York University Press, 2000), 13–50; On Howard: "Formal Opening of the Stenographers' Association," *BPM-W* 15 (17 February 1890): 100–102; "The Typewriter Girl: Her Habits and Peculiarities Clearly Described by an Accurate Observer," *BPMRJ* 10 (February 1885): 36 [*Exchange*]; On losing to marriage: Asmodeus,

"Difficulties of Securing Good Typewriter Operators and Stenographers," *BPW* 15 (17 November 1890): 659–61 [*New York Sunday World*]; John Robertson, "Is the Number of Women Stenographers Decreasing?" *PW* 5 (September 1889): 4.

22. Michael Denning, *Mechanic Accents: Dime Novels and Working-Class Culture in America* (London: Verso, 1987), 185–200; On flirt: "The Girl and the Machine," *BPMRJ* 14 (February 1889): 43–44 [*Exchange*]; "Womanly Dignity," *IPW* 9 (June 1894): 313 [*Ladies Home Journal*]; "Starting Out Right!" *IPW* 9 (September 1893): 32 [*Business Education*]; A Frisco Girl, "From a San Francisco Girl," *IPW* 10 (July 1895): 265; Margery W. Davies, *Woman's Place Is at the Typewriter: Office Work and Office Workers, 1870–1930* (Philadelphia: Temple University Press, 1982), 81–82; Ethyl B. Palmer, "A Telephone Proxy," *TPW* 23 (February 1904): 111–14.

23. On beauty as naturally female and dangerous: Kathy Peiss, *Hope in a Jar: The Making of America's Beauty Culture* (New York: Metropolitan Books, 1998), 24, 28–29, 183; Linda Frost, "The Circassian Beauty and the Circassian Slave: Gender, Imperialism, and American Popular Entertainment," in *Freakery: Cultural Spectacles of the Extraordinary Body,* ed. Rosemarie Garland Thomson (New York: New York University Press, 1996): 257; On typists as stupid, aloof, and frivolous: "Guarding Her Employer's Secret," *IPW* 12 (June 1897): 359 [*Chicago Daily News*]; "The Scorn of the Typewriter Girl," *BPMRJ* 12 (August 1887): 250 [*Tid-Bits*]; Frank H. Risteen, "Should Stenographers Marry?" *PW* 7 (June 1892): 393 [*London Phonographer*]; Robert Barr, "The Typewritten Letter: A Difficult Bit of Dictation From 'The Face and the Mask,'" *TPW* 26 (November 1905): 268; On railway clerks portraying women as distracting in the office: Janet F. Davidson, "'Now That We Have Girls in the Office': Clerical Work, Masculinity, and the Refashioning of Gender for a Bureaucratic Age," in *Boys and Their Toys? Masculinity, Class, and Technology in America,* ed. Roger Horowitz (New York: Routledge, 2001), 73.

24. Ellis Wood, "Two Men and a Maid," *TPW* 18 (February 1902): 565–66, 568, 570–71, 563, 570, 572; Male lawyers feared that beautiful female lawyers might sway the jury via seduction: Virginia G. Drachman, *Sisters in Law: Women Lawyers in Modern American History* (Cambridge: Harvard University Press, 1998), 85–86.

25. Peiss, *Cheap Amusements,* 156; "Dangerous Typewriters," *BPMRJ* 13 (July 1888): 204 [*New York World*].

26. "Where She Drew the Line," *BPMRJ* 13 (July 1888): 204 [*Chicago Times*].

27. Kathryn Chatoid, "The Fem-Sten's Retreat: The Efficiency of Women Stenographers," *TPW* 15 (May 1900): 530.

28. Peiss, *Cheap Amusements;* 59–62, 88–114, 122–38; For an example of the extensive literature on these criticisms in the Progressive reform agenda: Mary E. Odem, *Delinquent Daughters: Protecting and Policing Adolescent Female Sexuality in the United States, 1885–1920* (Chapel Hill: University of North Carolina Press, 1995), 95–127; McBee, *Dance Hall Days,* 82–90; John F. Kasson, *Rudeness and Civility: Manners in Nineteenth-Century Urban America* (New York: Hill & Wang, 1990), 124–26, 199, 207–10; Murolo, *Common Ground of Womanhood,* 25, 41, 163–64.

29. The quote in the heading designates the preferred, but problematic, office woman. Carey, "Reminiscences of a Shorthand Writer," 182–84.

30. For a discussion on blurring respectability for men: Brian P. Luskey, "Riot and Re-

spectability: The Shifting Terrain of Class Language and Status in Baltimore during the Great Strike of 1877," *American Nineteenth Century History* 4 (Fall 2003): 80.

31. "Womanly Dignity," 313; "Starting Out Right!" and editor's comments, *IPW* 9 (September 1893): 32 [*Business Education*].

32. S. S. Packard, "The Girl Amanuensis," *PW* 4 (October 1888): 40.

33. Harriet L. Husted, "Advice to a 'Pretty Type-writer,'" *PW* 5 (June 1890): 302.

34. On images of the lady: Fine, *Souls of the Skyscraper,* 61–66; Meyerowitz, *Women Adrift,* 117–27, 33; Sarah Eisenstein, *Give Us Bread but Give Us Roses: Working Women's Consciousness in the United States, 1890 to the First World War* (London: Routledge & Kegan Paul, 1983), 77–84; Mary Clemmer Ames, *Ten Years in Washington: Life and Scenes in the National Capital as a Woman Sees Them* (Hartford, CT: A. O. Worthington, 1875), 351–56; "Success of Our Instruction Reporting," *S-PV* 1 (February 1865): 115-11 [*Ames' College Monthly*]; "Slurs on Women," *S-PV* 3 (14 December 1868): 464 [*Packard's Monthly*]; "Women as Government Clerks: Their Work and Their Play—Play Fair," *Washington Capital,* 4 November 1871, 1; "The Lady of the Treasury," *Washington Capital,* 12 March 1871, 1; Mabel Deutrich and Virginia C. Purdy, eds., *Clio Was a Woman: Studies in the History of American Women* (Washington, DC, 1980), 2; Cindy Sondik Aron, *Ladies and Gentlemen of the Civil Service: Middle-Class Workers in Victorian America* (New York: Oxford University Press, 1987), 57; William E. Barton, *The Life of Clara Barton: Founder of the American Red Cross* (Boston: Houghton Mifflin, 1922), 91; One article reported that obscene letters barred "female" employment from the dead letter office: "Dead Letters," *S-PV* 3 (21 December 1868): 484; "Women to the Front," *BPM* 3 (December 1878): 220–22; Mrs. E. B. Burns, "Gentlewomen and Womanly Men," *BPM* 3 (July 1878): 128; "Personal," *BPM* 1 (January 1876): 35; "Personal," *BPM* 1 (June 1876): 95; "Woman," *BPM* 3 (December 1878): 230–31; "Lady Stenographers of New York," *BPM* 3 (December 1878): 222; "Something about the Girls: A Lady Stenographer," *BPM* 3 (December 1878): 233; "Second Annual Dinner of the Stenographers of Chicago," *BPM* 4 (February 1879): 23–26; Mary S. McCalla, "Interesting to Ladies," *BPM* 4 (February 1879): 36; "The Stenographic Profession for Ladies," *BPM* 4 (November 1879): 237; Teresa Anne Murphy, *Ten Hours' Labor: Religion, Reform, and Gender in Early New England* (Ithaca: Cornell University Press, 1992), 143; Ann Russo and Cheris Kramarae, eds., *The Radical Women's Press of the 1850s,* 2nd ed. (London: Routledge, 2001), 2: 105; Mary H. Blewett, *Men, Women, and Work: Class, Gender, and Protest in the New England Shoe Industry, 1780–1910* (Urbana: University of Illinois Press, 1988), 222–24; Gabler, *American Telegrapher,* 116, 127; Thomas C. Jepsen, *My Sisters Telegraphic: Women in the Telegraph Office, 1846–1950* (Athens: Ohio University Press, 2000), 85; Benson, *Counter Cultures,* 24; "Positions: Opportunities for Boys," *BPW* 16 (27 April 1891): 213; Lucy Larcom, *A New England Girlhood,* with an introduction by Charles T. Davis (1889; reprint, Gloucester, MA: Peter Smith, 1973), 201; Enstad, *Ladies of Labor,* 49–51, 68–78.

35. "Good Typewriting Won a Worthy Husband," *BPM-W* 15 (13 January 1890): 25; "Personal—Doings of Stenographers," *BPMRJ* 9 (December 1884): 357–58; "Personal—Doings of Stenographers," *BPMRJ* 14 (August 1889): 246 [*Michigan Exchange*].

36. "Personal—Doings of Stenographers," *BPM* 14:246; Miss Reynolds A. Sh. S., "Shorthand for Women," *BPW* 17 (25 January 1892): 51; B.C., "A Woman Stenographer's

Plea for Rights," *IPW* 7 (August 1892): 501–2; "Shorthand for Girls—What A Business Man Thinks," *BPMRJ* 11 (June 1886): 125–26 [*Exponent*]; "Lady Stenographers and Their Compensation," *BPMRJ* 8 (June 1883): 148–49; "Our Sisters in the Profession Are Not Interlopers," *BPW* 15 (16 June 1890): 343–44.

37. Aron, *Ladies and Gentlemen of the Civil Service,* 47–50; Murolo, *Common Ground of Womanhood,* 10; Quote on fit for exclusive society: editorial, *PM* 4 (May 1890): 134 [*Gossiper*]; On lady-in-distress style: "'Typewriter an Ambiguous Word," *BPMRJ* 14 (2 December 1889): 363–64 [*St. Louis Exchange*]; Pauline S. Roe, "The Lady Stenographer," *BPMRJ* 9 (June 1884): 148–50 [*Chicago Current*].

38. On etiquette and power: C. Dallett Hemphill, *Bowing to Necessities: A History of Manners in America, 1620–1860* (New York: Oxford University Press, 1999), 194–212; For one of the many examples on women's moral authority: Peggy Pascoe, *Relations of Rescue: The Search for Female Moral Authority in the American West, 1874–1939* (New York: Oxford University Press, 1990), xvii; Nurses used "motherly authority and skill" to protect against accusations of sexual interest in male patients: Reverby, *Ordered to Care,* 43.

39. E.L.C., "The Typewriter Girl," *PM* 6 (October 1892): 423–26; Quote on Rockman: Aron, *Ladies and Gentlemen of the Civil Service,* 164; Hattie Witherington Sutton, "The Will and the Way: A Common Experience in Many Offices—May the Outcome Be Always as Happy for the Stenographer," *TPW* 26 (August 1905): 79; Eisenstein, *Give Us Bread,* 87–93; Quote on common courtesies: Clara M. Binning, "What Shall I Demand of My Employer," *PM* 7 (15 March 1893): 104–6; In the face of improper remarks, a female columnist advised, "You will, of course, be entitled to assert your dignity": Husted, "Advice to a 'Pretty Type-writer,'" 302–3; On advice on how to deal with a boss who smokes or has other habits offensive to women: "Some Hints to the Girls in Particular," *PM* 4 (May 1890): 140; On women controlling etiquette in leisure: Murolo, *Common Ground of Womanhood,* 62–64; On expectation of politeness: Amy G. Richter, *Home on the Rails: Women, the Railroad, and the Rise of Public Domesticity* (Chapel Hill: University of North Carolina Press, 2005), 45–47.

40. "Feminine Stenographers," *BPMRJ* 12 (March 1887): 78–79 [*Boston Globe*]; Robertson, "Is the Number of Women Stenographers Decreasing?" 4; Quote on "Mr. A": "There is Too Much Truth in It," *PW* 8 (July 1893): 294 [*Ladies Home Journal*]; "Pacific States: Woman's Work," *BPMRJ* 11 (October 1886): 226–28; Fiction quote: Wood, "Revolt of the Abominated,"158.

41. Irland, "New York State Stenographers' Association," 17.

42. Ava Baron, "Contested Terrain Revisited: Technology and Gender Definitions of Work in the Printing Industry, 1850–1920," in *Women, Work, and Technology: Transformations,* ed. Barbara Drygulski Wright et al. (Ann Arbor: University of Michigan Press, 1987), 70–72; Karen Berger Morello, *The Woman Lawyer in America: 1638 to the Present* (Boston: Beacon, 1986), 174; it was assumed that women doctors would faint during an operation: Regina Markell Morantz-Sanchez, *Sympathy and Science: Women Physicians in American Medicine* (New York: Oxford University Press, 1985), 118; On stenographers: Fine, *Souls of the Skyscraper,* 55; Davies, *Woman's Place Is at the Typewriter,* 89–91; "The 'World's' Pictures of Popular American Stenographers," *PW* 3 (March 1888): 147–48; "Why Some Women Fail," 53; Davidson, "Girls in the Office," 75; On modesty and wages:

"Lady Stenographers and Their Compensation," 148–49; On modesty and courts: Carey, "Reminiscences of a Shorthand Writer," 182–84; Ballantyne, "Woman Stenographers," 131; Jane Jerome Camhi, *Women Against Women: American Anti-Suffragism, 1880–1920* (Brooklyn: Carlson, 1994), 15; On the ornamental image, the middle class resolution of idleness and the lady by advocating usefulness: Virginia Penny, *Think and Act*, 237.

43. On marriage: Fine, *Souls of the Skyscraper*, 62; S., "Another View of Female Stenographers," *BPMRJ* 11 (December 1886): 292; On business secrets: Asmodeus, "Difficulties of Securing Good Typewriter Operators," 659–61.

44. On discourse: Nancy Lee Sobal, "Curing and Caring: A Literary View of Professional Medical Women" (Ph.D. diss., University of Cincinnati, 1984); 51–62; Barbara Bardes and Suzanne Gossett, *Declaration of Independence: Women and Political Power in Nineteenth-Century American Fiction* (New Brunswick: Rutgers University Press, 1990), 130–52; Fifty-one percent of nineteenth-century women lawyers married, compared to 25 to 35 percent of doctors, but other professionals married even less frequently; Preceding statistics: Drachman, *Sisters in Law*, 100; On rationalization and practicing with husbands: Drachman, *Sisters in Law*, 101–8. On doctors' discourse and practicing with husbands: Regina Markell Morantz-Sanchez, "The Many Faces of Intimacy: Professional Options and Personal Choices among Nineteenth and Early Twentieth-Century Women Physicians," in *Uneasy Careers and Intimate Lives: Women in Science, 1789–1979*, eds. Pnina G. Abir-Am and Dorinda Outram, with a foreword by Margaret W. Rossiter (New Brunswick: Rutgers University Press, 1987), 45–59; idem, *Sympathy and Science: Women Physicians in American Medicine* (New York: Oxford University Press, 1985), 135–43.

45. Felicia Luz Carr, "All for Love: Gender, Class, and the Woman's Dime Novel in Nineteenth-Century America" (Ph.D. diss., George Mason University, 2003); Historians emphasize the marriage bar resolution that women remained temporary workers who would not move up the career ladder, which also explains how women became accepted in the office as different from men, rather than as equals: Fine, *Souls of the Skyscraper*, 63–65, 69; For the boundaries set by the marriage ideal: Kessler-Harris, *Out to Work*, 128; Sharon Hartman Strom, *Beyond the Typewriter: Gender, Class, and the Origins of Modern American Office Work, 1900–1930* (Urbana: University of Illinois Press, 1992), 190–96; On marriage attractions: Ileen A. DeVault, *Sons and Daughters of Labor: Class and Clerical Work in Turn-of-the-Century Pittsburgh* (Ithaca: Cornell University Press, 1990), 160–67; Jerome P. Bjelopera, *City of Clerks: Office and Sales Workers in Philadelphia, 1870–1920* (Urbana: University of Illinois Press, 2005), 120.

46. "The Typewriter Girl as Wife-Material," *IPW* 11 (June 1896): 381 [*Post-Intelligencer*]; Elizabeth Colberg Washabaugh, "Eleanor's Investment Which Yielded Better Returns Than Even She Had Hoped For," *TPW* 23 (May 1904): 335–38; Calvert, "Love versus Business," 141–46.

47. "Typewriter Notes," *PM* 7 (July 1891): 207 [*New York Sun*]; Marriage announcement: *IPW* 11 (December 1895): 118; "More Hearts Made Happy," *IPW* 11 (April 1896): 30; Angel Kwolek-Folland, *Engendering Business: Men and Women in the Corporate Office, 1870–1920* (Baltimore: Johns Hopkins University Press, 1994), 127; Fine, *Souls of the Skyscraper*, 68–69; "Matrimony," *BPMRJ* 14 (April 1889): 120; Five heroines married as a reward for good work, six married as a relief from work (although their stories were by

only three different authors), and four married for some mixture; Three of the stories advised against office romance; Carr, "All for Love."

48. Carole Srole, "'Beyond One's Control': Life Course and the Tragedy of Class, Boston, 1880 to 1900," *Journal of Family History* 11, no. 1 (1986): 43–54; Carr, "All for Love," 166.

49. On Rosa Wald: "Marriages," *TPW* 11 (November 1895): 84; Quotes on businessman and printer: "Cupid among the Stenographers," *TPW* 11 (December 1895): 126; Quote on Clinton: "More Hearts Made Happy," *TPW* 11 (April 1896): 303; Quote on millionaire: "Good Typewriting Won a Worthy Husband," 25; Quote by Scott-Browne: "Typewriting Girls and Love," *BPMRJ* 13 (April 1888): 118–19; "Type-Writer Notes," 207. "Marriages," *PW* 11 (November 1895): 84; "Cupid among the Stenographers," *PW* 11 (December 1895): 126; "Good Typewriting Won a Worthy Husband," 25; "More Hearts Made Happy," *PW* 11 (April 1896): 303; "Typewriting Girls and Love," *BPM* 13 (April 1888): 118–19; "Type-Writer Notes," 207.

50. Edith Azalia Adams, "'In Her Place:' The Stenographer Did Her Full Duty, and Faithfulness Brought Its Just Reward," *TPW* 25 (March 1905): 185; Marion Mitchell Barr, "A Mistake in Identity: Caused By the Blunders of a Bachelor and a Benedick," *TPW* 24 (October 1905): 203–7.

51. "Cupid among the Stenographers," *IPW* 11 (January 1896): 154 [*St. Louis Republic*].

52. Karen Lystra, *Searching the Heart: Women, Men, and Romantic Love in Nineteenth-Century America* (New York: Oxford, 1989), 113–17, 206; Carr, "All for Love," 170–72; Barr, "Mistake in Identity," 203–207; "'Wanted—a Stenographer' and This Law Firm Still Requires One; Do You Want the Job," *TPW* 28 (November 1906): 344–46; On Grace Brown: Edith Azalia Adams, "The One Thing Needful: The Stenographer Resigns but Makes Another Engagement," *TPW* 27 (February 1906): 77; On Thomasine Jadwin: Irene Harrington Wright, "Old Peter Murray's Millions: A Game That Two Could Play At, and—the Stenographer Won," *TPW* 25 (January 1905): 3–9; Mrs. C. H. Brake, "One Way: How a Plucky Girl Stenographer Demanded and Obtained a First-Class Situation," *TPW* 22 (August 1903): 91. The image of saleswomen is surprising considering how few men shopped in department stores. See Benson, *Counter Cultures,* 99, 135; Hapke, *Labor's Text,* 77, 87–88; Rebecca Harding Davis, *Margaret Howth: A Story of To-day* with an afterword by Jean Fagan Yellin (New York: Feminist Press, 1990); Allen, *Horrible Prettiness,* 201–4; Laura Hapke, *Daughters of the Great Depression: Women, Work, and Fiction in the American 1930s* (Athens: University of Georgia Press, 1995), 209, O. Henry, "Romance of a Busy Broker," 85–88.

53. Carr, "All for Love," 170, 181; On John and Grace: Marie A. Watson, "John Burton's Wife: It Took a Thunder-storm to Clear the Stenographic Atmosphere!" *TPW* 22 (November 1903): 381–83.

54. Lystra, *Searching the Heart,* 186; Sutton, "Failure!" 341–49; E. K. Stevens, "The Little Typist: Her Dream of 'Annexation,' or How She Studied Law," *TPW* 20 (October 1902): 288–95; One of the few love stories written by a man: Barr, "Typewritten Letter," 267–72; Watson, "John Burton's Wife," 381–83; Adams, "The One Thing Needful," 76–77; Barr, "Mistake in Identity," 203–7; Fine, *Souls of the Skyscraper,* 71–72; and David Graham Phillips, *The Grain of Dust* (New York: D. Appleton, 1911).

55. "Feminine Stenographers," 78–79 [*Boston Globe*]; Scott-Browne quote on advis-

ing marriage: Editor, "Women in the Profession," *BPM-W* 15 (6 January 1890): 4–5; "Typewriting Girls and Love," 118–19; Bjelopera, *City of Clerks,* 40.

56. "It Is the Truth," *BPW* 15 (7 July 1890): 389–90 [*New York Truth*].

57. "A Perfect Picture of Happiness," *BPW* 15 (28 April 1890): 260–61; Mrs. G. H. Lamb, "Getting Rid of the Girls," *BPM-W* 15 (31 March 1890): 197; Kate Armstrong, "Lady Stenographers and Salaries," *IPW* 12 (August 1897): 463; B.C. "A Woman Stenographer's Plea for Her Rights," 501–2; Eisenstein, *Give Us Bread,* 125–45; Willice Wharton, "Life of a Typewritist," *BPM-W* 14 (9 December 1889): 377–79; Fine, *Souls of the Skyscraper,* 63–64; Midcentury working women preferred marriage to work: Susan L. Porter "Victorian Values in the Marketplace: Single Women and Work in Boston, 1800–1850," in *Women of the Commonwealth: Work, Family, and Social Change in Nineteenth-Century Massachusetts,* ed. Susan L. Porter (Amherst: University of Massachusetts Press, 1996), 17–42.

58. Martha Ellsbeth, "For the Sake of the Office," *TPW* 22 (May 1902): 249–53; "The Female Stenographer Question," *BPMRJ* 12 (March 1887): 75–76; A Frisco Girl, "San Francisco Girl," 265; Quote by Eliza B. Burnz, "Shorthand Amanuenses and Schools," *PW* 6 (August 1891): 398; idem, "Dress for Business Women," *PW* 5 (January 1890), 136.

59. Dale M. Bauer and Jean Marie Lutes, "Beauty," in *The Oxford Companion to Women's Writing in the United States,* ed. Cathy N. Davidson, Linda Wagner-Martin, Elizabeth Ammons, et al. (New York: Oxford University Press, 1995), 97; "Typewriting Girls and Love," 118–19; Jessie M. Wood, "Are Women Any Good as Workers?" *IPW* 10 (May 1895): 227–29 [*Illustrated American*]; Clara Bell, "The Pretty Typewriter: Her More Homely Sister is Now in More Demand among Business Houses," *BPMRJ* 13 (April 1888): 104–5 [*New York World*]; "Bidlington's Miss Stubbs," *PW* 2 (August 1887): 245 [*Boston Transcript*].

60. Ellsbeth, "For the Sake of the Office," 249–53.

61. "Good Typewriting Won a Worthy Husband," 25; S. S. Packard, "The 'Pretty Typewriter,'" *PW* 5 (March 1890): 201; idem, "Girl Amanuensis," 40–41.

62. Viola Hopkins Winner, "Abigail Adams and 'The Rage of Fashion,'" *Dress* 28 (2001): 73; Halttunen, *Confident Men and Painted Women,* 66; Even advice for men recommended simple clothes: Joselit, *Perfect Fit,* 80–82, 178, 86; Fine, *Souls of the Skyscraper,* 60.

63. O. Henry, "Romance of a Busy Broker," 86; "The Woman in Business," *PW* 8 (March 1893): 231 [*New York World*]; Quotes on jewelry to attire: "Rainy-Day Costume: An Appropriate and Becoming Business Dress for Our Fair Amanuenses," *TPW* 17 (April 1901): 112.

64. Peiss, *Cheap Amusements,* 24.

65. Anne Guilbert Mahon, "A Christmas Dinner in a Law Office: The Stenographer Pursued the Path of Duty, and Won Out in the Good Old-Fashioned Way," *TPW* 25 (February 1905): 92; Sutton, "Failure!" 341; Adams, "One Thing Needful," 74.

66. Ethyl B. Palmer, "Brown's Amanuensis," *TPW* 21 (April 1903): 328–32.

67. Ibid., 328.

68. Ibid., 331; There is no physical description of Ralph Dexter, but Mr. Brown is referred to as one who "carried an old head on young and very finely-built shoulders,"

which were "his most striking feature," and he is said to be "smooth shaven and clear-eyed": ibid., 330.

69. Marie St. Felix [Harriet Louise Husted (Lynch)], *A Little Game with Destiny* (New York: Saalfield & Fitch, 1892), 9, 18, 31, 54–55, 65; idem, *Two Bad Brown Eyes* (New York: Western & Co., 1894); idem, *Patricia* (New York: Merriam, 1895); idem, *Told by Two: A Romance of Bermuda* (Chicago: M. A. Donahue, 1902); Husted, "Advice to a 'Pretty Typewriter,'" 302–3.

70. On men's fashion advice: Judy Hilkey, *Character Is Capital: Success Manuals and Manhood in Gilded Age America* (Chapel Hill: University of North Carolina Press, 1997), 136; Joselit, *Perfect Fit,* 80–83; For an example of a blurring of masculine and feminine clothes: Mary W. Blanchard, "Boundaries and the Victorian Body: Aesthetic Fashion," *American Historical Review* 100 (February 1995): 26–35, 49; "The Woman in Business," 231; Fine, *Souls of the Skyscraper,* 60; "The Fem-Sten's Retreat," *TPW* 15 (March 1900): 398; "The Fem-Sten's Retreat," *TPW* 15 (June 1900): 593; Schorman, *Selling Style,* 77, 51, 66, 69.

71. Enstad, *Ladies of Labor,* 8–10, 55; Elizabeth Ewen, *Immigrant Women in the Land of Dollars: Life and Culture on the Lower East Side, 1890–1925* (New York: Monthly Review Press, 1985), 67; Joselit, *Perfect Fit,* 116; Working-class women who worked as telegraph and telephone operators appreciated the status advantages of "respectable dress": Stephen H. Norwood, *Labor's Flaming Youth: Telephone Operators and Worker Militancy, 1878–1923* (Urbana: University of Illinois Press, 1990), 278; Gabler, *American Telegrapher,* 127–28; Virginia G. Drachman, *Women Lawyers and the Origins of Professional Identity in America: The Letters of the Equity Club, 1887 to 1890* (Ann Arbor: University of Michigan Press, 1993), 23, 30, 177.

72. "Emma Anderson," *PM* 10 (15 March 1896): 85; By 1896, the drooping sleeve reached its widest: Severa, *Dressed for the Photographer,* 457–60, 514, 528; Example of logo: "The Fem-Sten's Retreat," *TPW* 16 (September 1900): 21; On class conflicts and fashion: Enstad, *Ladies of Labor,* 61; On ambivalence in a feminist magazine, which both critiqued fashion and featured "fashion notes" on the newest styles: Schorman, *Selling Style,* 74, 68; On the railway clerks' union during World War I including "beauty pages" of women clerks: Davidson, "Girls in the Office," 74.

CHAPTER 6

1. "The Typewriter Girl," *IPW* 12 (November 1896): 130 [*Boston Courier*].

2. Helen L. Hinckle, "The Lady Court Stenographer," *PW* 8 (March 1893): 254.

3. For examples of the extensive literature on the New Woman: Karen J. Blair, *The Clubwoman as Feminist: True Womanhood Redefined, 1868–1914* (New York: Holmes & Meier, 1980); Joyce Antler, "'After College, What?' New Graduates and the Family Claim," *American Quarterly* 32 (Fall 1980): 409–34; Ellen Gruber Garvey, "Reframing the Bicycle: Advertising-Supported Magazines and Scorching Women," *American Quarterly* 47 (March 1995): 72, 85–94; Amy G. Richter, *Home on the Rails: Women, the Railroad, and the Rise of Public Domesticity* (Chapel Hill: University of North Carolina Press, 2005); Jane H. Hunter, *How Young Ladies Became Girls: The Victorian Origins of American Girl-*

hood (New Haven: Yale University Press, 2002); For working-class and lower middle-class versions: Priscilla Murolo, *The Common Ground of Womanhood: Class, Gender, and Working Girls' Clubs, 1884–1928* (Urbana: University of Illinois Press, 1997), 155–56; Edwin Gabler, *The American Telegrapher: A Social History, 1860–1900* (New Brunswick: Rutgers University Press, 1988), 99–105; Middle-class women's close relationship to their own mothers may explain why they rarely criticized them: Sherna Gluck, ed., *From Parlor to Prison: Five American Suffragists Talk about Their Lives; An Oral History* (New York: Vintage, 1976), 34–35, 44, 65; Yet fiction portrayed mothers as old-fashioned: Linda W. Rosenzweig, *The Anchor of My Life: Middle-Class American Mothers and Daughters, 1880–1920* (New York: New York University Press, 1993), 66, 70–113; Elaine Showalter, ed., *These Modern Women: Autobiographic Essays from the Twenties* (Old Westbury, New York: Feminist Press, 1978), 49, 54, 88; On rejecting the mothers' generation: Carroll Smith-Rosenberg, "The New Woman as Androgyne: Social Order and Gender Crisis, 1870–1936," in *Disorderly Conduct: Visions of Gender in Victorian America* (New York: Oxford University Press, 1985), 247–48, 256–57.

4. Lisa M. Fine sees clerical workers as New Women but emphasizes their success rather than their independence: *The Souls of the Skyscraper: Female Clerical Workers in Chicago, 1870–1930* (Philadelphia: Temple University Press, 1990), 65–75.

5. Dorothy S. Pam, "Exploitation, Independence, and Solidarity: The Changing Role of American Working Women as Reflected in the Working-Girl Melodrama, 1870–1910" (Ph.D. diss., State University of New York, 1980), 123–25; Ann Schofield, ed., *Sealskin and Shoddy: Working Women in American Labor Press Fiction, 1876–1920* (New York: Greenwood, 1988), 3–5, 10; Michael Denning, *Mechanic Accents: Dime Novels and Working-Class Culture in America* (London: Verso, 1987), 191–94; Nancy Catherine Enstad, "Compromised Positions: Working-Class Women, Popular Culture, and Labor Politics, 1890–1920" (Ph.D. diss., University of Minnesota, 1993), 35, 47–52, 56; Nan Enstad, *Ladies of Labor, Girls of Adventure: Working Women, Popular Culture, and Labor Politics at the Turn of the Twentieth Century* (New York: Columbia University Press, 1999), 20, 32–46, 74, 76; Robert E. Weill, *Beyond Labor's Veil: The Culture of the Knights of Labor* (University Park: Pennsylvania State University Press, 1996), 195–230.

6. Joanne J. Meyerowitz, *Women Adrift: Independent Wage Earners in Chicago, 1880–1930* (Chicago: University of Chicago Press, 1988), 55–60.

7. Ibid., 48, 53; Elizabeth Colberg Washabaugh, "Eleanor's Investment Which Yielded Better Returns Than Even She Had Hoped For," *TPW* 23 (May 1904): 335–38; Anne Guilbert Mahon, "Ill Blows the Wind That Profits Nobody: The Stenographer Bravely Followed the Path of Duty and Found That It Led To Happiness," *TPW* 21 (January 1903): 107–11; Only another story by Washabaugh and one more of the forty-four stories about women sounded like the woman adrift.

8. On low wages: "Lady Stenographers and Their Compensation," *BPMRJ* 8 (June 1883): 148–49; "A Deplorable Outrage," *BPMRJ* 11 (May 1886): 102–4; Jno. M. Hines, "Correspondence: Women Stenographers Should Demand Better Salaries," *PM* 7 (15 December 1893): 462–63; Willice Wharton, "Life of a Typewritist," *BPM-W* 14 (9 December 1889): 377–79; "Correspondence," *BPW* 16 (5 January 1891): 4–5; On Marion Orner: Edith Azalia, "'In Her Place': The Stenographer Did Her Full Duty, and Faith-

fulness Brought Its Just Reward," *TPW* 25 (March 1905), 180; On Helen Cartwright: Mrs. E. C. Washabaugh, "Just in Time! Through Difficulties and Dangers the Stenographer Pursued the Path of Duty, and Found Her Just Reward," *TPW* 25 (June 1905): 443–47.

9. Meyerowitz, *Women Adrift*, 125–34; Denning, *Mechanic Accents*, 193; Enstad, *Ladies of Labor*, 50–60; Felicia Luz Carr, "All for Love: Gender, Class, and the Woman's Dime Novel in Nineteenth-Century America" (Ph.D. diss., George Mason University, 2003), 163, 179.

10. Emily Ruth Calvin, "Laura's Mother," *TPW* 27 (June 1906): 361–62.

11. Karen Lystra, *Searching the Heart: Women, Men, and Romantic Love in Nineteenth-Century America* (New York: Oxford University Press, 1989), 158–65; Carr, "All for Love," 123, 169–73; Mrs. C. H. Brake, "One Way: How a Plucky Girl Stenographer Demanded and Obtained a First-Class Situation," *TPW* 22 (August 1903): 91; Irene Harrington Wright, "Old Peter Murray's Millions: A Game That Two Could Play At, and—the Stenographer Won," *TPW* 25 (January 1905): 3–9.

12. Robert Barr, "The Typewritten Letter: A Difficult Bit of Dictation from 'The Face and the Mask,'" *TPW* 26 (November 1905): 268.

13. A.H., "Women and Their Work: Lesson of a Young Woman Stenographer's Career," *TPW* 20 (August 1902): 94 [*New York Evening Post*].

14. Brake, "One Way," 91–95.

15. "Personal," *BPM* 1 (January 1876): 35; "Woman," *BPM* 3 (December 1878): 230–31.

16. Fine, *Souls of the Skyscraper*, 65–70; "Testing Her Speed," *TPW* 15 (December 1900): 206–7; Leander G. Bowers, "The Typewriter Telegram: How a Plucky Girl Operator in Colorado Prevented a Terrible Catastrophe," *TPW* 22 (July 1903): 3–6; Enstad, *Ladies of Labor*, 72–75.

17. "Another Woman Official Stenographer," *IPW* 10 (July 1894): 334.

18. Showalter, *Modern Women*, 50–51.

19. XYZ, "Communications: All About the Boston Boys," *BPMRJ* 6 (February 1881): 24–26; "Women's Salary," *BPMRJ* 8 (March 1883): 65–66; U.S. Commissioner of Labor, "A Compilation of Wages in Commercial Countries from Official Sources," in *Fifteenth Annual Report*, 2 vols. (Washington, DC, 1900) 1:148–52, 312–18; 2:1407–8.

20. Massachusetts Bureau of Statistics of Labor, "The Working Girls of Boston," in *Fifteenth Annual Report* (Boston: Wright & Potter, 1884), 41, 53, 76–81; U.S., Commissioner of Labor, "Work and Wages of Men, Women, and Children," *Eleventh Annual Report* (Washington, DC, 1897), 61–474, 482, 508, 644–45; Massachusetts Bureau of Statistics of Labor, "Mercantile Wages and Salaries," *Thirty-third Annual Report* (Boston: Wright & Potter, 1902), 123–24; Susan Porter Benson, *Counter Cultures: Saleswomen, Managers, and Customers in American Department Stores, 1890–1940* (Urbana: University of Illinois Press, 1986), 197–98; K.F.W., "Reminiscences," *Exponent* 1 (October 1883): 193–94; Cindy S. Aron, "'To Barter Their Souls for Gold': Female Clerks in Federal Government Offices, 1862–1890," *Journal of American History* 67 (December 1981): 161–62; Ileen A. DeVault, *Sons and Daughters of Labor: Class and Clerical Work in Turn-of-the-Century Pittsburgh* (Ithaca: Cornell University Press, 1990), 52, 56, 61; Fine, *Souls of the Skyscraper*, 42–43, 98–99.

21. U.S. Department of the Interior, *Register of Officers and Agents, Civil, Military, and Naval, in the Service of the United States* (Washington, DC, 1869), 737–39; U.S. Department of the Interior, *Official Register of the United States Containing a List of Officers and Employes [sic] in the Civil, Military, and Naval Service* (Washington, DC), 1871, 325–28; 1879, 1:151–55, 2:383–86; 1889, 1:170–75, 2:845–50; 1901, 1:203–7, 2:523–31; 1881, 1:169–70, 173; 1:633–36; 1895, 483–90; Aron, "'To Barter Their Souls,'" 44–45, 127; By the end of the century, gains in teaching salaries reversed the differential, as the lowest paid teacher earned $972, but the highest income of government clerical women remained competitive: Boston School Committee, *Annual Report* (Boston, 1895), 36; idem, *Annual Report* (Boston, 1896), 24–25; see appendix, table D2; Alice Flagg Simons to Elise Simons du Pont, 27 May 1889, Francis Gurney du Pont Papers, Hagley Museum and Library, Delaware (I thank Cindy Aron for this citation).

22. U.S. Commissioner of Labor, "Compilation of Wages," 1:83–103, 148–52, 176–85, 254–73, 312–18, 455–57, 1407–8, 1535; 2:946–47, 1057–70, 1112–17, 1121–29, 1164–67, 1244–50, 1275–76, 1407–8, 1535; Miss H., "Questions and Answers," *BPM* 1 (April 1876): 65; From the popular press: "A Profession for Women," *IPW* 11 (July 1896): 419 [*Philadelphia Telegraph*]; "Gleanings: The Typewriter Girl and What Her Qualifications Must Be," *BPW* 15 (11 August 1890): 468–69 [*Chicago News*]; "Stenographers in the Courts of Massachusetts," *BPMRJ* 14 (December 1889): 357–59; "Official Reporters' Salary," *BPM* 1 (December 1875): 18–19.

23. Albert W. Niemi Jr., "The Male-Female Earnings Differential: A Historical Overview of the Clerical Occupations from the 1880s to the 1970s," *Social Science History* 7 (Winter 1983): 97–107; Fine shows these distinctions for 1920s: *Souls of the Skyscraper,* 98–99, Cindy Sondik Aron, *Ladies and Gentlemen of the Civil Service: Middle-Class Workers in Victorian America* (New York: Oxford University Press, 1987), 83; "Personal," *BPM* 1 (February 1876): 48; Bessie A. Rogers, "Correspondence," *SJ* 6 (March 1877): 7; "Correspondence," *SJ* 6 (May 1877): 16.

24. Maria Susanna Cummins, *The Lamplighter,* ed. Nina Baym (1854; reprint, New Brunswick: Rutgers University Press, 1988), 1, 7, 18, 87, 129.

25. Enstad, *Ladies of Labor,* 76–77; Melodramas prefigured dime novel working-girl themes: Enstad, "Compromised Positions," 51, 52, 61–63; Pam, "Exploitation, Independence, and Solidarity," 50–61.

26. I searched for uses of the words *ambition* and *ambitious* in Project Gutenberg (http://www.gutenberg.org/), finding three about men in Rebecca Harding Davis's *Margaret Howth,* one about a man in her *Life in the Iron Mills,* and two about desire in Elizabeth Stuart Phelps's *Men, Women, and Ghosts.* In contrast, Louisa May Alcott's *Little Women* had nineteen positive references about women's ambition, in chapters 24 and 42.

27. William Dean Howells, *The Rise of Silas Lapham,* ed. Edwin H. Cady (1885; reprint, Boston: Houghton Mifflin, 1957), 127–241, 278–79; Theodore Dreiser, *The Titan* (1914), chap. 16, Project Gutenberg, http://www.gutenberg.org/.

28. "An Enterprising Lady," *TPW* 15 (September 1899): 27; U.S. Manuscript Census, 1900, Lowell, Enumeration District 450, 44.

29. Dorothy Richardson, *The Long Day: The Story of a New York Working Girl,* in *Women At Work,* ed. William O'Neill (1905; reprint, Chicago: Quadrangle, 1972), 269–73.

30. Lyde Cullen Sizer, *The Political Work of Northern Women Writers and the Civil War, 1850–1872* (Chapel Hill: University of North Carolina Press, 2000), 173–84, 245–78; Nancy Lee Sobal, "Curing and Caring: A Literary View of Professional Medical Women" (Ph.D. diss., University of Cincinnati, 1984); 51–62; Barbara Bardes and Suzanne Gossett, *Declaration of Independence: Women and Political Power in Nineteenth-Century American Fiction* (New Brunswick: Rutgers University Press, 1990), 130–52; Thomas C. Jepsen, *My Sisters Telegraphic: Women in the Telegraph Office, 1846–1950* (Athens: Ohio University Press, 2000), 119–38; Amal Amireh, *The Factory Girl and the Seamstress: Imagining Gender and Class in Nineteenth Century American Fiction* (New York: Garland, 2000), 139–40; Elizabeth Stuart Phelps, *Chapters from a Life* (Boston: Houghton Mifflin, 1896), 79.

31. B.C. , "A Woman Stenographer's Plea for Her Rights," *PW* 7 (August 1892): 501–2.

32. Alice Kessler-Harris, *Out to Work: A History of Wage-Earning Women in the United States* (Oxford: Oxford University Press, 1982), 135–39; "Biographical Sketch of Miss Mary Rowe of Brooklyn, New York: Chief Stenographer of the Norwich Union Fire Insurance Society of This City," *BPMRJ* 10 (January 1885): 9; "President Harrison's Stenographer," *PW* 5 (March 1890): 200; "President Harrison's Lady Stenographer," *BPM-W* 14 (2 December 1889): 360.

33. On opportunities: "Women to the Front," *BPM* 3 (December 1878): 220–23; "A New Field for Woman's Work," *BPMRJ* 5 (February 1880): 23; "The Stenographic Profession for Ladies," *BPM* 4 (November 1879): 237; On independence: "Migration of Stenographers," *BPMRJ* 10 (November 1885): 272–73; "How Poor Girls May Learn a Profession," *PW* 4 (April 1889): 159 [*Business Woman's Journal*]; Ellis Wood, "A Modern Instance in Which Ambition, Coupled with Willingness and Hard Work, Won Position and a Good Income," *TPW* 20 (November 1902): 341–44.

34. "Miss Cora Elisabeth Burbank," *TPW* 15 (February 1900): 356; "Personal—Brief Sketch of the Life of Miss Alice C. Nute," *BPM* 3 (December 1878): 226; "American Court Reporters and What Systems of Shorthand They Write," *PW* 8 (July 1893): 296–99.

35. Hinckle, "Lady Court Stenographer," 254.

36. "Hotel Stenographers," *PM* 1 (March 1887): 5 [*New York Mail and Express*]; "The 'World's' Pictures of Popular American Stenographers," *PW* 3 (March 1888): 147–48; "Edna I. Tyler," *PM* 5 (April 1891): 106–7; "The Rosenfield Sisters," *IPW* 9 (June 1894): 316; "Rosenfield Sisters, New York," *IPW* 13 (June 1898): 466.

37. "Certified Teachers—Alice W. Baker," *PM* 8 (1 February 1894): 43; "Miss Mary E. Pearce," *TPW* 14 (February 1899): 278.

38. "Certified Teachers—Elizabeth W. Walter," *PM* 6 (September 1892): 384–85; On Dyke: "Unknown Stenographers of Well-Known Men," *IPW* 9 (September 1893): 22–23; "Miss Rachel Brown," *TPW* 15 (May 1900): 541; "Personal—Miss Netta McLaughlin," *PM* 11 (15 February 1897): 63; "Mary F. Seymour," *PM* 4 (October 1890): 294–95.

39. According to a recalculation of Virginia G. Drachman's summary of a 1920 Bureau of Vocational Information questionnaire, 43.7 percent of lawyers previously had been stenographers, secretaries, court reporters, civil service, or deputy clerks, compared with 34 percent of former teachers or principals: *Sisters in Law: Women Lawyers in Modern American History* (Cambridge: Harvard University Press, 1998), 258; idem, *Women Lawyers and the Origins of Professional Identity in America: The Letters of the Equity Club, 1887 to 1890* (Ann Arbor: University of Michigan Press, 1993), 122, 109, 114, 169.

40. Jerome P. Bjelopera, *City of Clerks: Office and Sales Workers in Philadelphia, 1870–1920* (Urbana: University of Illinois Press, 2005), 41, 116–22; Miss Frances M. Fox, "Woman's Work," *PW* 3 (May 1888): 197; Walter E. Ingersoll, comp., *Shorthand, the Open Door to Opportunity; Some Distinguished Persons Who Write Shorthand* (New York: Gregg Publishing, 1915), 20–23.

41. S. S. Packard, "The Girl Amanuensis," *PW* 4 (October 1888): 40.

42. Geraldine Hussey, "The Shop-Girl and Shorthand," *PW* 4 (November 1888): 52; Quotes from idem, "Has Public Life Really Benefitted Women?" *IPW* 10 (September 1994): 15.

43. Hussey, "Shop-Girl and Shorthand," 52; On similar class resentment in the 1920s: Sharon Hartman Strom, *Beyond the Typewriter: Gender, Class, and the Origins of Modern American Office Work, 1900–1930* (Urbana: University of Illinois Press, 1992), 341–42.

44. On depositing negative traits of womanhood on working-class women: Christine Stansell, *City of Women: Sex and Class in New York, 1789–1860* (New York: Knopf, 1986), 19–30; Mrs. E. E. Doherty, "The Crowded Ranks," *PM* 2 (March 1888): 56; Minnie C. Pratt, "The Shiftless Student, the Poor Stenographer," *IPW* 12 (July 1897): 407; Grace Lincoln Hall, "Who Should Learn Shorthand and Who Should Not," *PW* 8 (November 1892): 62.

45. Calvin, "Laura's Mother," 361–62.

46. Hattie A. Shinn, "In Defense of the 'Pretty Typewriter,'" *BPMRJ* 14 (June 1889): 172 [*Chicago Tribune*]; Mrs. S. Louise Patteson, "The Woman Stenographer," *PM* 10 (15 June 1896): 202–3.

47. Ballantyne speech: Fred Irland, "The New York State Stenographers' Association," *PW* 3 (September 1887): 15–19; M. Jeanette Ballantyne, "Woman Stenographers," *PM* 10 (1 May 1896): 131 [*Rochester Post-Express*].

48. Angel Kwolek-Folland, *Incorporating Women: A History of Women and Business in the United States* (New York: Twayne, 1998); Frances B. Cogan, *All-American Girl: The Ideal of Real Womanhood in Mid-Nineteenth-Century America* (Athens: University of Georgia Press, 1989), 232–37; Jepsen, *Sisters Telegraphic*, 84–93; Wendy Gamber, *The Female Economy: The Millinery and Dressmaking Trades, 1860–1930* (Urbana: University of Illinois Press, 1997), 172–76; Pitman cited in Roger B. Landroth, "The History and Development of Pitmanic Shorthand in the United States, 1843–1976" (Ed.D. diss., New York University, 1977), 106; "Editorial Items," *S-PV* 3 (June 1868): 60; "Women and the Typewriter," *BPMRJ* 8 (September 1883): 225–26 [*St. Paul Pioneer Press*]; "Young Stenographers," *BPMRJ* 9 (March 1884): 57–60; "Is It Good Business for Girls," *PM* 2 (September 1888): 200; "What Salary Does a Bookkeeper-Stenographer Command?" *BPW* 16 (16 March 1891): 115.

49. "Are Lady Stenographers Desirable?" *BPMRJ* 11 (January 1886): 11; "Young Women Who Do Eat with Their Employers," *TPW* 18 (October 1901): 252; For similar language on doctors: Regina Markell Morantz-Sanchez, *Sympathy and Science: Women Physicians in American Medicine* (New York: Oxford University Press, 1985), 120.

50. "What Beautiful Hair You Have," *IPW* 10 (April 1895): 213 [*St. Louis Republican*]; "It Is the Truth," *BPW* 15 (7 July 1890): 389–90 [*New York Truth*]; "Gush, Charged at Time Rates," *IPW* 10 (March 1895): 188 [*Boston Journal*]; Hinckle, "Lady Court Stenographer," 254; Alice McKee, "Queer!" *TPW* 17 (September 1901): 22.

51. Fine, *Souls of the Skyscraper,* 156.

52. Cogan, *All-American Girl,* 232.

53. Irland, "New York State Stenographers' Association," 14; Eliza B. Burnz, "Dress for Business Women," *PW* 5 (January 1890), 136; *In Memoriam: Eliza Boardman Burnz* (New York: Burnz, 1906), 29–31. For general discussion of masculine woman: Laura L. Behling, *The Masculine Woman in America, 1890–1935* (Urbana: University of Illinois Press, 2001).

54. S. Louise Patteson, "Dress for Business Women," *PW* 5 (March 1890): 195; Kathryn Chatoid, "The Fem-Sten's Retreat," *TPW* 15 (June 1900), 593; Richardson disapproved of a "mannish shirtwaist": *Long Day,* 11.

55. Mary S. McCalla, "Deportment of Lady Stenographers," *BPMRJ* 7 (1882): 151.

56. Frances H. Cleveland, "Advice to Girls Entering the Business World," *IPW* 13 (April 1898): 341.

57. Editorial, *PM* 4 (May 1890): 134 [*Troy Telegram*]; "Are Lady Stenographers Desirable?" 11; Last two quotes: Ballantyne, "Woman Stenographers," 131; Ballantyne modesty quote: Irland, "New York State Stenographers' Association," 14.

58. Fine, *Souls of the Skyscraper,* 60; John Harvey, *Men in Black* (Chicago: University of Chicago Press, 1995), 195; Joan L. Severa, *Dressed for the Photographer: Ordinary Americans and Fashion, 1840–1900* (Kent: Kent State University Press, 1995), 456; Quote on avoiding showy clothing: Chatoid, "The Fem-Sten's Retreat," 593–94; For an example of appropriate clothing: "Waiting for the Verdict," *TPW* 17 (May 1901): 231; Angel Kwolek-Folland found the terms *business girls* and *office girls* were used to soften the businesswoman: *Engendering Business: Men and Women in the Corporate Office, 1870–1930* (Baltimore: Johns Hopkins University Press, 1994), 178.

59. International Congress of Shorthand Writers, *Proceedings of the Annual International Congress of Shorthand Writers* (Chicago: Western Label, 1882), 43–45.

60. T. C. Rose, "Stenographic Amanuenses, The Best Mode of Training Them with a View to Value and Efficiency," *PW* 1 (February 1886): 115–16; "Intelligence," *PM* 5 (May 1891): 131 [*The Press*]; Doherty, "Crowded Ranks," 56; "Shorthand at the U.S. Capitol," *PW* 6 (March 1891): 230–31.

61. Janice Weiss, "Educating for Clerical Work: The Nineteenth-Century Private Commercial School," *Journal of Social History* 14 (Spring 1981): 413; "Gossip Bureau: Personal Items of Interest from Our Different Shorthand Schools," *IPW* 13 (April 1898): 327; Bjelopera, *City of Clerks,* 70.

62. Richard L. Bushman and Claudia L. Bushman, "The Early History of Cleanliness in America," *Journal of American History* 74 (March 1988): 1213–38; Suellen M. Hoy, *Chasing Dirt: The American Pursuit of Cleanliness* (New York: Oxford University Press, 1995); On order: Jane Addams, "Utilization of Women in City Government," in *The Feminist Papers: From Adams to de Beauvoir,* ed. Alice S. Rossi (New York: Columbia University Press, 1973; Bantam, 1974) , 604–12; Lillian M. Growdy, "The Amanuensis Girl: Being a Truthful Narrative of How She Brought Order, Neatness, Efficiency, and Comfort on Her Train," *IPW* 7 (July 1896): 412; For another professional solution: Daniel J. Walkowitz, *Working with Class: Social Workers and the Politics of Middle-Class Identity* (Chapel Hill: University of North Carolina Press, 1999), 101–2, 104.

63. Mary E. Folsom, "The Competent Stenographer: A Symposium," *IPW* 13 (August 1898): 528–29; Harriet L. Husted, "Advice to a 'Pretty Type-writer,'" *PW* 5 (June 1890):

302–3; "The Fem-Sten's Retreat—Be Systematic," *TPW* 16 (December 1900): 204; Frank Rutherford, "What Is the Difference between a Male and a Female Stenographer?" *IPW* 9 (October 1893): 55.

64. Kwolek-Folland, *Engendering Business*, 85, 49, 53, 57; Benn Pitman, *Manual of Phonography* (Cincinnati: Phonographic Institute, 1855), 16–17; S. C. Rogers summarized the advantages of court reporters for settling disputes, relieving judges of note taking, shortening court terms and saving money, providing testimony for appeals, and undermining a "scheming witness": "The Mind of the Profession: Eptracts [*sic*] from the Contributions of Stenographers to Phonographic Literature," *BPMRJ* 8 (July 1883): 170–71.

65. A.H., "Women and Their Work," 95, 98; Samuel Haber, *The Quest for Authority and Honor in the American Professions, 1750–1900* (Chicago: University of Chicago Press, 1991), xii.

66. Fine, *Souls of the Skyscraper*, 69; Wood, "Modern Instance," 342–43.

67. Anne Guilbert Mahon, "The Too Obliging Miss Blake: An Investment That Brought the Amanuensis Rich Returns," *TPW* 23 (June 1904): 407–10.

68. E. K. Stevens, "The Little Typist: Her Dream of 'Annexation,' or How She Studied Law," *TPW* 20 (October 1902): 290; G., "An Iowa Girl's Opinion of Female Stenographers," *BPMRJ* 12 (May 1887): 140–41; "Lady Stenographers of New York," *BPM* 3 (December 1878): 222; Quote on Pulsifer: "Women to the Front," 220–22.

69. Susan M. Reverby, *Ordered to Care. The Dilemma of American Nursing, 1850–1945* (Cambridge: Cambridge University Press, 1987), 143–58; Joan Jacobs Brumberg and Nancy Tomes, "Women in the Profession: A Research Agenda for American Historians," *Reviews in American History* 10 (June 1982): 287.

70. For similar arguments about caring and nurses' professionalism: Tom Olsen and Eileen Walsh, *Handling the Sick: The Women of St. Luke's and the Nature of Nursing, 1892–1937* (Columbus: Ohio State University Press, 2004), 92.

CHAPTER 7

1. Mary Arnold, "Association News," *PW* 8 (September 1892): 22.

2. Ibid.

3. "The Shorthand Writers' Association," *BPMRJ* 8 (August 1883): 197; National Union of Stenographers, *Rules, Regulations, and Scale of Prices of the National Union of Stenographers* (Chicago: A. B. Reid, 1886); Lisa M. Fine, *The Souls of the Skyscraper: Female Clerical Workers in Chicago, 1870–1930* (Philadelphia: Temple University Press, 1990), 15; "Railway and Transportation Stenographers," *PW* 5 (August 1890): 382–83; G. E. Rider, "The 'National American Union of Stenographers and Typewriters,'" *IPW* 10 (December 1894): 101 [*St. Louis Globe-Democrat*]; "Association News," *IPW* 7 (July 1896): 419 [*Omaha World-Herald*]; Henry Demarest Lloyd, "The Lords of Industry," *North American Review* 331 (June 1884), *Modern History Sourcebook*, http://www.fordham.edu/halsall/mod/1884hd lloyd.html; "Intelligence," *PM* 5 (May 1891): 131 [*New York Press*].

4. Lloyd, "Lords of Industry"; "Railway and Transportation Stenographers," 382–83; National Union of Stenographers, *Rules*, 6.

5. "Railway and Transportation Stenographers," 382–83; "National Union of Stenographers," *BPMRJ* 11 (June 1886): 123–24.

6. On the signature "Fraternally Yours": F. Michinard Jr., "The Situation in New Orleans," *PW* (April 1886): 146; On "fair rate of wages": "National Union of Stenographers," 123–24; On other union language: National Union of Stenographers, *Rules,* 1–6; Quotes on "that fraternal feeling" and "helping hand": *PW* 1 (April 1886): 143; On regalia: "Railway and Transportation Stenographers," 382–83. The Brotherhood of Railway and Steamship Clerks and Brotherhood of Railway Car Men had racially discriminatory clauses, unlike the Retail Clerks National Protective Association: Jürgen Kocka, *White Collar Workers in America, 1890–1940: A Social-Political History in International Perspective,* trans. Maura Kealey (London: Sage, 1980), 74, 305n; Mary Ann Clawson, *Constructing Brotherhood: Class, Gender, and Fraternalism* (Princeton: Princeton University Press, 1989), 136–39; Robert E. Weir, *Beyond Labor's Veil: The Culture of the Knights of Labor* (University Park: Pennsylvania State University Press, 1996), 231–49; Fine, *Souls of the Skyscraper,* 15.

7. WSTU of New York meeting: "Intelligence," *PM* 5 (May 1891), 131; On a few early clerical women's unions: Roslyn L. Feldberg, "'Union Fever': Organizing among Clerical Workers, 1900–1930," *Radical America* 14 (May–June 1980): 53–67; On mutuality: "National Union of Stenographers," 123–24; "Proceedings of Societies," *PM* 5 (June 1891): 163.

8. "National Union of Stenographers," 123–24.

9. National Union of Stenographers, *Rules,* 2, 8; "A Questionable Enterprise," *PW* 1 (June 1886): 198–99; Ranking characterized fraternal organizations as well: Clawson, *Constructing Brotherhood,* 181.

10. National Union of Stenographers, *Rules,* 1–2.

11. Quote on legitimate purposes: Rider, "'National American Union of Stenographers and Typewriters,'" 101; Other quotes: "Questionable Enterprise," 199; see also Charles H. White, "An Open Letter to the Stenographers of North America," *IPW* 7 (September 1891): 14.

12. "Railway and Transportation Stenographers," 382–83; National Union of Stenographers, *Rules,* 1, 5–10.

13. "Questionable Enterprise," 199.

14. "Extract from the Remarks of Joseph Howard, Jr., before the Association as Printed by Mr. Howard in the N.Y. 'Press,'" in Stenographers' Association of the City of New York, *Souvenir* (New York, 1891).

15. White, "Open Letter," 14; While stenographers blamed teachers for training women who worked for too little, tailors condemned greedy employers: Ileen A. DeVault, "'To Sit among Men': Skill, Gender, and Craft Unionism in the Early American Federation of Labor," in *Labor Histories: Class, Politics, and the Working-Class Experience,* eds. Eric Arnesen, Julie Greene, and Bruce Laurie (Urbana: University of Illinois Press, 1998), 268.

16. "Questionable Enterprise," 199; Rider, "National American Union of Stenographers," 101; The NUS stated that the union "may act in concert with other trade organizations . . . [for the] advancement of the working classes": National Union of Stenographers, *Rules,* 5.

17. American retail clerks' unions' solidarity with the working class hurt membership: Kocka, *White Collar Workers,* 55–58, 68–79, 84–92; Clerk T. Fulton Gantt pitched the Knights of Labor to government clerks in his 1887 novel *Breaking the Chains: A Story of*

the Present Industrial Struggle, in *The Knights in Fiction: Two Labor Novels of the 1880s,* ed. Mary C. Grimes (Urbana: University of Illinois Press, 1986), 95–96; Clerks in twelve Knights' locals in New York, Massachusetts, and Illinois were probably retail clerks: Jonathan Garlock, comp., *Guide to the Local Assemblies of the Knights of Labor* (Westport, CT: Greenwood, 1982), 66, 80, 202–3, 205, 299, 303, 313, 316, 328, 333, 345; The Brotherhood of Railway Clerks was founded in the same years (1899): Janet F. Davidson, "'Now That We Have Girls in the Office': Clerical Work, Masculinity, and the Refashioning of Gender for a Bureaucratic Age," in *Boys and Their Toys? Masculinity, Class, and Technology in America,* ed. Roger Horowitz (New York: Routledge, 2001), 65, 87n; Edwin Gabler, *The American Telegrapher: A Social History, 1860–1900* (New Brunswick: Rutgers University Press, 1988), 51–57, 61–78, 100–105, 145, 159; Thomas C. Jepsen, *My Sisters Telegraphic: Women in the Telegraph Office, 1846–1950* (Athens: Ohio University Press, 2000), 148–55; Stephen Norwood, *Labor's Flaming Youth: Telephone Operators and Worker Militancy, 1878–1923* (Urbana: University of Illinois Press, 1990), 31–63.

18. "National Union of Stenographers," 123–24; William H. Brown, "Association," *PW* 1 (July 1886): 203; "Questionable Enterprise," 198.

19. John R. McKivigan and Thomas J. Robertson, "The Irish American Worker in Transition, 1877–1914: New York City as a Test Case," in *The New York Irish,* eds. Ronald H. Bayor and Timothy J. Meagher (Baltimore: Johns Hopkins University Press, 1996), 304–5.

20. Rider, "National American Union of Stenographers," 101; On images of professionals in success literature: Judy Hilkey, *Character Is Capital: Success Manuals and Manhood in Gilded Age America* (Chapel Hill: University of North Carolina Press, 1997), 113–16; For examples of the huge literature on late nineteenth-century professionalism and images of professionals: Burton J. Bledstein, *The Culture of Professionalism: The Middle Class and the Development of Higher Education in America* (New York: Norton, 1976), 85–87, 90–92; Samuel Haber, *The Quest for Authority and Honor in the American Professions, 1750–1900* (Chicago: University of Chicago Press, 1991), 193–358; Bruce A. Kimball, *The "True Professional Ideal" in America: A History* (Cambridge, MA: Blackwell, 1992); Susan M. Reverby, *Ordered to Care: The Dilemma of American Nursing, 1850–1945* (Cambridge: Cambridge University Press, 1987), 121–58; Barbara Melosh, *"The Physician's Hand": Work Culture and Conflict in American Nursing* (Philadelphia: Temple University Press, 1982), 21–24; On professionalizing salesmen: Angel Kwolek-Folland, *Engendering Business: Men and Women in the Corporate Office, 1870–1930* (Baltimore: Johns Hopkins University Press, 1994), 81.

21. "Netta McLaughlin," *PM* 7 (15 February 1897): 63; "Colored Stenographers," *TPW* 21 (April 1903): 297 [*Baltimore Herald*]; "Eighth Annual Dinner of the Law Stenographers' Assoc'n of the City of New-York [*sic*]," *BPMRJ* 6 (January 1881): 5–11; New York State Shorthand Reporters' Association, *Constitution, By-Laws, &c. of the New York State Law Stenographers' Association* (Ithaca: Norton & Conklin, 1877); "Shorthand Societies," *BPMRJ* 14 (May 1889): 153–54; "The Omaha Shorthand Association," *PW* 4 (June 1889): 210; "Two Boston Associations," *BPMRJ* 8 (October 1883): 276; Arnold, "Association News," 22; *Proceedings of the Fifth Annual Meeting of the New England Shorthand Reporters' Association,* vol. 3 (Providence, 1895), 6–7; Roger B. Landroth, "The History and Development of Pitmanic Shorthand in the United States, 1843–1976" (Ed.D. diss., New

York University, 1977), 160–62, 209–12; Julius Ensign Rockwell, "The Teaching, Practice, and Literature of Shorthand," in U.S. Department of the Interior, Bureau of Education, *Circular of Information of the Bureau of Education,* no. 2 (Washington, DC, 1884), 58; National Shorthand Reporters' Association, *Officers, Charter Members, and Constitution and By-Laws,* (Greenville, SC: Shannon, 1899); C. H. Rush, "The World's Congress of Stenographers," *PW* 8 (August 1893): 318.

22. Accounting associations also disagreed about immigration: Paul J. Miranti Jr., *Accountancy Comes of Age: The Development of an American Profession, 1886–1940* (Chapel Hill: University of North Carolina Press, 1990), 29–85; Mary N. Woods, *From Craft to Profession: The Practice of Architecture in Nineteenth-Century America* (Berkeley: University of California Press, 1999), 138–66; Keith P. McMillan, "The Institute of Accounts: A Community of the Competent," *Accounting, Business & Financial History* 9 (March 1999); 18–24; George C. Romeo and Larissa S. Kyj, "The Forgotten Accounting Association: The Institute of Accounts," *Accounting Historians Journal* 25 (June 1998): 36–42; Eileen Walsh and Thomas Olson, *Handling the Sick: The Women of St. Luke's and the Nature of Nursing, 1892–1937* (Columbus: Ohio State University Press, 2004); Ruth Oldenziel, *Making Technology Masculine: Men, Women, and Modern Machines in America* (Amsterdam: Amsterdam University Press, 1999).

23. "Membership Roll of the Chicago Stenographers [*sic*] Association," in Chicago Stenographers' Association, *Constitution and By-Laws* (Chicago, 1889), 2; "A Flourishing Organization of Stenographers," in Stenographers' Association of the City of New York, *Souvenir* (New York, 1891), 28.

24. Quote: New York State Shorthand Reporters' Association, *Constitution,* 2, 5–7, 9; House Committee on the Judiciary, *Stenographers in United States Courts,* "Licensing Stenographers in Courts of Record," *IPW* 11 (October 1895), 50–51.

25. "Official Reporters' Salary," *BPM* 1 (December 1875) 19; In 1876, Scott-Browne called for states to adopt statutes similar to California's examination by lawyers or "before a board of phonographic professors and reporters": "Personal," *BPM* 1 (February 1876): 48; "Not Quite Right, Mr. Dana, Not Quite Right," *BPMRJ* 8 (July 1883): 169–70; "Incompetent Stenographers," *PM* 6 (January 1892): 43; "Licensing Stenographers," 50–51; "Licensing Stenographers in Courts of Record," *IPW* 11 (November 1895): 87–89.

26. Charles Currier Beale, "A Unique Examination," *IPW* 14 (October 1898): 73; On accountants: Miranti, *Accountancy Comes of Age,* 29–85, 56–61.

27. Accountants also disagreed over ethnic inclusiveness: Miranti, *Accountancy Comes of Age,* 43–45.

28. Minutes of the Universal Association of Stenographers, 21 October 1893, O'Keefe Collection, box 4, NYPL.

29. Minutes of the Universal Association of Stenographers, 23 December 1893, O'-Keefe Collection, box 4, NYPL; Namedas, "A 'Plea for Professional Organization,'" *BPW* 16 (4 May 1891): 227–28; idem, "Plea" (11 May 1891): 243; idem, "Plea" (8 May 1891): 259.

30. "A 'Plea for Professional Organization,'" *BPW* 16 (25 May 1891): 276–77.

31. National Shorthand Reporters' Association, *Annual Meeting at Put-in-Bay, Ohio . . . 14–17 August 1900, Program* (Spartanburg, SC, 1900), n.p.

32. Only one of Suffolk County's official court reporters during the 1890s did not belong to the New England Shorthand Reporters' Association: "List of Members of the

New England Shorthand Reporters' Association, September 25, 1900," in *Proceedings of the New England Shorthand Reporters' Association, 1899–1900,* vol. 4 (Boston, 1900), 112–13; A higher percentage of the few women were teachers in the NSRA. "American Court Reporters and What Systems of Shorthand They Write," *PW* 8 (July 1893): 296–99; Quote: F. J. Squibb and I. S. Dement, "Our Courts," *PW* 3 (November 1887): 57; "The Chicago Combine," *BPM-W* 15 (27 January 1890): 53–54 [*Chicago Herald*]; Fred Irland, "The New York State Stenographers' Association," *PW* 3 (September 1887): 14–22.

33. New York State Shorthand Reporters' Association, *Constitution,* 7–8; Queen City Stenographers' Club of Cincinnati, *Constitution and By-Laws of the Queen City Stenographers' Club* (Cincinnati: C. Frigenspan, 1894), 3; Metropolitan Stenographers' Association, *Annual Announcement* (New York: 1891), 3; The Brooklyn Stenographers' Association specifically noted their lack of connection with the court reporters: "Associations," *PW* 8 (March 1893): 224; No court reporters attended their dances or belonged on their executive boards: "Ball of the Metropolitan Stenographers' Association," *MS* 1 (20 February 1890), 95; Stenographers' Business Association of St. Paul, *Constitution and By-Laws of the Stenographers' Business Association of St. Paul* (St. Paul: Price, McGill, 1890), 5; Trenton Stenographers' Association, *Constitution* (Trenton, 1891), 2.

34. Stenographers Club of Chicago, *Constitution, By-Laws* etc. (Chicago: Western Label, 1892), n.p.; Boston Shorthand Club, *Constitution and By-Laws* (Boston: George R. Libby, 1893), 7; "Intelligence," *PM* 3 (March 1889): 51; Even Gregg's top-down promotional clubs set standards of seventy-five words per minute: "The Gregg Shorthand Association of Chicago," 2, Gregg Collection, box 126, NYPL.

35. "Stenographic Association of the New Century Guild of Working Women," *PW* 4 (June 1889): 210; Priscilla Murolo, *The Common Ground of Womanhood: Class, Gender, and Working Girls' Clubs, 1884–1928* (Urbana: University of Illinois Press, 1997), 21; National Shorthand Reporters' Association, *Annual Meeting,* n.p.; Of 202 stenographers and typewriters in northeastern clubs, the lowest weekly wage rates were between $3 and $12.50, with the highest between $12 and $25: U.S. Bureau of Labor Statistics, "Industrial Education of Working Women," in *Thirty-seventh Annual Report* (Washington, DC, 1906), 26–27.

36. National Association of Women Stenographers, *Articles of Association and By-Laws of the National Association of Women Stenographers, organized April 22, 1891* (Chicago: C. E. Crone, 1892), n.p.; Stenographers' Business Association of St. Paul, *Constitution,* 5; "Membership of the Chicago Stenographers' Association," 2; Queen City Stenographers' Club of Cincinnati, *Constitution,* 3; National Shorthand Reporters' Association, *Constitution,* 15; New York State Law Stenographers' Association, *Constitution,* 7; "Flourishing Organization of Stenographers," 28; Since some Irish and English names are difficult to distinguish, the numbers approximate ethnic differences: *Proceedings of the New England Shorthand Reporters' Association, 1899–1900,* vol. 4 (Boston, 1990), 112–13; "Membership Roll of the Chicago Stenographers' Association," n.p.; Fine, *Souls of the Skyscraper,* 33.

37. Chicago Stenographers, *The Second Annual Dinner,* 11 January 1879 (Chicago: Blakely, Brown & Marsh, 1879), 10, 17–18; In 1891, the twenty-eight members of NESRA were male; by 1900, women comprised 37.3 percent of the fifty-one members: Yerrinton quote: *Proceedings of the New England Shorthand Reporters' Association, 1889–1892*

(Boston: George H. Ellis, 1892), 21, and see also 4–5, 8–9, 47, 79; Haskell quote: *Proceedings of the New England Shorthand Reporters' Association, 1899–1900,* 3–5, 112–13; At the New York Law Stenographers' Association's quarterly meeting in 1882, all thirty attendees were men: "New York Law Stenographers Association," *BPMRJ* 7 (January 1882): 2–3; In 1891, 43.9 percent of the 173 were women: *How's Directory of Stenographers of the United States* (New York: How Publishing, 1891); "Miss Wellington," *TPW* 21 (April 1903): 246.

38. "Flourishing Organization of Stenographers," 28; Trenton Stenographers' Association, *Constitution,* 8.

39. National Shorthand Reporters' Association, *Officers, Charter Members, and Constitution,* 3–13; *Proceedings of the New England Shorthand Reporters' Association, 1899–1900,* vol. 4, 112–13; National Shorthand Reporters' Association, "Paid Members, NSRA for 1904," 15 June 1904, O'Keefe Collection, box 15, NYPL; "Membership Roll of the Chicago Stenographers' [*sic*] Association," 2; "Flourishing Organization of Stenographers," 28 (200 out of 307 members); Women made up 11 percent in 1893: "American Court Reporters and What Systems of Shorthand They Write," *PW* 8 (July 1893): 296–99.

40. One organization's dues were two dollars for members, one dollar for associates: Stenographers' Business Association of St. Paul, *Constitution,* 5; New England Shorthand Reporters' Association, *Constitution & By-Laws* (Boston: Croke Printing, 1891), 4; Irland, "New York State Stenographers' Association," 14.

41. A. J. Peters, "New Orleans Phonographers' Association," *PW* 5 (September 1889): 12; "News of the Associations," *MS* 1 (20 April 1890): 123; "Our Visitors," *PS* 1 (May 1890): 16; John R. Geary, "Metropolitan Association," *BPM-W* 15 (21 April 1890): 230–31; On women's dominance of union social activities: Dana Frank, "Gender, Consumer Organizing, and the Seattle Labor Movement, 1919–1929," in *Work Engendered: Toward a New History of American Labor,* ed. Ava Baron (Ithaca: Cornell University Press, 1991), 280; Irland, "New York State Stenographers' Association," 14–15.

42. New York State Shorthand Reporters' Association, *An Author List of the Papers Read at the Convention of the New York State Stenographers' Association, 1876 to 1912,* (New York, 1912), NYPL; Editor, "New-York [*sic*] State Stenographer's [*sic*] Association," *BPMRJ* 11 (September 1886): 194.

43. Special Correspondent, "From Oakland California," *PW* 2 (October 1886): 37; "Comments and Chat," *BPW* 16 (12 October 1891): 484; Trenton Stenographers' Association, *Constitution,* 8; Metropolitan Stenographers' Association, *Annual Announcement of the Metropolitan Stenographers' Association of New York City* (New York, 1890), 5.

44. On Brooklyn Stenographers' Association: E. F. Treat, "Proceedings of Societies," *PM* 6 (June 1892): 221–22; E. F. Treat, "Association News," *PW* 8 (May 1893): 224; E. J. Walsh, "A Chicago Love Story," *IPW* 13 (November 1897): 118; Metropolitan Stenographers' Association, *Annual Announcement* (1890), 3.

45. "That Coming Brooklyn Stenographers Association," *MS* 1 (20 November 1889): 39; "News of the Associations," *MS* 1 (20 March 1890): 107–8; H. J. Rippel, "The Brooklyn New York Stenographers' Association," *PW* 6 (June 1891): 331; Early accounting societies attracted bookkeepers but were led by accountants or educators: Miranti, *Accounting Comes of Age,* 29.

46. "Proceedings of Societies," *PM* 7 (July 1891): 193.

47. *Proceedings of the New England Shorthand Reporters' Association, 1889–1892,* vol. 1, 3; National Shorthand Reporters' Association, *Annual Meeting,* 1900, n.p.; New York State Shorthand Reporters' Assocation, *Constitution,* n.p.; Stenographers' Association of Western Pennsylvania, *Programme of Social Meetings,* 14 June 1900, Pittsburgh, Pa.; "Colored Stenographers, 297.

48. McMillan, "Institute of Accounts," 21; "The Shorthand Writers' Assocation," 197; Boston Shorthand Club, *Constitution,* 5, 7; "Its object . . . securing positions for its members . . .": Metropolitan Stenographers' Association, *Annual Announcement* (1890), 2–4; "From Oakland California," 37; "Association News," *IPW* 11 (July 1896): 419 [*Omaha Herald*]; *Chicago Shorthand Writers Association* (Chicago: Western Label, 1881), n.p.; "Intelligence," *PM* 2 (May 1888): 97–98 [*St. Louis Republican*]; "Shorthand Societies," *BPM-W* 15 (13 January 1890): 29–30; The Stenographers Club of Chicago met Tuesdays at the Haymarket Theater for "social and literary enjoyment": Stenographers Club of Chicago, *Constitution,* n.p.; National Association of Women Stenographers, *Articles of Association,* n.p.; "Proceedings of Societies," *PM* 11 (15 November 1897): 349 [*Inter-Ocean*].

49. "The Brooklyn Stenographers Association," *MS* 1 (20 May 1890): 141–42; On evening high school: Alville B. Nickerson, "Intelligence," *PM* 2 (June 1888): 121; Jerome P. Bjelopera, *City of Clerks: Office and Sales Workers in Philadelphia, 1870–1920* (Urbana: University of Illinois Press, 2005), 84–85; "Gregg Shorthand Association of Chicago," 2; Minutes of the Gregg Shorthand Association of Chicago, 1896, Gregg Collection, NYPL.

50. "National Organization of Colored Stenographers," *IPW* 11 (October 1895): 47; On Baltimore stenographers: "Colored Stenographers," 297; "Presidents of the State Stenographers' Associations," *PM* 9 (1 December 1895), 358.

51. National Shorthand Reporters' Association, *Annual Meeting,* n.p.; "Shorthand Societies," *BPM-W* 15:29–30; A. J. Peters, "New Orleans Phonography Association," 12.

52. Metropolitan Stenographers' Association, *Annual Announcement* (1890), 3; On Brooklyn Stenographers: "Proceedings of Societies," *PM* 7:193; Rippel, "Brooklyn New York Stenographers' Association," 331. "Association News," *PS* 1 (November 1890): 17; "Shorthand Cyclers," *Stenographer* 8 (August 1895): 5; "Lady Stenographers' Camp Out," *Stenographer* 8 (September 1895): 76; "The Gregg Shorthand Association of Chicago," Gregg Collection, box 126, NYPL; Minutes of the Gregg Shorthand Association of Chicago, 1896, Gregg Collection, NYPL; "They Have a Lynching Bee," *Chicago Evening News,* 6 March 1896, n.p., clipping, Gregg Collection, NYPL; *The Term End Club,* ca. 1910s, pamphlet, O'Keefe Collection, box 16, NYPL.

53. Gabler, *American Telegrapher,* 191; Many fraternal club members were office clerks: Mark C. Carnes, *Secret Ritual and Manhood in Victorian America* (New Haven: Yale University Press, 1989), 35, 145; Clawson, *Constructing Brotherhood,* 95, 97, 104; Weir, *Beyond Labor's Veil,* 232–37, 244–45; On Brockaway: "A Badge for Stenographers," *PW* 7 (3 September 1891): 3; On later badge: "Association News," *PW* 8 (March 1893): 224.

54. Marie St. Felix [Harriet Louise Husted (Lynch)], *A Little Game with Destiny* (New York: Saalfield & Fitch, 1892), 53; GenCircles: http://www.gencircles; Female stenographers may not have approved of badges that advertised that they worked: Kathy Peiss, *Cheap Amusements: Working Women and Leisure in Turn-of-the-Century New York* (Philadelphia: Temple University Press, 1986), 173; Years before, Edward F. Underhill, un-

der the pseudonym Q. K. Philander Doesticks, also lampooned clubs in *The History and Records of the Elephant Club* (New York: Livermore & Rudd, 1856), 39–42.

55. Irland, "New York State Stenographers' Association," 14–22.

56. Bjelopera, *City of Clerks*, 156–57, 79–81, 94.

57. Karen Halttunen, *Confidence Men and Painted Women: A Study of Middle-Class Culture in America, 1830–1870* (New Haven: Yale University Press, 1982), 30–32; Richard L. Bushman, *The Refinement of America: Persons, Houses, Cities* (New York: Knopf, 1992), 61–99, 207–350; John F. Kasson, *Rudeness and Civility: Manners in Nineteenth-Century Urban America* (New York: Hill & Wang, 1990), 182–256; Susan R. Williams, introduction to *Dining in America, 1850–1900*, ed. Kathryn Grover (Amherst and New York: University of Massachusetts Press and Margaret Woodbury Strong Museum, 1987), 17.

58. On domesticating public spaces: Kwolek-Folland, *Engendering Business*, 99–105; Amy G. Richter, *Home on the Rails: Women, the Railroad, and the Rise of Public Domesticity* (Chapel Hill: University of North Carolina Press, 2005), 59–112; On male consumerism as female pleasure: Mary Ann Clawson, "Masculinity, Consumption, and the Transformation of Scottish Rite Freemasonry in the Turn-of-the-Century United States," *Gender & History* 19 (April 2007): 115–16.

59. "Flourishing Organization of Stenographers," 28.

60. Metropolitan Stenographers' Association, *Annual Announcement* (1890), 2–3; Metropolitan Stenographers' Association, *Annual Annoucement* (1891), 2; Brooklyn Stenographers' Association, *Annual Entertainment of the Brooklyn Stenographers' Association, 1893–95, Fourth Annual, Souvenir Programme* (Brooklyn, 1893–95), 7; "Proceedings of Societies," *PM* 5:193; On Peirce College alumni's clubhouse: Bjelopera, *City of Clerks*, 94; A Knights of Labor local in Massachusetts renovated an opera house for meetings: Weir, *Beyond Labor's Veil*, 295.

61. "N.Y. State Stenographers' Association," *PW* 2 (December 1886): 67.

62. "Association News," *PW* 8 (March 1893): 224.

63. Stenographers Club of Chicago, *Constitution*, n.p.; *Annual Meeting of the California State Stenographers' Association* (San Francisco, 1900), n.p.; Roy Rosenzweig, *Eight Hours for What We Will: Workers and Leisure In an Industrial City, 1870–1920* (Cambridge: Cambridge University Press, 1985), 67–69; "The Fem-Sten's Retreat," *TPW* 12 (August 1900): 673; National Shorthand Reporters' Association, *Annual Meeting*, n.p.; On union brochures: Weir, *Beyond Labor's Veil*, 295.

64. Cindy S. Aron, *Working at Play: A History of Vacations in the United States* (New York: Oxford University Press, 1999), 127–55; Peiss, *Cheap Amusements*, 117–21; *Souvenir Program of the National Shorthand Reporters' Association*, 18–21 August (Cincinnati, 1903), n.p.; National Shorthand Reporters' Association, *Fourth Annual Convention*, Boston, 19–22 August (Boston, 1902), n.p.; Irland, "New York State Stenographers' Association," 19; Peirce College spent eighteen thousand dollars between 1892 and 1913 mostly for socializing: Bjelopera, *City of Clerks*, 84.

65. Rosenzweig, *Eight Hours for What We Will*, 140–42; Frances G. Couvares, *The Remaking of Pittsburgh: Class and Culture in an Industrializing City, 1877–191* (Albany: State University of New York, 1984), 103; "Intelligence," *PM* 3 (September 1889): 194; "Iowa State Stenographers' Association, 1891," *PW* 7 (September 1891): 15; Knights of Labor leisure included boating excursions, dancing, and picnics with games like pole vaulting,

football, sack races, and a "'fat woman's race'" that became rough; in the mining regions, they participated in "blood sports like cockfights, pigeon shoots and prize fights": Weir, *Beyond Labor's Veil,* 285, 296; Bjelopera, *City of Clerks,* 87–88, 93–98.

66. Willard C. Gompf, "The Bicycle—a Blessing to Stenographers," *PW* 2 (November 1891): 97; "Wheelmen's Department," *PW* 8 (September 1892): 24–7; F. R. Madeira, ed., "Wheelmen's Department," *PW* 8 (December 1892): 124.

67. On 1920s telephone operators' conventions: Norwood, *Labor's Flaming Youth,* 234–38.

68. Inez L. Hopkins, "Proceedings of the Societies," *PM* 6 (December 1892): 485.

69. *Proceedings of the New England Shorthand Reporters' Association, 1899–1900,* vol. 4, 66; W. J. Rorabaugh, "Beer, Lemonade, and Propriety in the Gilded Age," in Grover, *Dining in America,* 42, 45; Kasson, *Rudeness and Civility,* 206–7; New York State Stenographers' Association, *Complementary to the New York State Stenographers' Association, at the Twenty-Third Annual Meeting,* 25 August 1896 (Averill Park, NY, 1898); Chicago Stenographers, *The Second Annual Dinner,* n.p.; Mark Twain's wife served sherry, claret, and champagne in the 1880s: Karen Lystra, *Dangerous Intimacy: The Untold Story of Mark Twain's Final Year* (Berkeley: University of California, 2004), 6.

70. Lawrence W. Levine, *Highbrow/LowBrow: The Emergence of Cultural Hierarchy in America* (Cambridge: Harvard University Press, 1988), 108, 136–46; Rippel, "Brooklyn New York Stenographers' Association," 331; Robert C. Allen, *Horrible Prettiness: Burlesque and American Culture* (Chapel Hill: University of North Carolina Press, 1991), 180–85; *Annual Entertainment of the Brooklyn Stenographers' Association, 1893–95, Fifth Annual, Souvenir Programme* (Brooklyn, 1893–95), 11–13; For similar Knights of Labor extravaganzas: Weir, *Beyond Labor's Veil,* 295; Bjelopera, *City of Clerks,* 129–40.

71. *Proceedings of the American Federation of Labor, 1897–1898* (Bloomington, IL: Pantagraph Printing, 1905), 93, 96, 100; *Proceedings of the American Federation of Labor, 1889–1892* (Bloomington, IL: Pantagraph Printing, 1906), 11, 41, 43, 46; Brotherhood of Carpenters and Joiners of America, *Proceedings of the Fifth General Convention,* Detroit, 6–11 August 1888 (Philadelphia, 1888); Rosenzweig, *Eight Hours for What We Will,* 67–69; On rowdy working-class leisure of sing-along, clapping, and drums on sawdust-covered floors: Lillian Taiz, *Hallelujah Lads and Lasses: Remaking the Salvation Army in America, 1880–1930* (Chapel Hill: University of North Carolina Press, 2001), 79–90; Peiss, *Cheap Amusements,* 117–18; "Social Statistics of Workingwomen," *Massachusetts Labor Bulletin* 18 (May 1901): 39–45; On Knights of Labor and quote: Weir, *Beyond Labor's Veil,* 283–95; *Proceedings of the New England Shorthand Reporters' Association, 1889–1892,* vol. 1, 6; On working girls' clubs: Murolo, *Common Ground of Womanhood,* 62–64; On growing working-class involvement in the consumer economy: Lawrence B. Glickman, *A Living Wage: American Workers and the Making of Consumer Society* (Ithaca: Cornell University Press, 1997), 108–28; Nan Enstad, *Ladies of Labor, Girls of Adventure: Working Women, Popular Culture, and Labor Politics at the Turn of the Twentieth Century* (New York: Columbia University Press, 1999).

72. For a drawing of a woman playing pool: Stenographers' Association of the City of New York, *Souvenir,* 7; Mel Adelman, "Neglected Sports in American History: The Rise of Billiards in New York City, 1850–1871," *Canadian Journal of History of Sport* 12, no. 2 (1981): 1–28; On elite men's clubs: Howard P. Chudacoff, *The Age of the Bachelor: Creat-*

ing an American Subculture (Princeton: Princeton University Press, 1999), 115–21; On late night dancing: Rippel, "Brooklyn New York Stenographers' Association," 331; On wee hours: "The Banquet," *PS* 1 (June 1890): 12; On "milkman's call": Association News," *PS* 1 (June 1890): 14; "Hall of the Metropolitan Stenographers' Association," *MS* 1 (20 February 1890): 95; Peiss, *Cheap Amusements*, 100–102; On mixing of class styles among telegraphers: Gabler, *American Telegrapher*, 85–105.

73. Chudacoff, *Age of the Bachelor*, 150; On gendering office space: Kwolek-Folland, *Engendering Business*, 94–128; "Comments and Chat," 484; Stenographers' Association of the City of New York, *Souvenir*, 4; Arnold, "Association News," 22.

EPILOGUE

1. "From the President," *NSR* 5 (January 1917): 7.

2. "Membership Statistics," *NSR* 1 (May 1940): 285; "Membership Statistics," *NSR* 1 (March 1940): 225; On membership, fluctuating between 1,012 and 992 members: Joyce P. Jacobsen, "Occupational Segregation and the Tipping Phenomenon: The Contrary Case of Court Reporting in the United States," *Gender, Work and Organization* 14 (March 2007): 136 table 2.

3. Shorthand Club of New York, "Organization," *NSR* 1 (April 1913): 86–87; National Shorthand Reporters' Association, *Bulletin . . . Fifteenth Annual Convention*, Chicago, August 1913 (Chicago, 1913), 170–77; "Notes from the Secretary," *NSR* 1 (May 1913): 106.

4. O. L. Detweiler, "Is Standardization Impossible?" *NSR* 2 (July 1914): 149–52; *Do You Gregg?* (Liverpool: Gregg Shorthand Institute, 1909), 5, 8–9; *What They Say of Each Other* (New York: Gregg Publishing, 1908), Gregg Collection, box 103, NYPL; National Court Reporters Association Web site, History of NCRA, "NSRA Starts Testing Program," http://www.ncraoneline.org/about/history/NCRA.shtml; NSRA Collection, NYPL.

5. Arthur Bailey to Robert S. Taylor, 21 February 1935, National Shorthand Reporters' Association Records, box 1, NYPL; Edwin G. Knepper, *History of Business Education in United States* (Bowling Green, OH: Edwards Brothers, 1941), 145. By 1910, twice as many schools taught Gregg than any other system.

6. "Silver Jubilee of Gregg Shorthand," *NSR* 1 (December 1913): 287; "How to Organize a Gregg Shorthand Association," *GAW* 1 (April–May 1916): 1; Knepper, *History of Business Education*, 141–45; Jacobsen, "Occupational Segregation," 135 table 1.

7. Gordon L. Elliot, ed., *Shorthand Reporters: A Digest of Statutes and Legal Decisions Relating to Official Stenographers and Their Reports*, 2nd ed. (Des Moines, IA: Homestead Printing, 1916); "Compensation of Official Reporter," *NSR* 1 (August 1913): 191–92; Willard B. Bottome, "Legislation Affecting Shorthand Reporters," *NSR* 1 (May 1913): 107–8, 110; NCRA Web site, History of NCRA, "A Steady Decade of Progress for NSRA" and "NSRA Starts Testing Program"; Jacobsen, "Occupational Segregation," 135–36.

8. "William C. Booth Promoted to the Supreme Court in New York City," *NSR* 1 (December 1913): 279; "In Memoriam," *NSR* 1 (November 1939): 50; "In Memoriam," *NSR* 26 (December 1964), 142.

9. "Who's Who in NSRA: Director J. L. McAttee," *NSR* 1 (1940): 66; "In Memoriam," *NSR* 18 (April 1957): 233–34; "Mr. Charles L. Swem Accompanies the President to the

Peace Conference: Shorthand Is the Open Door to Opportunity," *Greggite* 5 (January 1919): 3–4.

10. "In Memoriam," *NSR* 28 (May 1967): 41–42.

11. Jacobsen, "Occupational Segregation," 137 table 3. "In Memoriam," *NSR* 8 (May 1946): 286–87; Philip H. Burt, "Eight Decades of Court Reporting," *NSR* 25 (February 1964): 173–75; National Shorthand Reporters' Association, *Celebrating Our Heritage: National Shorthand Reporters [sic] Association Diamond Jubilee Convention,* Washington Hilton, 2–7 August 1976, Washington, DC (Arlington, VA, 1976), 14.

12. Horace A. Edgecombe, "Office Methods," *NSR* 1 (August 1913): 177–84; Frederick H. Gurtler, "President's Message," in National Shorthand Reporters' Association, *Our Silver Jubilee,* ed. Herbert Dore (Chicago: Silver Jubilee Committee, 1924), 21, 27; NCRA Web site, History of NCRA, "NSRA Starts Testing" and "NSRA Celebrates Program's 50 Years."

13. Jacobsen, "Occupational Segregation," 135 table 1, 154 figs. 20 and 26, 139–44, 148–50, 156, 137 table 3; Greg Downey, "Constructing 'Computer-Compatible' Stenographers: The Transition to Real-Time Transcription in Courtroom Reporting," *Technology & Culture* 47 (January 2006): 1–26; NCRA Web site, History of NCRA, "A Turning Point for the Association"; Tara Bahrampour, "Court Reporters Hear the Tap, Tap, Tap of Obsolescence," *New York Times,* 13 February 2000, sec. 14, p. 4.

14. "Proceedings of the Fifteenth Annual Convention of the N.S.R.A.," *NSR* 1 (September 1913): 199; Jacobsen, "Occupational Segregation," 137 table 3; In 1955, the Indiana state president and all of the officers were female, as were the past presidents: "Indiana," *NSR* 17 (October 1955): 47.

15. Darius Dust, "What about the Shorthand Man?" *NSR* 1 (October 1913): 232.

16. James Abbot, "Brains in Shorthand: A Talk before the Munson Shorthand Association at Chicago, 19 December 1916," *NSR* 5 (1917):12.

17. Gurtler, "President's Message," 23.

18. "Report of Historian," 8, O'Keefe Collection, box 4, NYPL.

19. W. L. James, "Advice to the Ambitious," *NSR* 1 (January 1913): 23; Dust, "What about the Shorthand Man?" 230.

20. "Fourteenth Annual Dinner of the National Shorthand Reporters' Association," *NSR* 1 (April 1913): 96; Bailey to Tayor, 21 February 1935; "California's Answer to Sound Recording," *NSR* 27 (March 1965): 245.

21. Darius, "What about the Shorthand Man?" 230; Lawrence E. Orr, "Reporter or Stenographer," *NSR* 7 (1946): 129–30 [*Utah Shorthand Reporter*]; Morris L. Fried, "Status Claims and the Nonperson: The Case of the Court Reporter," *Buffalo Studies* 3 (December 1967): 121, 129; Jacobsen, "Occupational Segregation," 153.

22. U.S. Census Bureau, "Estimated Median Age at First Marriage, by Sex: 1890 to the Present," 2006, http://www.census.gov/population/socdemo/hh-fam/ms2.pdf; Nancy Woloch, *Women and the American Experience,* 4th ed. (Boston: McGraw Hill, 2006), A-2.

23. For a supply-side explanation on the rise of married women's employment: Claudia Goldin, *Understanding the Gender Gap: An Economic History of American Women* (New York: Oxford University Press, 1990), 119–210; Jacobsen explains the feminization

of court reporting by pointing to the recruitment from female-dominated secretarial skills classes, the expansion of part-time work in the "freelance sector," and the ease of falling back to secretarial jobs if they fail, but she misses the general changes in the number and character of women's employment in the 1970s: "Occupational Segregation," 137 table 3, 144–50, 152–55; National Shorthand Reporters' Association, *Directory of Shorthand Reporters in the United States and Canada, and a Two Hundred Year Calendar* (n.p., 1932); Accounting did not reach 52.7 percent female until 1990: Charles W. Wooton and Barbara E. Kemmerer, "The Changing Genderization of the Accounting Workforce in the U.S., 1930–90," *Accounting, Business & Financial History* 10 (July 2000): 175.

24. Richard Lederer, "25 Years of 'Lederer on Language,'" *JCR* 68 (November–December 2006): 61; "Book Review," *NSR* 48 (February 1987): 46; "Interview: Dr. Anne Graffam Walker, Part I," *NSR* 49 (February 1988): 12–21; Santo J. Aurelio, "Why the Record Must Be Verbatim," *NSR* 49 (February 1988): 34–37; Karen Yates, "People: 'It's One of the Greatest Professions in the Whole World,'" *JCR* 68 (October 2006): 15–16.

25. Bahrampour, "Court Reporters Hear the Tap, Tap, Tap of Obsolescence," sec. 14, p. 4; Quote from "Q&A: An Energizing Winner," *JCR* 68 (November–December 2006): 18; "In Your Association," *JCR* 68 (November–December 2006): 94–96; Richard Sherman, "Ask Mr. Modem!" *JCR* 68 (November–December 2006): 70.

26. JoAnn Yates, *Control through Communication: The Rise of System in American Management* (Baltimore: Johns Hopkins University Press, 1989), 45; Sharon Hartman Strom, *Beyond the Typewriter: Gender, Class, and the Origins of Modern American Office Work, 1900–1930* (Urbana: University of Illinois Press, 1992), 46, 185, 242, 245; 39–42; Mary Christine Anderson, "Gender, Class, and Culture: Women Secretarial and Clerical Workers in the United States, 1925–1955" (Ph.D. diss., Ohio State University, 1986), 19–22, 39–42; Two-thirds of American companies did not use the machines: On dictating machines and 1967 study: Brian Dewalt, "Men, Women, and Machines: Time Management and Machine Dictation in the Modern Office," *Material History Review* 52 (Fall 1900): 19, 26–28; Sandra Lynn Whitcomb, "A Comparative Follow-up Study of Gregg Shorthand Students and Stenograph Students Who Were Graduated from Alhambra (California) High Schools during the Years 1968–1972" (master's thesis, California State University, Los Angeles, 1974), 4.

27. Edward J. McNamara, "Personality of the Secretary," 1920, sec. 4, p. 2, O'Keefe Collection, box 4, NYPL.

28. Ibid., sec. 4, pp. 4, 9; Edward J. McNamara, "How the Secretary Organizes Work," O'Keefe Collection, box 4, NYPL; Clark Davis, *Company Men: White-Collar Life and Corporate Cultures in Los Angeles, 1892–1941* (Baltimore: Johns Hopkins University Press, 2000), 40–66, 152–60.

29. Strom, *Beyond the Typewriter,* 232–33, 240, 284–85, 249, 317–26, 343–51.

30. By the mid-1920s, Leffingwell's approach lost popularity, as the late nineteenth-century language no longer resonated: Strom, *Beyond the Typewriter,* 247–50; Edward Wiest, "Round-Table Conferences: Secretarial Training Schools of Business," in *Journal of Business of the University of Chicago* 3, no. 4, part 2: *Proceedings of the Twelth Annual Meeting of the American Association of Collegiate Schools of Business* (October 1930): 60; *You Can't Take It with You,* dir. George Cukor (1938).

31. Margery W. Davies, *Woman's Place Is at the Typewriter: Office Work and Office*

Workers 1870–1930 (Philadelphia: Temple University Press, 1982), 130–31, 135–36; Edward J. McNamara, *Secretarial Training Course—Secretarial Typewriting Standards* (Brooklyn: Brooklyn Institute of Commerce, 1920), A1–3, 4, 1, 8, 6. O'Keefe Collection, box 4, NYPL.

32. Lisa M. Fine emphasizes the respectability of female characters in film and fiction, missing the lingering embedded discourse of the typewriter girl: *The Souls of the Skyscraper: Female Clerical Workers in Chicago, 1870–1930* (Philadelphia: Temple University Press, 1990), 142–51; Cora Jackson, "Not to the Swift: A Play of the Business World in Three Acts," in *Commercial Clubs: Organizations, Programs, and Plays,* ed. and comp. Archibald Alan Bowle (New York: Gregg Publishing, 1926), 193–209; Sinclair Lewis, *Babbitt,* chap. 3, and *Main Street,* chap. 18, Project Gutenberg, http://www.gutenberg.org/; Anita Loos, *Gentlemen Prefer Blonds* and *But Gentlemen Marry Brunettes* (1925; reprint, New York: Penguin, 1998), 24; *Grand Hotel,* dir. Edmund Golding (1932); *Red-Headed Woman,* dir. Jack Conway (1932).

33. Margaret Thomas Buchholz, ed., "Josephine: The Washington Diary of a War Worker, 1918–1919," *Washington History* (Fall–Winter 1998–99): 22; Strom, *Beyond the Typewriter,* 346–47.

34. Los Angeles Marriage Records, 1908, 1923; Buchholz, "Josephine," 22–23.

35. Marye [*sic*] Golding, "The Trailer of Errors," in Bowle, *Commercial Clubs,* 175, 181.

36. *Wife vs. Secretary,* dir. Clarence Brown (1936), starring Clark Gable, Myrna Loy, and Jean Harlow.

37. Dewalt, "Men, Women, and Machines," 25; cartoon, *NSR* 28 (December 1966): 33.

38. Andrew R. Heinze, "Schizophrenia America: Aliens, Alienists, and the 'Personality Shift' of Twentieth-Century Culture," *American Quarterly* 55 (June 2003): 231; Davies, *Woman's Place Is at the Typewriter,* 151–52; Quote given in Strom, *Beyond the Typewriter,* 321; Thomas Winter explains how the concept of personality became a central articulation of class through manhood as a symbol of manly leadership around World War I: *Making Men, Making Class: The YMCA and Workingmen, 1877–1920* (Chicago: University of Chicago Press, 2002), 116–42.

39. "A Group of Recent Books," *Los Angeles Times,* 27 April 1930, B16.

40. John L. Scott, "Take a Letter, Darling's Ingenious Light Comedy," *Los Angeles Times,* 5 June 1942, 17; E. V. Durling, "On the Side with E. V. Durling," *Los Angeles Times,* 31 March 1939, A1; "Office Wife Given Term as Slayer," *Los Angeles Times,* 23 December 1938, 6.

41. "Storeroom Vault of Memories: Office Wife," *Los Angeles Times,* 7 May 1928, A20.

42. Lorania King Francis, "Washington's Secretaries," *Los Angeles Times,* 5 January 1936, H9.

43. Davies, *Woman's Place Is at the Typewriter,* 144–45.

44. An Ex-"Office-Wife," "I'm Glad I Lost My Job," *Los Angeles Times,* 18 June 1933, H11; Lydia Lane, "Advice on Slenderizing and Coiffure Given," *Los Angeles Times,* 18 April 1941, A8.

45. On National Secretaries Association: "Secretaries Quash Idea They Live to Romance with Their Bosses," *Los Angeles Times,* 2 October 1949, 21; Hubbard Hoover and Isabelle Macrae Hoover, "Pursuit of Happiness: "'Wife Can Easily Out-Wife Her Office Rival,'" *Los Angeles Times,* 26 December 1948, C11; On wife who took up golf: Anonymous, "My Husband Had an Office Wife," *Coronet* 25 (1949): 118–22; Abigail Van Buren,

"Dear Abby: Woman Can't Be Doormat Unless She Wants to Be," *Los Angeles Times,* 18 August 1969, C2; Abigail Van Buren, "Dear Abby: It's Past Time to Cut Cord," *Los Angeles Times,* 20 May 1970, F2.

46. Barbara Howar, "Book Review: Profiles of the Women of Watergate," *Los Angeles Times,* 12 October 1975, X1, 8; Marlene Cimons, "Voice for the Lowly Go-Fer," *Los Angeles Times,* 15 March 1972, 12.

47. By the turn of the twentieth century, the term *office wife* referred to women who developed close office friendships, even as equals: John Intini, "She's My Office Wife," *Maclean's* 119 (23 January 2006): 42.

48. Advertisement, *Secretary,* April 1963, n.p.; Quote given in Ruth Gallinot, "The Image of Performance," *Secretary,* August 1961, 1; "NSA International Board of Directors," *Secretary,* August 1961, n.p.

49. International Association of Administrative Professionals (formerly National Secretaries Association) Web site, http://www.iaap-hq.org/.

50. Joan Greenbaum, *Windows on the Workplace: Computers, Jobs, and the Organization of Office Work in the Late Twentieth Century* (New York: Monthly Review Press, 1995); Yolanda O'Bannon, "Living What You Do Every Day," National Public Radio, *This I Believe,* November 2006, http://www.npr.org/templates/story/story.php?storyId=6431548.

51. International Association of Administrative Professionals, "Administrative Professionals Week and Day," http://www.iaap-hq.org/apw/apwindex.htm; Cathleen Lynn Armstead, "Clerical Workers and Secretaries: Gender and Resistance in the Office and Home" (Ph.D. diss., University of California, Irvine, 1994), 134–35, 176–77; Ivy Kennelly, "Secretarial Work, Nurturing, and the Ethic of Service," *NWSA Journal* 18 (Summer 2006): 182–83.

Appendix

ABBREVIATIONS OF SHORTHAND JOURNALS

A-S—Anglo-Saxon
BPM, BPMRJ, BPM-W, BPW—Browne's Phonographic Monthly (1875–79), *Browne's Phonographic Monthly and Reporters' Journal* (January 1880–December 1889), *Weekly Edition of Browne's Phonographic Monthly* (January 6, 1890–May 9, 1890), and *Browne's Phonographic Weekly* (June 9, 1890–December 18, 1893)
GAW—*Gregg Association World*
JCR—Journal of Court Reporting
MS—The Metropolitan Stenographer
Munson's—Munson's Phonographic News/Munson's Phonographic News and Teacher
NSR—National Shorthand Reporter
PM—The Phonographic Magazine
PW, IPW, TPW—The Phonographic World (September 1888–August 1893), *Illustrated Phonographic World* (September 1893–August 1899), *The Typewriter and Phonographic World* (September 1899–December 1908)
SJ—Student's Journal
S-PV—The Standard-Phonographic Visitor
UP—Universal Phonography

MANUSCRIPT COLLECTIONS

NYPL—New York Public Library, New York

Charles Currier Beale
John Robert Gregg
Jerome B. Howard
David O'Keefe
National Shorthand Reporters' Association Records (NSRA)

NYHS—New York Historical Society

Robert McCoskry Graham
Henry A. Patterson
Edward N. Tailer

DESCRIPTION AND LINKING OF SOURCES

The data sets used in this project came from federal censuses, city directories, and school records. Unless otherwise specified, they included Boston and the communities that became part of Boston during the century, such as Brighton and West Roxbury. Each of the data sets are here described in terms of their selection and tracing procedures.[1]

Female Clerical Workers, 1860, 1870, 1880, and 1900

I gathered the names of all female clerical workers from the U.S. Manuscript Census for Boston for 1860, 1870, and 1880, which numbered 114, 277, and 524, respectively. For 1900, only names of nonclerks were gathered, a total of 4,861. I located most families in the city directory closest to the census in order to find correct or alternative spellings of names, addresses, and occupation changes. If there was more specific information on a father's occupation or a different occupation, it was also coded.

Clerical Men and City Directories

I gathered the names of all clerks, bookkeepers, secretaries, scriveners, accountants, and those listed as "in office" from the Boston City Directory for 1821, 1834, and 1840—numbering 97, 288, and 389, respectively—and traced them all at least ten years. Because I did not have the 1831 directory, I traced the 1821 cohort to 1834. In some ways, this gave them more opportunity to achieve some stability. But it also meant that they had more time to disappear from the records. For 1821, 45.4 percent were confidently traced to 1834: 40 were lost, 10 not sure, and 3 without occupations. For 1834, 130 were lost, 4 died, and 23 were found but without occupations, leaving 131, or 45.5 percent, successfully traced. For the last cohort, traced from 1840 to 1850, 131 of the 389 were lost, and 39 more had no occupation, meaning that 56.3 percent were located.

Clerical Men Ages Twenty-five and Younger

Samples of clerical men twenty-five and younger were gathered for each of the federal census years of 1860, 1870, 1880, and 1900: one out of five in 1860, or 1,471; all in 1870, or 1,386; one out of two in 1880, minus 10 percent of the rest, for a total of 860; one out of five in 1900, plus a random sample of bookkeepers, for a total of 873. Because so many were unspecified clerks in 1860, I included a subgroup of clerical men with occupations other than clerk, such as bank clerks, bookkeepers, and accountants. The subgroup was not used when calculating the proportion of clerical men in each class. It was used when comparing men of different occupations or different classes. The sample of bookkeepers added in 1900 was also used in the same restricted circumstances.

Because of the disruption of the Civil War, I linked the men from 1860 only to the nearest following city directory, to check on fathers' occupations. In the other samples, each man was traced fifteen years through the city directories. Men were traced fifteen years because it took them until their late twenties or early thirties to become proprietors or partners. Office boys, some of whom were only thirteen years old when first located in the census, were at least in their late twenties. Still, most of them, as well as most others, were in their thirties. Some men and their families were never found: 18.4 percent in 1870, 11.6 percent in 1880, and 11.8 percent in 1900. Other men were never found, although their families were. Slightly more of the boys themselves were never found because they were too young to be listed in the city directories: 26.8 percent of the 1870 sample, 19.9 percent of the 1880 sample, and 19.5 percent of the 1900 sample. After fifteen years, two-fifths in 1870 and slightly under half in the other years were still found in the Boston City Directory: 39.7 percent of the 1870 sample, 47.4 percent of the 1880 sample, and 45.4 percent of the 1900 sample. Also after fifteen years, nearly three-fifths of family members were still found in each year: 53.9 percent of the 1870 sample, 61.6 percent of the 1880 sample, and 62.1 percent of the 1900 sample. Obviously, some family members remained in Boston even when others died or migrated.

Nearly half of the men were without fathers or stepfathers: 48.4 percent in 1870, 44.1 percent in 1880, and 45 percent in 1900. It was easier to trace those with fathers. Among men with fathers traced between 1880 and 1895, 54.1 percent (260 of 481) were located, compared to 39.3 percent (149 of 379) of fatherless men. In the 1900–1915 sample, the differences were 50.9 percent (244 of 479) and 38.4 percent (151 of 393), respectively. As expected, single men often moved when their fathers died, while married men with families were less mobile.

Of those with fathers, it was easier to trace the higher-class men. In the 1870–85 sample, 60 percent (33 of 55) of the sons of professionals and business executives, 49.3 percent (140 of 284) of the sons of clerks and salesmen, and 45.1 percent (147 of 326) of sons of men in manual occupations, except sons of general laborers, were found. Only 22.4 percent (11 of 49) of sons of general laborers were located. In the next sample, for 1880–95, 44 percent (11 of 25) of the sons of professionals and business executives, 59.2 percent (100 of 169) of the sons of clerks and salesmen, and 58.1 percent (126 of 217) of the sons of men in manual occupations, except sons of laborers and factory operatives, were found. Slightly under one-third (31.9 percent, or 22 of 69) of sons of laborers and factory operatives were found. By 1900–1915, the identical proportion of sons of professional and business executives and salesmen and clerical men, 54.5 percent (12 of 22 and 90 of 165), were found, with all of the working class at 48.9 percent (107 of 219). Sons of laborers and factory operatives did not stand out from other working-class sons, at 47.1 percent (33 of 70).

Although married men were more likely to reside apart from their fathers, more of them were found: 43.5 percent compared to 39.7 percent of single men in 1870–85. In the later years, the discrepancies were even greater: 55 percent and 46.9 percent in 1880–95 and 52.4 percent and 44.9 percent in 1900–1915.

The sample from the 1880 census was linked to the published names of grammar school and high school graduates. One hundred and forty-six, or 17 percent, were located. Of these, two-thirds graduated from grammar school but not high school.

Clerical Men Ages Twenty-six and Older

For 1860, 1870, and 1880, I collected information on all clerical men ages twenty-six and older: 2,246, 1,405, and 2,523, respectively. From 1870 on, I excluded nonspecific clerks, ones who could not be verified to work in an office, factory, and so on. Since these data were only used for counting the numbers of clerical workers, the possible differences in class background did not matter. For 1900, I collected one out of five, or 1,085. These were weighed and used to compute the total number of clerical workers in the earlier years when the published census records did not specify clerical workers.

OCCUPATIONAL CATEGORIES

All clerical workers in the following occupations were tabulated from the U.S. Manuscript Census for 1860, 1870, and 1880: accountants, bookkeepers, copyists, unspecified clerks, clerks in offices, secretaries, stenographers, and typewriters. I excluded clerks in pharmacies, hotels, groceries, and stores and others that appeared to be in stores. I included clerks in manufacturing, wholesale trade, insurance companies, railroads, banks, societies, and offices of professionals, as well as others. For 1900, I did not include unspecified and specified clerks.

Throughout this work, I have used fathers' occupations as a proxy for income, social status, and class, even though it means none of those. However, occupation correlates with each of these categories.[2] Working-class occupations ranged from skilled workers to transitionally skilled workers, service workers, factory operatives, and general laborers. Skilled workers included construction craft workers like carpenters, plumbers, and fitters, as well as cutters, compositors, printers, engravers, and milliners. They were the most difficult to categorize, because they belonged with the middle class in some cases but with the working class in others. As the nineteenth century came to a close, fewer of the skilled workers were artisans, and more factory workers were semiskilled. The experiences and behavior of the various groups of the working class converged somewhat. The transitionally skilled workers included men and women whose occupations had been skilled occupations in 1880 but who became semiskilled or unskilled by 1900. Among the occupations of the transitionally skilled were jobs like baking, which still included skilled workers in 1900, although the proportion had decreased.

NOTES

1. For more details on these data sets, see Carole Srole, "'A Position That God Has Not Particularly Assigned to Men': The Feminization of Clerical Work, Boston 1860–1915" (Ph.D. diss., University of California, Los Angeles, 1984), app. I.

2. Stephen Thernstrom, *The Other Bostonians: Poverty and Progress in the American Metropolis, 1880–1970* (Cambridge: Harvard University Press, 1973), 296–302; Daniel D. Luria, "Wealth, Capital, and Power: The Social Meaning of Home Ownership," *Journal of Interdisciplinary History* (Fall 1976): 266.

TABLES

A. Male Clerical Workers

TABLE A1. Occupations of Clerks and Office Workers, Boston, 1821 and 1834, in Percentages

Occupations	1821	1834
Clerks in Mercantile/Manufacturing	41.3	55.9
Unspecified clerks	26.9	55.2
Miscellaneous clerks	4.1	
Counting	10.3	0.7
Institutional Clerks	39.2	27.4
Government	20.6	13.9
Banking	18.6	13.5
Other Office Workers	19.6	16.7
Insurance	8.3	8.0
Secretaries	5.2	
All others	3.1	
Intelligence offices	3.1	1.7
Accountants/Bookkeepers	1.0	3.8
Scriveners	5.2	
Others	2.0	3.1
N	97	288

Source: Boston City Directory, 1821, 1834.

TABLE A2. Fathers' Occupations of Clerical Men Aged Twenty-five and Younger Living with Fathers, Boston, 1860, 1870, 1880, and 1900, in Percentages

Father's Occupation	1860	1870	1880	1900
Professionals and executives	5.4	7.7	4.3	3.6
Small businessmen	27.7	24.9	17.3	13.1
Clerical workers, salesmen, etc.	12.0	14.8	13.1	17.1
Skilled workers	17.6	18.7	18.1	21.4
Transitionally skilled workers[a]	9.9	9.2	11.6	9.0
Service workers	13.8	13.0	16.0	17.9
Factory operatives	6.0	4.6	7.5	8.8
General laborers	6.2	6.9	12.1	8.1
Miscellaneous	0.0	0.1	0.0	0.7
Unemployed	1.4	1.3	0.2	0.2
N	484	715	481	420

Source: U.S. Manuscript Census, Boston, 1860, 1870, 1880, 1900.

[a]The transitionally skilled were employed in occupations de-skilled between 1880 and 1900.

TABLE A3. Career Patterns of Male Clerical Workers, Boston, 1821–34 and 1834–44

Occupation	Percentage and Number Who Became Proprietors or Presidents	Percentage and Number Untraceable	Percentage and Number of Those Traced Who Became Proprietors or Presidents
Unspecified Clerks			
1821–34	23.1 (6/26)	69.2 (18/26)	75.0 (6/8)
1834–44	15.7 (25/159)	50.3 (80/159)	52.1 (25/48)
Government Clerks			
1821–34	0.0 (0/20)	50.0 (10/20)	0.0 (0/10)
1834–44	17.5 (7/40)	32.5 (13/40)	24.1 (7/29)
Bank Clerks and Bookkeepers			
1821–34	5.6 (1/18)	38.9 (7/18)	0.9 (1/11)
1834–44	7.7 (3/39)	48.7 (19/39)	15.0 (3/20)

Source: Boston City Directory, 1821, 1834, 1844.

TABLE A4. Occupations of Male Clerical Workers, Fifteen Years Later, by Father's Occupation, 1885, 1895, 1915, in Percentages

	Father's Occupation in 1870		
Clerical Worker's Occupation in 1885	Professionals and Executives	Small Business/ Clerical and Sales	Manual Workers
Professionals and executives	24.2	2.9	2.5
Small businessmen	6.1	27.9	17.7
Clerical workers, salesmen, etc.	36.4	53.3	50.6
Skilled workers	30.3	12.9	19.0
All others	3.0	2.9	10.1
N	33	140	158

	Father's Occupation in 1880		
Clerical Worker's Occupation in 1895	Professionals and Executives	Small Business/ Clerical and Sales	Manual Workers
Professionals and executives	0.0	6.0	6.1
Small businessmen	18.2	22.0	6.8
Clerical workers, salesmen, etc.	63.6	50.0	54.1
Skilled workers	18.2	13.0	17.6
All others	0.0	9.0	15.5
N	11	100	148

	Father's Occupation in 1900		
Clerical Worker's Occupation in 1915	Professionals and Executives	Small Business/ Clerical and Sales	Manual Workers
Professionals and executives	16.7	6.7	7.1
Small businessmen	8.3	16.7	5.0
Clerical workers, salesmen, etc.	50.0	64.4	58.6
Skilled workers	25.0	7.8	10.0
All others	0.0	4.4	19.3
N	12	90	140

Source: U.S. Manuscript Census, Boston, 1870, 1880, 1900, Boston City Directory, 1870–1915.

B. Female Clerical Workers

TABLE B1. Clerical Women's U.S. Residency by Generation, Boston, 1860–1900, in Percentages

Generation	1860 (all clerical)	1860 (office clerks only)	1870	1880	1900
First	9.8	2.6	4.9	7.3	13.6
Second	4.5	2.6	13.3	19.4	32.2
Mixed[a]	5.4	2.6	2.7	7.3	13.9
Third or More	80.4	92.3	79.1	65.9	40.3
N	112	39	264	504	4,824
Total First, second, mixed	19.7	7.8	20.9	34.0	59.7

Source: U.S. Manuscript Census, Boston, 1860, 1870, 1880, 1900.
[a]One parent was second-generation, another third-generation or more.

TABLE B2. Fathers' Occupations of Clerical Women Living with Fathers, Boston, 1860, 1870, 1880, and 1900, in Percentages

Father's Occupation	1860 (all clerical)	1860 (office clerks only)	1870	1880	1900
Professionals and executives	0.0	0.0	8.3	2.0	2.0
Small businessmen	6.7	9.1	28.1	17.2	12.1
Clerical workers, salesmen, etc.	10.0	9.1	7.3	8.9	12.8
Skilled workers	66.7	54.5		25.5	26.2
Transitionally skilled[a]			44.8	14.1	7.4
Service workers	3.3	9.1	9.4	16.1	19.9
Factory operatives, general laborers	6.7	9.1	2.1	16.2	19.5
No occupation and retired	6.7	9.1	0.0	0.0	0.1
"Working-class" occupations	76.7	72.7	56.3	71.9	73.0
N	30	11	96	192	1,994

Source: U.S. Manuscript Census, Boston, 1860, 1870, 1880, 1900.
[a]The transitionally skilled were employed in occupations de-skilled between 1880 and 1900.

TABLE B3. Clerical Women's Living Arrangements, Boston, 1860–1900, in Percentages

Other Household Members	1860 (all clerical)	1860 (office clerks only)	Single Women Only 1870	Single Women Only 1880	Single Women Only 1900
Both parents	24.3	28.2	32.5	37.4	38.5
Father only	4.5	2.6	3.3	2.3	4.8
Mother only	14.4	12.8	24.1	25.0	24.0
Siblings	15.3	17.9	7.7	8.3	10.7
Other relatives			2.5	2.2	
Alone[a]	41.4	38.5	32.5	24.6	19.7
Fathers present	28.8	30.8	35.8	39.8	43.3
N	111	39	274	484	4,598

Source: U.S. Manuscript Census, Boston, 1860, 1870, 1880, 1900.

[a]The category "Alone" includes those women living with "Other relatives" (i.e., relatives other than parent(s) or siblings) in 1860 and 1870.

C. Male and Female Clerical Workers

TABLE C1. Numbers of Male and Female and Total Clerical Workers and Percentage Female, Boston, 1860–1920

	Male		Female			
Year	Published Data	Unpublished Data	Published Data	Unpublished Data	Total	% Female
1860		5,624		114	5,738	2.0
1870		2,791		277	3,068	9.0
1880		4,433		524	4,957	10.6
1885	9,290		1,975		11,265	17.5
1890	12,529		4,217		16,746	25.2
1895	12,607		4,230		16,837	25.1
1900	14,379		7,885		22,264	35.4
1905	15,831		10,884		26,715	40.7
1910	15,156		13,671		28,827	47.4
1915	21,753		18,427		40,180	45.9
1920	24,192		26,243		50,435	52.0

Source: U.S. Manuscript Census, Boston, 1860, 1870, 1880; Massachusetts Bureau of Statistics of Labor, *The Census of Massachusetts, 1885: Population and Social Statistics,* vol. 1, pt. 2 (Boston: Wright & Potter, 1887), 342; U.S. Department of Interior, Census Office, *Eleventh Census of the United States, 1890: Report on the Population of the United States,* vol. 1, pt. 2 (Washington, DC: 1897), 638; *Census of the Commonwealth of Massachusetts, 1895: Population and Social Statistics,* vol. 4 (Boston: Wright and Potter, 1900), 1048–53; U.S. Department of Interior, Census Office, *Twelfth Census of the United States, 1900: Population,* vol. 2, pt. 2 (Washington, DC: U.S. Census Office, 1901), 554; Massachusetts Bureau of Statistics of Labor, *Census of the Commonwealth of Massachusetts, 1905: Occupations and Defective Social and Physical Conditions,* vol. 2 (Boston: Wright & Potter, 1910), 141, 145; U.S. Bureau of the Census, *Thirteenth Census of the United States, 1910: Population,* vol. 4 (Washington, DC: GPO, 1913), 541; Massachusetts Bureau of Statistics, *The Decennial Census of the Commonwealth of Massachusetts, 1915* (Boston: Wright & Potter, 1918), 194; U.S. Bureau of the Census, *Fourteenth Census of the United States, 1920: Population,* vol. 4 (Washington, DC: GPO, 1923), 1064–65.

TABLE C2. Clerical Workers by Occupation and Sex and Percentage Female, Boston, 1860–1920

	Bookkeepers/Accountants			Clerks/Copyists[a]			Stenographers/Typewriters			Miscellaneous Clerical		
Year	Male	Female	% Female	Male	Female	% Female	Male	Female	% Female	Male	Female	% Female
1860	896	35	3.8	4,702	78	1.6				26		0.0
1870	1,121	170	13.2	1,525	141	8.5				145	6	4.0
1880	1,858	349	15.8	2,395	150	5.9				180	24	11.8
1885	2,056	—	—	6,851	—	—	68	58	46.0			
1890		1,977			1,641			599				
1900	3,026	3,564	54.1	10,998	2,144	16.3	355	2,177	86.0			
1905	2,822	4,449	61.2	12,572	2,772	18.1	437	3,663	89.3			
1910	3,666	5,636	60.6	10,880	2,911	21.1	610	5,124	89.4			
1920	3,833	7,533	66.3	15,848	8,836	35.8	573	9,317	94.2			

Source: U.S. Manuscript Census, Boston, 1860, 1870, 1880; *Eleventh Census of the United States, 1890: Report on the Population of the United States*, vol. 1, pt. 2 (Washington, DC: GPO, 1897), 638; *Twelfth Census of the United States, 1900: Population*, vol. 2, pt. 2 (Washington, DC: U.S. Census Office, 1901), 554; *Thirteenth Census of the United States, 1910: Population*, vol. 4 (Washington, DC: GPO, 1913), 540–51; *Fourteenth Census of the United States, 1920: Population*, vol. 4 (Washington, DC: GPO, 1923), 135, 1064–65; Massachusetts Bureau of Statistics of Labor, *The Census of Massachusetts, 1885: Population and Social Statistics*, vol. 1, pt. 1 (Boston: Wright & Potter, 1887), 342; *Census of the Commonwealth of Massachusetts, 1895: Population and Social Statistics*, vol. 2 (Boston: Wright & Potter, 1897), 141.

Note: For the published censuses, dashes indicate a lack of comparable data. The 1885 census divided women into bookkeepers and clerks in offices (140) and other clerks and bookkeepers (1,777), and so the data were not comparable with the data on the men. The 1890 census combined all male bookkeepers, clerks, and so on (12,529). For the manuscript censuses, the dash means a lack of recorded data. The manuscript census for 1890 was destroyed, and so figures for males in 1890 are not available.

[a]The published census combined clerks and copyists.

TABLE C3. Fathers' Occupations of Young Male and All Female Clerical Workers, Boston, 1860, 1870, 1880, and 1900, in Percentages

	1860		1870		1880		1900	
Father's Occupation	Men	Women	Men	Women	Men	Women	Men	Women
Professionals and executives	5.4	0.0	7.7	8.3	4.3	2.1	3.6	2.0
Small business/clerical and sales	39.7	16.7	39.7	35.4	30.4	26.1	30.2	24.9
Manual workers	53.5	76.7	51.3	56.3	65.1	71.9	66.0	73.0
Unemployed	1.4	6.7	1.3	0.0	0.2	0.0	0.2	0.1
N	484	30	715	96	481	192	420	1,994

Source: U.S. Manuscript Census, Boston, 1860, 1870, 1880, 1900.

TABLE C4. Generations of U.S. Residency of Female and Young Male Clerical Workers by Type of Job, Boston, 1900, in Percentages

	Bookkeepers		Stenographers		Typewriters	
Generation	Women	Men	Women	Men	Women	Men
First	14.3	15.6	12.2	14.9	16.2	23.7
Second	35.3	28.0	26.9	16.0	35.3	33.9
Mixed[a]	14.6	9.7	13.2	7.0	12.6	6.8
Third or more	35.7	46.8	47.8	62.2	36.1	35.6
First and second combined	49.6	43.6	39.1	30.9	51.5	57.6
N	2,830	668	1,690	444	216	59

Source: U.S. Manuscript Census, Boston, 1900.
[a]One parent was second-generation, another third generation or more.

TABLE C5. Fathers' Occupations of Female and Young Male Clerical Workers by Type of Job, Boston, 1900, in Percentages

	Bookkeeper		Stenographer	
Father's Occupation	Women	Men	Women	Men
Professionals and executives	1.8	2.9	2.3	1.4
Small businessmen	12.6	13.3	12.4	17.1
Clerical workers, salesmen, etc.	10.5	5.8	16.5	11.4
Skilled workers	26.4	18.5	25.1	22.9
Transitionally skilled workers[a]	8.3	11.6	6.4	10.0
Service workers	19.9	21.4	19.6	17.1
Factory operatives	16.4	20.8	13.9	17.1
General laborers	4.0	5.8	3.8	2.9
N	1,210	173	704	70

Source: U.S. Manuscript Census, Boston, 1900.
[a]The transitionally skilled were employed in occupations de-skilled between 1880 and 1900.

D. Salaries

TABLE D1. Daily Wage Rates and Differentials of Male and Female Clerical Workers, Northeastern United States, 1875–99

a. Daily Wage Rates

	Male			Female		
	N	Constant 1913 Dollars	Actual Dollars	*N*	Constant 1913 Dollars	Actual Dollars
Bookkeepers						
1875–79	68	2.99	2.78	4	1.85	1.71
1880–84	93	2.77	2.70	10	1.89	1.85
1885–89	236	2.82	2.89	40	1.54	1.59
1890–94	1,216	2.39	2.55	33	1.16	1.25
1895–99	284	2.52	2.98	119	1.27	1.49
1895–99/1885–89 ratio		89.4	103		82.5	93.7
Stenographers						
1885–89	28	2.48	2.54	24	1.78	1.83
1890–94	53	1.61	1.72	75	1.19	1.29
1895–99	17	1.88	2.22	82	1.40	1.66
1895–99/1885–89 ratio		75.8	87.4		78.7	90.7
Typewriters						
1885–89	7	1.77	1.81	37	1.56	1.60
1890–94	12	1.28	1.37	8	.097	1.04
1895–99	2	1.98	2.33	58	1.19	1.40
1895–99/1885–89 ratio		too few	too few		76.3	87.5

b. Differentials (in dollars)

	Bookkeepers		Stenographers		Typewriters	
	Constant 1913 Dollars	Actual Dollars	Constant 1913 Dollars	Actual Dollars	Constant 1913 Dollars	Actual Dollars
1875–79	1.14 (61.9)	1.08 (61.5)				
1880–84	0.88 (68.2)	0.86 (68.5)	—	—	—	—
1885–89	1.28 (54.6)	1.30 (55.0)	0.70 (71.8)	0.71 (72.0)	0.21 (88.1)	0.21 (88.4)
1890–94	1.23 (48.5)	1.31 (49.0)	0.41 (73.9)	0.44 (75.0)	0.31 (75.8)	0.33 (75.9)
1895–99	1.26 (50.4)	1.49 (50.0)	0.48 (74.5)	0.56 (74.8)	0.79 (60.1)	0.93 (60.1)

Source: U.S. Commissioner of Labor, "A Compilation of Wages in Commercial Countries from Official Sources," in *Fifteenth Annual Report,* 2 vols. (Washington, DC, 1900), 1:148–52; 2:1407–8, 1535. This U.S. Commission of Labor study summarized various studies on wages and hours. I summarized those north of Maryland and Virginia. To arrive at a constant, I computed the constant wage for each study for each year and then the mean per five-year period.

Note: *N* = the total number of employees; too few = too few for meaningful comparison; — = no data. Figures in parentheses are male/female ratios.

TABLE D2. Salary Differences between Male and Female Postal Clerks, Boston, 1879–1901

	Dollars per Year			
Year	Male	Female	Differential (male – female)	Number of Women
1879	849	559	290	5
1889	806	686	120	34
1901	847	885	38	41

Source: U.S. Department of the Interior, *Official Register of the United States Containing a List of Officers and Employes* [*sic*] *in the Civil, Military, and Naval Service,* 2 vols. (Washington, DC: GPO, 1879–1905), 1879, 1:383–86; 1889, 2:845–50; 1901, 2:523–31.

Note: Many more men than women held temporary jobs in 1901, probably delivering mail. This accounts for women's higher annual wage.

TABLE E1. Membership in Professional Associations by Sex and Occupation, 1899 and 1900, in Percentages

	New England Shorthand Reporters' Association, Sept. 25, 1900			National Shorthand Reporters' Association, Charter Members, 1899		
	Women	Men	All	Women	Men	All
Official reporters	31.6	56.3	47.0	31.2	54.8	52.4
Former official reporters		12.5	7.8			
Court or law reporters	31.6	3.1	13.7	12.5	14.4	14.3
Public stenographers	5.2	3.1	3.9			
Teachers/authors	15.8	12.5	13.8	25.0	11.4	12.9
Shorthand	15.8		5.9			
Shorthand reporters		12.5	7.8			
General stenographers				12.5	8.4	8.8
Business/government stenographers				18.75	10.7	11.6
Total number	19	32	51	16	131	147
Percentages of official reporters (current or former) and court or law reporters	63.2	71.9	68.5	43.7	69.2	66.7

Source: "List of Members of the New England Shorthand Reporters' Association, September 25, 1900," in *Proceedings of the New England Shorthand Reporters' Association, 1899–1900,* vol. 4 (Boston, 1900), 112–13; National Shorthand Reporters' Association, *Officers, Charter Members, and Constitution and By-Laws* (Greenville, S.C.: Shannon, 1899).

Index